Created and Directed by Hans Höfer

INSIGHT GUIDES

BRAZIL

Edited by Edwin Taylor
Photography by Vautier de Nanxe, H. John Maier
and others
Revised and Updated by Deirdre Ball

APA PUBLICATIONS

BRAZIL

Second Edition (Reprint)

Printed in Singapore by Höfer Press Pte. Ltd

ABOUT THIS BOOK

With *Insight Guide: Brazil*, Apa Publications adds another exciting destination to its series of internationally acclaimed travel books. The world's fifth-largest nation, Brazil has a magical allure typified by its fame as the land of carnival. The explosive colors of this dynamic nation, its unique culture and history, the spontaneous, fun-loving nature of its people and the multitude of travel options awaiting its visitors all are in glorious evidence here. As always, *Brazil* follows the same imaginative and innovative style that has marked the *Insight Guides* series.

Brazil project editor **Edwin Taylor** is a long-time resident of the country. Taylor is an American journalist-writer who has written extensively about Brazil from all its varied angles—politics, economics, history and culture, as well as travel. Taylor is editor and publisher of the *Brasilinform Newsletter*, recognized as one of Brazil's most authoritative and influential newsletters on economics and politics. Taylor has also written dozens of articles for travel publications in the United States, Europe and Brazil. He is coauthor and editor of *Fodor's Guide to Brazil*, editor for Brazil of *Fodor's South American Guide* and in 1988 launched the first English-language travel newsletter on Brazil called *Brazil Travel Update*.

To produce *Insight Guide: Brazil*, Taylor put together a team of experienced, professional writers and journalists, all of them residents of the country. **Tom Murphy**, an American journalist from New Jersey, used his expert knowledge of Brazil's leading city, São Paulo, to provide a compelling portrait of the world's third largest metropolis. Murphy also traveled to the interior state of Minas Gerais, researched Amazon legends and wrote a definitive guide to the greatest spectacle on earth—Carnival—for the chapters on Minas, Amazon Dreams and Eat Drink and Be Merry. The well-documented piece on Brazil's racial mix, The Colors of Brazil, is also the work of Murphy, who has written for publications including *The Wall Street Journal*, *The International Herald Tribune*, Pan Am's *Clipper Magazine* and *The Christian Science Monitor*.

The task of handling Brazil's more adventuresome destinations fell to British journalist **Richard House**, who traveled to the Amazon and Brazil's still untamed western frontier as well as the northeastern state of Ceará. For this, House was well prepared, having compiled in his career an impressive list of rugged journeys, including a 1,200 mile sojourn down the Indus River from near the Khyber Pass to Hyderabad. Writing for *Insight Guide: Brazil* was a homecoming for House, who, during a stint in the Orient in the late 1970s, worked briefly for Apa Publications. Besides his travel pieces, he wrote the excellent chapter on Brazil's Indians.

Another expatriate British journalist, **Moyra Ashford**, drew from her own love affair with the exotic rhythms of Brazilian popular music to produce an all-encompassing chapter on Song and Dance. A former art student in London, Ashford, in her words, "fell into journalism," a fall that has been steadied by her obvious talent. She has written for *Euromoney*, the *London Sunday Times*, *Macleans Magazine*, *The Chicago Sun Times*, and *The Daily Telegraph* of London.

While Brazil in general is different from the rest of South America, no state is more different than Bahia, as shown in the chapter written by American journalist **Elizabeth**

Taylor

Murphy

House

Ashford

Herrington, who also traveled through the northeast for her piece on this legendary region of Brazil. Herrington is a veteran travel writer, having written extensively on the country's innumerable attractions.

American novelist and playwright **Sol Biderman** ably handled the chapters on Brazil's art scene and the panoply of the country's spiritual life. Few residents of Brazil are as well qualified as Biderman for these two subjects. A recognized expert on Brazilian art, the author of *Bring Me to the Banqueting House* has also studied and researched religion and spirituality in Brazil.

Michael Small, the first secretary of the Canadian Embassy in Brasília, took on the challenge of describing Brazil's capital city. "Once people arrive," says Small, "they want to know why does this place exist and then, does it work? In answering both questions I've tried to combine an anthropologist's eye for hidden meanings with a diplomat's sense of significant understatement."

Brazil without soccer would not be Brazil, a fact ably demonstrated by **Steve Yolen** in his chapter on the national passion. American journalist Yolen is a former UPI chief for Brazil and is currently editor and publisher of *Rio Life*, the foreign community newsletter of Rio de Janeiro.

The revising, re-editing and updating of the book for the more recent editions was done by **Dierdre Ball**, a São Paulo-based writer and editor. Ball first worked for Apa as the project editor for their *Argentina* guide.

Updates for the History chapter, the Introduction's section on the Amazon and other pieces scattered throughout the book, as well as invaluable editorial assistance, came from **Alexander Shankland**. Based in São Paulo, Shankland has written for the *Daily Telegraph* and *The Guardian* and is currently working with Brazil's Yanomani Commission and Forest Peoples' Alliance.

The tricky task of bringing Brazil's economic picture up-to-date was handled by **Christopher Wells**, a marketing manager at a major São Paulo-based company. He is a former editor of the English-language edition of *Gazeta Mercantil*, Brazil's top business newspaper.

To handle the photos for *Brazil*, Apa called on the services of a talented group of international photographers. Paris-based **Vautier de Nanxe** provided excellent photos of the northeast, Bahia and the Amazon. American photographer **H. John Maier Jr.** handled Rio de Janeiro, where he works out of the Time-Life News Service bureau. São Paulo was shot by Brazilian photographer **Vange Milliet**, who also provided the bulk of the book's historical photos. Also supplying photos was the **F-4** photo agency, one of Brazil's best.

No guidebook can succeed without painstaking research, a responsibility that fell to **Kristen Christensen**. An American from Minnesota, Christensen abandoned the cold winters of her hometown, Duluth, for the tropical sun of Rio in 1971. She has worked as a journalist, translator and English teacher. For *Brazil*, Christensen researched and wrote the fact-filled Travel Tips as well as the chapter on the country's national meal, *feijoada*. She also served as editorial assistant to project editor Taylor, providing invaluable assistance at all stages of the guide.

Special thanks must also go to the officials of the Brazilian National Tourism Authority (Embratur) and state tourism authorities throughout Brazil. Finally, thanks to Kodak of Brazil for developing the photos of Rio.

Small

Maier

Christensen

CONTENTS

History

Maps

Tropical Thrills

Features

TRAVEL TIPS

TREASURES TO DISCOVER

Since its settlement by the Portuguese in the 16th century, Brazil has been a constant fascination to foreigners. First it was gold, then rubber and coffee and more recently the exotic sights and sounds of the world's fifth largest nation. No less fascinated have been the Brazilians. Genuinely in love with their nation, the Brazilians, like the foreigners, have always been slightly dazed by the size of their country. The sensation is that, hidden under the rug in some far corner may be an immense treasure just waiting to be discovered. The problem is knowing which corner and which rug.

Over the last 400 years, Brazilians and foreigners alike have been looking, in the process gradually filling in the enormous empty spaces of this continent-sized country. They have filled them in with some 140 million souls, composing one of the world's most heterogeneous populations. Brazilians are black, brown, white and yellow and all the shades in between. They live in modern splendor amidst sprawling cities and they live in squalid deprivation in rural backwaters. They work in high tech industries preparing for the 21st century and they push wooden plows behind laboring beasts. Within the confines of the same Brazil live near-stone age Indians, feudal peasants and lords, pioneers hacking out jungle settlements and yuppie princes and princesses.

And all of this is constantly in movement. Perhaps nowhere on earth is the process of development as tangible as in Brazil. The dynamism of the country is its greatest achievement. Even in the midst of a period of stagnation in the 1980s, Brazilians have continued to get on with the process of nation building. The once-impregnable Amazon is being pushed back, quickly, many say too quickly, and is the last great frontier of a nation that after four centuries of existence is still not entirely explored.

What unites the contradictions of Brazil are a common language, Portuguese; a common religion, Catholicism (over 90 percent of Brazilians are Roman Catholic); and a common dream, that sometime, somehow, Brazil will be a great nation. A concomitant of this dream, though, is a common frustration with the slow pace of Brazil's path towards greatness. Nevertheless, despite often enormous social and economic difficulties, Brazilians are a remarkably happy lot. Spontaneous, enthusiastic and high-spirited, the Brazilian is a creature of the moment. Nothing is as real or as important as what he is doing right now at this precise second. Cautious, long-range planning types go mad when faced with the Brazilian "charge the ramparts" style of living. For Brazilians, however, nothing could be more natural. In the land of carnival, seize the moment. After all, at any moment, you may just turn up the right rug.

Preceding pages: Bahian girls carry load of cooking pots; calm waters at Morro de São Paulo in Bahia; Brasília's cathedral; open-pit mining at Serra Pelada; Amazon river country. Left, creating a picture in a bottle with colored sand.

SPARKLING BEACHES TO THE AMAZON

Brazil is the smallest big country in the world. Although it is the fifth largest nation on the planet, although it is four times the size of Mexico and over twice as large as India, although it is bigger than the continental United States, the Brazil where most Brazilians live, work and play is only a small fraction of the country's total land mass. A full 25 percent of the population is crowded into five metropolitan areas located in the southern part of Brazil.

Together, the southern and southeastern states contain 58 percent of Brazil's population yet account for only 16 percent of the country's area. In effect, 78 million Brazilians live in an area slightly smaller than Alaska while another 57 million populate an area the size of the continental United States minus Texas. What Brazil has is space, enormous regions of vast, empty space.

The country's two largest regions are also its least populated. The north, home to the mighty Amazon rain forest, occupies 42 percent of the Brazilian land mass, an area large enough to accommodate all of Western Europe.

Yet its population is smaller than that of New York. Located just south of the Amazon is the central-west, dominated by a vast elevated plateau, and covering 22 percent of Brazil's territory. However only 7 percent of the country's population live in the region. These two great land masses, together larger than most of the world's nations, are both the promise and the challenge of Brazil's future.

Unsolved mystery: The legendary Amazon is one of the planet's last unsolved mysteries. The world's largest river basin, it contains not only one fifth of Earth's fresh water but also its greatest rainforest, a teeming biological storehouse whose true potential remains almost unknown.

Despite the encroaching devastation along the forest's frontiers, it is still possible to fly for hours over the Amazon and see no break in the carpet of greenery other than the sinuous curves of the region's rivers. On boat journeys, the wall of vegetation at the

Preceding pages, government buildings in Brasilia. Left, colonial city in Minas Gerais.

river's edge rolls by for days on end broken only by the occasional wooden hut.

These huts, however, are clues to a fact which has been largely ignored both by Brazil's development planners and by many of the ecologists who campaign to protect the forest as the "lungs of the world": the Amazon is no empty wilderness. Aside from the remnants of the populous Indian nations who once ruled the jungle, an estimated three million people live scattered over this huge area, following traditional ways of life adapted to the demands of a region which has defied all attempts to tame it. Collectively known as *cabaclos*, these true Amazonians are rubber-tappers, Brazil nut gathers, fishermen and subsistence farmers along the rivers' fertile floodplains.

With Brazil's latest and most violent attempts to "integrate" the vast and enigmatic region which makes up almost half of its national territory, the forest's people have fallen victim along with its trees. Encouraged by government incentives, cattle barons and land speculators carved up swathes of virgin forest, and waves of migrants followed the highways hacked into the jungle. The Indians were driven from their traditional lands, and rubber-tappers were forced into the city slums as the forest on which they depended was slashed and burned.

Resistance: In the state of Acre, along the southwestern border of the Brazilian Amazon, the people of the forest began to organise resistance. A rubber-tapper called Chico Mendes worked to form his fellow-workers into a union and led them on peaceful blockades of ranchers' attempts to tear down the forest. On December 22, 1988, Chico Mendes became the world's first ecological martyr when he was gunned down on the orders of angry cattle barons.

The international outcry prompted by Mendes' murder put pressure on Brazil to reconsider its senselessly destructive development policies. This pressure contributed to the realization of one of Chico Mendes' dreams, with the creation of "Extractive Reserves"—areas where the forest is handed over to its traditional inhabitants, who protect it while continuing their sustainable harvesting of its natural riches. Behind the Extractive Reserves is a new vision, one

Left, resting in a shillside doorway.

Medellín
Bogotá
San Pedro de Armeno
Pto. Ayacucho
Orinoco
VENEZUELA
Sta. Elena
2579 Cerro Marahuaca
Boa Vista
GUYANA
SURINAME
FRENCH GUYANA
Cayenne
Calçoene
COLOMBIA
Mitu
Tapacuquara
Caracaraí
Macapa
Rio Negro
Almeirim
Oriximina
Santarém
Amazonas
Manaus
Madeira
AMAZONAS
Benjamin Constant
Jacareacanga
Purus
Humaita
Cruzeiro de Sul
Pucallpa
Pto. Velho
BRAZIL
Abuná
Rio Branca
RANDONIA
PERU
Ucayali
SERRA DOS PARECIS
Lima
CORDILLERA DE LOS ANDES
Vilhena
MATO GROSSO
Lucas
Iça
Nevado Coropuna 6425
Nevado Chachini 6075
Lago Titicaca
Cuiabá
Gojas
Goiânia
Arequipa
La Paz
BOLIVIA
Santa Cruz
PANTANAL DO RIO NEGRO
Mineiros
Nevado Sajama 6520
Cochabamba
MATO GROSSO DO SUL
Lago de Poopo
Corumba
Arica
Sucre
F.C. Eugenio Garay
Campo Grande
São José do R. Prêto
Pacific Ocean
Mariscal Estigarribia
Bela Vista
Volcán San Pedro 5974
Paraná
Paranapame
PARAGUAY
Londrina
Antofagasta
Salta
Joaquin V. Gonzalez
Asunción
Foz do Iquacu
Curitiba
CHILE
S. Miguel de Tucumán
Resistencia
Corrientes
Santiago del Estero
RIO GRANDE DO SUL
Mercedes
ARGENTINA
Sta. Maria
Porto Alegre
Coquimbo
La Mar Chicquita
Rosário do Sul
LAGOA DOS PATOS
Salto
Santa Fe
Cerro Aconcagua 6959
Córdoba
Parana
Rio Grande
URUGUAY
LAGOA MIRIM
San Juan
Rosario

which recognizes that the Amazon's true riches lie not in the soil but in the forest itself. Nevertheless, the battle is far from won. Brazilian policymakers still tend to see it as a heroic national duty to occupy the Amazon at any price, and suspect sinister plots to "internationalize" the region's vast mineral resources behind foreigners' calls for preservation. The destructive consequences of this attitude will only stop when Brazil replaces the urge to conquer the rainforest with the urge to understand it.

The central-west: In Brazil's other great void, the central-west, the pace of development has slowed after a quick burst in the 1970s. The planned capital of Brasília was placed in the central plateau as a magnet to attract settlers and integrate this region with the coastal areas. But while Brasília has matured into a city of over 1 million, it has failed to spawn the growth hoped for by its planners. In terms of its geography, the central-west offers none of the natural barriers of the Amazon. An elevated plateau at 3,300 feet (1,000 meters) above sea level, the *Planalto Central* is divided into areas of forest and woodland savanna known as *cerrado*. The forest is mainly confined to the northern part of the region and amounts to an extension of the Amazon rain forest while the *cerrado* dominates most of the plateau.

Made up of stunted trees and grasslands, the *cerrado* appears to be a scrubland with little value. Experience has shown, however, that once cleared, the *cerrado* land is extremely fertile. Following initial investments by wealthy São Paulo businessmen, farmers from southern Brazil have turned areas of the *cerrado* into sprawling farms and ranches including the world's largest soybean farm. The grasslands of the southern part of the region have also been adapted to pasture and some of Brazil's largest cattle herds now graze here.

The northeast: Brazil's third largest region, the northeast, occupying 18 percent of the country, is the nation's most tragic. Although sugar plantations made it the original economic and political center of the country during the colonial period, the northeast has not kept pace with the development that has occurred in the southern and southeastern states. Unlike the north and central-west, the northeast is neither isolated nor underpopulated. Its fatal flaw has been its climate.

The region is divided into four zones: its northernmost state, Maranhão, combines characteristics of the northeast and the Amazon; along the coast from the state of Rio Grande do Norte to Bahia runs a narrow 60-120 mile (100-200 km) wide strip of fertile land known as the *zona da mata*; just west of this strip begins a transition zone of semi-fertile land called the *agreste*; the final zone occupies the bulk of the interior of the northeast's states, a dry, arid region known as the *sertão*. It is the *sertão* that has given Brazil its most devastating poverty. It is an area of periodic drought, of parched earth, of temporary rivers that swell to flood stage in times of rain, of a thorny scrub called *caatinga* and of widespread human suffering. The last drought, the worst of the century, ended in 1984 after five years. The certainty that other droughts will come has propelled millions of the *sertão's* residents to the urban centers of the southeast, mainly to São Paulo and Rio de Janeiro.

Sparkling beaches: The irony of the northeast is that only a few hours from the despair of the *sertão* is the coastal zone where white sand beaches sparkle beneath the tropical sun. It is here that Brazil's famed coastal beaches begin stretching the length of the country from Maranhão to the southernmost state of Rio Grande do Sul. Altogether, Brazil's coastline encompasses 4,600 miles (7,700 km)—the longest continuous coastline in the world.

Blessed with adequate rainfall, the northeast coast is home to the bulk of the region's agricultural production which is concentrated in sugar and cocoa and home to a constantly increasing percentage of the region's population.

Lacking investment capital, the economy of the northeast has remained dominated by farming with a few isolated pockets of industry. Tourism, however, may prove to be the northeast's real saviour. The region's excel

Right, river slum houses built on stilts.

lent beaches and year-round tropical climate have won the northeast an international reputation that is now producing a boom in hotel construction.

São Francisco River: Running along the southern edge of the northeast is the São Francisco River, the second of Brazil's main river systems. Beginning in the central plateau, the river flows east for over 1,000 miles, reaching into the northeast at its southernmost state of Bahia and providing a historic link between the northeast and central Brazil. In addition, the São Francisco has added a reliable source of water for the interior through which it passes, creating a narrow belt of productive farm land for a region that has never been able to feed itself.

The southeast: On the other side of the development pole from the northeast is the southeast region which comprises only 11 percent of the national territory but is home to Brazil's three largest cities, São Paulo, Rio de Janeiro and Belo Horizonte, and 45 percent of the country's population. The region is divided between a narrow coastal zone and an elevated plateau, with a coastal mountain region (the escarpment) beginning in Bahia and running the length of the coast to Rio Grande do Sul.

The dense tropical foliage of the *mata atlantica* has encrusted the coastal mountains with a rich, deep cloak of green. The very development that has brought prosperity to the southeast, however, is now also threatening the survival of this tropical vegetation. In many parts of the state of São Paulo, the forest has been destroyed by pollutants in the air, a by-product of the state's industrial park, the largest in Latin America. The best preserved example of Brazil's coastal tropical forest is found in the southern state of Parana.

With the exception of the coastal cities of Rio and Santos (Brazil's two largest ports) the southeast's main population centers are located on the plateau at an average altitude of 2,300 feet (700 meters). This area of rolling hills and temperate climate, where there is a clear distinction between winter and summer, has been the center of Brazil's economic growth since the 19th century.

Left, fans packed together at a soccer game. Following pages, Bahian woman prepares snacks to sell at the beach.

Minas Gerais, the only state in the region without a seacoast, owes its early development to its mineral wealth. Minas Gerais' red earth provides graphic testimony to its iron ore deposits. Part of Brazil's mammoth Pre-Cambrian shield area, Minas in the 18th century was the world's leading gold producer. In modern times it has made Brazil a leading producer of iron ore and gemstones.

The southern region: The south is the smallest of Brazil's regions, accounting for only 7 percent of total national territory. Like the southeast it was blessed with rapid development in the second half of the century and today is home to 16 percent of the nation's population. Located below the Tropic of Capricorn, the south is the only region of Brazil characterized by a subtropical climate with all four seasons, including frosts and occasional snowfall in the winter. In part due to the climate, the three states of the southern region attracted large numbers of immigrants from Italy, Germany, Poland and Russia at the start of this century, giving the region a distinctive ethnic mix that is still apparent today.

The rolling farmlands of Parana and Rio Grande do Sul have made these states, together with São Paulo, the breadbasket of Brazil, raising primarily wheat, corn, soybeans and rice.

The region is also Brazil's traditional cattle producer, although it has been losing ground to the central-west. In the western half of Rio Grande, pampas grasslands or prairie are home to many of Brazil's largest farms and cattle ranches. The eastern half of the state is marked by mountainous terrain with deep, forested valleys where Italian and German immigrants established Brazil's wine and grape industries.

Besides its rich farmlands, the state of Parana has benefitted from its vast pine forests, which have been a primary source of lumber for Brazil's construction industry, although they are now being rapidly depleted. Marking the state's western border is the Paraná River, which together with the Paraguay farther to the west forms the country's third great river system. The force of these rivers has been harnessed to produce energy for the industries of the south and southeast, particularly the Paraná, where Brazil has built the world's largest hydroelectric project, the Itaipú Dam.

A Quiet Past

Despite its size, Brazil has tended to play a secondary role in the shaping of the world today. Brazil does not possess a millennial culture with roots running back to a proud Indian past, à la Mexico and Peru. It has been on the sidelines of major developments in modern history, more an observer than a participant. Fortunately, it has not been marked by the type of violent upheavals that have occurred frequently in Latin America. Change in Brazil has in general come peacefully, although not always quietly, a tribute to the ability of Brazilians to resolve their disputes through compromise rather than confrontation. For Brazilians, the lack of an heroic past is an oversight to be corrected in the future. Brazil is a country that is planted firmly in the present with its eyes on the future and with very little sense of the past. According to a popular saying, Brazil is a country without a memory.

However, Brazil does have a history, one which sets it apart from the rest of South America. In addition to its size, which dwarfs that of its neighbors, Brazil stands out because of its language, Portuguese, its colonial period, in which it became the seat of government of the mother country, its mostly bloodless path towards independence and its largely peaceful relations with its neighbors.

Cabral: Brazil's discovery in 1500 by explorer Pedro Alvares Cabral was part of a series of exploratory voyages launched by the great Portuguese navigators in the 15th and 16th centuries. Cabral's voyage was destined for India via the Cape of Good Hope but officially was blown off course.

At first this Portuguese explorer thought he had discovered an island and named it Ilha de Vera Cruz. Later when it became obvious that the island was the east coast of a continent, the name was changed to Terra de Santa Cruz, eventually evolving into Brazil because of one of the new colony's primary products, *pau brasil* or brazilwood, highly valued in Europe for its red dye extract.

Colonization: Finally, in 1533, the Portuguese crown made its first determined effort to organize the colonization of Brazil. The coastline, the only area of the colony that had been explored at that point, was divided into 15 parts called captaincies which were given to Portuguese noblemen who received hereditary rights over them, creating a form of fiefdom. The owners of the captaincies were expected to settle and develop them, using their own resources, thus sparing the crown this expense. The two most important captaincies were those of São Vicente in the south (today the state of São Paulo) and Pernambuco in the north where the introduction of sugar plantations quickly made this area the economic center of the colony.

The captaincies, however, proved ineffective in satisfying the needs of either the colonists or Portugal. Left to the whims and financial means of their owners, some were simply abandoned. Further, there was no coordination among the captaincies, with the result that Brazil's coastline fell prey to constant attacks by French pirates. In 1549, Portuguese King João III finally lost patience with the captaincy system and imposed a centralized colonial government on top of the existing divisions. The northeastern city of Salvador, today the capital of the state of Bahia, became the first capital of Brazil, a status maintained for 214 years. Portuguese nobleman Tomé de Sousa was installed as the colony's first governor general, the formal representative of the crown.

With this administrative reform, colonization again picked up. From 1550 to the end of the century, a mixed bag of colonists arrived—mostly noblemen, adventurers and Jesuit missionaries entrusted with the task of converting the Indians. Several leading Jesuits, such as Father José de Anchieta in São Paulo, established the firm principle that the Indians were to be protected not enslaved, a moral stand that put them in direct conflict with the interests of the colonizers. Besides converting the Indians, the Jesuits built schools and missions, around which Indian villages sprang up, an effort to protect them from slave traders. Because of the insistence

Preceding pages: 1657 painting by Frans Post depicts Cidade Mauricia and Recife. Left, Emperor Dom Pedro II's summer palace in Petrópolis.

of the Jesuits and their initial success in preventing enslavement of the Indian population, the colony turned to Africa to supply it with manpower. Soon slave ships were unloading blacks taken from the west coast of Africa.

French occupation: For the remainder of the 16th century, the colony consolidated itself along the Atlantic seacoast. In 1555, the French occupied what is now the city of Rio de Janeiro, the first step in what was planned to be a major French colony in South America. However they were unable to attract colonists from Europe and finally in 1565 the Portuguese drove them out. Two years later the Rio was founded by the Portuguese.

The *Bandeirantes*: During the same period, in the south of Brazil, bands of adventurers called *bandeirantes*, or flag carriers, began to march out from their base in São Paulo in search of Indian slaves and gold. The great marches *(bandeiras)* of the *bandeirantes*, composed of up to 3,000 colonizers and Indian allies, took them west, south and north into the hinterlands, with some of these treks lasting for years. Through the efforts of the *bandeirantes*, the colony for the first time launched a conscious effort to discover and define its frontiers. The *bandeirantes* clashed with the Jesuits, the Indians' protectors, but there was nothing the missionaries could do to stop the great *bandeiras*, which

This would be the last challenge to Portuguese control of Brazil until 1630, when the Dutch West India Company sent out a fleet which conquered the economically important sugar-growing region of Pernambuco in the north. This conquest was a direct consequence of Portugal's alliance with the Spanish Empire in 1580, a union that was to last until 1640 and which brought Brazil under fire from Spain's enemies. The Dutch established a well functioning colony in Pernambuco that remained under their control until 1654, when they were driven out by a rebellion inspired and led by the colonists themselves with little help from Portugal.

reached in the south to Uruguay and Argentina, in the west to Peru and Bolivia and in the northwest to Bogota, Colombia. In the process, the *bandeirantes* crossed the imaginary line of the Tordesillas Treaty signed by Spain and Portugal, which divided the possessions of these two empires in South America. At the time this had little significance, since the two nations were united, but after 1640, when Portugal again became an independent nation, the conquests of the *bandeirantes* were incorporated into Brazil over the protests of Spain.

As part of this period of nation building, Jesuit missionaries moved into the Amazon and the powerful landholders of the northeast expanded their influence and control into the arid backlands of this region. Uniting this huge colony was a common language and culture, Portuguese, a factor that made clear the distinction between Brazil and Spanish South America. The Treaty of Madrid with Spain in 1750 and succeeding treaties recognized the incursions of the *bandeirantes* and formally included these areas in the colony of Brazil.

Rural society: The colony in the 18th century had grown into a predominantly rural society still largely located along the coastline. Wealth was concentrated in the hands of a few landholding families and the principal products were sugar, tobacco and cattle, with coffee and cotton acquiring increasing importance. Despite the efforts of the Jesuits, the *bandeirantes* had managed to reduce drastically the Indian population through enslavement, disease and outright massacre. The population of black slaves, however, had increased sharply. Trade for the colony was restricted to Portugal and, other than the marches of the *bandeirantes*, there was little contact between Brazil and its neighbors. All of this, however, was about to change, thanks to a discovery made at the end of the 17th century.

In the mountains of Brazil's central plateau, the *bandeirantes* finally found what they had been looking for from the beginning—gold. Immediately a gold rush began, bringing thousands of settlers to what is today the state of Minas Gerais, the first massive settlement of Brazil's vast interior. Towns sprang up in the mountains of Minas, and in 1750 the city of Ouro Preto had a population of 80,000. The gold found in Minas Gerais made Brazil the world's largest producer of the precious metal in the 18th century. All of this wealth, however, went to Portugal, a fact that was not lost upon the colonists who were already feeling more Brazilian than Portuguese.

The gold also brought other consequences, shifting the colony's center of wealth from the sugar producing areas of the northeast to the southeast. This was the main factor behind the decision in 1763 to move Brazil's capital from Salvador to Rio de Janeiro. At the same time, the remaining captaincies were taken over by the crown and the Jesuits were kicked out of Brazil.

Liberal ideas: While isolated, Brazil was not entirely shut off from the outside world and by the second half of the 18th century,

Left, *Founding of São Paulo, 1554*, painting by Oscar Pereira da Silva. Above, *Independence or Death*, 1880 painting by Pedro Americo.

the liberal ideas then popular in Europe began to enter the national consciousness. In 1789, the country experienced its first independence movement, centered in the gold rush boom town of Ouro Preto. The catalyst was a decision by Portugal to increase the tax on gold. But the Inconfidencia Movement of Minas, as it was called, ended badly, with the arrest of its leaders. One of these, Joaquim José da Silva Xavier, a dentist better known as Tiradentes, or tooth-puller, was hanged and quartered.

It is probable that other movements would have followed this but for developments in Europe. In 1807, Napoleon conquered Portugal, forcing the Portuguese royal family into exile. King João VI fled to Brazil, in the process making the colony the seat of government for the mother country, the only instance of such a turnaround during the colonial period. An immediate result of Brazil's changed status was the crown's decision to open up commerce with other nations, in particular England, Portugal's ally against Napoleon.

When King João at last returned to Portugal in 1821, he named his son, Dom Pedro, as regent, making him the head of government for Brazil. The Portuguese parliament, however, refused to recognize Brazil's new situation and attempted to force a return to the days of colonial dependence. Realizing that the Brazilians would never accept this, Pedro, on September 7, 1822 declared independence from Portugal, in the process creating the Brazilian Empire, the first monarchy in the Americas.

With Portugal still recovering from the Napoleonic wars, Brazil faced little opposition from the mother country. Helped by a British soldier of fortune, Lord Alexander Thomas Cochrane, the Brazilian forces quickly expelled the remaining Portuguese garrisons. By the end of 1823 the Portuguese were gone and the new nation's independence secured. The following year, the United States became the first foreign nation to recognize Brazil, and in 1825 relations were re-established with Portugal.

Internal divisions: The ease with which independence was won, however, proved to be a false indication of the young nation's immediate future. During its first 18 years, Brazil struggled to overcome bitter internal divisions, which in some cases reached the point of open revolt. The first disappointment of the post-independence period was the emperor himself. Pedro was far better at declaring freedom than in defending it. Rather than adopting liberal policies as his subjects wanted, Pedro insisted on maintaining the privileges and power of an absolute monarch. When a constitutional assembly drew up a liberal document reducing his powers and introducing parliamentary rule, Pedro shut down the assembly and wrote his own constitution. Eventually he agreed to the creation of a parliament but fought with it constantly. Already widely disliked, Pedro then plunged Brazil into a reckless and unpopular war with Argentina over what was

then the southernmost state of Brazil, Cisplatina. The costly war ended with the Brazil's defeat and the loss of Cisplatina, which became the nation of Uruguay.

Tired of the unending political battles that marked his reign, Pedro at last abdicated in 1831, naming his five-year-old son, Pedro II, the prince regent. From 1831 to 1840, Brazil was ruled by a triple regency composed of political leaders who ran the nation in the name of young Pedro. This system, however, proved untenable, as the lack of a strong leader encouraged regional groups to challenge the monarchy. These 10 years were the most tumultuous period of Brazil's history, with revolts and army rebellions in the northeast, the Amazon, Minas Gerais and the south. Throughout these years, Brazil appeared to be on the verge of all-out civil war as regional factions fought for their own autonomy, threatening to tear the nation apart. One of the most serious threats came from an independence movement in the south, known as the war of the *farrapos*, which lasted for 10 years and nearly resulted in the loss of what is today the state of Rio Grande do Sul.

Golden age: Out of desperation, the country's political leadership agreed in 1840 to declare Pedro of age and hand over rule of the country to the then 15-year-old monarch.

For the next 48 years, Pedro II reigned as emperor of Brazil, using his extraordinary talents to bring domestic peace to the nation and giving it its longest continuous period of political stability. A humble man, Pedro had none of the autocratic ways of his father but was still blessed with enormous personal authority which he used to direct the path of the nation. Under this scholarly monarch regional rivalries were kept in check and Pedro's own popularity extended the control of the central government over the nation. In the midst of the American Civil War, Abraham Lincoln once remarked that the only man he would trust to arbitrate between north and south was Pedro II of Brazil.

Left, Avenida Beira Mar in Botafogo. Above, Rua do Ouvidor in downtown Rio.

But while Pedro was successful in restoring internal peace to the nation, his foreign policy put Brazil into armed conflict with its neighbors to the south. Determined to maintain regional parity, Pedro insisted on interfering in political developments in Uruguay, Argentina and Paraguay, with the result that Brazil fought three wars between 1851 and 1870, the last time in its history that the nation was to enter into open warfare with any of its neighbors (since 1870, Brazil's only involvement in foreign wars was its limited participation in World War II on the side of the Allies). To ensure free navigation on the vital River Plate and its tributaries, a policy that Brazil shared with England, in 1851, Pedro sent his troops to invade Uruguay, gaining a quick victory. After this, Brazil and Uruguay joined forces to attack Argentina and overthrow the Argentine dictator Juan Manuel Rosas. By the end of 1852, governments friendly to Brazil were in control in Uruguay and Argentina and Pedro had achieved his goals.

War with Paraguay: A second incursion against Uruguay in 1864, however, ended by provoking a war with Paraguay. Allied with the losing side in Uruguay was Paraguay's ruler Francisco Solano Lopez, who struck back against both Brazil and Argentina. In 1865, the so-called triple alliance was formed, joining the apparently invincible forces of Brazil, Argentina and Uruguay against Paraguay. But after initial successes, the alliance suffered a series of surprising setbacks at the hands of the outgunned and outnumbered Paraguayans. Instead of ending quickly, the war dragged on until 1870, becoming in the process the longest and bloodiest in South America in the 19th century. With Brazil carrying the bulk of the fighting, Paraguay was finally defeated, after having lost half of its male population. For Brazil, the losses in combat were heavy, but the ultimate consequence of the war was its elevation to prominence of the nation's military leaders.

The increased influence of the military was eventually to be the main factor leading to Pedro's downfall. Given his accomplishments and unquestioned popularity, it is at first difficult to understand why Pedro was overthrown. The emperor, however, came into conflict with powerful opposition forces and ideas at the end of his reign. Although the industrial revolution began to be felt in Brazil in the latter half of the 19th century, the economy was still overwhelmingly agricultural. Slaves continued to play a major role, especially in the northeast, and the slave ships from Africa did not stop traveling to Brazil until 1853. In the 1860s, an abolitionist movement took hold, gradually gaining political support until in 1888 the institution of slavery was banned. This act won the emperor the opposition of the nation's landholders. By themselves they could not have

overthrown Pedro but they found support from the military.

Combined, these forces proved too strong for Pedro to resist. Without the backing of the landowners, Pedro was unable to put down a military revolt on November 15, 1889. Ironically, the most popular leader Brazil was ever to have was forced into exile.

The armed forces: The end of the monarchy marked the arrival of what was to become Brazil's most powerful institution—the armed forces. Without exception, from 1889 to the present day, the military have been at the center of every important political development in Brazil. The first two governments of the republic were headed by military men, both of whom proved better at spending than governing. By the time a civilian president took office, the country was deeply in debt, a problem that was addressed by the country's second civilian president, Manuel Ferraz de Campos Salles (1898-1902), who negotiated the first re-scheduling of Brazil's foreign debt, and is credited with saving the country from financial collapse. Campos Salles and his successor, Francisco de Paula Rodrigues Alves (1902-06) put Brazil back on its feet but set an example that few of their successors were able to follow.

Alternating good and bad presidents, Brazil went through a period of dramatic social change between 1900 and 1930. Large numbers of immigrants arrived from Europe with Italians forming the main contingent. They settled for the most part in São Paulo, adding to that state's heterogeneous population and providing its rich farm area and emerging industry with a new source of cheap manpower. Coffee had now become the dominant crop and with it, the economic force of São Paulo, site of the nation's largest coffee plantations, was virtually unchallenged. In second place came Minas Gerais, blessed with mineral wealth and productive farm land. Losing out to these two southeastern giants were the former kingpins of the northeast—Bahia and Pernambuco. As economic power shifted to the southeast, so also did political power. In the first 20 years of this century, São Paulo and Minas controlled the presidency in a political back and forth that became known as "coffee and cream" due to São Paulo's role as coffee producer and Minas' dairy products.

This control, however, demonstrated another of the problems facing Brazil's republic. While certain states had great power and influence, the federal government had very little of either, becoming increasingly a prisoner of regional and economic interests, parties who decided the vital political issues including the choice of the president.

Economic woes: After World War I, in which Brazil declared war on Germany but did not take an active role, economic woes again beset the country. Spendthrift governments emptied the public coffers while rumors of widespread corruption and graft led to public unrest. Military movements also reappeared with an attempted coup in

1922 and an isolated revolt in São Paulo in 1924 put down with enormous destruction by the federal government, whose troops bombarded the city of São Paulo at will. The dissatisfaction in the barracks was led by a group of junior officers who became known as the *tenentes* (the lieutenants). These officers were closely identified with the emerging urban middle class which was searching for political leadership to oppose the wealthy landholders of São Paulo and Minas.

The political crisis reached its zenith following the 1930 election of establishment candidate Júlio Prestes, despite a major effort to mobilize the urban masses in favor of opposition candidate Getúlio Vargas, the governor of Rio Grande do Sul. The opposition refused to accept the election result. With the support of participants and backers of the lieutenants movement of the 1920s, a revolt broke out in Minas Gerais, Rio Grande do Sul and the northeast. Within two weeks, the army had control of the country, overthrowing the president and installing Vargas as a provisional president.

The Vargas era: The rapid ascension of Getúlio Vargas signalled the beginning of a new era in Brazilian politics. A man linked to the urban middle and lower classes, Vargas represented a complete break from the previous rural controlled political machine. The coffee barons of São Paulo and the wealthy landholders of other states and regions, the political power brokers of the Old Republic, were suddenly out. Instead of backroom politics dominated by a powerful elite, the focus of political action in Brazil was shifted to the common man, the masses of Brazil's fast growing urban centers.

Ironically, however, this dramatic upheaval did not lead to increased democracy for the country. Intent on retaining power, Vargas initiated a policy marked by populism and nationalism which succeeded in keeping him at the center of Brazil's political life for 25 years. During this period, Vargas set the model for Brazilian politics for the remainder of the 20th century, which saw the country alternate between populist political leaders and military intervention.

Vargas' basic strategy was to win the support of the urban masses and concentrate power in his own hands. Taking advantage of the growing industrialization of the country, Vargas used labor legislation as his key weapon: laws were passed that created a minimum wage and a social security system, paid vacations, maternity leave and medical assistance. Vargas instituted reforms that legalized labor unions but also made the unions dependent on the federal government. He quickly became the most popular Brazilian leader since Dom Pedro II. In the new constitution, which was not drafted until 1934 and then only after an anti-Vargas revolt in São Paulo, Vargas further increased the powers of the central government.

Left, Grand Salon in Catete Palace, Rio de Janeiro. Right, Praça Visconde de Rio Branco in Belém.

Dictatorship: With the constitution approved, Vargas' "interim" presidency ended and he was elected president by Congress in 1934. The constitution limited him to one four-year term, with elections for a new president scheduled for 1938, but Vargas refused to surrender power. In 1937, using the invented threat of a communist coup and with the support of the military, Vargas closed Congress and threw out the 1934 constitution, replacing it with a new document giving him dictatorial powers. The second part of the Vargas reign, which he glorified under the title The New State, proved far more tumultuous than his first seven years. Growing political opposition to Vargas' repressive means threatened to topple him but the president saved himself by joining the allies in World War II, declaring war on Germany in 1942. Vargas sent a Brazilian expeditionary force of 25,000 soldiers to Europe, where they joined the allied Fifth Army in Italy, making Brazil the only Latin American country to take an active part in the war. Although Brazilian losses were light (approximately 450 dead), the country's war effort served to distract the public and lessened the pressure on Vargas.

With the war winding down, however, the attention centered on him again. Under threat from the same military that had put him in power, Vargas approved measures legalizing opposition political parties and calling for a presidential election at the end of 1945. But while he bargained with the opposition to prevent a coup, Vargas also instigated his backers in the labor movement to join forces with the communists in a popular movement to keep him in office. Fearful that Vargas might succeed, the military on October 29, 1945 ousted him from power, ending Vargas' 15-year reign.

Vargas' exit, however, proved to be temporary. In the presidential election of 1945, Vargas' former war minister, General Eurico Gaspar Dutra, was elected president, serving a five-year term during which a new, liberal constitution was approved. In 1950, Vargas was back in power, this time elected by the people.

End of Vargas era: Vargas' final years in office stood in marked contrast with the success of the previous period. Vargas tried to save his government with nationalistic measures, including the nationalization of petroleum exploration and production, but found himself continuously losing ground. A political crisis sparked by an attempt on the life of one of Vargas' main political opponents, allegedly planned by a Vargas aide, finally brought the Vargas era to an end. Given an ultimatum by the military either to resign or be overthrown, Vargas chose a third route and on August 24, 1954, committed suicide in the presidential palace.

Vargas' removal from the political scene cleared the way for new faces to appear. The first to emerge came again from the twin poles of Brazilian 20th-century politics, São Paulo and Minas Gerais. Juscelino Kubitschek from Minas and Jânio Quadros from São Paulo both used the same path to reach the presidency, first serving as mayors of their state capitals and then as governors. Populism, nationalism and military involvement, the three leading themes of modern Brazilian politics, all played a part in the careers of Kubitschek and Quadros. Two new factors were added: the increasing linkage of economic growth with political developments and Brazil's growing economic and political ties with the outside world.

Dynamic leader: Kubitschek, an expansive, dynamic leader with a vision of Brazil as a world power, was elected president in 1955 promising to give the country "50 years of progress in 5". For the first time, the country had a leader whose primary concern was economic growth. Under Kubitschek's command, industrialization expanded rapidly. Foreign automakers were invited into Brazil, providing the initial impetus for what was to become an explosion of growth in the

city and state of São Paulo. Highways, steel mills and hydroelectric plants were built with government funds and/or incentives, creating the precedent of direct government involvement in infrastructure projects. But Kubitschek's biggest project was the building of Brasília.

The construction of a new federal capital in the heart of the country became an obsession for Kubitschek. Upon taking office, he ordered the plans drawn up, insisting that Brazil would have a new capital before his term ended. The idea was to develop the nearly deserted central plain of the country by moving the thousands of civil servants from Rio to Brasília. Since nothing existed at the site he chose, Kubitschek faced enormous opposition from bureaucrats who had no desire to leave the comforts and pleasures of Rio de Janeiro for an inland wilderness. From 1957 to 1960, the construction continued at full speed until on April 21, 1960, Kubitschek proudly inaugurated the capital he had built. But while Brasília became a living symbol of Kubitschek's dynamism, it also became an unceasing drain on the country's national treasury. As a result of Brasília and other grandiose public works projects, the Kubitschek administration left office having produced not only rapid growth, but also a soaring public debt, high inflation and vast corruption.

Self-styled reformer: The situation seemed ready-made for Quadros, a self-styled reformer who used the broom as his campaign symbol, promising to sweep the government clean of corruption. Instead, Quadros embarked on a short but memorable administration culminating in an institutional crisis that ultimately brought an end to Brazil's experiment with democracy. Quadros proved to be an impossible leader, impatient, unpredictable and autocratic. Insisting that everything be done exactly his way (at one point he banned bikinis from Brazil's beaches), Quadros attempted to ignore Congress, sparking an open confrontation with the legislative branch. He surprised his followers by moving Brazil closer to the bloc of non-aligned nations and shocked the military by presenting a medal to Cuban revolutionary Che Guevara. At last, in a typical Quadros move, without warning, he resigned from the presidency on August 25, 1961, seven months after taking office, citing "terrible forces" aligned against him.

Quadros' resignation created an immediate crisis, again bringing the military to the center of political developments. Top officials of the armed forces threatened to prevent Quadros' leftist vice president, João Goulart, from taking office. Goulart, though, was able to gather support from military units in his home state of Rio Grande do Sul. Fearing a civil war, the military agreed to negotiate a solution to the impasse, permit-

Left, Av. Paulista on its inaugural day, 1891 watercolor by Jules Victor André Martin. Above, Getúlio Vargas (center in riding boots).

ting Goulart to assume the presidency but also instituting a parliamentary system of government with vastly reduced powers for the president.

Populist policy: This compromise solution, however, failed to work in practice and in 1963 a national plebiscite voted to return Brazil to presidential rule. With his powers enhanced, Goulart launched a populist, nationalistic policy that moved the country sharply to the left. Goulart announced a sweeping land reform program, promised widespread social reforms and threatened to nationalize foreign firms. His economic policies, meanwhile, failed to stem the inflation that he had inherited from his predecessors. The cost of living soared, contributing to a wave of strikes supported by Goulart's followers in the labor movement. Opposition grew, centered in the middle class of São Paulo and Minas Gerais whose political leaders appealed to the military to intervene. Finally, on March 31, 1964, claiming that Goulart was preparing a communist takeover of the government, the military moved against the president. The bloodless coup was over by April 2 when Goulart fled into exile in Uruguay.

While the 1964 coup was the fourth time since 1945 that the military had intervened in the government, this was to be the only instance where the generals remained in power. For the next 21 years, Brazil was governed by a military regime, as the armed forces clamped down on civilian corruption and launched a bid to stamp out leftist influence and transform the political system. Five army generals occupied the presidency during this period. The first was Humberto de Alencar Castello Branco, who concentrated on resolving the country's delicate economic situation. He introduced austerity measures to attack inflation and reduced government spending sharply. Through these and other economic reforms, the Castello Branco government restored economic stability, setting the stage for the strong growth years that were to follow. His administration also adopted measures to limit political freedom—the existing political parties were suspended and replaced by a two-party system, one party (Arena) supporting the government and the other (the MDB) representing the opposition; mayors and governors were appointed by the military and the president"s election was made indirect (all the presidents of the military regime were chosen in secret by the army).

New constitution: During the presidency of General Arthur da Costa e Silva, the successor of Castello Branco, the military introduced a new constitution making Congress clearly subordinate to the executive branch. A wave of opposition to the military in 1968, including public demonstrations and acts of armed resistance, led Costa e Silva to clamp down. The closing of Congress and the severe restriction of individual rights marked the beginning of the most repressive years of the military regime. Employing the doctrine of national security, which gave the government the right to arrest and detain without habeas corpus, the military embarked on a war against "subversion". Organized guerrilla groups were crushed, government critics were arrested and often tortured and the press was censored. The military repression reached a peak of ruthlessness during General Emílio Garrastazu Medicis government. He assumed the presidency after Costa e Silva suffered a stroke in 1969, later dying.

The Medici years were the most dramatic of the military regime not only because of the severe suppression of human rights but also due to the economic growth Brazil enjoyed during this period. Starting with Medici and continuing through the term of his successor, General Ernesto Geisel (1974-79), the Brazilian economy surged ahead. The Brazilian Miracle, as the high growth years of the 1970s were called, brought the country into the international spotlight and spurred the dream of ex-president Kubitschek to make Brazil a major world power. These boom years brought unprecedented prosperity to the country, providing full employment for the urban masses and high salaries for middle class professionals and white collar workers. As a result, Brazilians were inclined to accept military rule and overlook the restriction of personal and political freedoms. The increasing economic clout of Brazil led the military to adopt a more independent foreign policy, breaking with the country's traditional adherence to U.S.-backed positions.

Left, Juscelino Kubitschek at the inauguration of Brasilia. Above, military president Medici.

Hard times: With the advent of the 1980s, however, the military regime fell on hard times. Economic growth first slowed then slumped. Following a debt moratorium by Mexico in 1982, the Latin American debt crisis exploded on the country. New foreign loans dried up while the interest charges on previous loans outstripped the resources of the government. General João Figueiredo, the last of the military presidents, was also fated to be the least popular. Upon taking office in 1979, Figueiredo promised to return Brazil to democracy and that same year announced an amnesty for all political prisoners and exiles. Following this, the government moved ahead with other liberalizing steps: press censorship was lifted, new political parties were founded, elections for governors and Congress were held. The increasing political freedom, however, did nothing to offset the sense of gloom that gripped the country as it struggled with an economic recession from 1981 to 1983.

Civilian rule: In January, 1985, an electoral college composed of Congress and state delegates chose Tancredo Neves as Brazil's first civilian president in 21 years. Neves was then the governor of Minas Gerais and considered the most astute of the opposition politicians. A moderate who had opposed the military regime, he was acceptable to

both conservatives and liberals. Brazil's transition to democracy, however, was marked by tragedy as Neves took ill the night before he was to be sworn in. After a month-long struggle with an internal infection, Neves finally succumbed, once more plunging Brazil into a political crisis. Neves' vice president, José Sarney, took office as president but Sarney, a conservative, had little support among the liberals who were now returning to power.

Once in office, Sarney attempted populist measures such as an ill-fated land reform program to secure the support of the liberals who controlled Congress. The country's economic difficulties, however, worsened. Weighted down with foreign debt and lacking the resources for investments, the government was unable to provide effective leadership for the economy.

By the start of 1986, with inflation running at an annual rate of 330 per cent, Sarney was facing a slump in popularity and pressure from the left for a direct presidential election to be held immediately. His response was the Cruzado Plan, an unorthodox economic package which froze prices while letting wages continue to rise. After years of seeing their spending power eroded by inflation, Brailians threw themselves into the ensuing consumer boom. The President's popularity rose sharply; claiming co-responsibility for the plan, the politicians of the liberal Democratic Movement Party (PMDB) who now supported Sarney swept to landslide victories in the congressional and state elections of November 1986.

High Inflation: However, the long-term success of the Cruzado Plan depended on cuts in government spending, which Sarney, keen to hold on to his new-found popularity, was reluctant to make. Inflation was soon back with a vengeance, and was to survive a sequence of increasingly ineffectual economic packages introduced throughout the remaining years of the Sarney administration.

The return of high inflation in 1987 coincided with the start of the National Constituent Assembly, charged with drafting Brazil's new democratic constitution. Promulgated in 1988, the Constitution included significant advances ranging from the end of censorship to recognition of Indian land rights to increased worker benefits, but powerful lobbies and the formation of an informal conservative majority within the Assembly blocked progress on controversial issues such as land reform. In addition, the upsurge in nationalism which had contributed to Brazil's declaration of a moratorium on its debt with foreign banks in February 1987 led to the inclusion in the Constitution of a series of measures directed against foreign capital.

Direct Elections: By liberally distributing political favours and government concessiions, Sarney won Congressional approval to extend his term in office until March 1990. But he was unable to form any consistent base of support, and while inflation accelerated and discontent grew his government became more ineffectual. In the municipal elections of November 1988, control of many state capitals (including Brazils largest metropolis, São Paulo) was won by the left-wing Workers' Party (PT), a new political force based on the trade unions and free fron any association with the old-style politicians who had supported the military and Sarney. And when the long-awaited direct presidential elections were held in November 1989, it was the PT candidate, union leader Luís Inácio "Lula" da Silva, who emerged as the strongest contender on the left, displacing veteran populist Leonel Brizola.

No fewer than 22 candidates entered the field in the election's first round, some in spectacular fashion. Silvio Santos, Brazil's most popular game-show host and owner of the country's second largest T.V. network, tried to join the race just a few days before the vote but was barred by a judicial decision. Led by the PMDB, the traditional parties suffered overwhelming rejection of their candidates, while two "outsiders" ended up going through to the election's final round a month later. One of them was Lula. His opponent was the forty-year-old former governor of the insignificant Northeastern state of Alagoas, running on the ticket of the all-but-nonexistent National Reconstruction Party: Fernando Collor de Mello.

Collor had won an early lead in the first-round through a series of spirited attacks on the unpopular Sarney government. Mixing an appeal to youth and modernity with a moralizing discourse which reminded many of Jâmop Quadros, and including a hefty dose of preaching against Lula's "communism", he held on to this lead and beat the PT candidate by a narrow margin. Taking office in March 1990 with the authority of Brazil's first directly-elected president in three decades, Collor wasted no time in attacking inflation (which in 1989 had climbed to an annual rate of over 1700 percent) with a brutal fiscal squeeze which included confiscation, in the form of an 18 month "compulsory loan", of 80% of the national's savings. Having forestalled the imminent threat of hyperinflation, Collor's austerity policies plunged Brazil into an instant recession. Betting heavily on attracting injections of foreign capital with promises of a more open economy and reduced state interference, the new government then set about the daunting task of tyring to steer Brazil back towards growth.

Left, José Sarney, whose presidency marked the return to civilian rule. Above, Collor on the campaign trail.

COUNTRY OF THE FUTURE

Brazil is the land of the future, and always will be.

— A popular Brazilian saying

Potential is Brazil's middle name. Born fully grown as the fifth largest nation on earth, Brazil has since added people to its empty spaces, making it today not only the sixth largest in population but also one of the world's largest consumer markets. On top of this, Brazil possesses an enormous store of natural resources, much of which is still untapped, and one of the world's most extensive industrial parks.

What amazes most about Brazil is that it has managed to accomplish so much so quickly so quietly. The country's geographical position, far from the news capitals of the world, its tendency towards isolation and its propensity to undervalue its own achievements have combined to keep much of the Brazil story under wraps. Here are a few highlights:

—With a gross domestic product of $313 billion, Brazil today is the eighth largest economy in the western world, double the economies of Mexico and Saudi Arabia, four times the size of South Africa and Nigeria, $50 billion ahead of Spain, $80 billion in front of India and $100 billion on top of Australia.

—Among developing nations in the world, Brazil is by far the most industrialized, with the most highly developed domestic consumer market.

—Brazil is the seventh largest steel producer in the world.

—Its auto industry is the world's ninth largest.

—Brazil's hydroelectric potential surpasses that of any other nation and the world's largest hydroelectric plant is Brazilian.

—The country is the number two producer of iron ore, the eighth largest producer of aluminium, third largest of manganese and bauxite and number two in tin.

Preceding pages, petrochemical plant near Salvador. Left, steel worker at open blast furnace.

—In addition to being the largest exporter of coffee, Brazil also leads the world in sugar production, is currently number two in soybean and cocoa production and number three in corn and its cattle herd is the second largest in the world.

—Agriculture, which once dominated the Brazilian economy, today accounts for only 13 percent of gross domestic product, while manufacturing adds up to 35 percent and services 52 percent.

—In the '70s and '80s, consumer spending in Brazil rose by an average that was significantly higher than that for the industrialized countries.

—Coffee is no longer the king of Brazilian exports. Today industrial goods account for 67 percent of the total. Brazil exports automobiles, steel products, shoes and airplanes and is the fifth largest arms exporter in the world.

These achievements have provided Brazil with a modern and diversified economy that has placed it on the threshold of graduation to the ranks of the economic heavyweights. For economists this is simply a matter of time. With its large industrial base, its growing domestic and foreign markets and its vast natural resources, Brazil's continued ascension in the rankings seems assured.

Progress for the country, however, has not been painless. Since colonial times, Brazil has gone through alternating cycles of boom and bust.

Industrialization came late to Brazil. From colonial days until midway through this century, Brazil was a primarily rural society with a one-product economy. First it was wood, then sugar, shifting in the 18th century to gold; after the rubber boom, coffee emerged as the economy's work horse. As late as the 1950s, coffee still provided over half of Brazil's export revenue, 65 percent of the work force was farm-based and the main function of the banking system was to supply credit to farmers.

Modernization: World War II provided the first stimulus to industry when the conflict cut off Brazil's supplies of manufactured goods, forcing the development of local substitutes. To expand further, however,

Brazil's infant industries needed a strong push and this came from the government specifically, President Juscelino Kubitschek. Upon taking office in 1955, Kubitschek vowed to modernize the Brazilian economy.

He made economic growth the primary goal of his administration, a policy that has been followed by all succeeding governments. He also established the development model that was copied with modifications by his successors: active government involvement in managing the economy and an important role for foreign capital.

Kubitschek poured government money into infrastructure projects (highways and power plants) while inviting foreign auto makers to establish plants in São Paulo. Government loans also financed the private sector, with the result that for the period 1948-61, the Brazilian economy grew at an average annual rate of 7 percent.

At this point, however, two of the great evils of Brazil's 20th century history—high inflation and political instability—brought the first spurt of economic growth to a halt.

With the coup of 1964 Brazil's new military rulers turned to austerity measures to trim down inflation. By 1968, inflation was under control and the economy was poised for a historic takeoff.

Beginning in 1970, Brazil enjoyed four straight years of double digit economic growth, topped by a 14 percent expansion in 1973. Although the rate of growth slowed for the remainder of the decade, it never fell below 4.6 percent and averaged 8.9 percent a year for the period between 1968 and 1980.

These boom years, known as the period of the Brazilian Miracle, changed the face of Brazil forever. Led by São Paulo, the country's major cities underwent rapid industrialization, attracting waves of peasant migrants fleeing their precarious existence in the nation's rural areas in search of jobs. Between 1960 and 1980, Brazil changed from a majority rural nation (55 percent of the population) into a majority urban nation (67 percent), perhaps the most thorough peacetime transition any large nation has ever undergone.

Nowhere was this more apparent than in the state of São Paulo. With São Paulo city receiving the bulk of new investments in the private sector, the state's industrial park exploded, emerging as the largest in Latin America and one of the most modern in the world.

São Paulo's miracle has continued to the present day, where the state has a gross domestic product of $75 billion, larger than that of any nation in Latin America except Mexico.

National psyche: But the miracle years brought more than dramatic social and economic changes. They also produced a profound effect on the national psyche. Accustomed to playing down both the value and potential of their country, Brazilians in the 1970s saw this sleeping giant suddenly begin to stir and climb to its feet.

Ecstatic with the success of their economic programs, the generals abandoned their initial goal of providing the framework for growth and embarked on a wildly ambitious scheme to turn Brazil into a world power by the end of the century. Moderation

attractive investment opportunities, the bankers turned their eyes to the countries of the Third World. None of these nations possessed the growth record of Brazil, let alone its potential. It was a perfect marriage.

Soon pin-striped bankers were flying down to Rio, Brasília and São Paulo from New York and London, followed shortly by colleagues from Frankfurt, Tokyo, Paris, Toronto, Geneva, Chicago and Los Angeles. The rules of the game were disarmingly simple. The generals presented their blueprints for superpowerdom and the bankers unloaded the dollars. The only collateral necessary was the obvious potential of Brazil. This country could not go wrong.

was abandoned and the military drew up massive development projects for all areas of the economy. The problem, however, was finding a way to finance these dreams. The government, the private sector and the foreign companies did not have the resources required. Clearly another partner was needed.

In 1974, that partner appeared. Following the 1973 oil shock, international banks were overflowing with petro-dollars. In search of

<u>Left</u>, assembling electronic products at Philips factory. <u>Above</u>, robot solders cars on Volkswagen assembly line.

Borrowing binge: In 1974, Brazil borrowed more than it had in the preceding 150 years combined. When the decade finally bowed out five years later, a total of $40 billion had been transferred to Brazil. Money during these years did not flow into Brazil, it poured. It poured into transportation (new highways, bridges and railroads, and subways for Rio and São Paulo), into industry (steel mills, a petrochemical complex and consumer goods factories), into the energy sector (power plants, nuclear reactors, an alternative energy program and oil exploration), into communications (television, postal service and a telecommunications system) and in some instances into the pockets of generals and technocrats.

Then in 1979 the bubble burst. The second oil shock doubled the price of Brazil's imported petroleum while at the same time interest rates shot up and the prices of commodities on international markets came crashing down. Brazil's trade balance recorded a deficit in 1979 nearly three times that of 1978.

At first, however, neither the generals nor the bankers were willing to admit that the party was over. The borrowing continued, only now the incoming dollars went to pay for imported oil and to cover previous loans now falling due.

In 1981 the situation worsened with a recession in the United States which was felt immediately by Brazil. Economic growth went from 9.1 percent in 1980 to a negative 3.4 percent in 1981, recovering slightly to 0.9 percent in 1982 before falling back to minus 2.5 percent in 1983.

Three-year recession: The three-year recession in Brazil had the effect of a prolonged depression. Unemployment soared, business failures increased sharply and the generals' dream of a Grand Brazil faded away. It appeared that once more Brazil's future had escaped its grasp, leaving only a melancholy, nostalgic aftertaste. As the denouement to this tragedy, Mexico in 1982 declared a moratorium on its foreign debt, triggering the Latin American debt crisis and shutting off all sources of development loans for Brazil.

Besides recession and debt crisis, the country has confronted renewed inflation (climbing to nearly 1,800 percent in 1989), five years of a discredited civilian president, following the exit of the even more discredited generals in 1985, and a dearth of new investments. Bad as all this sounds, however, the country has not thrown in the towel.

In truth, even in the midst of crisis, investing in Brazil is a gamble worth taking. While today Brazilians openly bemoan the borrowing orgy of the military, the results of that binge are very evident and promise to play a key role in the country's next growth surge. Many of the 1970's mega-projects gave the country the means to substitute for imports, thus reducing foreign dependency.

Oil Suffiency: A major offshore oil exploration project turned the country from one of the world's biggest oil importers in the 1970s to being capable of producing about 60 percent of its needs. Recent massive offshore finds have moved the country to within sight of self-sufficiency, which should come in the 1990s.

Thanks to these investments, the country

has gone from importing to exporting steel, cars, aircraft, paper, and even engineering services; the only raw materials that still are a major slice of the import bill are oil, wheat, copper and fertilizers. The rest of imports are made up of machinery and industrial parts to modernize factories.

Export drive: Before the debt crisis, Brazil exported primarily raw materials and agricultural products, the aim of which was to bring in funds to pay for imports of oil and capital goods. With the cut-off of foreign loans, the country was forced to increase its exports to simultaneously hike the trade surplus and pay off its annual debt service.

The resulting export drive has conquered overseas markets for Brazilian-made products and given Brazilian industries a valuable option to the domestic market. Brazil's ability to sell abroad has seen the country emerge as the South Korea of Latin America, with its trade balance mushrooming from a deficit of $2.8 billion in 1980 to a surplus of $2.8 billion in 1980 to a surplus of $16.1 billion in 1989, behind only West Germany and Japan. This amazing turnabout demonstrates the enormous sophistication and flexibility of the Brazilian economy today.

Left, oil rig off Brazilian coast. Above, industrial worker.

What is missing at the moment is a new round of investments to prepare Brazil for the 1990s, when it is hoped that the country will retain its newly conquered space abroad and at the same time enjoy a fresh spurt of domestic growth.

The slump at the start of the 1980s left Brazil's productive capacity frozen at the high point reached in 1980. Only in 1986 did Brazilian industrial output return to the levels it had reached six years earlier. Before production can exceed these levels, investments will have to be made to increase industrial capacity.

Fortunately, the current difficulties have also pointed the way towards a solution. The growth model employed from the Kubitschek administration through the 21 years of the military regime stressed heavy government involvement, not only as a dispenser of resources through low-cost loans but also as a direct participant. State companies sprouted in virtually every sector, leaving Brazil in 1987 in the incongruous position of being a capitalist country where 60 percent of the economy is controlled by the government.

As in all state-directed economies, the Brazilian model has given birth to rampant inefficiency. State companies have become patronage plums stuffed with political appointees. Deficits are routinely covered by the federal treasury, a comfortable situation that leaves state firm executives with little incentive to generate profits but which produces an enormous drain on the government's limited resources.

Expansion: During the high growth years, these failings were covered by the overall success of the economy. Since 1980, however, even government officials have come to admit that for the Brazilian economy to modernize and expand, state control must be reduced. Plans have now been drawn up for a long overdue privatization program, closing down inefficient state firms and selling others, either wholly or in part, to the private sector. In addition to cutting back on the government's overwhelming presence in the economy, this program will also help reduce the administration's chronic overspending. Huge budget deficits have contributed greatly to Brazil's nagging inflation woes. From the glory days of the 1970s, when inflation averaged around 20 percent a year, increases in the cost of living have exploded in the 1980s to an average in excess of 170 percent yearly.

Brazil has tried to adapt to high inflation by indexing virtually everything in the economy, in the process making market forces a hostage to government policies. Salaries, loans, tax arrears, rental and leasing contracts, savings accounts, financial statements, time deposits and all other monetary contracts are indexed to inflation, receiving monthly adjustments.

Prices have been indexed, then controlled, then frozen, then controlled in a constant back and forth that has left corporate planners dizzy. From 1986 to 1990, the currency has been changed three times.

The proliferation of a variety of indexers, coupled with the penchant of the government to experiment at regular intervals with new combinations of controls and index mechanisms, have given voodoo economics a new meaning for Brazil. Shudders would run down the spines of businessmen at each rumor of a new government economic package.

These constant changes of the rules of the game have thus far done nothing to attack inflation but have made life miserable for businesses attempting to plan ahead. Projections are rarely made beyond the next quarter and then only with a series of variables. With each month's inflation rate, plans are updated and revised, creating an ongoing nightmare for cost-conscious managers. Thus far, however, the government has refused to trust in the marketplace to define such key variables as prices and wages.

Multinational firms: Looking on with concern at Brazil's economic troubles are multinational companies, for whom the 1980s have been particularly difficult. Besides facing price controls and occasional freezes, foreign firms have also been subjected to a wave of nationalism that has followed the end of the military regime. Nationalism grew in the final years of the military's control over the country as an extension of the generals' belief in inevitable superpower status for Brazil. With the military out, leftist influence has increased, bringing with it an antagonistic attitude towards multinational investments.

This emotional attitude, however, overlooks the important contribution made by foreign investment to the Brazilian economy in the post-war period.

One of the main reasons why Brazil was slow to industrialize was that there was a shortage of risk capital. In the 1950s, as the country sought to replace imports with domestic production, foreign firms stepped up their investments.

Through the 1960s, multinationals and the Brazilian government were the primary sources of long-term investments in the industrial sector. Volkswagen, General Motors, Ford, Mercedes-Benz, Fiat, Volvo and Saab-Scania poured hundreds of millions of dollars into Brazil, creating the Third World's largest auto industry and also providing thousands of skilled jobs for Brazilian workers. Concentrated in São Paulo, the auto industry in turn gave birth to a Brazilian-owned auto parts industry, and it provided a ready market for Brazil's steel mills coming on line in the 1960s and the 1970s.

In the 1970s, multinationals increased their investment level, accompanying the spurt in growth, bringing in new technologies and opening up export markets for Brazilian products. By the end of 1987, total multinational investment and reinvestment in Brazil stood at $23 billion, led by the United States (33 percent), West Germany (13 percent), Japan (9 percent), Switzerland (8 percent), Great Britain (6 percent) and Canada (4.5 percent).

Thanks to these investments, Brazil was able to achieve its unprecedented level of industrialization in such a short period of time. Today multinational companies are responsible for 23 percent of industrial production, 28 percent of Brazil's manufactured exports and 35 percent of total corporate taxes paid by industry in Brazil. They employ 18.5 percent of the industrial work force and pay, on the average, 39 percent more than Brazilian capital firms. Their productivity level is 60 percent greater than that of Brazilian private sector firms and five times that of the state companies.

Future growth: Brazil spent the 1980s grappling with the problems of foreign debt, inflation and recession while patiently completing its transition to full democracy. The chaos on the economic front earned the 1980s the title of the "lost decade"; whereas from 1970 to 1981 per capita income jumped 82 percent, it nudged up only 3 percent from 1981 to 1989. Despite this loss of momentum, Brazil entered the 1990s with an asset it lacked in 1980: a democratically elected president and congress. Brazil is now the world's third most populous democracy after India and the United States.

The new president, Fernando Collor de Mello, launched the nation into its most radical anti-inflation plan yet on the day after his inauguration on March 15, 1990. The

Left, hoeing sugarcane field. Above, harvesting coffee.

toughest part of his plan, and precisely the point where the previous ones had failed, is the measures aimed at cutting the federal budget deficit.

That is a hard task in any democracy, as it throws people out of government jobs and slahes job-creating subsidies, and harder still in Brazil, where a million young people join the labor force each year. Collor nevertheless seems intent on becoming the man who finally killed inflation.

The foreign debt issue continues to drag on, but now under different conditions. The banks who so gleefully poured money into the country in the 1970s have now assume they will never get most of it back, and have made provisions to protect themselves if the $80 billion owed to private creditors remains just that —owed. (Brazil also owes $15 billion in short-term credits to the banks and $15 billion to foreign governments and multilateral organizations such as the World Bank).

The private banks' protection against a default means that Brazil has lost its most powerful card in convincing them to soften repayment terms: the threat of breaking several blue-chip New York or London banks.

In the 1990s, the country will have to rely on direct investments by multinationals, and not loans, as the prime source of foreign financing. That means Brazil will have to polish the jewel that attracts foreign capital: its industry, backed by minerals and abundant farmland.

One major step toward this polishing would be a reversal of the formerly successful policy of import substitution. Brazil, in the post-war period, built up its industry by placing barriers on imports; now the best way to keep on building is to remove those barriers.

Some sectors of industry (such as electronics and cars, singled out by Collor) have become cozily inefficient because imports were just plain prohibited. In order to sharpen up competitiveness, the government is slowly but surely knocking down import bans and tariffs. This in turn will enable the country to export more.

Minerals will continue to play a key role, having already placed Brazil in the select company of such mining powers as South Africa and Australia. In fact, Brazil is beginning to overtake these two countries in production of gold and "high-tech" minerals such as titanium, vanadium, zirconium, beryllium, niobium and quartz, which will be in great demand as the world moves toward special alloys, newfangled ceramics and computer-driven everything.

The right environment: Industralization is a messy business and Brazil is experiencing all the side-effects seen decades ago in Europe and the United States.

Brazilians are well aware that they are getting plenty of criticism for the damage being done to the Amazon forest by mining companies, gold prospectors, ranchers, woodpulp factories and pig iron mills. The country is slowly waking up to its responsibility as a protector of a huge tract of the Earth's surface.

Although shocking scenes of flaming trees and polluted rivers appear on television in Brazil as frequently as they do abroad, Brazilians' view of the problem is slightly different from that of citizens of wealthier countries.

Many feel that they are being criticized for the same crimes as those that are committed by the rich nations during the last century. They point to how the United States achieved world supremacy while slaughtering both animals and Indians, building dirty steel mills and strip mining once-beautiful mountains.

Fortunately, both the government and converned citizens' groups have taken steps to fight pollution, restrain the worst aspects of exploitation in the Amazon and try to patch up the country's image abroad. To achieve more progress, Brazil will need aid, as more pressing priorities — such as housing, health and education — take first claim on the government's resources.

The environmental issue is helping to teach this young giant that, like it or not, Brazil cannot solve all its problems on its own. In addition, the world's new set of environmental priorities give the country a growing importance.

The challenge for its leaders is to expand on Brazil's ranking as the eighth largest economy of the capitalist world and move it into the big league of mature, interdependent powers.

Right, bank building in downtown São Paulo.

BANCO FRANCÊS
E BRASILEIRO

THE COLORS OF BRAZIL

Brazil is a diverse nation. Her people share only a common language and a vague notion of their country's geographic and cultural shape. They worship a dozen different gods and their ancestors came from the far reaches of the globe. Brazilians don't really know what color they are and many of them don't care either.

Much of the reason Brazil's "melting pot" continues to simmer has to do with the nation's colonial past. Among the countries of the New World, Brazil's heritage is unique. Where the Spanish-American colonies were ruled by rigid bureaucracies and the future United States of America by a negligent England, Brazil's colonial society followed a flexible middle course. The Portuguese colonists were not like the Puritans of New England, who were outcasts from their native land. Nor were they grasping courtiers, anxious to soak the colonies during a few brief years of colonial "service," before returning to Iberia. They were men—and for decades, *only* men—who retained their allegiance to the old country but who quickly developed an identity with the new one into which they were settling nicely.

The Spanish grandees hated the New World, the Puritans were stuck with it, but the Portuguese came, and stayed, because they *liked* Brazil—particularly its native women. Historians cite a phrase from the 18th century to describe this difference: "The Englishman, in the name of his God, shot the Indians. The Portuguese, with a slight nod towards his God, slept with them." The colonizers' desire and the indigenous females' attractiveness were the beginning of a new race.

The first members of that race—the first true Brazilians—were called *mamelucos*, the progeny of Portuguese white men and native Indian women. Later other races emerged as a result of the mixing—the *cafuso*, those of Indian and Negro blood, and the *mulatto*, progeny of blacks and whites.

Octávio Paz, in his trenchant essay on the Mexican character, *The Labyrinth of Solitude*, notes the ambivalence of the Mexican toward his mestizo past. There is not, in all of Mexico, a single monument to the conquistadores, he observes, yet most Mexican mestizos look to the time when their blood will be "purified" and their progeny can pass legitimately as white.

In Brazil the fusion of white and red is more complete. Pedro Alves Cabral is honored by all Brazilians as the country's discoverer, yet the Indian past is not disdained. Diplomat William Schurz, in his 1961 book *Brazil,* notes that numerous Indian family names have come down from colonial times to the present. He lists *Ypiranga, Araripe, Peryassu* and others, adding that some belong to distinguished families in Pernambuco and Bahia.

The influence of the Indian language is also great. Schurz developed a long list of words from the Tupi-Guarani language which have influenced modern Portuguese and English: *abacaxi, urubu* and *caatinga* are among the 20,000 indigenous words which are part of the modern Portuguese language, while tobacco, hammock, tapioca, manioc and jaguar are Tupi-Guarani words which have found their way into the English vocabulary.

In contemporary Brazil, Schurz might have pointed out, the Indian is only a shadow to the other races. Historians believe as many as 4 million Indians lived in the area at the time of the European discovery in 1500. According to Indian leader Ailton Krenak, chairman of the Brazilian Indian Nations League, approximately 700 tribes have disappeared from Brazilian soil since the discovery, having fallen victim to disease, extermination or gradual absorption through miscegenation. Krenak believes about 180 tribes, speaking 120 languages or dialects, have survived, mostly on government reservations in Mato Grosso and Goiás or in villages deep in the Amazon. He puts the total number of pure-blood Brazilian Indians at a maximum of 220,000.

Brazil's mestizo population, meanwhile, has tended to melt into the white category. Only about 3 to 4 percent of Brazilians, mostly in the Amazon or in Amazon-border regions (Maranhão, Piaui, Goiás and Mato

Left, white child with black nanny.

Grosso States), consider themselves mestizos. Nevertheless, throughout the north and northeast, many who are nominally caucasian are mestizos.

The African culture: The evolution of the black and the mulatto through Brazilian history has been complex. Brazilians have traditionally been ambivalent about their black heritage. In the past, racism was simply denied, but in recent years an awareness of both Brazilian racism and the rich legacy of the blacks has emerged.

Gilberto Freyre, the great Pernambucan sociologist, brings a scholarly eloquence to the subject. He crystalizes this point in his epoch-making 1936 volume *Casa Grande e Senzala*; "every Brazilian, even the light-skinned and fair-haired one, carries about with him in his soul, when not in soul and body alike, the shadow, or even the birthmark, of the aborigine or the negro. The influence of the African, either direct or remote, is everything that is a sincere reflection of our lives. We, almost all of us, bear the mark of that influence."

Starting in colonial days, entire portions of African culture were incorporated wholesale into Brazilian life. Today, they are reflected in the rhythmic music of samba, in the varied and highly-spiced cuisine of Bahia and in the growing influence, even in urban centers, of African-origin "Spiritist" religions. And "the mark of that influence," as Freyre hinted, goes far beyond mere religious and culinary conventions.

Bahian writer Jorge Amado, in his masterly short novel *Tent of Miracles*, showed how a mulatto medical assistant and amateur scholar named Pedro Archanjo fought a tide of racism in the 1930s by proving that most of the proud "First Families of Bahia" had rich admixtures of black blood in their veins, which was a fruit of Brazil's miscegenist heritage.

In the past, however, many Brazilians would have denied "the mark of that influence". A turn-of-the-century painting, "*The Redemption of Ham*," by Modesto Brocos, is a typical example. The canvas depicts an elderly black woman sitting on a sofa next to her *mulatto* daughter and white son-in-law. The daughter is proudly holding a bouncing pink baby on her knee while the elderly woman lifts her eyes to heaven as if to say "Thanks be to God!" There is little doubt how the artist and his subjects felt about race.

And yet there is a fascinating contradiction in Brazil. The dominant white classes hold racist views while, at the same time, they permit their male heirs to marry supposedly inferior *mulatas*. Statistically, this has been the trend throughout the 20th century in what sociologists call the "bleaching" of Brazil. According to official census records, the black population of Brazil has dropped dramatically since 1940, when 14.6 percent of Brazil's people were black, to 5.9 percent in 1980.

The caucasian portion of the population has also declined, from 63.5 percent to 55 percent. However, the mulatto population has risen sharply, from 21.2 percent to 38.5 percent. Where Brazil was a black and white nation in 1940, today it is an increasingly brown one.

The bastion of the disappearing Brazilian black is still Bahia. Salvador, one of Brazil's oldest and most fascinating cities, is the nation's largest predominantly black state capital. The mulatto is more prominent in coastal regions north and south of Bahia, and in the vast interior state of Minas Gerais, west of Rio, where slavery was introduced during the prolonged 18th-century gold rush.

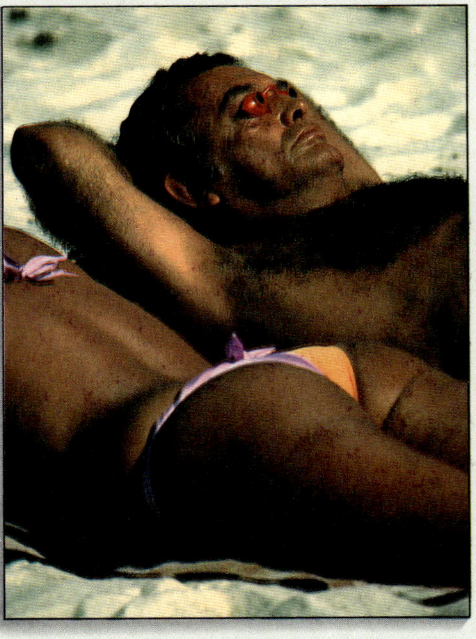

Change in racial views: Recent years have seen the rediscovery and redefinition of Brazil's black past. Just as racist beliefs about the contemporary world are undergoing revision, so are racist views of history.

Left, young street vendors. Above, in pursuit of the perfect tan.

Brazilian history books at the turn-of-the-century often contained racist passages. One text described Brazil's earliest black slaves as "generally accepting the most grotesque of fetishes". Another noted that "negros of the worst quality, generally those from the Congo, were sent to the fields and the mines". The preamble of an early 20th-century immigration law stated "it is necessary to preserve and develop the ethnic composition of our population by giving preference to its most desirable European elements."

Contemporary social scientists, beginning with Freyre, have catalogued the real achievements of Brazil's earliest black residents. In doing so, they have discovered that the African brought with him to the New World more than just a strong back.

For one thing, he often possessed highly developed manual skills in woodworking, masonry and mining. Much of the best baroque carving which still graces the colonial churches of Bahia was accomplished by African slaves.

In Minas Gerais mulatto artisan Antônio Francisco Lisboa, called Aleijadinho ("the little cripple") because of his deforming arthritis, led Brazilian sculpture and architecture into the high baroque. He started late in the 18th century with his elegant Igreja de São Francisco in Ouro Preto, and the larger, more elaborate São Francisco in the eastern Minas Gerais town of São João del Rei. He also created 78 soapstone and cedar carvings at the Basílica do Senhor Bom Jesus de matosinhos in Congonhas do Campo in eastern Minas Gerais. The statues, 66 of them representing the "*Stations of the Cross,*" breathe with sinuous human life as if Aleijadinho had been present at the Cruxificion.

But the miracle of Aleijadinho, the illegitimate son of a Portuguese builder and a black slave woman, is that he created an informed yet innovative artistic idiom at the edge of western civilization.

During his 80 years he never studied in a school and he never saw the ocean. Yet his Congonhas statues have been numbered among the greatest collections of baroque art anywhere in the world.

However, the blacks contributed more than their artistic attributes and economic skills. Many Africans, especially the Yorubás, who dominated in Bahia, also brought sophisticated political and religious practices with them. Contemporary historians note that they practiced Mohammedanism and were literate in Arabic. Their culture was also rich in music, dance, art and unwritten but majestic literature. Writes Freyre, "In Bahia, many accomplished in mind and statuesque of body, were, in every respect but political and social status, the equal or superior of their masters."

Brazilian slavery: These proud black men and women did not always accept their bondage with equanimity. Much of Brazil's previous view of African slavery as "less rigorous than that practiced by the French, English or North Americans" has been revised by contemporary historians, who note that nine violent slave rebellions rocked the province of Bahia between the period 1807 and 1835.

A German visitor to a Bahian plantation in the 19th century, Prince Adalbert of Prussia, wrote "the loaded guns and pistols hanging up in the plantation owner's bedroom showed that he had no confidence in his slaves and had more than once been obliged to face them with his loaded gun."

The story of Brazilian slavery is every bit as harrowing as that of the "peculiar institution" in North America. Historians believe as many as 5 million Africans were captured and shipped to Brazil between 1532 and the outlawing of the Brazilian slave trade in 1850. Of that number about 20 percent, or 1 million Africans, died before they could reach Brazilian shores.

Once in Brazil, white masters often treated their slaves as a cheap investment. The average life span of a black youth enslaved by a Brazilian sugar plantation or gold mine owner during colonial times was only about eight years. It was considered cheaper to buy new slaves than to preserve the health of the existing ones.

By 1835, the year of a bloody slave revolt in the interior of Bahia, there may have been more blacks in Brazil, counting both slaves and freemen, than whites. Rising black consciousness and violence against the white ruling class led four Brazilian provinces to enact racial segregation laws against free men.

When not in revolt, the slaves of the northeast were often in flight. Historians know of at least ten large-scale *quilombos,* or slave retreats, which were formed during colonial days in the deep interior of the northeast. The largest, Palmares, had a population of 30,000 at its peak and flourished for 67 years before being crushed by the colonial militia in 1694. Palmares, like the other great *quilombos* of the 17th and 18th centuries, was run like an African tribal monarchy, with a king, a royal council, community and private property, a tribal army and a priest class.

In some respect, however, Brazilian slavery was more liberal than its equivalents in other New World colonies. Owners were prohibited by law from separating slave families and were required to grant a slave's freedom if he could pay his fair market price.

A surprising number of slaves were able to do this, even in the earliest colonial days. Freed slaves often formed religious brotherhoods, with the support and encouragement of the Roman Catholic Church, particularly the Jesuit missionaries.

The brotherhoods raised money to purchase the freedom of even more slaves, and some of them became quite wealthy. In Ouro Preto, one such brotherhood built the magnificent baroque jewel box, the Igreja da Nossa Senhora do Rosário dos Pretos, one of the most beautiful chur-ches in Brazil. In an ironic turnabout, Rosá-rio dos Pretos discriminated against whites.

Brazilian slavery finally died on May 13, 1888 when Princess Regent Isabel de Orleans e Bragança, signed a law abolishing the institution, which immediately freed an estimated 800,000 slaves. Brazil was the last country in the Western Hemisphere to put an end to slavery.

Socio-economic development: For the most part, however, Brazil's black and brown population was unprepared for the 20th century about to dawn. Contemporary Brazil suffers from a lag in socio-economic development among blacks and mulattos—a vicious circle—which has resulted in persistent discrimination against them.

According to São Paulo human rights attorney Dalmo Dallari, "we have, in our Constitution and laws, the explicit prohibition of racial discrimination. But, it is equally clear that such laws are merely an expression of intentions with little practical effect." Dallari and other rights advocates, point to persistent episodic discrimination. Blacks barred at the doors of restaurants and hotels, black women told to "go to the service entrance" by doormen at high-rise apartment buildings, are among many examples.

There is also a more subtle face to Brazilian racial discrimination. Says São Paulo State Government Afro-Brazilian Affairs Coordinator Percy da Silva, "while it may be true that blacks are no longer slaves, it is also a fact blacks do not have the same opportunities as whites. We are, to a great extent, stigmatized, seen as inferior. We must show a double capacity, both intellectual and personal, to be accepted in many places, especially the workplace." The result, says da Silva, is that Brazil has no black cabinet officers, no black diplomats, few black corporate leaders and only a handful of black legislators. "The face Brazil shows the world," he says, "is a white face" even though Brazil is more than 40 percent black and brown. Statistically, the black economic condition was amply documented in a 1983 report published by Brazil's official Geographic and Statistical Institute (IBGE). The report showed that, while whites formed 56.6 percent of the work force, they earned 71.1 percent of the personal income. Mulattos, on the other hand, constituted 30.8 percent of the work force but earned only 19.8 percent of personal income.

Meanwhile, blacks earned 5.2 percent of personal income, accounting for 9.5 percent of the work force. The study also found that 8.5 percent of all whites in the Brazilian work force had college degrees against only 1.1 percent for blacks and 2.7 percent for mulattos. At the other end of the educational scale, 15.5 percent of whites were described as illiterate against 42.4 percent for blacks and 31.5 percent among mulattos.

Yet the surprising thing in Brazil is precisely the lack of black and brown consciousness. "The truth is," says University of São Paulo social scientist João Baptista Pereira, "blacks in Brazil don't know whether they suffer discrimination because they are black or because they are poor."

Racial tensions in Brazil may appear muted for cultural reasons as well. Says noted *carioca* playwright Millôr Fernandes, "you don't hear much about racism in Brazil for a very simple reason. The black man knows his place. If blacks ever had a spokesman in Brazil like Martin Luther King, you'd see racism. The racists would come out of the closet."

The notion, put forward in the past by some scholars, that Brazil is an emerging "racial democracy," has been seriously

Left, Minas Gerais farm worker. Above, woman in Bahian costume.

questioned against the background of today's subtle discrimination and insipient racial tension. Yet, if the "face" Brazil presents to the world is white—55 percent white to be exact—its whiteness is by no means uniform. One Brazilian image which has not been shattered is that of a still bubbling "melting pot."

Brazil, like the United States, is a nation of immigrants, and not just immigrants from Portugal, the original colonizing country. Rodrigues, Fernandes, De Souza and other Latin names dominate the phone book in some Brazilian cities.

In others, names like Alaby or Geisel, Tolentino or Kobayashi, even an occasional

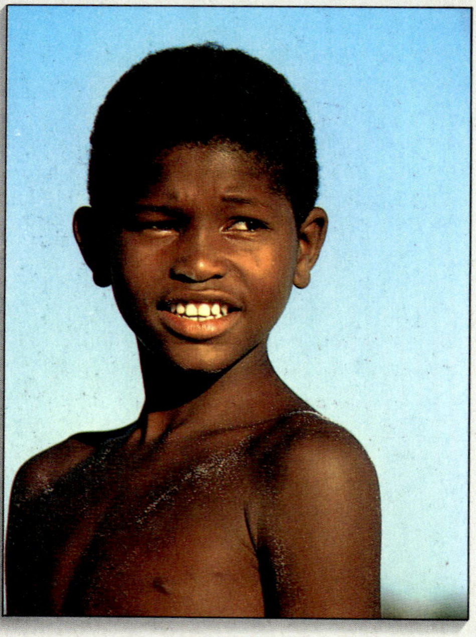

MacDowel, appear more than once.

European immigrants: The presence of many ethnic groups on Brazilian soil dates from the 1850s, when the imperial government encouraged European immigration to help rebuild the labor force after the slave trade was banned. The first immigrants were German and Swiss farmers, who settled mainly in Brazil's three southern states of Rio Grande do Sul, Santa Catarina and Parana, where soil and climate were most similar to European conditions.

For decades some communities, such as Novo Hamburgo in Rio Grande do Sul and Blumenau in Santa Catarina, were more German than Brazilian. Protestant religious services were as common as Roman Catholic ones and German, rather than Portuguese, was spoken as the first language by most residents. Even today such towns show the distinctive mark of their Tutonic heritage, with Alpine-style architecture dominating the landscape and restaurant menus offering more *knockwurst* and *eisbein* than *feijoada*.

Later in the 19th century, Italian immigration predominated, especially in the state of São Paulo. The Italians were not all farmers like the first immigrants. Many were skilled workmen and a smattering of white-collar professionals were mixed in.

Starting in the 1870s, the Italians flooded São Paulo state, and many of them worked on the rich coffee plantations in the state's interior. A sizable contingent entered the growing urban work force in São Paulo and neighboring cities. Within one generation the Italians were established in the trades and professions.

Within two they were a new elite, complete with their own *nouveau riche* industrial millionaire families such as the Martinellis and the Matarrazzoa. One of the first skyscrapers erected in Brazil, which still dominates São Paulo's old downtown, was the Martinelli Building.

A few years later an even more imposing monument, the 41-story Itália Building, was built on the corner of bustling Ipiranga and São Luis Avenues, and it is still South America's tallest building.

By the turn of the century, Brazil was hosting immigrants from around the globe. According to Foreign Ministry records, a total of 5 million immigrants arrived on Brazilian shores between 1884 and 1973, when restrictive legislation was adopted.

Of that total, the largest number, 1.4 million, were Italians. Portugal sent 1.2 million of its sons and daughters, Spain 580,000, Germany 200,000, Russia 110,000, including many Jews who settled in São Paulo and Rio de Janeiro. An additional half million came from European origins as diverse as Poland, Lithuania and Greece.

Eastern immigrants: The call for immigrants reached beyond the borders of Europe. Starting in 1908, with the arrival in Santos Harbor of the immigrant ship *Kasato*

Maru, 250,000 Japanese transferred permanently from their homeland to the wilds of Brazil. Most descendants of those hardy Japanese, who were fleeing crop failures and earthquakes in their native islands, still live in metropolitan São Paulo.

The Japanese presence is most apparent in São Paulo's Liberdade section, which is a veritable "Japantown" near the old downtown. Signs in the windows of row after row of Japanese restaurants are bilingual. The movie theaters show Japanese-language films and a colorful street fair on Sundays sells Japanese handicrafts and food (see the chapter on "Liberdade: A Touch of Tokyo").

The Middle East sent 700,000 immigrants, mostly from today's Syria and Lebanon, during the first decades of the 20th century.

Two sprawling commercial districts—one centered on Rua do Ouvidor in Rio de Janeiro, the other around Rua 25 de Março in São Paulo—feature hundreds of retail shops owned by Mideastern immigrants and their descendants. The stores, which pack together on narrow streets bazaar-style, sell everything from fresh flowers to Persian rugs. In both cities, store owners are proud that Jewish and Arab merchants work side by side in harmony.

Regional diversity: And yet the process of molding diverse populations into a single "Brazilian race" is far from complete. One result is the continued strength of regionalism in Brazil.

The nation's complex and intricate pattern of ethnic heritages includes differences so pronounced that Euclydes da Cunha, author of the seminal *"Os Sertões,"* (a saga about the southern soldiers who marched in the 1897 Canudos campaign in Bahia), wrote, "they were in a strange land now, with other customs, other scenes, a different kind of people, another language even, spoken with an original and picturesque drawl. They had, precisely, the feeling of going into another country."

Despite the impact of mass communications and the trend toward political centralization, regionalism still flourishes in Brazil. Indeed, it is precisely in examining regionalism that all the different colors of the racial mosaic seem to blend together.

Left, Bahian boy. Right, *Favela* kids.

The white *gaucho*, with his stoic Catholicism and die-hard *machismo*, still stalks the southern plains. The aggressive *paulista,* who practises religions that range from Islam to Shintoism and has a varied ethnic origin, staffs the nation's banks, industries and offices. The *carioca*, whose tan may or may not be skin deep, seems to practise all religions, but is actually agnostic.

The *mineiro*, stolid and hard-working, whose family members are caucasian, mulatto and black, is almost Puritanical in his worship, severe in his maleness and infinitely patient and practical in his politics. The *nordestino* is of brown or black skin,

light of heart, colorful in personality, and practices a flamboyant blend of Catholic and African religions, with the accent on the African.

And finally, there is still the *sertanejo*, the man of the back country, whose religious beliefs may include a profound respect for the works of the Devil.

The incredible *sertanejo*, whose origins may reflect Indian, caucasion and black roots, is still trekking the dusty roads of the vast *sertão,* fleeing from the alternate scourges of floods and drought and hoping one day to return to what he proudly calls his country.

National

THE INDIANS: A LOST RACE

"Do not trust the whites. They are the men who control the lightning, who live without a homeland, who wander to satisfy their thirst for gold. They are kind to us when they need us, for the land that they tread and the plains and rivers they assault are ours. Once they have achieved their goals they are false and treacherous."

—Rosa Borôro, 1913

The first contact Brazil's Indians had with the future colonists was in 1500, when Pedro Alves Cabral's ship arrived. The Indians' innocence and generosity impressed the travelers and one writer noted "their bodies are so clean and so plump and so beautiful they could not be more so."

Amerigo Vespucci, a Florentine adventurer after whom the Americas are named, wrote an account in 1503 of the Indians and it became an instant best-seller in Europe, forging the notion of the noble savage. "I fancied myself to be near the terrestrial paradise," he told eager readers.

Early slavery: At first the Indians were treated with respect and some were even brought back to be shown to European royalty. The coastal tribes helped the Portuguese load their caravelles with logs of highly-profitable Brazil dyewood. While the Indians' interest in the metal cutting tools they received as barter was soon satisfied, the colonists' demands for their backbreaking labor was not. As greed replaced enchantment, the Portuguese sought an excuse for enslaving the Indians.

They found just such an excuse when the coastal Tupi Indians made the mistake of eating a shipwrecked Portuguese bishop. Soon after the incident, despite a papal ruling that Brazilians were free sons of Adam and could not be enslaved, Indian captives from "just wars" against hostile tribes were enslaved, as were many Indians providentially saved from the cooking pot by white colonists. Though hundreds of other Indian nations rejected cannibalism, a moral excuse for white domination had been found.

Left, traditional body painting and adornments mix with wristwatch and tape recorder.

In 1552 Indians captured Hans Staden, a German soldier who narrowly escaped being eaten, and he wrote the first detailed account of tribal life. "Their main purpose in gnawing the dead down to the bones is to fill the living with horror," he wrote. Diogo Alvares was a Portuguese sailor washed ashore in Bahia with musket and gunpowder, which he used to mystify the Indians. Renamed *Caramuru,* the god of fire and thunder, he married two Indian princesses and even brought one back to France.

Other early captives taught military tactics to the violent coastal tribes, which provided the Portuguese with another excuse for bloody retribution. Tribes helping the French, Dutch or British gain a foothold in the New World were wiped out as the colonists learned to divide and rule the warring Indians who still vastly outnumbered them.

The original inhabitants: At the time of contact, Brazil's Indian population was estimated to be between 2.5 and 4 million. There were four language groups. Two, the Arual and Carib, are found throughout Central America and the Caribbean basin, suggesting a common origin. Until recently anthropologists agreed that the ancestors of Indians in both Americas had migrated from Central Asia across the Bering Strait about 10,000 years ago. Ancient pottery finds in the mid-Amazon and the wide variety of Indian cultures suggest to some experts that the origins of Brazil's first inhabitants may stretch back much further, and even across the Pacific.

Tropical forest provides abundant timber but is a poor source of stone, and the Indians' shifting life-style left few lasting monuments that are considered the mark of advanced civilizations. Even today much Indian culture is ephemeral. Warriors spend days adorning their bodies with complex designs in *urucúm* vegetable dye, and flower or feather decorations which are discarded after the dance or ritual. Only the superb *cokar* or feather headdresses may survive in some western museum.

The introduction of iron tools quickly undermined stone-age cultures, and western medicines replaced the spiritual remedies of the *page* or tribal healer. Though some Indian groups, such as the Nambikuara in Rondônia, were among the most primitive on the planet, the Caduveo of Mato Grosso, visited in the 1930s by the French anthropologist Claude Levi-Strauss, had such an absurdly aristocratic culture he likened them to the royalty of *Alice in Wonderland*.

The Indians' demise: The Indians' undoing was the triple scourge of slavery, religion and disease brought by the white man. Jesuit missionaries who arrived in 1549 were appalled at the depradations of ruthless gangs of *bandeirantes* or slave-raiders fanning out from the tiny settlement of São Paulo. The missionaries tried to protect and convert the Indians by "reducing" forest-dwelling tribes

to *aldeias* or settlement-dwellers. Conflicts soon developed with the colonists, whose demand for slave labor was insatiable.

Slavery or "ransoming" was abolished in 1609, but because Portugal's colony was going bankrupt, it was re-introduced just two years later.

Without any resistance to imported diseases and living in crowded, unhealthy *aldeias*, entire tribes were wiped out by influenza, measles, smallpox and even bubonic plague, while the colonists clamored for forced labor.

In 1639 the Spanish Jesuit Cristóbal de Acuña wrote that Amazon "Indian settlements are so close together that one is scarcely lost sight of before another comes into view... imagine how numerous are the Indians." He described a vibrant culture living off the fertile floodplain and the abundant river, farming river turtles, and trading pottery and cotton goods. However, he found no trace of the legendary tribe of Amazons, those classical women-warriors who fascinated Europeans.

Just decades after Acuña visited, it was possible to travel days along the river without seeing a single Indian. Officials proudly swore they had killed 2 million in the lower Amazon. "It is awesome to contemplate the destruction caused by these few settlers. The mighty Amazon was almost depopulated and the populous villages gone, their tribes fled or annihilated by the white man's diseases and extortion," writes noted historian John Hemming.

The Portuguese interest in the Indians as people was negligible; they represented heathen souls to convert, shiftless but profitable manpower, or potent enemies who still outnumbered those in the fledgling colonies. Above all, the Portuguese never accepted the Indians as people who had any right to the land. Even today the Indians are wards of the state and do not enjoy full sovereignty over their reserves.

Their only mentor was the Jesuit, António Vieira, who was expelled from Brazil in 1755 for encouraging the Indians to resist slavery. Later, his influence in the Portuguese court opened the still unresolved debate whether Indians should be supervised by missionaries or laymen.

The Jesuit missions replaced Indian culture with religion and hard labor. The Spanish Jesuits resisted a 1750 treaty that handed their seven flourishing settlements to Portugal and encouraged the Indians to resist inevitable enslavement. The historic conflict was the subject of the 1986 film "*The Mission*", and there is still lively debate over whether Jesuit missions defended or helped crush the Indians.

The end of slavery: In 1755 Portugal freed all Indians from slavery, but the effects were negligible. The Jesuits were expelled and their missions in southern Brazil and Paraguay put under the control of lay directors who could make profits from the Indians' forced labor. Under the Jesuits the seven

Guaraní missions held 30,000 Indians. By 1821 only 3,000 survived.

Indian labor was so scarce it was supplemented by African slaves. The Indians worked on plantations or were forced to row expeditions up rivers, to work on road building or in royal shipyards. Accustomed to shifting agriculture and forest life, their response to the harsh life was to flee up the tributaries of the Xingu and Madeira rivers to impenetrable sanctuaries where some still survive today. The advance of cattle ranchers across the northeastern plains, and of goldminers to the south, caused more bloodly conflicts. By the time the Portuguese Royal Family fled to Brazil in 1808, the whites outnumbered the Indians. Though they ceased to represent a threat, a new edict was issued permitting enslavement of hostile Indians in the south.

In the 19th century, the first scientists penetrated Brazil's interior and brought back shocking reports of life in Indian settlements. "They decay morally and physically in the most pitiful hybrid way of life," wrote two Germans. Disease, slavery and the introduction of alcohol bowed Indians to the point where white society regarded them as lazy and shiftless, incapable of integration. In 1845 the Indians were restored to mission life by the new Brazilian government, just in time for their labor to be tapped by the debt-slavery system used to extract rubber from the Amazon forest.

By then the river basin was the object of development dreams in which Indians had no place. "The Indians cannot endure the higher culture that Europe wishes to implant among them…it irritates them like destructive poison," wrote the German travelers Spix and Martius.

Scientific arguments were used to justify extermination of the Indians, believed to be an inferior race. "Immigration by a vigorous race will, in the struggle for survival of which Darwin speaks, annihilate them by assimilation," wrote a Brazilian intellectual.

Not all the blame can be heaped on the Portuguese and their descendants. In 1908 Hermann von Ihering, director of the São Paulo Museum, defended the extermination of all remaining Indians in the southern states of Santa Catarina and Paraná who threatened German and Italian immigrants. Diplomats from these countries also demanded energetic steps to protect their colonists against Indians whose territory was parcelled out to Europeans. In the early 1900s, *bugreiros*, Indian-hunters hired by the colonists, prided themselves in poisoning, shooting or raping Kaingáng Indians who were attempting to stop a railroad line pushing westward. By then, fewer than a million Indians survived.

The Indians' plight was heard: Ironically, von Ihering's outburst helped turn public opinion in the cities to the Indians' cause,

Left, young Indian mother with baby. Above, man wears brilliantly-colored feathered head-dress.

just as Candido Rondon, explorer and man of action, was sending back reports describing his pacification of Indians in Mato Grosso, where he was opening a telegraph line. Rondon's dedication to Indians was summed up in his standing orders to his troops: "Die if you must, but never shoot!" Rondon, a humanist, disapproved of missionaries and understood that Indians could only survive if their lands were guaranteed. In 1910 he successfully formed the Indian Protection Service, an attempt to pay the nation's debt to the Indians.

Though in its early years officers of the service carried out campaigns of pacification that cost dozens of lives, nothing could stop the decline of the Indians . Anthropologist Darcy Ribeiro found in 1960 that one third of the 230 tribes existing in 1900 had vanished. Today only an estimated 200,000 Indians survive.

"Entire tribes stubbornly refused to adapt to the invading civilization…some fought heroically to defend their lands, their freedom and their way of life. Others tried to accommodate the new values, but failed," historian John Hemming wrote.

Indian victories have been pitifully few. Chief amongst them is the creation of the Xingú Park, a natural refuge where several different tribes coexist. The park is the work of three veteran anthropologists, the Villas Boas brothers, who spent three decades amongst the Indians.

Today, Xingú Indians retain their tribal organization because contact with civilization is limited. They still deform their lower lips with large wooden discs, but many have developed business activities and in 1982 they even saw one of their leaders elected to the national congress. Every year TV crews pay handsomely to film the colorful dances of the Guarupa festival. Even with carefully-controlled exposure to civilization, Orlândo Villas Boas doubts the Indians will retain their cultural identity by the century's end. "People are romantic, but Indians aren't exotic—they are people who need help," he says without fanfare.

The survivors: Today the Indians are cared for by FUNAI, the government's Indian agency, which is also responsible for the still-uncompleted task of delineating Indian tribal land as protection against the tide of farmers, gold prospectors and logging companies. Legislation protecting the Indians is excellent, but in remote areas gun law often prevails.

Foreign missionaries are still responsible for the welfare of many Amazon tribes. Acculturated Indians have united to gain political force. The Xavante are imposing warriors whose belligerence in the court room won them back tribal lands taken over by modern farmers.

Today they run communal farms equipped with tractors and harvesters. In the lower Amazon unexpected prosperity has come to the tribes through royalties from gold prospectors. One group has a plane to fly in fresh bread, and a video camera to record rituals before their memory is lost forever.

A handful of uncontacted tribes still exist, but the integration of the Amazon basin into the world economy by means of massive development projects, dams and highways, has dislodged many survivors, whom urban Brazilians believe, and insist, stand in the way of "progress."

Probably the last and largest unassimilated tribe is the Yanomami, a nation straddled across the Brazil-Venezuela border in mountainous Roraima. Airborne missionaries first contacted many of the 8,000 living in the region in the 1950s and iron tools were introduced only a century ago. "Yanomami" simply means "humanity" and the isolated nomadic groups still hunt and skirmish amongst themselves with bows and arrows.

Roraima, where early explorers located El Dorado, is enjoying a mining boom, and the government is determined to settle its northern frontier. Thousands of illegal gold prospectors, know as *garimpeiros*, have poured into Yanomani territory, bring violence, pollution and epidemics of diseases which have brought the tribe face to face with extinction.

The Indians may soon vanish, but modern Brazilians are reminded of them daily through place names, foods, the spiritist rituals of *umbanda*—and even the national passion for cleanliness. The unhappy history of contact with whites means that today visitors are not welcome in reserves administered by FUNAI. Only "bona fide" researchers who are willing to wait months will get through the discouraging bureaucratic curtain erected by FUNAI and Rio's Museu do Indio, which processes all foreigners' applications.

Reaching outlying reserves often means chartering an expensive air taxi, as government planes are scarce. Life at isolated FUNAI posts is spartan. Visitors are expected to bring their own food and hammocks, and be in good health. Many Indian groups unreservedly request payment for photography or their company, which can be made with barter goods purchased at the government post.

Right, men play long pipes in Xingú reservation ceremony.

GB
AGO/87

VENDE-SE
ESTA-CASA

RICH MAN POOR MAN

Although no map will ever show them, there are in fact two Brazils, inhabiting the same space and living side by side.

One is a country of enormous potential with vast human and natural resources, a true land of opportunity. In this country, an individual can make it and make it big and once he's made it, unimaginable privileges and status are suddenly open to him.

The second country, though, is a land of deprivation, of blight and human misery. There are no opportunities in this country and there is little hope, save one: to escape to that other Brazil.

Since its inception as a nation, Brazil has been an imperfect and largely unjust society, sharply divided among social classes, with a small minority exercising complete control over the nation's political and economic life. Unlike other nations of the Americas, Brazil won its independence only to become a near carbon copy of its colonial past.

Elitist rule: Rather than rid itself of the trappings of monarchy bestowed by Portugal, Brazil embraced them. The country went from colony to empire, in the process replacing Portuguese noblemen with Brazilian clones and establishing the concept of elitist rule as a guiding precept of Brazilian society.

Since then, while the composition of the elite has changed (the nobles became landholders, then rubber barons, coffee barons, and today the industrial and business lords of the southeastern states), the basic divisions of society have remained unchanged: a few on top, a few more in the next level and a great many on the wide base of the Brazilian pyramid.

Today the upper 10 percent of Brazilian society accounts for 47.5 percent of total national income. The bottom half of the society accounts for 12 percent, less than the 14.5 percent of national income earned by the top one percent.

In a nation that prides itself on being the tenth largest economy in the world, only one-and-one-half percent of wage earners receive annual income in excess of $17,000. Two percent earn between $8,500 and $17,000 a year, 30 percent bring home between $2,000 and $8,500 yearly, while 52 percent earn less than $2,000 each year. Another 12 percent exist in the sub-world of the underemployed, earning loose change washing cars, selling sundry items on Brazil's street corners or simply begging.

These wage levels have long forced Brazilians, especially those on the bottom of the pyramid, to supplement their incomes. Among the poor, it is common for children to begin work at age ten, and increasingly women have joined the job market, today composing 33.5 percent of the work force. The extra incomes push up household earnings with the result that among Brazilian households, 4.5 percent earn in excess of $17,000 and 8.5 percent total between $8,500 and $17,000. Still, though, the bottom is where the bulk of households are found: 68 percent have total incomes of less than $4,300 a year.

Other divisions: The inequality of income distribution is just one dividing line between the two Brazils. The 13 percent of Brazilian households that enjoy a middle class or higher standard of living have access to quality health care, proper nutritional intake, good schooling for their children and adequate housing.

Their Brazil is a country of modern consumer goods, of shopping centers and fashionable boutiques, high-rise apartment buildings, medical clinics, chic restaurants, late model cars, private schools and university education.

For the two-thirds of Brazilian households on the far side of the division, there is none of this. Education, when available, is through the underfinanced and often overcrowded public school system. Health care is through a precarious public health system and housing conditions are deplorable, with millions of Brazilians living in shantytowns and tenement slums. While starvation on the level of Ethiopia is unknown, malnutrition is widespread.

Regional disparities: Examples of the two Brazils are found in every city and state but

<u>Preceding pages</u>, mansion protected by grating. <u>Left</u>, improvised slum housing.

there are also enormous regional disparities. For most of the colonial period, the northeast was the dominating economic force of Brazil, the center of the colony's rich sugar plantations. But as sugar lost its importance and was replaced by gold, general commerce and other cash crops, the region fell into decay.

The final blow was the industrial revolution that has swept Brazil this century, shifting all economic and political power to the factory-clogged cities of the southeast and south. Lacking industry and plagued by periodic droughts and an archaic tenant farming system, the northeast has become the symbol of the "other Brazil."

According to government figures, an extraordinary 86 percent of the children in the northeast suffer from some form of malnutrition. A majority of the country's victims of infectious diseases live in the northeast, where the infant mortality rate is 120 per 1,000 births compared to 87 for the nation and 61 for the southern states. Life expectancy in the region is only 55 years versus 64 for all of Brazil and 67 in the southeast.

Nearly 60 percent of the region's workers earn less than $900 a year, compared with 26 percent in the more prosperous southeast. While the northeast is home to only 28 percent of Brazil's total population, half of the country's illiterates are from the region. The illiteracy rate in the northeast is 47 percent versus 17 percent in the southeast and 26 percent for the nation as a whole. Only 2 percent of northeasterners have a high school education compared with 6 percent in the southeast.

Government attempts to remedy these inequalities and diminish the gap between the two Brazils have largely failed. The 1970s saw a spurt of economic growth and a major influx of foreign loans. These loans, however, went primarily to finance large infrastructure projects such as hydroelectric dams and highways. Social problems were mostly ignored, as the country's military rulers believed firmly in the trickle down effect of economic growth.

Social debt: With the arrival of the 1980s and the international debt crisis, the flow of foreign loans dried up and Brazil's new civilian rulers found themselves facing an enormous social debt.

As economic growth first slowed and then slumped into recession, the social question assumed critical proportions. The basic problem confronting Brazil is that the economy must grow at a rate of at least 3 percent annually in order to absorb the 1.5 million youths who enter the job market each year. At the same time massive investments must be made in education, housing, health and basic sanitation to compensate for the decade of neglect in the 1970s. Working against government efforts to address these questions have been unstable economic growth in the 1980s and an inefficient and unwieldy bureaucracy which in 1988 consumed over 80 percent of Brazil's federal tax receipts just to meet payroll costs. In addition, there is the controversial question of population growth. Even with stable economic expansion, the government will be hard pressed to provide services for a population that is doubling every 30 years.

Population explosion: At the moment Brazil's population is 140 million and growing at a rate of 2.3 percent a year. At this rate, the country's population will double by the year 2015.

Also doubling will be the number of children living in poverty (45 million today, 90 million in 2015), the number of children suffering from malnutrition (today 15 million, in 2015, 30 million) and the number of abandoned children (estimated at 12 million today, 24 million in 2015). In fact poverty statistics may more than double due to a higher birth rate among the lower classes (in the northeast the average number of children per family is five in the rural areas and four in the cities while the average in the southeast is 2.9).

Left, gracious living for the wealthy. Above, river slum in Bahia.

Birth control: Should population growth remain at 2.3 percent annually, the country would have 600 million inhabitants in the year 2050. Seen in this light it seems obvious that Brazil must take immediate steps to slow population growth. Thus far, though, opposition from the Catholic Church, leftists and a small but influential part of the armed forces has blocked all attempts to develop a nationwide birth control program.

The main barrier to effective population control is misinformation, not only among the general population but within the government as well. Officials tend to consider the matter secondary and also are easily convinced that it will resolve itself. The birth rate has fallen in the 1980s and will undoubtedly continue to decline. Some highly optimistic projections estimate that by the end of the century, population growth will be down to 1.7 percent annually. It seems more probable, however, that without massive government intervention, the rate will not reach this level before 2010.

One critical aspect of population growth in Brazil is where it is growing. In 1981-85, the backward northeast actually recorded a growth rate below that of the more advanced southeast, 2.1 percent versus 2.5 percent. But this does not mean that poor northeasterners are ahead of their more prosperous countrymen to the south in the practice of birth control. The difference is due to high infant mortality rates and low life expectancy in the northeast, plus one additional and crucial factor—the migration of northeasterners to the south in search of jobs.

Shifting population: This shifting of population from the rural northeast to the urban southeast began in the 1960s and still shows no sign of abating. The result is that today 25 percent of Brazil's population lives in the metropolitan areas of São Paulo, Rio de Janeiro, Belo Horizonte, Curitiba and Porto Alegre, the leading cities of the south and southeast. Between 1970 and 1980, the population of the metropolitan area of São Paulo was swelled by the arrival of 3 million immigrants, most of them from the impoverished northeast.

Through this process, unskilled, poor rural peasants are being exported to the industrial centers of the south and southeast, providing a steady source of cheap manpower but also an enormous and growing social problem. In addition to stretching public services to their limits, this mass of poor immigrants is contributing to the growth of fetid urban slums and an accompanying crime problem. Today 5 million residents of São Paulo, half of the city's population, live in sub-standard housing. Over 800,000 live in *favelas* or shantytowns, an increase of 1,039 percent since 1973, compared with the city's population growth of 60 percent during this period.

City officials estimate São Paulo's housing shortage at 1 million units. These figures indicate that because of the higher population growth among the poor, the Brazil of the have nots is invading the Brazil of the haves.

Thus far the only brake on Brazil's population growth has been the slowly increasing awareness among the poor of birth control techniques, not all of which are available to them because of costs. There is no sex education in Brazilian public schools and despite three announced government programs in the 1980s to provide free birth control information and devices, little has been done. Efforts have been stalled by opposition from the church, inadequate funding and bureaucratic inefficiency.

Ambiguous policy: Behind all of these factors, however, is the basic ambiguity of the government's position. Top ministers have admitted the need for population control, but official government policy remains one of non-interference in family planning, meaning in practice that the government refuses to encourage Brazilians to have fewer children. Because it is virtually impossible to provide birth control devices without encouraging men and women to use them, the government has been constantly accused by the left and the church with promoting birth control. This puts the government on the defensive and inevitably slows or blocks program implementation.

Despite this indecision in the government, there is ample evidence that poor Brazilians need and want government help. The most graphic proof of this is the fact that in the world's largest Catholic nation, where abortion is strictly forbidden, the number of abortions each year is equal to the number of births, which is approximately 3 million (the number of newborn Brazilians each year is also equal to annual births in the United States and the Soviet Union combined). A Gallup poll taken in Rio de Janeiro and São Paulo in 1987 showed that 63 percent of the respondents favored a government role in providing access to birth control devices and information.

Visible contrasts: For visitors, the contrasts between the two Brazils become quickly evident. Beggars line the beachfront sidewalks of Rio, while maids wash the windows of luxury high-rise apartments across the street. On the streets of São Paulo, Mercedes Benz limousines whisk by ragged men pushing hand carts filled with old newspapers to be sold for recycling.

What is not so apparent are the two lifestyles of the residents of the two Brazils. For the wealthy and near wealthy being at the top of the pyramid provides obvious material rewards. Sumptuous mansions line the streets of São Paulo's Morumbi neighborhood while in Rio, million dollar apartments form a phalanx of privilege along the beachfront in Ipanema. The rich of these and other Brazilian cities also own vacation homes in popular mountain and beach resorts. With labor cheap, the rich are surrounded by platoons of servants: maids, cooks, cleaning women, nannies, chauffeurs, gardeners, seamstresses and increasingly, security guards. A typical São Paulo mansion may have 10 to 15 servants (household servants are also common in middle class homes, which will usually have at least one live-in maid).

Left, wealthy home in São Paulo's Morumbi district.

What distinguishes Brazil's wealthy from their counterparts in other countries, though, is not their possessions but their power. The elite-driven nature of Brazilian society means that those on top have nearly unchallenged authority. There are white collar crimes in Brazil but there are no white collar criminals.

Today's business elite, the top layer of the upper crust and concentrated in São Paulo, does not wash its dirty linen in public, a practice that is also followed by Brazilian governments. Cases of fraud or corruption are in general handled quietly if possible behind closed doors. The elite is careful to protect its members.

For the residents of the other Brazil, there are no protective barriers between themselves and the hardships of life. On the contrary, they live on the cutting edge of misery. The most visible are those who inhabit the thousands of shantytowns scattered across the country, ranging from wooden shacks built on sticks above polluted waterways to the more affluent brick and concrete homes that now dominate the *favelas* of Rio and São Paulo.

Rio's *favelas*: Rio was the first major Brazilian city to become a home for these ubiquitous shantytowns. *Favelas* have been a part of the Rio scene since the start of the century, when federal troops discharged after putting down a rebellion in the northeast came to the city, setting up shacks on a near-downtown hillside. They named their community *favela* after the site of their encampment during the fighting in Bahia. Since then all shantytowns have been called *favelas* and they have grown steadily, assuming sometimes frightening proportions.

There are, according to the government, 480 *favelas* in Rio, with a population estimated at 1 million out of the city's total population of 5.6 million, and they are growing at the rate of 5 percent a year, double the growth rate of the city. At first confined to the downtown area, the *favelas* began to expand with the expansion of the city. They sprouted on the mountains behind Copacabana, moving on next to Ipanema, always following the steady southward movement of construction sites and jobs.

Attractive mosaic: While those on the mountainsides are the most prominent, with the colors of their shacks creating an oddly attractive mosaic in the midst of the gray rock and green forest, in recent years the *favelas* have also spread to the flatlands of the northern and southern suburbs of Rio.

Their existence is graphic evidence of the pressures of population growth on a city whose topography drastically limits its physical expansion. Since colonial times, Rio's residents have chosen to live close to the sea with the mountains to their backs, an aesthetically correct choice that has made Rio a city with clear boundaries between social classes as well as an unending nightmare for city planners.

With property values exploding for the limited land close to the beaches and downtown jobs, the poor have been forced to move steadily farther away, increasing the time and cost of travel to their work. Accompanying this trend has been a growing shortage of housing in the lower class neighborhoods of the city. The answer to both of these problems has increasingly been the *favela*.

Rocinha: Nowhere is this process more evident than in the Rio *favela*, Rocinha, Brazil's largest and possibly the largest in South America. In this swarming anthill of narrow alleys and streets, over 60,000 people live (some estimates are double this), most of them in makeshift brick houses and shacks, pressed tightly side-by-side. Rocinha began in the 1940s with a group of squatters taking over vacant land on a south zone hillside. By the 1960s, the *favela* had become a permanent feature of Rio, although its size was still restricted. During these years, several of Rio's larger *favelas* were removed by the city government and their inhabitants forcibly relocated in distant housing projects.

Rocinha, however, escaped this fate. Since the 1970s, the *favela* has undergone its own population explosion, first with a construction boom in the nearby Barra da Tijuca neighborhood. More recently it has received immigrants from Rio's distant northern slums seeking to move closer to their work, plus the overflow from other, crowded south zone *favelas*. Sprawling across a mountainside, Rocinha today is a city within a city, looking down at five-star hotels, luxury condominiums and a golf course, its unwilling neighbors in São Conrado, a popular, upper income beach area where hang gliders float serenely overhead.

The most urbanized of Rio's *favelas,* Rocinha has electricity, and an estimated half of its dwellings have at least running water. The slum also has a thriving commerce of its own—clothing shops, grocery stores, bars, lunch counters, drugstores, butcher shops, bakeries and a bank branch, all of them providing jobs to the *favelados* (squatters' rights give ownership after five years but in reality few of the properties in Rocinha have been legalized, although today the size of the shantytown makes removal unthinkable). In addition, Rocinha supplies the doormen, maintenance crews and other auxiliary help for the hotels and condominiums of São Conrado as well as providing cheap labor for Ipanema and other nearby neighborhoods.

But while relatively well off compared to other slums, Rocinha is far from being called a paradise. There are no sewers and garbage collection is at best infrequent. Health conditions are for the most part deplorable (Rocinha with its city-size population has only one poorly-equipped health clinic) and there is the constant danger of landslides during the rainy season.

Rocinha has also of late become the main source of illicit drugs, especially cocaine and marijuana, for the area's high rollers, a fact that has transformed the *favela* into a profitable center for Rio's drug trade.

Drug trafficking has also spread to other *favelas*, where, as in Rocinha, the economic power of the traffickers has made them the dominant force. Gangs of drug dealers now control the majority of Rio's hillside *favelas*.

For the immediate future there is no possibility of a significant change in the divisions of Brazilian society. Movement from the Brazil of the have nots to the Brazil of the haves is virtually unthinkable and those on top never fall back. A Brazilian economist once wrote a parable describing a country where a small minority enjoyed the standard of living of a Belgium while the overwhelming majority was trapped in the poverty of India. He called this nation Belinda. Its real name is Brazil.

Right, girl playing with kite in front of family's home.

ART OF COMPROMISE

Like other Latin American countries, Brazil is a land of extremes, of great wealth and wretched poverty, of rural backwardness and urban modernity.

Unlike its neighbors, however, Brazil has largely avoided open clashes between its extremes. There have been no bloody revolutions or civil wars in the history of Brazil, although on paper the elements have always been present.

What has saved this country from a history of confrontation and strife has been the uncanny ability of Brazilians to compromise, to find the middle ground and settle matters. This skill is an all-encompassing facet of the national character, expressed not only in politics but in ethics, justice, finances and all the myriad aspects of human interaction. There are extremes in Brazil but there are few if any absolutes—everything is open to negotiation.

Interpretations: One of Brazil's leading 20th-century politicians, the late President Tancredo Neves, was fond of saying, "It's not the fact but the interpretation that counts." Since "interpretations" change, so also do the "facts." In line with Neves' precept, Brazil is a land of unending interpretations and precious few facts, the ultimate kingdom of situation ethics.

Take for example the case of the traffic light. In Brazil, as in all other nations, traffic lights are red, yellow and green. One would assume that, as in the rest of the world, drivers would stop at a red light. Wrong. Drivers stop at red lights when it is absolutely necessary to stop but how often is it really necessary? There are clearly moments when a red light is no more than a meaningless nuisance or worse, a potential danger. If there is no one coming from the cross street, why should you waste your time waiting for the light to change colors? And in the dead of night, why should you be forced to stop in the street, and become a sitting duck for any passing criminal, just because the light is the wrong color?

In this manner, Brazilians have developed a unique skill at providing personal interpretations to supposedly universal facts.

The laws: There are, of course, laws in Brazil, thousands of them. But laws in Brazil tend to be like vaccines, some take and others don't. And why should a generally law-abiding citizen be forced to obey an obviously stupid law?

There is also a Supreme Court in Brazil, but very rarely is it called upon to judge the constitutionality of Brazil's laws. This act is performed daily by the country's 140 million citizens using their innate common sense to correct glaring injustices. Through this process, laws change and evolve naturally and humanely without the noise and inconvenience of legal challenges, court battles, etc. Congress is also spared the task of re-writing laws. Bad laws don't die, they just fade away.

In some cases, though, even ridiculous laws have their supporters and lobbies. For instance, there is a law in Brazil that regulates the profession of journalism. By this law every form of publication must employ card-carrying Brazilian journalists whether they need them or not, an artifice of the journalists union to guarantee jobs for its members. The law could be an enormous obstacle for companies with in-house organs and client newsletters for whom professional journalists would be an unwanted and unnecessary expense.

Enter Brazilian ingenuity. To avoid an unpleasant confrontation with the union, these companies hire a legitimate journalist and put his name on their mastheads. The journalist is paid very little but in compensation he does no work. Thus, the union is happy, the journalist is happy and the company is happy and in theory the law is obeyed.

Such inventive solutions fall under the general heading of *jeito*, a Portuguese word that has defied lexicographers and translators for centuries. Brazil's leading Portuguese dictionary devotes nearly one-third of a page in a valiant but fruitless attempt to define the word.

While its meanings are various, *jeito* is most often used in the expression *dar um jeito*, defined by the dictionary as "to find a

Left, a thoughtful moment.

solution or way out for a specific situation". Since "specific situations" in Brazil, like facts, are open to interpretation, there is an infinite variety of potential solutions for each of them, thus giving rise to what is a legitimate Brazilian art form—the creation of *jeitos.*

Bureaucratic red tape: Although one could argue as to which came first, the bureaucracy or the *jeito,* neither could survive long without the other. In a country buried up to its neck in officious bureaucrats and time-wasting red tape, the *jeito* is a national life saver. In 1979, the government attempted to cut its own red tape by creating a National Debureaucratization Program. Despite its unpronounceable name, the program was an immense success, but the bureaucracy has fought back and today with the program largely abandoned, individuals are once more left to their own solutions. Brazilians, however, take justifiable pride in their ability to come up with sometimes brilliant solutions to impossible situations.

Most individual *jeitos* result from a confrontation between an average citizen and a bureaucratic regulation. An amazingly large number of such regulations have no rationale other than the basic fact that they exist and therefore must be obeyed.

A Canadian diplomat recently received permission to visit an Amazon Indian tribe but at the last minute he was told he needed a chest x-ray to make the trip. There was no time for the x-ray to be taken, though, a fact that at first seemed to doom the diplomat's trip. A solution, however, was very quickly found—another person's x-ray was substituted, thus in theory satisfying the regulation.

The fixers: Solutions such as this usually depend on the compliance of the other end of the *jeito* life chain, the bureaucracy. For this, a certain amount of friendly persuasion is recommended. Not all individuals, though, are adept at handling this type of persuasion and most have no idea how much to pay. To resolve this situation (in effect another *jeito*), an entire profession was created, that of the *despachante* or fixer. The *despachante* is a consummate middleman, an artful dodger who has learned the ins and outs of the bureaucratic labyrinth and sells his services as a professional guide. Thus, an individual wishing to open a business (for which an infinity of forms must be filled out and fees paid, all of which can take months), will choose to pay a fixer to run the gauntlet of the bureaucracy. The businessman pays the fixer a set amount and asks no questions. The bureaucrats charge the fixer flat fees for which the fixer asks no questions. At the end, the businessman has the proper forms and can start work, the fixer has his earnings and both the bureaucrats and the bureaucracy are satisfied.

Not everyone, of course, is happy with this system. For law and order types, the creativity of Brazilian *jeito* smacks of permissiveness and self-indulgence, not to mention outright corruption. Occasionally, a public

official announces a major crackdown, such as the periodic attempts in Rio to force drivers to park their cars on the streets instead of the sidewalks.

For the first two weeks, the program is a success and the sidewalks are free of cars. But then common sense once more takes hold: there really aren't enough parking spaces on the streets for the cars and after all what do you expect a driver to do with his car, eat it? This plus a little friendly persuasion slowly but surely brings the cars back to the sidewalks.

Legal *jeitos*: A classic example of the power of *jeito* occurred earlier this century, when Brazilians found themselves caught in a monumental contradiction. Because of the Catholic church's opposition, divorce was outlawed, but married couples separated anyway. What then was their legal status? After much thought, the government hit upon a thoroughly Brazilian solution. A new status was invented called *desquite*, which covered couples who were separated but not divorced since there was no divorce. *Desquite* guaranteed alimony and child support for ex-wives but neither party could marry again (although naturally this was ignored). Thus the legal question was resolved and church leaders could sleep easily knowing that divorce was **still** prohibited.

This case raised *jeito* to a new status, that of a law of the land.

While most Brazilians prefer to believe that *jeito* is a harmless aspect of their national character, not all fixes have happy endings. In particular, the compromises worked out by the country's politicians have sometimes led to disastrous results. In 1961, the president of the country suddenly resigned, precipitating an enormous political crisis. According to the constitution, the vice president should have assumed the presidency, but the vice president was a leftist opposed by the military. Army generals threatened to overthrow the government. The vice president, however, also had support in the armed forces and suddenly the nation seemed on the verge of civil war.

To get themselves out of this mess, the congress and the generals negotiated a compromise, Brazilian style: the vice president was allowed to become president but the system of government was changed to parliamentary rule, with most of the power in the hands of a prime minister acceptable to the generals.

This clever solution, though, backfired. The president eventually persuaded congress to hold a national plebiscite in which the parliamentary system was rejected. With power in his hands, he then guided Brazil steadily towards the left, until in 1964, the military staged a coup, one situation for which no *jeito* has yet been invented.

Quick fixes have also gotten the government into trouble in the economic area. In one famous case in 1982, the government was informed that a leading brokerage house was about to go under. Concerned that this might lead to other failings, the ministers devised a "market solution" by which they convinced another brokerage to take over the collapsing firm with the promise of future benefits. Two years later, the merged firm, by now thoroughly debt-ridden, was caught turning out falsified bills of exchange. A total of $500 million worth were bought by unsuspecting clients, the largest financial fraud in Brazilian history. The brokerage's owner, however, argued that he did it all with the knowledge and permission of the government as part of their 1982 "deal." To date, no one has been punished in this fraud.

Despite such bad examples, *jeito* remains a firm and viable Brazilian institution. From the bottom to the top of society, Brazilians instinctively look for the easy way out of life's daily impasses, avoiding or postponing confrontations. In the midst of heated debate on Brazil's new constitution in 1987, a senator examined calmly what appeared to be an impossible division between left and right. "What will we do?" he asked. "We'll debate and scream and threaten. And then we'll sit down and compromise. It's always that way."

<u>Left</u>, drivers find parking space on sidewalk. <u>Above</u>, black market dollar rate displayed openly in São Paulo.

SAINTS AND IDOLS

Visitors to Brazilian beaches in December, January and February often find flowers, cakes of soap still in their wrappers or perfume bottles tossed on the shore strewn with burnt-out candles. These are the offerings of the followers of perhaps Brazil's largest religious cult after Catholicism, *umbanda*, in honor of the Afro goddess of the sea, *Iemanjá*. In the Valley of the Dawn, not far from Brasília, thousands of worshippers who believe in the imminent end of the world have set up a community under the "protection" of the spirits of Aluxá and Jaruá, with altars honoring Jesus Christ, White Arrow and the medium Aunt Neiva.

In the northeastern city of Juazeiro, women wear black every Friday and on the 20th day of the month in mourning over the death of Padre Cicero, who according to legend did not really die, but was translated (like Enoch, Elija and Santa Catarina) to heaven, and whose fingernail clippings possess therapeutic properties.

In the north-east, farmers draw magic circles around their sick cows and pray to Santa Barbara or her Afro-cult equivalent, Iansa, that their cow not die. They also place six lumps of salt outside their homes on the night of Santa Lucia, December 12. If the dew dissolves the first lump, it will rain in December, if on the second lump, January, and so on. If no dew dissolves the salt, drought will plague the *sertão*, the northeastern backlands.

Spiritual energy: The more time you spend in Brazil the more you discover that the country's inhabitants are charged with a spiritual energy that more often than not fails to fit in the patterns of traditional religion. Brazil has the largest Catholic population in the world but millions of the faithful light candles at more than one altar and feel no discrepancy whatsoever.

Brazil is one of the few countries in the world in which you can choose the century you want to live in. If you prefer a hectic 20th-century urban civilization, São Paulo, Rio de Janeiro and several other large cities are at your beck and call. Should you choose the 19th century, small towns and rural areas offer a way of life which differs little from that of the past century. There are pockets of the Middle Ages where religious cults live in communities and await with varying degrees of anxiety the end of the world. Should you wish to return to the stone age, there are Indians in the Amazon who have not yet conquered the use of iron.

And Brazil is one of the few countries in the world where you choose from several different forms of religion and immerse yourself in all the internal and external expressions of the cult, from animistic Indian rites, through messianic and end-of-world beliefs, to the philosophical doctrines of existential Protestantism, the Liberation Theology of rebel Catholic priests, or modern and traditional Judaism.

Left, worshippers at Vale da Aurora outside Brasilia. Right, pilgrim prays with rosary in Juazeiro.

Indian influence: The nation's Indian heritage is partly responsible for the deep-rooted mystic beliefs. Even today the Indian tribes that have not been fully assimilated continue to make artifacts which are gradually losing their religious meaning. The clay sculptures of the Karajas represent birth and death. The myth of the origin of medicinal plants is associated with the ritual flutes of the Nambikara. The figures on the Aparai baskets represent their myths, and the Bororo, Macro, Je, Urubu and many other tribes use diadems, bracelets or necklaces made of feathers of birds emblematic of magic, health, disease or death. Indians of the Amazon evoke dead ancestors rising out of totem tree trunks as the men paint their body with symbolic colors and wrestle and dance and play giant flutes and chant night and day. The tribal villages themselves assume a mythical configuration. The north huts and the south huts of the Bororo follow the trajectory of the sun and the west is a circular area called "Path of the Souls".

African religious cults: African rites are the second major influence in Brazilian religious culture. Perhaps the most African of the rituals is *candomblé*, practised primarily in the northeastern state of Bahia, where priestesses are ordained with the ceremonial shaving of heads, ritual baths, the smearing of hen's or goat's blood and chicken feathers on their foreheads.

The ceremony is accompanied by *atabaque* drums, chants in African languages and frenetic dancing until the initiates fall in a trance. *Quimbanda* contains other influences as well as African and is characterized by what Brazilians call "black magic", meaning destructive hexes against others, with sacrifices of black hens, roosters or goats. In some services the deities are served heads and feet of animals while the priests keep the more delectable parts for themselves. *Umbanda* is also associated with "white magic", including invocations for healing and rites and prayers promoting a more positive form of sympathetic magic. *Umbanda* is strongly influenced by non-African cults, although it is often classified under the umbrella of *macumba*, an Afro-Brazilian term comparable with voodoo.

Voodoo cults, similar to those in Haiti and the rest of the Caribbean, found roots in a few parts of Brazil. In Maranhão and on the northern border with the Guianas, descendants of runaway slaves cultivated African tribal patterns and cults far from the domination of the white man until early in the 20th century.

Black heritage: One by-product of Brazil's thriving African cults has been the maintenance of an oral history of the blacks in Brazil. It has been far easier for Brazilian blacks to trace their ancestry back to Africa than for American blacks. Leading priestesses of *candomblé*, such as the late Olga Olekatu and Mãe Menininha de Gantau, could recite the names of their ancestors and the ancestors of the members of their community, going back as far as their African homeland. They described in detail how their ancestors were bound and transported on slave ships to Brazil. Before the priestesses died they transmitted this knowledge to the new spiritual leaders of the community, who memorized the immense genealogy. Even today spiritual leaders are the scribes and notary publics in parts of tribal Africa, learning by heart the genealogy of their people.

Religious blending: The mixture of Indian, African and European cults results in a unique form of syncretism or blending of

religions in Brazil, where Catholic Santa Barbara is Iansa of the Afro-Brazilian cults, where Iemanjá, the goddess of the sea, often assumes the form of the Virgin Mary and Xango, the god of thunder, St. George.

Syncretist cults such as *umbanda* may also include the god of war, Ogun, the orixãs or godlike figures, and the demonlike forces, Exus, which are part of the *candomblé* and other African rituals. *Umbanda* is part of a mystic movement called spiritism, which mingles the African-inspired figures along with purely Brazilian semi-deities or mediums such as Pai João, Caboclo and Pomba Gira, plus the mystical theological concepts of Allan Kardec, a European spiritual figure. Then there is the Brazilian spiritual leader, Chico Xavier, whose books sold in the millions to his followers and are said to be transcodifications of messages from the beyond. Some of the most popular images on the *umbanda* and spiritist altars are St. Cosme and St. Damyan, St. George slaying the dragon, and Iemanjá in her white flowing robes, or the cigar-smoking Uncle Tom-like figure, Pai João.

Iemanjá is sometimes characterized as the Virgin Mary, sometimes as a sea goddess or a mermaid. On December 13, in Praia Grande, São Paulo, December 31 in Rio de Janeiro and February 2 in Bahia, her worshippers offer flowers, perfume and face powder at the edge of the sea (Iemanjá is a vain goddess, appeased only by flowers and cosmetics). If the offerings sink in the water or are carried out to sea, Iemanjá is said to accept them. If they return to shore she rejects them.

Imagery from Europe: Religious imagery from Europe arrived with the first Portuguese colonizers, who brought with them the

Far left, offering on a Rio beach and left, chicken blood dripped on *candomblé* initiate. Above, sea celebration and right, man wears both Christian and Afro-Brazilian religous symbols.

most frequently worshipped Catholic saints and, above all, the manger scene. Nativity scenes were supposed to be mounted for seven years in a row or the family would suffer divine retribution. Every year a new figure had to be added and the Christ Child's clothes could not be changed. New clothes were added on to the old each Christmas. In some manger scenes, Brazilian animals abound, including the armadillo and native butterflies.

Patron Saints: The patron saint of Brazil is Nossa Senhora de Aparecida, the Virgin of the Conception. Three centuries ago, a broken terra-cotta image "appeared" in a fisherman's net in the Paraiba River between Rio and São Paulo. The custom in those days was to throw broken images into the river as it was considered bad luck to have a broken saint in the house. The custom continued well into the 20th century.

Today the Basilica of Aparecida, located on the highway between Rio and São Paulo, houses the terra-cotta image and receives more than 3 million pilgrims a year, exceeded only by the Virgin of Guadalupe in Mexico and Czechestowa in Poland. A number of legends, stories, superstitions and presumed miracles have been woven around the image.

In the late 1970s it was broken by a fanatic and restored by specialists from the São Paulo Art Museum. Every year on the October 12 saint's day, hundreds of thousands of worshippers will flock to the sanctuary, some crawling on their bleeding knees. There are orders of cavaleiros—horsemen who ride on pilgrimages for hundreds of miles. It is said one man walked a thousand miles carrying an enormous cross to fulfill a "promise".

Another popular representation of the Virgin is Our Lady of the "O", a euphemism for the pregnant Virgin. The upper clergy tried to suppress this cult in favor of Our Lady of the Conception (with no distended belly). Some Brazilians call Our Lady of the "O", "Our Lady of March 25", that is to say she conceived nine months before Christmas. Due to the perils of childbirth, Our Lady of the "O" is worshipped by pregnant women.

Therapeutic properties: Other saints have therapeutic properties. Santa Lucia is supposed to cure bad eyesight and blindness. Santa Barbara protects against lightning. Single girls pray to Saint Anthony to find them a husband. Santo Antonio normally carries the Christ Child in his arms, but in a form of sympathetic magic, the marriageable girls remove the Christ child, which presumably makes the saint so upset he would do everything in his power—even find the girls a husband—to get little Jesus back. Only after the wedding does the successful bride return the Christ Child to Saint Anthony's arms.

São Bras, the Bishop, protects against sore throats and choking on fish bones. Another popular saint carved in wood or molded in plaster of paris is Saint Jude, who always wears tall boots. This is the same Saint Jude known in Europe as the patron of lost causes.

Carrancas: Many images which once bore a religious connotation have survived without their former mystic aura. The carranncas were wooden figureheads attached to the prows of paddle-wheel steamers and other vessels sailing up and down the São Francisco River from 1850 to about 1950. Today on the beach in Nazare, Portugal, fishermen paint eyes on the prows of ships to "see" the dangers underwater. Similar prow figures served the same purpose in Guiné and other parts of Africa.

The Brazilian carrancas were carved in the form of monsters, to frighten off the spirits of the waters that were a menace to shipping. The carranca gazed down and the crew aboard ship saw only the elaborate mane so as not to be "frightened" by its terrible features. The São Francisco River is rich with legends of water spirits, "the Water Bitch", "the Water Monster", and the *Caboclo da Agua* ("Backwoodsman of the Water"), which send ships down to a watery grave.

The spiritual force of woodcarving continues to this day in the São Francisco Valley and the Brazilian central plateau, where the Brazilian artist GTO, Geraldo Teles de Oliveira, makes sculptures with rings of winged forms mounted like spokes on a wheel similar to the circular medieval representations of the hierarchies of angels. GTO's angels, however, look alike and have no differentiating features like the medieval distinctions between the cherubim, seraphim, archangels, thrones, powers, glories and dominations.

A popular subject for Brazilian artists

throughout the centuries has been the crooked angel. Some of the gilt carved angels in the São Francisco Church and other churches in Bahia have malicious features—wall-eyed, cross-eyed, presbyopic. In a similar tradition,

Marino Araujo, a contemporary sculptor from Minas, creates his angels, priests, monks, and manger scene centurions with bulging guppy eyeballs, with one eye looking north-northwest and the other looking south-southeast.

Besides angels, the arts and crafts fairs all over Brazil are literally flooded with carved sculptures of the saints. Among the most original of these are the no-neck images of Santa Ana made by woodcarvers of the northeastern state of Ceará.

Padre Cicero: Hundreds of woodcarvers have also sculpted images of the most famous religious figure of the northeast, Padre Cicero, and literally millions of plaster of paris images have been sold throughout the country.

Some of Padre Cicero's followers honor him by wearing black on the day of his death (June 20). Cicero was considered a messiah who would turn the dry backlands green, into a paradisiacal garden where hunger and poverty would cease. A verdant valley of the region was named the "Horto" or Garden of Gethsemane and the city of Juazeiro was called the "New Jerusalem". Some of his more fanatic followers were said to collect his fingernail clippings, which, like water used to wash his soutane, were said to have magical properties.

He first gained fame when an elderly woman, Maria Araujo, received the host from his hands at Mass then fell on the floor in convulsions. Blood in the form of the "sacred heart" was said to form on the host. Balladeers wandered throughout the *sertão* singing praises of the miraculous priest and the "miracle of the Sacred Heart". Other, more cautious observers, suggested that Maria Arauja suffered from tuberculosis and had coughed up blood or suffered from bleeding gums. One detractor, Pedro Gomes of nearby Crato, hinted that the host was made of litmus paper and that Padre Cicero's "miracle" was nothing but an acid test known to every student of chemistry. Padre Cicero's fame spread throughout the land like wildfire and one balladeer went so far as to sing: "Padre Cicero is one of the three of the Holy Trinity."

The "miracle of the host" occurred in 1895, shortly before the outbreak of the

Above, interior of Roman Catholic church. Right, in contemplative mood.

Canudos War, in which troops of the newly founded Brazilian Republic were sent to crush a movement by Antonio Conselheiro, a religious fanatic who prophesied a rain of stars and the imminent end of the world. The Brazilian government thought Conselheiro represented the forces of the deposed Brazilian emperor. Conselheiro and his followers thought that the new Republic was the Antichrist for refusing to recognize religious marriages.

The Republic sent thousands of troops to stamp out Conselheiro's community in Canudos. Conselheiro's men repelled four government incursions. However, in 1897 the Army got the upper hand and literally decimated thousands of Conselheiro's followers, including women and children. Some who survived wandered to Juazeiro and swelled the ranks of Padre Cicero's worshippers.

Through woodcarvings, songs and verse published in chapbook form, the Padre Cicero legend has been carried forward. A statue of the priest was built in Horto in the 1960s and his church has become a popular shrine that annually attracts thousands of followers.

The church in Juazeiro is filled with *ex votos* or votive offerings carved in wood in the shape of injured limbs or parts of human bodies. When someone is cured of an illness he fulfills a promise by carving an image of the wounded part of his body and after making a pilgrimage to Juazeiro hangs the carving in the *ex voto* chamber of the church as a token of gratitude.

Churches in Caninde and Salvador are filled with *ex votos*, the more recent ones made of wax at the encouragement of the priests, who melt them down and later sell them as candles.

There are delicately carved femur tibias, hands, elbows, pockmarked heads, eyes, perforated abdomens, etc. One elderly woman who watched over the *ex voto* room in Juazeiro was famed for the curses she hurled at anyone who tried to steal the votive offerings: "Steal those eyes and Padre Cicero will blind you. Steal those lungs and Padre Cicero will give you tuberculosis. Steal that leg and Padre Cicero will curse you with leprosy."

One of the most famous Padre Cicero woodcuts is called "The Girl Who Turned into a She Dog Because She Cursed Padre Cicero on Good Friday." Metamorphosis, or the transformation of a human into an animal, is a punishment frequent in Brazilian chapbooks when someone violates the moral and religious codes of the region.

Since the death of Padre Cicero, numerous messianic cults have appeared, the most famous in the northeast being centered around Frei Damião, a Calabrian priest who arrived in Brazil 60 years ago and who preaches with the same fire and brimstone images used by Antonio Conselheiro, Padre Cicero and a host of other prophetic figures over the past three centuries.

Mysticism: A religious movement known as the Valley of the Dawn (*Vale do Amanhecer*) has sprung up near Brasília, where thousands of followers eagerly await the millennium in the belief they will be among the chosen few to survive the end of the world.

They have built an enormous temple filled with new deities and religious figures, including Aluxá, Jaruá, the Indian White Arrow and the medium Aunt Neiva, the founder of the movement. About 35 miles (60 km) from Brasília, the Valley of the Dawn is currently the largest center of mysticism in Brazil.

The movement was founded by Aunt Neiva in 1959 and moved to the Brasília suburb of Planaltina in 1969. Today it has 4,000 inhabitants, a school for 300 students, a cafeteria, two restaurants, an ice cream parlor, hotel and two policemen assigned by the Brasília police department.

On arriving at the Valley of the Dawn, visitors can see dozens of women in long robes decorated with silver sequins in the shapes of stars and quarter moons. They wear veils and gloves that match their dresses (usually black, blue or red). The men wear brown trousers, a black shirt, a ribbon which crosses their chests and carry a leather shield. These are the mediums who lead thousands of the sect.

Aunt Neiva, the founder, believed there were 100,000 Brazilians with the supernatural powers of a medium, and she herself registered 80,000, according to her follower Mario Sassi. "Two thirds of humanity will disappear at the end of the millennium, but we, here in the Valley of the Dawn, will be saved," Aunt Neiva preached.

The Valley of the Dawn is the latest of the messianic and end-of-world movements of Brazil. Hundreds of years before, the followers of King Sebastião, the Portuguese king who disappeared in combat with the Moors in Morocco, believed he would reappear in Brazil and turn the dry lands green and turn the sea to dry land.

Brazil has always been synonymous with mystic energy and religious expectation and as the century ends this energy and expectation will no doubt intensify.

Left, *umbanda* ceremony. Above, Catholic procession.

BODYBOARD

XYZ
XYZ

Gov. Portela
Petrópolis
SERRA DO COUTO
SERRA DOS ORGÃOS
Guapimirim
Xerém
Inhomirim
S. Aleixo
Imbarié
Majé
Rio Iguaçu
Mauá
Nova Igauçu
Baia de Guanabara
Rio Macacu
Duque de Caxias
Int. Rio Airport
Ilha de Governador
S. João de Meriti
Nilópolis
São Gonçalo
Niterói
Rio de Janeiro
15km
Oceano Atlântico
R. Basilo de Brito Galileu
JACARÉ
R. P. de Silva
R. Lino Teixeira
R. Sousa Barros
Av. Ana Neri
Av. Quatro de Majo
R. Mar Rondon
R. Mar Rondon
R. Br. de Bom Retiro
SERRA DO ENGHO NOVO
VILA ISABEL
R. Santa Isabel
R. Vinte e Oito de
R. Prof Valadares
MARACANÃ
R. Br.
R. Maxwel
ANDARAÍ
de Mesquita
R. Leopoldo
R. Maracanã
R. Conde de Bonfim
SERRA DOS TRÊS RIOS
Estrada da Cascatinha
PEDRA DO CONDE
Cascatinha
Estrada
Estrada do Redentor
FLORESTA DA TIJUCA
ALTO DA BOA VISTA
PARQUE NACIONAL DA TIJUCA
Mesa do Imperador
Cascatinha
Estrada de Vista Chinese
Vista Chinesa
FURNAS
Estr. da Perdra da Gávea
Estr. das Furnas
PEDRA BONITA
Viaduto das Canoas
Ten. Arantes Filho
GÁVEA
Estr. da Barra Tijuca
Estr. da Barra Tijuca
CANOA
ITANHANGÁ
R. Capuri
Túnel Dois Irmãos
PEDRA DIOS
S. CONRADO
Joá est da
Pref. Mendes de Morais
PEDRA DA GÁVEA

Rio de Janeiro
2km
Av. Brasil
SÃO CRISTÓVÃO
R. Beja Escobal
Av. Rio de Janeiro
Cais de Porto
Av. Rodrigues Alves
Av. Perimetral
SAUDE
Cabral
GAMBOA
Ilha das Corbas
Ilha Fiscal
R. Luis Gonzaga
R. Exército
SANTO CRISTO
R. America
R. Senador Pompeu
Av. Rio
National Museum
Quinta de Boa Vista
R. Perdro II
Av. F. Bicalho
PRES. VARGAS
URUGUAIANA
CENTRO
CARIOCA
Av. Gal. Justo
Santos Dumont Airport
MARAKANÃ
Av. Presidente Vargas
CENTRAL
Branco
Av. Osvalao Aranha
PC. DA BANDEIRA
CIDADE NOVA
PC. ONZE
R. Frei Caneca
S. CHRISTÓVÃO
ESTÁCIO
Av. Mem de Sá
CINELÂNDIA
Av. Beira Mar
Ilha de Villegaignon
Estádio Maracanã
PARÇA DA BANDEIRA
Av. Paulo de Frontin
R. Riachuelo
Túnel Santa Barbara
Av. Maracanã
S. FCO. XAVIER
AFONSO PENA
RIO COMPRIDO
SANTA TEREZA
GLÓRIA
R. Conde de Bonfim
CATETE
Praia do Flamengo
Parque do Flamengo
Baía de Guanabara
R. Lima des Isidro
R. Junouilhos
Alexandrino
SUMARÉ
LARANJEIRAS
LGO. DE MACHADO
R. Pinheiro Machado
R. Almirante
R. Das Laranjeiras
FLAMENGO
Ponta de São Teodósio
COSME VELHO
FLAMENGO
SERRA DA CARIOCA
Av. Nacoes Unidas
Mirante Dona Marta 362m
Praia de Botafogo
URCA
PÃO DE AÇÚCAR
Sugar Loaf 404m
Estrada das Pianeiras
Late Club
Sumaré
Corcovado (Statue of Christ) 709m
Túnel Rebouças
BOTAFOGO
Mirante
R. Humaita
BOTAFOGO
R. Gen. Polidoro
Av. Princ. Isabel
Parque Lage
JARDIM BOTÂNICO
R. Pacheco Leão
R. Jardim Botânico
Av. Borges de Medeiros
LAGOA
R. Barata Ribeiro
Botanical Gardens
Lagoa Rodrigo de Freitas
Av. Epit. Pessoa
COPACABANA
Av. Atlântica
Praia de Copacabana
Padre Leonel França
LEBLON
Av. Epit. Pessoa
IPANEMA
Av. N. Senhora de Copacabana
Av. Ataulfo de Paiva
R. Visconde de Piraja
Av. Delfim Moreira
Av. Vieira Souto
Ponta de Copacabana
Av. Niemeyer
Praia do Leblon
Praia de Ipanema
Praia do Vidigal

BRAZIL'S GIFT

As its size would suggest, Brazil is a giant package with a multitude of gifts. Travelers looking for warm water, white sand and tropical beauty will be overwhelmed by the Brazilian coastline, the longest if not the most beautiful in the world. In an area that would fit all the beaches of the Riviera and Hawaii and still have hundreds of miles left over, the options range from isolated, palm-tree encrusted inlets to gently-curving crescents to miles-long straightways backed by sand dunes. One of the eternal arguments among Brazilians is exactly which of the country's mass of beaches is the best. No-one has yet discovered the answer.

In the north and northeast, colonial monuments dot the region's capital cities, the majority of which are located on the water. Salvador and Recife, former colonial capitals, offer the best combination of beach and history. In addition, Salvador is home to a culture of its own which is a unique mixture of black Africa and Portuguese Brazil.

The onslaught of beautiful beaches continues on south, reaching its zenith in the Americas' all-time leading beach city, Rio de Janeiro. But Rio is more than just the sum of its beaches. It is spectacular scenery (mountains and sea), samba, carnival and a relaxed, carefree existence. The newly popular resort areas of Buzios and Angra dos Reis, both within hours of Rio, beckon with unspoiled beaches and tropical islands, while in the mountains outside of Rio, sedate, European-style resort hotels offer a cool respite from the often searing heat of the coastal plain.

In São Paulo, Brazil stops playing and gets down to serious stuff. The center of the Third World's largest industrial park, São Paulo is the most dynamic city of South America. Its hodge-podge of nationalities and ethnic groups make it a wonderful Brazilian version of New York.

The farther south you travel in Brazil, the more European influences take over, culminating in the states of Paraná, Santa Catarina and Rio Grande do Sul, where Italian, German and Polish settlers have left their mark. Here, too, the accent is on sand and water, with the beaches of Santa Catarina taking first prize in the south.

Not all of Brazil is located on the coast. Inland travelers will discover some of the world's most remarkable natural wonders. Occupying one-third of the nation's territory is the Amazon rain forest, a home to legend and romance as well as the mighty Amazon river. Below the Amazon region, in an area drained by its rivers, is the Pantanal, an immense swampy area that serves as a natural sanctuary for fish, birds and animals. In the south, the wildly beautiful Iguaçu Falls is considered by many to be the greatest natural attraction of Brazil.

Preceding pages: Sugarloaf mountain guards the entrance to Rio's Guanabara Bay; a lazy day at the beach in Rio; map of Rio de Janeiro. Left, Christ the Redeemer statue.

RIO DE JANEIRO

Sprawling in majestic disarray across a strip of land between granite peaks and the South Atlantic, Rio de Janeiro is the final victory of fantasy over fact.

Each day Rio's streets and sidewalks support some 8 million persons transported by some 1 million cars, trucks, buses, motorcycles and scooters all competing for room in a space designed for one-third their number. This spectacular chaos, though, does nothing to dampen the enthusiasm of the *carioca*, Rio's imperturbable native son. For the *carioca*, all things are relative, except for one—the wonder and beauty of Rio de Janeiro.

Altogether there are 5.6 million *cariocas*, the residents of Rio proper, but an additional 4 million live in suburbs ringing the city. Many are poor by American or European standards, as many as 70 percent. But there is the beach and there is the samba and there is carnival and there is the comforting presence of Rio's extraordinary beauty.

Nothing quite prepares you for Rio, not the postcards, not the films, not the comments, nothing, not even living in Rio really does it. There are other cities that have grown up backed by mountains and fronted by the sea but there are none where the play of light, the shifting of shadows, the mix of colors and hues are so vibrant and mobile. Each day in Rio is slightly different from the previous day and all of them are strikingly beautiful.

History: The first tourists officially arrived in Rio on January 1, 1502. They were part of a Portuguese exploratory voyage headed by Amerigo Vespucci. Vespucci entered what he thought to be the mouth of a river, hence the name Rio de Janeiro or River of January. Vespucci's river was in reality a 147-sq mile (245-sq km) bay, still known today by its Indian name, Guanabara or "arm of the sea."

As the Portuguese slowly settled their colony, they concentrated on regions north and south of Rio, leaving in peace the Tamoio Indians inhabiting the land surrounding the bay. This peace was eventually broken by raids launched by French and Portuguese pirates who prowled the Brazilian coast in search of riches. In 1555, a French fleet arrived with the intention of founding France's first colony in the southern half of South America. The efforts to colonize the coastline were largely unsuccessful and in 1560, the Portuguese attacked, driving out the last remnants of the French colony in 1565.

From then on, Rio received increasing attention from Brazil's Portuguese masters. In 1567, the city of São Sebastião de Rio de Janeiro was founded. While named in honor of Saint Sebastian, on whose feast day the founding occurred, the city soon became simply Rio de Janeiro.

By the end of the 16th century, Rio was one of the four largest population centers of the colony and from its port sugar was exported to Europe. Its importance grew over the next 10 years, challenging that of the colony's capital of Salvador in the northeastern state of Bahia.

In the 18th century, a gold rush in the neighboring state of Minas Gerais turned Rio into the colony's financial center. Gold became the main export item and all of Brazil's gold went through Rio to Portugal. In 1763, the colonial capital was transferred from Salvador to Rio as recognition of Rio's newly-won status.

Pre-eminent city: Until the 1950s Rio was Brazil's pre-eminent city. When the Portuguese royal family fled from Napoleon's conquering army in 1808, Rio became capital of the Portuguese Empire. With Brazil's independence in 1822, Rio's title shifted to capital of the Brazilian Empire, changing again in 1889 to capital of the Republic of Brazil. Throughout these years, Rio was the economic and political center of Brazil, home to the pomp of the monarchy and the intrigue of the republic.

The 20th century brought a surge of economic growth in the state of São Paulo. By 1950, São Paulo had sur-

Preceding pages: hillside existence of Rio's poor; Rio's famous Copacabana beach. Below, clowns parade at Carnival.

passed Rio in population and economic importance, a lead that it has never relinquished. In 1960, Rio suffered the final humiliation when President Juscelino Kubitschek formally moved the nation's capital to the city he had built in the center of the country, Brasília.

Since losing its status as number one, Rio has floundered about. Its previous rankings as the country's leading industrial and financial center were also taken over by upstart São Paulo. Although Rio's upper crust refuse to admit it, the city has become increasingly dependent on tourism, today Rio's biggest money maker. But even in the uncomfortable role of number two, Rio remains at the heart of the nation's unending political intrigue. Decisions may be made in Brasília and São Paulo, but as *cariocas* proudly note, plots are hatched in Rio.

Historical downtown: For visitors to Rio, there is little sense of the city's historical past, a result of sporadic construction booms and the *carioca's* insatiable thirst for the new and modern. With space limited by the contours of Rio, something must usually go down before something else can go up. The wrecking ball has done away with much of old Rio, but there are still unique treasures hidden along the old downtown streets.

Perched on a hilltop overlooking Guanabara Bay is the most precious of these gems, the **Nossa Senhora da Glória do Outeiro** chapel, popularly known as simply the Glória Church. This petite 1720s church, with its gleaming white walls and classic lines, is one of the best-preserved examples of Brazilian baroque and a landmark of downtown Rio.

In the heart of the downtown area, at the **Largo da Carioca**, is the **Santo Antônio Monastery**. Construction spans several colonial periods starting from 1608. The main church was completed in 1780 and next to it stands the 1739 **São Francisco da Penitência Chapel**, whose interior is rich in gold leaf and woodcarvings.

Due north of Largo da Carioca is

Santa Teresa street car atop the old aqueduct.

Praça Tiradentes, a public square where Brazil's most famed revolutionary, Tiradentes, was hanged in 1793 after the Portuguese uncovered his plot to win independence for the colony. Urban decay has removed the square's historical aura, a problem that has also affected the **Largo de Sâo Francisco**, located behind Tiradentes. On the south side of the Largo, behind the rows of buses that hug the square's contours, is the **Igreja de São Francisco de Paulo**. Rococo design on the outside, the church's interior chapel is famed for its paintings by baroque artist Valentim da Fonseca e Silva.

Three blocks from the Largo da Carioca and across downtown's main thoroughfare, Av. Rio Branco, runs a maze of pedestrian streets crowded with businessmen, shoppers and the eternal army of downtown office boys. **Praça XV de Novembro** is home to the **Paço Imperial**, a classic structure dating from 1743 that first served as the capital building for Brazil's governor generals and later as the imperial palace. Recently restored, the Paço is now a culture center.

Nearby on **Rua Primeiro de Março** is the **Nossa Senhora do Carmo Church**, completed in 1761 and the site of the coronations of both Brazil's emperors, Pedro I and Pedro II. Next door, separated by a narrow passageway, is the **Nossa Senhora do Monte do Carmo Church**, 1770.

Four blocks west of Praça XV is Rio's most striking church, the **Igreja da Candelária**. Built between 1775 and 1877, the domed Candelária stands like a timeless guardian at the beginning of Av. Presidente Vargas which stretches out before it. Five blocks east on Av. Rio Branco and up a hill is the **São Bento Monastery**, dating from 1633. The monastery overlooks the bay, but more impressive and spectacular than the view from the hill is the splendor of the monastery's gold leaf-covered wood carvings.

Land fills: The hill on which the monastery stands is one of the few that survive in downtown Rio. The others

Bird kites for sale on Copacabana beach.

which existed during the colonial period have fallen victim to *carioca* progress, a penchant for removing hills to fill in the bay. The Candelária church, which once stood close to the water, is now far removed, thanks to land fills using dirt from the fallen hills.

The most tragic case was in 1921-22 when the downtown hill of Castelo was carted off together with most of Rio's remaining 16th and 17th century structures.

Before the hill disappeared, it formed a solid backdrop to Rio's most elegant avenue. Inaugurated in 1905, Avenida Central was built in response to President Rodrigues Alves' vision of a tropical Paris. Unfortunately Alves overlooked the fact that downtown Rio, unlike Paris, had no room to grow other than vertically.

Through the years the elegant three and five-story buildings of Avenida Central were replaced by 30-storey skyscrapers. In the process, the avenue also suffered a name change, becoming today's **Av. Rio Branco**. Of the 115 buildings that flanked Av. Central in 1905, only 10 remain. The three most impressive are: the **Municipal Theater**, a two-thirds replica of the Paris Opera with one of the world's most unusual restaurants downstairs in unforgettable Assyrian motif; the **National Library**, which is an eclectic mixture of neo-classic and *art nouveau*; and the **Museum of Fine Arts**, where the works of Brazil's greatest artists are on display.

Museums: Most of Rio's principal museums are located either downtown or nearby. Besides the fine arts museum there are: the **Museum of the Republic** in the **Catete** neighborhood, 10 minutes from downtown and the former residence of Brazil's presidents; the **National Historical Museum**, just south of Praça XV, containing Brazil's national archives; the **Naval and Oceanographic Museum**, one block north of the historical museum, famed for its detailed ship models; the **Museum of Modern Art**, on the bay beside the downtown airport (unfortunately the

Bus stop with 1986 World Cup soccer mural.

museum's valuable collection was completely destroyed by fire and a new collection is slowly amassing); the **Indian Museum** in the **Botafogo** neighborhood 10 minutes from downtown, an excellent source of information on Brazil's Indian tribes; the **Casa Rui Barbosa**, near the Indian museum, the former home of one of Brazil's most famed scholars and political leaders.

Fifteen minutes by car from downtown is the **National Museum**, the former residence of the Imperial family during the 19th century. The impressive palace, next door to Rio's zoo, houses natural history, archaeological and mineral exhibits. It is located at Quinta da Boa Vista.

Santa Teresa: Only a few minutes from the crowded streets of downtown Rio is the neighborhood of **Santa Teresa**, a tranquil nest of eccentricities perched atop the mountain spine that presses against the city below. According to legend, black slaves used Santa Teresa's mountain trails to escape from their owners during the 18th century, when Rio was Brazil's leading slave port. Santa Teresa began to receive more permanent residents when a yellow fever epidemic forced the city's population to flee to the hills to escape from the mosquitoes carrying the disease. By the end of the 19th century, Santa, as it is known to its residents, became a privileged address for Rio's wealthy whose Victorian mansions sprouted from its hillsides. Intellectuals and artists were also attracted by its cool breezes and tranquil setting, removed yet close to the hectic downtown area.

Today, hanging from its hillsides and flanking its winding, cobblestoned streets, the architectural hodge-podge of Santa Teresa's homes is one of Rio's most distinctive features.

Gabled mansions with wrought iron fixtures and stained glass windows stand beside more staid and proper edifices, all perfectly at home atop a mountain that provides a spectacular view of the bay below. While it is an undeniable pleasure to walk along the flowered streets of Santa Teresa, getting there is

Sunset stroll around the Lagoa.

easily half the fun.

Departing from downtown in front of the **Petrobrás** building (Brazil's state oil company) are open-sided trolley cars that make the picturesque climb up the mountain and along Santa's surprise-filled streets. The highlight of the trip is the crossing of the **Carioca Aqueduct**, known to locals as the **Arcos da Lapa**, downtown Rio's most striking landmark. Built in the 18th century to carry water from Santa Teresa to the downtown area, the aqueduct became a viaduct in 1896 when the trolley car service began.

Since then its massive granite arches have supported the trolleys on their trips up and down the mountain (while this is one of the most interesting day trips in Rio, tourists should be forewarned that the trollies of late have become the targets of petty thieves and pickpockets. Hold on to your purses, cameras and wallets).

Views are as plentiful as flowers and greenery in Santa Teresa. The best are from the second trolley station looking down at the bay; several public stairways that lead from Santa's streets to the neighborhoods of **Glória** and **Flamengo** hundreds of feet below; and the grounds of the **Chácara do Céu** (Little House in the Sky Museum) looking out over the city, the aqueduct and the bay.

The museum itself is one of Santa Teresa's main attractions. Located at **Rua Murtinho Nobre 93**, it contains a superb collection of works by Brazilian modernists including paintings by Brazil's greatest modern artist, Candido Portinari, as well as paintings by European masters Braque, Dali, Matisse, Moet and Picasso.

The Bay: Since its discovery in 1502, Rio's **Guanabara Bay** has been a must stop for visitors. One visitor, Charles Darwin, wrote in 1823: "Guanabara Bay exceeds in its magnificence everything the European has seen in his native land." In modern times, however, the bay has become a massive refuse dump for the *cariocas*, with an estimated 1.5 million tons of waste poured into it daily making it a virtual cesspool. Despite this, views of the bay are beautiful, accented by the two forts, one from the 17th century and the other from the 19th, that guard its entrance.

Trips across the bay to the city of Niterói on the far side or to the islands within the bay are easily arranged and offer spectacular vistas looking back at Rio and the lush green covering of its mountains. The cheapest trip is by ferry boat but more comfortable aerofoils also make bay trips (both the ferry and the aerofoils leave from Praça XV). Within the bay, the favorite stop is **Paquetá Island**, largest of the bay's 84 islands. Visitors may rent bicycles or take a magical trip around the island by horse-drawn buggy. Paquetá has beaches but they should be used only for sunbathing; swimming in the bay is to be avoided.

Although *cariocas* generally thumb their noses at Niterói, the city has attractions of its own. The **Parque da Cidade**, at the end of a winding uphill road in the midst of a tropical forest, provides stunning views of the bay and

***Carioca* beach bum.**

the mountains. At the foot of the hill upon which this viewpoint rests is the **Itaipu beach**, an ocean-side beach that offers the same panoramic view of Rio.

Sugarloaf: Undoubtedly the most famous landmark of Guanabara Bay is the solid granite prominence that rises at its entrance, known to the world as **Sugarloaf**. The Indians called this singularly shaped monolith *Pau-nd-Acuqua*, meaning high, pointed, isolated peak. To the Portuguese this sounded like *pão de açucar* (sugarloaf) and its shape reminded them of the clay molds used to refine sugar into a conical lump called a sugarloaf.

In 1912 the first cable car line was built from **Praia Vermelho** at the base of Sugarloaf to its top in two stages, the first stopping at the rounded **Urca Mountain** at the foot of Sugarloaf. The original 24-passenger German-made cable car remained in use for 60 years, after which it was finally replaced in 1972 by larger cars.

Now visitors are whisked up in Italian-made bubble-shaped cars that hold up to 75 passengers and offer 360-degree vision. Each stage takes just 3 minutes, with a car starting out from the top and the bottom simultaneously, zipping past each other in the middle of the ride. Departures from the Praia Vermelho station, where tickets are sold, are every half hour from 8.00 a.m. to 10.00 p.m.

From both the Morro da Urca and Sugarloaf visitors have excellent views on all sides, with paths leading to viewpoints. To the west lie the beaches of Leme, Copacabana, Ipanema and Leblon and the mountains beyond. At your feet are Botafogo and Flamengo leading to downtown, with Corcovado peak and its Christ statue behind. To the north, the high bridge across the bay connects Rio de Janeiro and Niterói, with the latter's beaches stretching away towards the east. At any hour the view from Sugarloaf is extraordinarily beautiful.

The beaches: While the bay's waters are not fit for swimming today, the beaches that ring it were once the main draw for *cariocas*. At the start of this century tunnels were constructed linking bayside Botafogo with the ocean beach of Copacabana, and Rio's beach life found a new home. Since then, the *carioca's* endless search for the best beach has carried him constantly south, first to Copacabana, then to Ipanema and Leblon, then São Conrado and today the Barra da Tijuca and beyond.

With the passage of time, a day on the beach has evolved from tranquil family outings into an all-encompassing cradle-to-grave lifestyle of its own. Today the beach is not part of the life of Rio, it *is* the life.

The beach is a nursery, school yard, reading room, soccer field, volleyball court, singles bar, restaurant, rock concert hall, exercise center and office all at once. Occasionally someone goes into the water but only for a refreshing pause before returning to more important activities. *Cariocas* read, gossip, flirt, jog, exercise, dream, think and even close business deals on the beach. On a glorious summer weekend, nearly the whole of Rio spends some time on the

Below, face of Rio and right, beautiful bodies of Rio.

beach, which is not to say they aren't there during the week too. One of the great mysteries of Rio is how anything ever gets done on a warm, sunny day.

Carioca sociologists claim that the beach is Rio's great equalizer in addition to being its great escape valve. According to this theory, the poor majority of the city's residents, the inhabitants of its mountainside *favelas*, its housing projects and northern slums, have equal access to the beach and are therefore satisfied being poor. Surprisingly, there is some truth to this romantic notion, although a rising crime rate in the 1980s indicates that not all of the poor are satisfied. The beach, though, remains open to all and it is free.

But while democratic and integrated, Rio's beaches are not entirely classless. A quick passage along the sands of Copacabana will take you past small "neighborhoods" of bathers each congregating its own social type or group—gays, couples, families, teenagers, yuppies, celebrities, etc. If you return the next day, you will find the same groups in the same places, a "beach corner society" that has become a permanent characteristic of Rio life.

Copacabana: Although aged and somewhat the worse for wear, **Copacabana** remains the centerpiece of Rio's beaches. Its classic crescent curve anchored at one end by the imposing presence of Sugarloaf has made Copacabana a world-class postcard for decades. The beach first gained fame in the 1920s after the opening of the **Copacabana Palace Hotel** in 1923, at the time the only luxury hotel in South America. Also in the early 1920s gambling was legalized in Brazil and Copacabana became home to many of Rio's liveliest casinos. With gambling and the continent's best hotel, Copacabana evolved into an international watering hole for the world's celebrities. Black tie evening at the Copa, as the hotel was baptized, became *de rigeur* for figures such as Lana Turner, Eva Perón, Ali Khan, Orson Welles, Tyrone Power and even John F. Kennedy, who dropped in once after the war.

Left, couple relax in a hammock. Right, a soccer match on the beach.

Casino gambling was finally outlawed in 1946, but the party rolled on into the 1950s. Copacabana suffered a slump in the 1960s, but with the construction of three major hotels and the refurbishing of others, including the landmark Copacabana Palace, the beach staged a comeback in the 1980s. Today, with its beach widened by land fill, it is again an essential stopping point for visitors.

Across its steaming sands on hot summer days pass literally hundreds of thousands of sun and water worshippers. Hawkers of beverages, food, sun tan lotions, hats, sandals and the distinctive bird-kites of Rio plod across the beach, adding a musical accompaniment to the flow of colors with their sing-song voices and the frantic rhythms with which they beat on small drums and whirl metal ratchets. Bathers linger beneath multi-colored beach umbrellas or canopies, then briefly wet themselves in the ocean before parading across **Avenida Atlântica**, the beach drive, for a cool beer at a sidewalk café.

On any given summer weekend, up to a half-million *cariocas* and tourists will promenade on Copacabana. The crush of the beach is an extension of the crush beyond the beach. The quintessential Rio neighborhood, Copacabana is composed of 109 streets on which live over 300,000 people, squeezed into high rises by mountains at their back and the Atlantic in front. For this urban mass, the beach is their final backyard.

Corcovado: Overlooking Rio's beach life is the famed statue of Christ the Redeemer, standing arms outstretched atop **Corcovado** or hunchback mountain. To reach the 2,340 foot (710 meter) summit you may go by rented car or taxi, but the most recommended means is the 2.3 mile (3.7 km) Corcovado Railroad with trains leaving every few minutes from a station in the **Cosme Velho** neighborhood, halfway between downtown and Copacabana. The scenic ride climbs up the mountainside, through tropical foliage with views of the mountain and the city below.

On the top is the **Christ Statue**, vis-

Brazilian bikinis leave little to the imagination.

ible day and night from most parts of Rio. Standing 100 feet (30 meters) tall, the granite statue is the work of a team of artisans headed by French sculptor Paul Landowsky and was completed in 1931. Since then it has competed with Sugarloaf for the titles of symbol of Rio and best viewpoint. One decided advantage that Corcovado has over Sugarloaf is that it provides the best view possible of Sugarloaf itself. Towering over the city, Corcovado looks down at Sugarloaf, the waters of the bay, Niterói on the far side, while to the right are the southern ocean beaches—Copacabana and Ipanema—and the beautiful Rodrigo de Freitas Lagoon.

The Tijuca Forest: Enveloping Corcovado is one of Rio's least known but most enchanting natural attractions, the **Tijuca Forest**, a tropical reserve that includes 60 miles (100 km) of narrow, two-lane roads, winding through the forest's thick vegetation interrupted by waterfalls. Along the way are several excellent viewpoints not to be missed: the **Mesa do Imperador**, according to legend the site where Brazil's emperor Dom Pedro II brought his family for royal picnics, looking down directly at the lagoon and the southern neighborhoods; the **Vista Chinesa** (Chinese View), looking towards the south with a sidewise glance at Corcovado; the **Dona Marta Belvedere**, just below the summit of Corcovado looking directly at Sugarloaf.

Ipanema: Along much of its route, the main road through the Tijuca Forest provides often spectacular glimpses of the beach and neighborhood of **Ipanema**, its extension, **Leblon** and the **Rodrigo de Freitas Lagoon** known to *cariocas* as the *lagoa*. This is the money belt of Rio, home to a mixture of traditional wealth and the *carioca nouveau riche*. Ipanema (an Indian name meaning dangerous waters) began as an adventure in land development in 1894, marked by dirt roads running through the existing sand dunes with a handful of bungalows along the sides of the roads. Considered a distant outpost on the fringe of civilization, the neighborhood was mostly ignored until the crush of Copacabana became too much for its well-to-do residents and they moved to the next beach south.

From the 1950s to the present day, Ipanema has undergone an extraordinary real estate boom and population explosion. Its early posh homes were replaced first by four-story apartment buildings and since the 1960s by a surging army of high rises, steadily turning the Ipanema skyline into an updated version of Copacabana.

For long-time residents of Ipanema, this transformation is a crime against humanity that they have vowed to fight. Forsaking the normal *carioca* attitude of what will be will be, the neighborhoods of Ipanema, Leblon, the lagoon and nearby Gávea and Jardim Botânico have launched Rio's first determined effort to preserve the city's natural and man-made charms, a welcome sign in a city that is showing deep scars along some of its most treasured routes.

That this conservation effort should happen in Ipanema is not surprising. In the 1960s, the neighborhood was swept by a highly romanticized wave of liberalism. Rio's bohemians and intellectuals gathered at Ipanema's sidewalk cafés and bars to philosophize over the movements of the decade—the hippies, rock and roll, the Beatles, drugs, long hair and free love. Humor was also present, expressed monthly through a satirical newspaper which proudly announced the founding of the Independent Republic of Ipanema.

Two of the republic's prominent members were poet Vinícius de Moraes and songwriter Tom Jobim. One day, Jobim, in the spirit of the period, became enchanted with a beautiful school girl who walked by his habitual perch in an Ipanema bar. Each day for weeks he followed her daily passage, inviting his pal Moraes to join him. Inspired, the two put to words and music their feelings, the result being the pop classic, *The Girl from Ipanema*.

This mystical blend of Camelot and Haight Ashbury received a severe blow with the 1964 military coup and subsequent crackdown on liberals. Today Moraes is dead, Jobim has become an internationally renowned composer and the "girl," Heloisa Pinheiro, is a still-beautiful businesswoman in her 40's and a mother of four. The street down which Heloisa walked is now named after Moraes and the bar is called *A Garota de Ipanema* (the girl from Ipanema).

Despite its briefness, this period defined the modern *carioca* spirit—irreverent, independent and decidedly liberal towards matters of the flesh and spirit. It also propelled Ipanema into the vanguard in determining *carioca* style, pushing Copacabana back into second class status.

Today, Ipanema is Rio's center of chic and sophistication. If it's not "in" in Ipanema then it's simply not in. Rio's poshest boutiques line the streets of Ipanema and Leblon (basically the same neighborhood; a canal linking the lagoon with the ocean divides the two, giving rise to separate names but a shared identity).

The trendiest of Ipanema's famed boutiques are located on the neighborhood's main street, **Visconde de Pirajá** and side streets running in both directions (**Rua Garcia d'Avila** is tops). Ipanema's shops cater to men, women and children, offering leather goods and shoes in addition to clothing and gifts. In the latter category, Ipanema of late has become Rio de Janeiro's jewelry center. Brazil is the world's largest producer of colored gemstones and samples of them all are found on the block of Visconde de Pirajá between **Garcia d'Alvila** and **Rua Anibal Mendonça**, home to seven jewelry stores including the world headquarters of H. Stern, Brazil's leading jeweler and one of the largest in the world.

Ipanema's beach is a smaller version of Copacabana, both in length and width. At the Copacabana end is a section called Arpoador, famed for its surfing. At the far end, standing sentinel, is the imposing **Dois Irmãos (Two Brothers) Mountain**, setting off one of Rio's most spectacular natural settings. In the morning, joggers and bicyclists

Left, family outing in Rio's Botanical garden. Right, an Ipanema artist.

fill the sidewalk while exercise classes go through their gyrations on the beach. During the day, the golden youth of Rio frequent the beach and waters (befitting its image of free-spirited youth and daring, Ipanema is virtually the only beach where women go topless, although even here not many do).

Palm trees add to the special, more intimate setting of Ipanema. At sunset, the sidewalk is crowded with lovers of all ages, walking hand in hand. Less boisterous and rambunctious than the beachfront of Copacabana, Ipanema preserves the romance of Rio more than any of the city's 22 other beaches.

Away from the beaches: Inland from Ipanema is another of the symbols of Rio's romantic side, the lagoon. This natural lake, originally part of a 16th-century sugar plantation, provides a breathing space from the crowded south beaches of Rio. Around its winding shore, joggers, walkers and bicyclists beat a steady path, enjoying the best of Rio's mountain scenery—Corcovado and the Tijuca Forest, Dois Irmãos Mountain and the distant flat top of Gávea Mountain. On weekends, picnickers frequent the lagoon or stroll through the **Catacumba Park** just across the street.

Continuing towards the mountains on the side of the lagoon farthest from the beach, is Rio's **Botanical Garden** on **Rua Jardim Botânico**, an area of 340 acres (140 hectares) containing some 235,000 plants and trees representing over 5,000 species. Created by Portuguese prince regent Dom João VI in 1808, the garden was used to introduce different varieties of plants and trees from other parts of the world. The tranquil garden is a refreshing respite from the heat and urban rush of Rio and deserves a long, studied walk through its myriad examples of tropical greenery. The majestic avenue at the Garden's entrance is lined with a double row of 134 royal palms which were planted in 1842.

The outlying beaches: South of Ipanema are the outlying beaches, the most isolated and therefore the most unspoiled of Rio. The first, São **Conrado**, rests in an idyllic natural amphitheater, surrounded on three sides by thickly forested mountains and hills including the **Gávea Mountain**, a massive block of granite more impressive in shape and size than Sugarloaf.

Closing the circle on this small, enclosed valley is the São Conrado beach which is popular among the affluent youth of Rio. São Conrado can be reached from Ipanema by a tunnel underneath Dois Irmãos Mountain but a far more interesting route is **Avenida Niemeyer**, an engineering marvel completed in 1917. The avenue hugs the mountain's cliffs from the end of Leblon to São Conrado, looking at times straight down into the sea with striking vistas of the ocean and Ipanema looking back. The best view is saved for the end, where the avenue descends to São Conrado and suddenly, the ocean beach and the towering presence of Gávea emerge into sight. In a city where the spectacular becomes commonplace, this is a view that startles with its suddenness and unmatched beauty.

***Favela* shacks cling to the mountainside.**

Vidigal: On the cliff side of Avenida Niemeyer is the neighborhood of **Vidigal**, an eclectic mix of rich and poor where the mountainside homes of the former have been slowly surrounded by the advancing shacks of the Vidigal *favela*, one of Rio's largest shantytowns. On the ocean side of the avenue is the **Sheraton Hotel**, one of only two resort hotels in Rio. Although access to beaches is guaranteed by law in Rio, the Sheraton's imposing presence which encompasses the entire width of Vidigal beach, gives it the added distinction of being the city's only hotel with a de facto private beach.

São Conrado: Space and the absence of the crush of Copacabana and Ipanema are the main factors that separate the outlying beaches from their better known neighbors. While compact in area, São Conrado has an uncrowded openness guaranteed by the 18-hole **Gávea Golf Course** which runs through its middle.

One of Rio's more exclusive addresses, São Conrado is also a near perfect microcosm of Rio society. On the valley floor live middle and upper middle class *cariocas* in sometimes luxurious apartments, homes and condominium complexes which line the beach front and flank the golf course. The links' privileged location makes it one of the most beautiful in the world and adds to the dominating presence of green in São Conrado. But as lush as São Conrado is, its beauty is marred by a swath cut out of the hillside vegetation where **Rocinha**, Brazil's largest *favela*, spreads like a blight across the mountain from top to bottom. In this swarming anthill of narrow alleys and streets, over 60,000 people live (some estimates are double this), most of them in tumble-down brick houses and shacks, pressed tightly together side-by-side.

Hang gliders: At the end of São Conrado, a highway surges past the massive Gávea, a point where hang gliders soar overhead preparing for their landings on the beach to the left. On the right, another road climbs up the mountainside leading to the takeoff

Hand-gliding over São Conrado.

FEIJOADA: A NATIONAL DISH

There is nothing more *carioca* than Saturday *feijoada*.

From humble origins, this bean dish with its traditional accompaniments has been elevated to the status of Brazil's national dish, a favorite of the rich, poor and visitors from abroad. Variations using different kinds of beans, meats and vegetables can be found all over Brazil, but it is the famous black bean *feijoada* of Rio de Janeiro that is considered *the feijoada*.

In Rio, *feijoada* for lunch on Saturday is an institution. Although technically a lunch, it is served all afternoon and *cariocas* often linger at the table for hours. Theoretically, it is possible to eat lightly at such a meal, but you will probably never meet anyone who has, maybe because there are just so many ingredients to try or simply because it's so tasty. Or perhaps because the custom of getting together with friends has made it a leisurely affair.

Whatever it is that leads people to eat so heartily when a *feijoada* is spread out before them, it is a good idea to arrive at the restaurant with a healthy appetite. Swimming or walking on the beach might help you get into shape for your first *feijoada*.

Wait until mid-afternoon to put a special edge on your appetite, then ask your hotel to recommend a good restaurant—some are famous for their *feijoada completa*, including several of Rio's best hotels: Sheraton, Caesar Park and Inter-Continental.

What is this *feijoada?*: The original version was eaten by slaves. To the pot of beans were added odds and ends, leftovers that were not welcome on the master's table.

Nowadays, a *feijoada* includes ingredients that the slaves never saw in their bean pot (although tradition calls for such delicacies as the ears, tail, feet and often the snout of a pig, the better restaurants today leave these out). Into the modern *feijoada* goes a variety of dried,

***Feijoada* served buffet-style.**

salted and smoked meats, including salt pork, dried beef, tongue, pork loin and ribs, sausage and bacon. The beans, which seem to be a mere pretext for eating all that, are seasoned with onion, garlic and bay leaves, and cooked for hours with the generous amounts of flavorful meats.

That is the basic dish; *feijoada* accompaniments are considered inseparable. First a *caipirinha* (lime slices crushed inside a glass with sugar, ice and *cachaca* or sugarcane liquor) is served as an *abrideira* (literally, opener) or appetizer. Side dishes include white rice, over which the beans are ladled, bright green kale (shredded fine and sautéed), orange slices, which counterbalance the fatty meats, and *farofa* which is made of manioc flour sautéed in butter, sometimes with onion, egg or even raisins. Many restaurants will also include crisply fried bacon with the rind (*torresmo*). Meats are usually served on a separate platter from the beans.

A special touch, which is optional, is hot pepper. Ask for *pimenta*, tiny *malagueta* chilies similar to Mexican *jalapeñas*. If you really like it hot, crush a few on your plate before dishing up your food. A special bean sauce with onions and hot pepper is also served separately and, depending on the restaurant, this can be extremely hot. It is best to try a drop of the liquid first to see how hot it is before proceeding.

Although most salt is soaked out of the meats before they're added to the beans to cook, you will soon feel the need for a cool refreshment, especially if you went for the *pimenta*. If you did well with your first *caipirinha*, try another, but be careful—they are potent. Good, cold Brazilian beer should down all that quite well.

You will probably be surprised that this rather heavy repast is popular all year round, even in the hottest summer months. And you may be amazed at how much you end up eating. But you will certainly take off your hat (and unbuckle your belt) to Brazil's most tempting national dish.

Cured meats add flavor to beans.

point for the bird men of Rio. This same road leads back to the Tijuca Forest and Corcovado, passing through the thick tropical forest and providing memorable views of the beaches below. For tourists who wish to experience the sensation of jumping off a wooden runway 1,680 feet (510 meters) in the air to glide down to the beach below, several of Rio's more experienced and trustworthy hang glider pilots offer tandem rides for $60. For information call the Rio Hang Gliders Association at 220-4704 or ask at your hotel.

Barra da Tijuca: From São Conrado, an elevated roadway continues on to the far southern beaches, twisting along the sharply vertical cliffs where the mansions of the rich hang suspended at precarious angles. Emerging from a tunnel, you are suddenly face to face with the **Barra da Tijuca**, Rio's current high-growth area for the middle class. This vast lowland with mountains filling the western horizon is Rio's answer to America's suburbia. Low rises and homes fill most of its streets, with high rises now shooting up along the beachfront. The Barra, as it is commonly called, is also where Rio's largest shopping center is located, a recent phenomenon that has captured the imagination of *carioca* consumers. Unlike the more traditional beach neighborhoods of Copacabana and Ipanema, where shops, supermarkets and stores are all within walking distance, in Barra, distances are greater and the car is king.

The Barra is where Rio's future lies, for *cariocas* and tourists alike. This is the only large beach area that has not yet been completely developed and space is Rio's most valued commodity. Coming from Rio's high density neighborhoods, the Barra is like an enormous breath of fresh air. Much of it is still vacant lots, waiting for the city's next real estate boom which will certainly occur here very soon.

Longest beach: The Barra beach, running on for 11 miles (18 km), is Rio's longest and during the week its most deserted. On weekends, it fills up with

A quiet moment by the sea.

bumper-to-bumper traffic on the beach drive, **Avenida Sernambetiba**. The long beach is now attracting the tourism trade, with several buildings along Sernambetiba converted to apart-hotels, one- and two-bedroom apartments with kitchens that are rented as hotel rooms. Most of them go for rates well below those of comparable hotels in Copacabana, Ipanema and São Conrado. Several of the apart-hotels are part of condominium complexes, providing guests with access to swimming pools, tennis courts, saunas and exercise centers.

What has been missing in the Barra has been an active nightlife, but this too is changing. In recent years, several excellent restaurants have opened up along the beachfront avenue and near the Barra Shopping Center. Fast food outlets, led by McDonald's, discotheques, small bars and samba clubs have also invaded the Barra, but the neighborhood's most distinctive nighttime feature is the myriad trailers that dot Avenida Sernambetiba.

The Barra's trailers: The Barra's answer to Copacabana's sidewalk cafes, the nondescript trailers sell cold drinks and hot food during the day to bathers, but on weekend nights they become convivial meeting points for couples and singles. Large crowds gather around the more popular trailers, some of which are converted at night into samba centers called *pagodes*. Originally confined to back yards in the city's lower class northern neighborhoods, *pagodes* were no more than samba singalongs where musicians, professional and amateur, engaged in midnight jam sessions. In the move to the affluent south zone of Rio, the *pagodes* have maintained their purist samba qualities but have acquired commercial overtones, becoming in effect open-air samba bars.

For romantics, however, there can be no quibbling over the splendid image of the Barra's beachside trailers with the sound of the surf crashing behind them, guitar and percussion instruments pounding out the samba in the night and scores of fun-seekers singing along—

Left, souvenir T-shirts for sale. **Right**, off to the beach on a motorbike.

just right for an evening out in Rio de Janeiro.

Romance and the Barra have a more palpable connection in an area where dozens of motels have sprung up over the years. In Rio, as throughout Brazil, motels are for lovers and rooms are rented out by the hour, replete with such facilities as saunas, whirlpools, and ceiling mirrors. Some of the Barra's love centers outshine Rio's five-star hotels in luxury and sheer indulgence. Originally aimed at providing young couples with privacy for romantic encounters, the motels have retained this function and added another—serving as meeting places for adult love affairs as well. Because of this, the Barra's motels are usually hidden behind high walls, with private garages for each room to protect guests from inquisitive eyes and chance encounters with the wrong person. Many married couples also frequent the motels in search of an added sense of adventure.

At the end of the Barra is the Recreio dos Bandeirantes, a small beach with a natural breakwater creating the effect of a quiet bay. From Recreio the road climbs sharply along the mountainside, descending to Prainha, a beach which is popular among surfers, and then to Grumari, a marvelously isolated beach where part of the movie *Blame It on Rio* was filmed. From Grumari, a narrow, pot-holed road climbs straight up the hillside. From the top is another of Rio's unforgettable views—the expanse of the Guaratiba flatlands and a long, sliver of beach stretching off into the distance, the Restinga de Marambaia, a military property that is unfortunately off limits to bathers.

Down the hill is **Pedra da Guaratiba**, a quaint fishing village with the best seafood restaurants of Rio (Candido's, Tia Palmira and Quatro Sete Meia). From Barra to Guaratiba is an exhilarating day trip which can be topped by a leisurely two-hour lunch over shrimp or fish dishes at any of the Guaratiba restaurants, the favorites of the Rio in-crowd.

Night-life: At night Copacabana still

Imaginative way to display colorful beachwear.

reigns as king of Rio. The lights that follow the curve of the beach and the darkened profile of Sugarloaf are sufficient for anyone's night of romance. For *cariocas* an evening out is serious business, for many of them more serious than the business of the day. To be in step with Rio time, a night out begins late with a dinner at 9 p.m. or later (most popular restaurants are still receiving dinner guests into the morning hours on weekends). Meals fall into two categories, either small and intimate (French restaurants with excellent views are favored) or sprawling and raucous (served best by Brazilian steak houses called *churrascarias* where *cariocas* gather with small armies of friends around long tables overflowing with food and drink). Either way, you will be well served in Copacabana.

The beach itself is an excellent starting point. Sidewalk cafes run the length of **Av. Atlântica**, gathering points for tourists and locals where cold draft beer is the favorite order. Copacabana at night is like a Persian bazaar with street vendors hawking souvenirs, paintings, wood sculptures and t-shirts along the median of the avenue. Prostitutes (female, male and transvestite) prowl the broad sidewalk with its serpentine designs, moving furtively through the midst of wistful couples. In Leme, **Maru's** at Av. Atlântica 290 is considered the city's best *churrascaria*, serving rounds of beef, pork, chicken and sausage in *rodízio* style—the waiter keeps serving until you say stop. Nearby, the faithful gather at the Italian restaurant **Le Fiorentina**. While famed more for its past as a watering hole for artists and actors, Fiorentina is still capable of attracting earnest bohemians of the present.

At the division between Leme and Copacabana stands the **Meridien Hotel**, one of the big five hotels in Rio. The others are the **Rio Palace** at the other end of Copacabana, the **Caesar Park** in Ipanema, the **Sheraton** on the road to São Conrado and the **Inter-Continental** in São Conrado. On top of the Meridien is the **Saint Honore** restau-

Stripper in Rio nightclub.

rant (under the direction of French master chef Paul Bocuse), a delightful combination of view and cuisine.

Across the street begins Copacabana's state-of-the-art red light district of international fame. As with the beach sidewalk, all tastes are served, with activity divided between heterosexual located to the east of the beach and homosexual to the west. With suggestive names such as **Pussy Cat, Erotika, Swing, Don Juan** and **Frank's Bar**, prostitute bars and clubs line the back streets between the Meridien and the **Lancaster Hotel**. Within their darkened interiors, customers will find overpriced drinks, erotic shows and both beautiful and not so beautiful women. At the western end of the beach homosexual bars and clubs are concentrated in the **Galeria Alaska**.

Dining out: Rio's cuisine varies tremendously, with the accent on international. Among Copacabana's top restaurants are: **Le Pré Catalan**, a respected temple of French nouvelle cuisine located in the Rio Palace Hotel; **Le Bec Fin**, a traditional French restaurant that is a Copacabana landmark in **Praça do Lido**; the restaurant of the **Ouro Verde Hotel** on Av. Atlântica, a home of excellence in international cuisine for three decades; **Enotria**, an excellent Italian restaurant famed for its wine list, at **Rua Constante Ramos 115**. For steaks try the **Bife de Ouro** in the Copacabana Palace Hotel or the popular steak houses, **Palace (Rua Rodolfo Dantas 16)** and **Jardim (Rua Republica de Peru 225)**; for seafood, **Grottamare** (between Copacabana and Ipanema at **Rua Gomes Carneiro 132**), **Shirley's (Rua Gustavo Sampaio 610)** and **Principe (Av. Atlantica 974-B)**. Close by to Copacabana atop the Rio Sul Tower is **Maxim's**, a faithful *carioca* branch of the famed Paris restaurant.

The sophistication of Ipanema and environs is amply supported by their restaurants: **Le Streghe**, a top-rated *nouva cucina* Italian restaurant resting atop one of Rio's most disputed disco/nightclubs: the **Caligula**, at **Rua Prudente de Morais 129**; **Petronius**, one of the fine restaurants of the **Caesar Park Hotel**; **The Lord Jim Pub**, an authentic London pub transplanted to Rio, a popular meeting place for Rio's foreign community, at **Rua Paul Redfern 63**; **Sal & Pimenta**, a mix of *nouva cucina* and Brazilian cuisine, popular among Rio celebrities, downstairs is the **Alo-Alo** piano bar, one of the city's best, at **Rua Barão de Torre 368** (on the same street is Rio's most exclusive private club, the **Hippopotamus**); **Claude Troisgros**, in the Jardim Botanico neighborhood, at **Rua Custodio Serrao 62**, *nouvelle cuisine* as it was meant to be; **Antiquarius, Rua Aristides Espinola 19**, an elegant Portuguese restaurant famed for its cod (*bacalhau*); **Florentino, Av. General San Martin 1227**, international cuisine and one of Leblon's top bars; **Satiricon, Rua Barão da Torre 192**, an attractive and reasonably-priced home to excellent seafood.

Fastidious diners will also not go wrong at either of Rio's two resort-style hotels, the Sheraton and the Inter-Continental. The Sheraton's **Valentino's** restaurant offers gourmet Italian cuisine in one of Rio's most elegant settings, while next door the hotel's **Mirador** restaurant serves an unbeatable *feijoada* on Saturdays.

The Inter-Continental is home to the **Monseigneur**, for intimate French dining and also the Rio branch of the famed Roman eatery, **Alfredo's**. Both hotels and their five-star cousins in Copacabana, the Meridien and Rio Palace, provide live entertainment (Brazilian music mixed with jazz and an international selection) at their chic piano bar/nightclubs.

For full-scale extravaganzas, Rio's leading nightclubs are the **Canecão**, close to Copacabana beside the Rio-Sul Shopping Center and in Leblon the **Scala** and **Plataforma**. Canecão and Scala showcase Brazilian and international attractions while the Plataforma presents a nightly review of Brazilian song and dance. Other popular nightspots are: **Help**, a mammoth discotheque on Avenida Atlântica in Copacabana; **Biblio's Bar**, a Rio rar-

Right, the samba fun is extended to the beach. Following page; another look-out point; scalloped shoreline and islands along the Green Coast.

ity—a singles bar, **Av. Epitacio Pessoa 1484** on the lagoon, with a view made for romance; **Chiko's**, next to Biblio's and with the same view, piano bar for the international set; **Jazzmania, Av. Rainha Elizabeth 769** in Ipanema, which together with **People** in Leblon at Av. Bartolomeu Mitre 370A dominates Rio's jazz scene.

Shopping: Although it wasn't until the start of the 1980s that Rio's first shopping center was built, *cariocas* have quickly caught on to the advantages of shopping in an air conditioned mall away from the the summer temperatures, which average around 90° F (35° C). As a result the city's best shops and boutiques are gravitating from Ipanema to the city's top malls and shopping centers.

The principal shopping centers are: **Rio-Sul**, located in the neighborhood of Botafogo a short distance from Copacabana, open 10 a.m. to 10 p.m. Monday through Saturday, with free buses from and to Copacabana's hotels; **Barra Shopping**, Brazil's largest, located in the Barra da Tijuca neighborhood with the look and feel of an American suburban mall, open 10 a.m. to 10 p.m. Monday through Saturday, with free buses to and from hotels; **Cassino Atlântico** on Copacabana's beachfront drive, Av. Atlantica, at the Rio Palace Hotel, small but with good souvenir shops, art galleries and antique shops, open 9 a.m. to 10 p.m. Monday through Friday and 9 a.m. to 8 p.m. on Saturday; **São Conrado Fashion Mall**, close to the Sheraton and Inter-Continental hotels in São Conrado, boutiques, restaurants and art galleries, open 10 a.m. to 10 p.m. Monday through Saturday.

Souvenir hunters should also check out the **Ipanema Hippie Fair** at Praça General Osorio, Sundays 9 a.m. to 6 p.m. A leftover from Ipanema's flower children days of the 1960s, the fair has a wide offering of wood carvings, paintings, hand-tooled leather goods and other assorted gifts, including a large selection of Rio's multi-colored tee-shirts. Many of the fair's vendors also sell their wares at night along the median of Copacabana's Av. Atlantica.

STATE OF RIO

While the city of Rio has captured most of the glory through the decades, the state of which it is the capital (also called Rio de Janeiro) is replete with attractions of its own. Like its capital, the state of Rio is an exciting contrast of forested mountains and sun-drenched beaches, all located within a few hours of the city.

Búzios: According to the history books, Búzios was discovered by the Portuguese at the start of the 16th century. Locals, however, know better. Búzios actually was discovered in 1964 by actress Brigitte Bardot. Convinced by an Argentine friend, Brigitte spent two well-documented stays in Búzios, parading her famed bikini-clad torso along the unspoiled beaches and in the process spreading the fame of Búzios across the globe. The town hasn't been the same since.

Búzios, or more correctly Armação dos Búzios, once was a tranquil fishing village fronting the lapping waters of a bay. After Bardot, however, it became a synonym for all that splendor in the tropics is supposed to be—white sand beaches, crystalline water, palm trees and coconuts, beautiful half-naked women and a relaxing, intoxicating lifestyle of careless ease.

What is amazing about Búzios is that all of this is true. It is one of only a handful of super-hyped travel destinations that does not delude or disappoint. It is not as good as the posters. It is even better.

Paradise found: Located 115 miles (190 km) east of Rio along what is known as the Sun Coast (Costa do Sol), Búzios has been compared to the fabled island of Ibiza in Spain. It is a sophisticated, international resort that for most of the year manages to retain the air of a quiet fishing village. The exception is high summer season, just before, during and after Carnival, when even tranquil Búzios is overrun by tourists, its population of 10,000 swelling to 50,000.

For the remaining nine months of the year, Búzios is the type of beach town that most travelers suspect exists only in their dreams. Unlike many popular resorts in Brazil, including Rio de Janeiro itself, Búzios has not lost control of its growth. It is a favorite retreat of Rio's social column set.

Búzios has undergone a major real estate boom since the 1970s but fortunately the city fathers have kept a firm hand on developers. Strict zoning laws limit building heights, with the result that Búzios has escaped the high rise invasion that has scarred many Brazilian beaches. The fashionable homes that dot the Búzios beach-scape for the most part blend in with the picturesque homes of the fishermen.

The city has also been spared an onslaught of hotels. Most of the accommodations in Búzios are *pousadas* or inns, quaint and small with no more than a dozen rooms (the largest hotel occupies an island off the coast, the **Ilha das Rocas**, with 70 rooms and an idyllic resort setting). This in turn has helped preserve the relaxed atmosphere of the town and provides visitors with an intimate setting to enjoy the sun and beach.

The beaches: Altogether, there are 23 beaches in the Búzios area, some fronting quiet coves and inlets and others the open sea. The main distinction, though, is accessibility. Beaches close in to the town or nearby, such as **Ossos, Geriba** and **Ferradura** are easily reached by foot or car.

As could be expected, the "best" beaches are those that require the most effort to reach, in the case of Búzios either long hikes, sometimes over rocky ground, or a drive along a dirt, pot-holed road. At the end are treasures like **Tartaruga**, **Azeda** and **Azedinha**, **Brava** and **Forno**, famed for their beautiful calm waters and equally beautiful topless bathers.

Visiting all of the beaches by land is not only tiring but also unnecessary. The fishermen of Búzios have become part-time tour operators and tourists can rent boats by the hour or for the day. Sailboats may also be rented as well as cars and dune buggies, bicycles, motorcycles and horses. Diving enthusi-

<u>Left</u>, burst of wild flowers on a mountainside near Petrópolis.

asts will also find equipment for rent.

A typical Búzios day begins late (no one wakes up before 11 a.m.) with a hearty breakfast at a *pousada*, one of the treats of Búzios' inns. Daytime activities center on the beach. Swimming, long leisurely walks or exploration of distant beaches all can be enjoyed with an occasional break for fried shrimp or fresh oysters washed down with cold beer or *caipirinhas*, Brazil's national drink, composed of lime slices, ice and sugarcane liquor. For shopping, there are fashionable boutiques along cobblestoned **Rua José Bento Ribeiro Dantas**, better known as **Rua das Pedras**, or street of the stones, and also on **Rua Manuel Turibe de Farias**.

Nightlife: At night, the bohemian spirit of Búzios takes charge. Though small in size, the city is considered the third best in Brazil for dining out, with over 20 quality restaurants, some of them rated among the country's finest. Gourmets have a wide choice, including Brazilian, Italian, French and Portuguese cuisines, as well as seafood and a local favorite—crêpes. **Le Streghe Búzios** (Italian), **Au Cheval Blanc** (French) and **Adamaster** (seafood) are considered the best of Búzios' excellent restaurants. Other small restaurants are constantly popping up, many of them superb. A word of caution, though, the bargain prices of Rio's restaurants are not to be found in Búzios.

After an inspiring meal, the in-crowd of Búzios gravitates to the city's bars, many of which have live entertainment. Bars like restaurants in Búzios are as famed for their owners as for what they offer. The town's numerous charms have waylaid dozens of foreign visitors since BB's first promenade. Brigitte left but many of the others have stayed, opening inns, restaurants and bars and providing Búzios with an international air. The Brazilian residents of Búzios have been joined by French, Swiss, Scandinavian and American expatriates, all vowing that they will never leave.

Amiable eccentrics: Among Búzios' amiable eccentrics and engaging drop-

outs are Madame Michou, owner of **Chez Michou**, Búzios' chic *crêperie*, where the young crowd gathers at night; François Le Mouellic and Vivianne Debon, owners of **La Nuance**, a popular meeting point with live music and where François Le Mouellic performs puppet shows and opens champagne bottles with a sword; Bruce Henry, an American jazz musician, who owns the **Estalagem**, an inn with a popular restaurant and bar; and Matthew, a New Zealand mural painter who lives in a beachside cave.

The Lake Region: Between Rio and Búzios are several beautiful beach areas, starting with what is known as the lake region, a series of lagoons separated from the sea by lengthy sand bars. The sea along this unbroken coastline east of Rio is marked by strong currents and large waves, making it a favorite area for surfers. Major surfing competitions are held in **Saquarema**, one of four beach resorts in the lake region (on the other side of the highway, state road 106, the lagoons are popular spots for windsurfing).

Near **Maricá** is the **Ponta Negra** beach, a spectacular, nearly deserted stretch of white sand and wild blue water. After Saquarema come **Araruama** and **São Pedro d'Aldeia**, popular among *cariocas* during vacation periods, especially Carnival, when the lake region's hotels and numerous campgrounds are filled till overflowing. Salt flats are also visible off the side of the road along this stretch, culminating in a large area of flats at **Cabo Frio**, officially the end of the lake region and the beginning of the Sun Coast.

Located 15 miles (25 km) from Búzios, Cabo Frio is famed for the white, powdery sand of its beaches and its dunes. During vacation season, Cabo Frio's population of 40,000 swells with *cariocas* on holiday. Unlike Búzios, Cabo Frio is an historical city, with ruins from the 17th century, including the 1616 **São Mateus Fort**, the 1666 **Nossa Senhora da Assunção Church** and the 1696 **Nossa Senhora dos Anjos Convent**.

Children play in the ocean near Búzios.

Undiscovered paradise: Only eight miles (14 km) from Cabo Frio is **Arraial do Cabo**, next to Búzios, the most beautiful attraction of the Sun Coast. Arraial has yet to be discovered by the tourist trade and has only a handful of small and unimpressive hotels (thus far, tourists have preferred to stay in Búzios and Cabo Frio, making day trips to Arraial).

Arraial has the clearest water in southern Brazil, making it the preferred site of scuba divers and spear fishermen. The city is located at the tip of a cape with a variety of beaches, some with quiet waters and stunning lush green mountain backdrops, while others, the surfer beaches, are swept by strong winds which drive the waves against the sand.

Off the coast is the **Ilha do Farol**, site of a lighthouse but more famed for the **Gruta Azul**, an underwater grotto with bright blue waters. The island, reached by boat, also offer excellent views of the mainland.

Like Búzios, Arraial began as a fishing village and is still known for the quality of the fresh catches brought in each day. The fishermen of Arraial climb to the top of sand dunes, from where they look into the water below in search of schools of fish, a testimony to the unspoiled clarity of the waters of Arraial do Cabo.

The Green Coast: On the western side of the city of Rio are a string of beaches and islands known collectively as the **Green Coast** (*Costa Verde*). Named for the dense vegetation which dominates the coastline and descends to the sea, the *Costa Verde* is nature at its best: a unique tropical mix of mountains, rain forest, beaches and islands. Green, in every imaginable shade, surrounds you, invading even the sea with a soft turquoise hue.

Access to the Green Coast is on coastal highway BR 101, known locally as the Rio-Santos Highway for the two port cities it connects. The scenic drive compares with that down Spain's Costa Brava or California's State Road 1. At times it seems as if you are going to take

Colonial Glória Church.

flight as the road rises high up a mountainside for a wide panoramic view. Then it drops and winds steeply back down to the shoreline. The road passes beside a national park, Brazil's only nuclear power plant, tourist resorts, fishing villages, ocean liner tanking stations, cattle ranches, a shipyard and the historical town of **Paraty**, a monument to Brazil's colonial past.

The most enticing attractions along the 160-mile (270 km) extension of the Green Coast are the beaches. Some are small, encased by rocky cliffs, with clear, tranquil lagoons, while others stretch on for miles, pounded by rough surf. The entire area is a haven for sports enthusiasts, offering everything from tennis, golf and boating to deep-sea fishing, diving and surfing.

Although it is possible to see the Green Coast in a single day, to explore it thoroughly and enjoy its beauty, plan on two to three days. Over the last 10 years, tourism has become the leading activity of the region and there is a growing number of fine hotels and restaurants, even on some of the islands. A word of caution: if you're renting a car, don't drive at night. Not only do you miss the scenery, but in the dark, the highway—with its sharp curves, unmarked shoulders and frequent and poorly lit construction sites—becomes extremely dangerous.

Tropical islands: The Green Coast begins 40 miles (70 km) outside of the city of Rio de Janeiro at the town of **Itacuruçá** (population 2,000). From the town's harbor, schooners holding up to 40 people depart every morning at 10 o'clock for one-day excursions to the nearby tropical islands in the surrounding **Sepetiba Bay**. The trips average US$20 a person and include a seafood lunch on one of the islands.

The schooners stop at several islands such as **Martins**, **Itacuruçá** and **Jaguanum** to allow passengers to swim or snorkel. Some of the smaller islands can be visited by hiring a boat and guide, usually a local fisherman (the islands of **Pombeba** and **Sororoca** are recommended). Also, for visitors who

Picturesque colonial Paraty.

wish to stay on the islands, there are several good hotels, including the **Hotel Ilha de Jaguanum** and the **Hotel do Pierre**.

The highway continues past **Muriqui** to **Mangaratiba**, site of a new 350-room **Club Mediterranée**. Further down the road is **Angra dos Reis** (King's Cove), the Green Coast's largest city (population 60,000). The city sprawls across a series of hills at the beginning of a 60-mile long (100 km) gulf. The Angra Gulf contains over 370 islands, 2,000 beaches, seven bays and dozens of coves. The water is warm and clear, a perfect sanctuary for marine life. Spearfishing along the rocky shores is a favorite pastime, as is fishing in deeper waters. The tourist information center, across from the bus station near the harbor, provides maps and information on hotels and boat tours. For golfing enthusiasts, the **Hotel do Frade** has the Green Coast's only golf course, a scenic 18 holes, where international tournaments are held every June and November.

Ninety minutes from Angra by boat is the paradisical island **Ilha Grande**, a nature reserve blessed with spectacular flora and fauna and some of Brazil's most beautiful beaches. The island can be reached by ferry boats that operate from Mangaratiba and Angra and disembark at **Abraão**, the only city on the island. In Abraão, small boats can be rented to visit the more distant beaches, such as **Lopes Mendes**, **das Palmas** and **Saco do Céu**. There are several campsites on the island but only two small hotels.

History preserved: From Angra, the coastal highway flanks the gulf, running past Brazil's only nuclear power plant and the picturesque fishing village of **Mambucaba**. At the far end of the gulf, three-and-a-half hours from Rio, is **Paraty**, (population 9,000), a colonial jewel that in 1966 was declared a national monument by UNESCO.

Paraty was founded in 1660 and in the 18th century gained fame and wealth as the result of the discovery of gold and diamonds in the neighboring state of

Left, an outing on a *saveiro*. Right, a fisherman and his boat.

Minas Gerais. The precious stones were transported by land to Paraty and from there either on to Rio or by ship to Portugal. The city also served as the main stopping-off point for travelers and commerce moving between São Paulo to the south and Rio. For over a century, Paraty flourished and prospered. Large mansions and estates attested to the wealth of its residents.

After Brazil declared independence in 1822, the export of gold to Portugal ceased and a new road was eventually built, bypassing Paraty and connecting Rio to São Paulo directly. Paraty lost its strategic position and was forgotten, and its colonial heritage was consequently preserved.

That heritage today awaits visitors in the form of colonial churches and homes in the relaxed, laid-back atmosphere of Paraty, a town trapped contentedly in a time warp. To get a feel for Paraty, walk around the colonial area where cars are not permitted to enter. Large, uneven stones provide often precarious footing on the narrow streets. To test your balance even more, the streets slope in towards the center to drain off rain water.

Bananas for sale along a mountain highway.

Standing out among Paraty's churches is **Santa Rita de Cássia** (1722), a classic example of Brazilian baroque architecture which today also houses the **Museum of Sacred Art**. Next-door, in what was once the town's prison, is the tourist information office.

All of Paraty's streets contain hidden surprises: art galleries, handicraft shops, quaint *pousadas* (inns) and colonial homes. From the outside the *pousadas* look like typical white-washed Mediterranean-style houses with heavy wooden doors and shutters painted in bright colored trim.

On the inside, however, they open up onto delicately landscaped courtyards with ferns, orchids, rosebushes, violets and begonias. Two of the most beautiful gardens are in the **Pousada do Ouro** (both in the main hotel and across the street) and **Coxixo**. Across from the latter is a pleasant, open-air bar and restaurant, which also triples as an antique shop.

Unlike Angra, Paraty is not famed for its beaches, but schooners such as the 80-foot (24-meter) long Soberno da Costa make day trips to the nearby islands. A different type of excursion can be made by car to **Fazenda Banal**, five minutes from Paraty on the old gold route up the hill to **Cunha**. The 17th-century ranch has something for everybody: a large zoo complete with wild cats, monkeys and rare birds, waterfalls to bathe in, a restaurant specializing in Brazilian country-home cooking, and an ancient but still operating *cachaça* (sugarcane wine) distillery, where you can sample and buy 10 potent flavors made with different herbs and fruits.

Mountain retreats: Dedicated as they are to the beach life, Rio's residents also feel an occasional need to get away from it all and escape to the cool, refreshing air of the mountains. This urge has existed since the first days of the Brazilian nation and was the principal reason behind the founding of Rio's two leading mountain resorts, **Petrópolis** and **Teresópolis**. The pastel hues and green gardens of these two *carioca* getaways are a 19th-century imperial inheritance left by independent Brazil's first rulers, Emperors Pedro I and Pedro II.

Petrópolis: This city of 270,000, only 40 miles (65 kms) from Rio, is a monument to Pedro II, emperor of Brazil from 1831 until his exile in 1889 (he died in France two years later).

The city was first envisioned in the 1830s by Pedro I, who purchased land in the spectacular **Serra Fluminense** mountain range for a projected summer palace. But it was his son, Pedro II, who actually built the palace and the quaint town surrounding it starting in the 1840s. The idea was to maintain a refreshing refuge from the wilting summer heat of Rio.

The road to Petrópolis is itself one of the state of Rio's prime scenic attractions. An engineering marvel, its concrete bridges soar over green valleys as the road curves around mountains and the flatlands below.

From sea level in Rio, the highway climbs 2,750 feet (840 meters) during the hour-and-a-quarter drive. On the way, visitors can still glimpse traces of the old Petrópolis **Highway**, a perilous, cobblestoned roadway that once kept royal workers busy the year round with repairs.

Life in Petrópolis is centered around two busy streets, **Rua do Imperador** and **Rua 15 de Novembro**, the only part of town with buildings over five stories tall. Temperatures are lower here than in Rio and the city's sweater and jacket-clad inhabitants give it an autumnal air during the cool months from June to September.

Perpendicular to Rua do Imperador is the **Avenida 7 de Setembro**, the city's lush boulevard used by kings of the past. The partially cobbled avenue is divided by a slow-moving canal, and horse-drawn carriages for rent by the hour form an old-fashioned taxi stand on its sun-dappled stones.

The area around the **Summer Palace**, now called the **Imperial Museum** is crowded with trees and shrubs and is

Paddling in the waters of Búzios.

criss-crossed by carefully kept pathways. The rose-colored palace, fronting Avenida 7 de Setembro, is modest for a royal dwelling. The palace-converted-museum is open from noon to 5 p.m., Tuesday through Sunday, and visitors are asked to wear felt slippers which pad quietly over the gleaming *jacarandá* and brazilwood floors. The museum's modest furnishings attest to the bourgeois character of its builder, Pedro II, who for the most part avoided the traditional trappings of nobility. Its second floor collection of kingly personal artifacts, including telescope and telephone, is a reminder of Pedro's scientific dabbling.

Among items of interest are the **crown jewels**—a glistening frame of 77 pearls and 639 diamonds—and the colorful skirts and cloaks of the emperor's ceremonial wardrobe, including a cape of bright Amazon toucan feathers. Royal photographs on the second floor, however, show that Brazil's second and last king felt more at home in their conservative business suits than in flowing robes.

Dom Pedro's Heirs: Across the square from the palace is the royal guesthouse, now the residence of Dom Pedro's heirs. Dom Pedro de Orleans e Bragança, Pedro II's great grandson, is the home's owner and chief representative of monarchism in Brazil. Although the house is closed to the public, Dom Pedro himself can be seen walking in the square chatting with local residents and, occasionally, with tourists.

A few blocks up Avenida 7 de Setembro is the French Gothic-style **Cathedral de São Pedro de Alcantara**. Begun in 1884, the imposing structure took 55 years to complete. From the cathedral a web of tree-shaded, cobblestoned streets spreads into residential Petrópolis.

The city is famed for its delightful, rose-colored homes, including many which were once the dwellings of members of the royal family. The city is also known for its numerous overgrown private gardens and public parks and the simple beauty of its streets.

Praia do Forte Beach in Cabo Frio.

A few blocks beyond the cathedral, on **Rua Alfredo Pachá**, is the 1879 **Crystal Palace**, a glass-and-iron frame still used for gardening and art exhibits. The palace was built almost entirely of panels shipped from France. Nearby is the unusual **Santos Dumont House** which displays a collection of eccentricities reflecting the unusual personality of its former owner.

Santos Dumont: Albert Santos Dumont is credited by Brazilians and many Europeans with being the inventor of the airplane.

In 1906, while living in Paris, he made the first fully-documented flight in a heavier-than-air machine, designed and built by him. The famed flight of the Wright Brothers occurred in 1903, but documentation for it was only produced in 1908.

Santos Dumont's home, designed by him, has only one room, no tables or kitchen (his meals were delivered by a local hotel), no staircases or bed.

It does have a variety of shelves designed for various purposes and a chest of drawers, on top of which the inventor slept. Santos Dumont committed suicide in 1932 at age 59, allegedly out of despondency over the use of airplanes in war.

Other Petrópolis attractions include the sprawling Normandy-style **Hotel Quitandinha**, a luxuriously appointed structure completed in 1945 to be Brazil's leading hotel casino.

Unfortunately, however, only a few months after its inauguration, gambling was outlawed and has remained so ever since. Today the still striking complex, which is located on the Rio-Petrópolis Highway five miles (eight km) from downtown Petrópolis, is a combination condominium and private club (by calling in advance, tourists can often find accommodations).

Quitandinha's lobby, night club and ballrooms are vast, gleaming expanses that look like sets from Hollywood musicals of the 1930s.

Teresópolis: Just 33 miles (53 kms) from Petrópolis, at the end of a one-hour drive along steep mountain roads, is Rio de Janeiro's other mountain gem, **Teresópolis** (population 115,000). Named after Pedro II's wife, the Empress Tereza Cristina, Teresópolis was planned in the 1880s but only incorporated in 1891, two years after the royal couple's exile.

The picturesque town, 57 miles (92 km) from Rio on the broad **Rio-Teresópolis Highway**, clings to the edge of the **Serra Fluminense** at 2,960 feet (902 meters).

The main attractions, besides the cool air, are an encompassing though distant view of Rio's **Gunabara Bay** and the city's proximity to the spectacular **Serra dos Orgãos National Park**. The park, landscaped with broad lawns, masonry fountains and patios, is dominated by a ridge of sharp peaks. The tallest, **Pedra do Sino**, is 7,410 feet (2,260 meters) above sea level.

But the range's most striking summit is the rocky spike called O Dedo de Deus (The Finger of God). On clear days, the chiseled profile of the Serra dos Orgãos can be seen from many points in Rio itself.

Below, shops on cobblestoned street in Paraty. Right, diving from the high prow of a *saveiro* near Angra dos Reis.

ASSICURAZIONI GENERALI
DI TRIESTE E VENEZIA

GARBO
MODA MASCULINA

SÃO PAULO

While there may be two Brazils—one a dynamic developing country, the other scourged by poverty and drought—there are many São Paulos, one for each of this city's multitude of ethnic and social groups.

The New York of Latin America, São Paulo is home to more ethnic communities than any other city in the region. Its 10 million inhabitants make it the fourth largest city in the world (after Shanghai, Mexico City and Tokyo). Its vast industrial park, one of the largest and most modern in the world, attests to the force of the São Paulo dynamo, just as the city's elegant apartment buildings and mansions demonstrate the wealth of its powerful business elite.

Also like New York, São Paulo is a city of contrasts. While it is the country's industrial and financial center, it is also saddled with teeming slums. Five million *paulistanos*, as residents of the city are called, live in tin-and-wood hovels or shabby tenements called *cortiços,* where a hundred people may share a bathroom and where children play with mud and garbage in the backyard. A hilly ring of working class suburbs is ill-lighted, ill-paved and stinks with a thousand miles of open sewers. Half the population survives on a family income of only US$100 a month or less.

Yet, even for its poor, São Paulo is a "carousel", according to one of the city's most respected journalists, Lourenço Diaféria. "São Paulo is a migrant city," he notes. "Many people manage to rise here, if only because their origins were so humble."

Immigrants: About one million *paulistanos* are of Italian descent and another million of Spanish or Spanish-speaking Latin origin. Large communities hail from Germany (100,000), Russia (50,000), Armenia (50,000), with another 50,000 from Balkan and Central European immigrant groups.

Preceding pages: the city of São Paulo; mural brightens city street. Left, rooftop sunbather.

As in American cities, the ethnic populations are mainly working and middle class while refugees from blighted rural areas have become the legion of urban poor. About 2 million *paulistanos* are migrants or scions of migrants from Brazil's impoverished northeast area.

Of São Paulo's important non-Caucasian population about 600,000 are of Japanese heritage, with another 100,000 of diverse Asian origins. In contrast to other big Brazilian cities, blacks and mulattos make up less than 10 percent of São Paulo's population.

São Paulo is one of Brazil's least Roman Catholic cities, with one-third of its population following other religions. These include Shinto and Buddhism among the sizable Oriental population, and Islam among the one million-strong Lebanese-origin community. The city has approximately 100,000 Jewish worshippers. Even among Roman Catholics there is diversity. At last count, Sunday mass was conducted in 26 languages.

Surrounding the city is the state of São Paulo—Brazil's largest (31 million population), most economically diverse and wealthiest. The state of São Paulo includes a little bit of everything, from the smoky industries of São Paulo city to beach resorts that rival Rio; to a string of pleasing mountain resorts; and finally to a fertile farm area that is the most productive in Brazil.

The state of São Paulo is Brazil's economic powerhouse. With 22.5 percent of the nation's population, São Paulo accounted for 39.2 percent of federal tax revenues in 1986, consumed 29.2 percent of Brazil's electric power, drove 38.5 percent of its 13 million motor vehicles and communicated on 4.1 million telephone lines, 39 percent of the Brazilian total.

Half of all Brazilian manufacturing concerns are members of the state industrial federation (Fiesp). Ten of Brazil's 20 largest privately-held corporations and 10 of the 20 biggest private banks are headquartered in the state.

The most striking element of São Paulo's modern development has been its startling velocity. During the first three and a half centuries of Brazilian history São Paulo was a backwater, home to a few half-breed traders and pioneers.

First settlements: São Paulo's story is as old as Brazil's. The coastal settlement of São Vicente was founded in 1532, the first permanent Portuguese colony in the New World. A generation later, in 1554, two courageous Jesuits, José de Anchieta and Manuel da Nóbrega, established a mission on the high plateau 42 miles (70 km) inland from São Vicente. They called the colony São Paulo de Piratininga.

Much of São Paulo's traditional dynamism can be traced to the early isolation of settlements like São Vicente and Piratininga, located far away from the administrative and commercial center of the colony in the northeast region.

Since few European women would venture the hardships of life on the wind-blown plateau, male colonists took Indian concubines, fathering a race of hardy half-breeds accustomed to privation and feeling little attachment to Portugal.

Within two generations the remote colony had produced its own brand of frontiersman—the *bandeirante*. On his Indian side, the *bandeirante's* heritage included pathfinding and survival skills. From his Portuguese fathers he inherited a thirst for gain and a nomadic streak that would send him roaming over half a continent.

Modern *paulistas* of São Paulo explain their state's vocation for capitalism, pointing to the spirit of rugged individualism personified by the fearless *bandeirante*.

For two centuries the *bandeirante* was the all-purpose frontiersman, exploring the vast Plata and Amazon river systems, securing the borders of the Portuguese New World against Spanish incursions, discovering gold and diamonds in Minas Gerais, Goiás and Mato Grosso, and dragging Indian slaves from the hinterland to serve sugar barons on the coast. His epic wilderness treks called *bandeiras* (Portuguese for "flags"), gave him his sobriquet *bandeirante*, or "flag-bearer". Such journeys could last a year or more and, counting Indian guides, bearers and even women and children, might include a thousand souls.

Bandeirante individualism carried over to the political arena, starting in the 19th century; *paulistas* are proud of the fact that Brazil's verbal declaration of independence was uttered by Prince Regent Pedro I on São Paulo soil—at a place called Ipiranga—on September 7, 1822. Pedro I was greatly influenced by *paulista* advisers led by José Bonifácio de Andrada e Silva. Later in the 19th century, *paulistas* led the fight against slavery and helped establish the 1889 Republic.

Economic growth: São Paulo's true vocation was business. Attracted by the growth of British textile manufacturing, *paulista* plantation owners first cultivated cotton in the early 19th century. Lacking a large slave population, however, the state's plantations soon faced a manpower shortage and cotton production fell behind the American competition.

The American Civil War resulted in a brief spurt of sales to the British, due to the four-year blockade of Confederate ports but, following the war, Brazilian cotton exports decreased again. It was then that *paulista* plantation owners made the first in a series of astute investment moves destined to make their state Brazil's richest.

With money from the cotton boom, they diversified into coffee, a product enjoying increased world demand but little producer competition. São Paulo's climatic conditions and the fertile red soil called *Terra Roxa* proved ideal for the finicky coffee bush.

Within a decade coffee surpassed cotton as São Paulo's chief cash crop. Meanwhile, plantation owners decided to end the labor shortage once and for all. Starting in the 1870s state commissions and private agents began a systematic campaign to attract European settlers. Between 1870 and 1920 this campaign in Brazil successfully attracted some 5 million immigrants. About half settled in São Paulo, most working for set contractual periods as coffee plantation laborers.

Coffee money rebuilt the once sleepy outpost of São Paulo de Piratininga. During the first decades of the 20th century, elegant public works like the Municipal Theater and the first skyscrapers, like the Martinelli Building, transformed a village into a metropolis. At the same time, the coffee barons began to look for investment hedges to protect themselves against a drop in world coffee prices.

Their chief strategy, as in the past, was diversification, this time into manufacturing. Key elements were: an innovative, dynamic business elite; ready capital from booming coffee exports; an enviable network of railroads; a first-class port; skilled, literate workers from the ranks of European immigrants; and because of the web of rivers flowing down the coastal mountains, the Serra do Mar, ample sources of cheap hydroelectric power.

The stage was set for São Paulo's leap to becoming an industrial and financial giant. World War I was the spark: lack of European manufactured imports left a vacuum eagerly filled by a rising class of entrepreneurs.

The 1930s depression began a process of internal migration which further satisfied the rapidly industrializing state's hunger for labor. The city's almost incredible population boom, largely from migration, made it the world's fastest growing major city during much of the 1960s and 1970s, with as many as 1,000 new residents coming to São Paulo per day.

The velocity of São Paulo's growth can be seen in comparative population figures. In 1872 São Paulo was Brazil's ninth largest municipality, a village of 32,000. Rio de Janeiro was a 276,000-population metropolis. Even in 1890 São Paulo was only fourth with 65,000 people against Rio's half million. But the expansion of manufacturing spurred by World War I made São Paulo into a working- and middle-class city of 579,000 by 1920, number two behind the 1.1 million-population of Rio de

Janeiro. In 1954 São Paulo surpassed Rio to become number one. By 1960 São Paulo had 3.8 million residents, rising to 8.5 million in 1980, against Rio's 3.3 million in 1960 and 5.1 million in 1980. In 1984 São Paulo passed the 10 million mark, with another six million in its endless suburbs.

Independent streak: Meanwhile, São Paulo's tradition of political and intellectual independence continued into the 20th century. One of the first stirrings against the conservative Old Republic was a 1924 São Paulo barracks revolt led by young army officers.

In 1932 the entire state mobilized in a three-month Civil War against federal intervention in state affairs. The revolt was crushed by provisional president Getúlio Vargas. But the shrewd Vargas knew he could never govern Brazil without *paulista* consent. The worst punishment he meted out to rebels was Uruguayan exile.

Paulistas were also in the forefront of a nationalist intellectual movement erupting in 1922. That year Brazil's government organized an exhibition in Rio de Janeiro marking the 100th anniversary of independence. A group of São Paulo artists and writers boycotted the official event, staging a parallel "Modern Art Week" at São Paulo's Municipal Theater. The generation of intellectuals who would dominate 20th-century Brazilian arts and literature—painter Anita Malfatti, novelist Mário de Andrade, critic Oswald de Andrade, sculptor Victor Brecheret and composer Heitor Villa-Lobos—railed against "slavish imitation" of French and English artistic trends, calling for "the Brazilianization of Brazil."

The goals of the 1922 movement were never fully met, not even in São Paulo itself. Yet, the continued mix of disparate elements, old and new, foreign and indigenous, is probably São Paulo's greatest charm. No other Latin American city is as eclectic. Few display their wealth or flaunt their status as flamboyantly as São Paulo.

Historical center: The hard knot marking the center of São Paulo is a breezy esplanade and a handful of white-walled structures called the **Páteo do Colégio**. It was here that the hardy Jesuits Anchieta and Nóbrega founded the São Paulo de Piratininga Mission in 1554. The houses and chapel were substantially reinforced during restoration work in the 1970s. The **Anchieta house** is now a cramped museum displaying artifacts of the village's earliest settlers.

It took nearly 100 years to add the first ring around São Paulo's humble settlement. In 1632 the **Igreja do Carmo** was built about 660 feet (200 meters) from Anchieta's chapel, just behind today's **Praça da Sé**. The mannerist façade is well-preserved though largely hidden by office buildings and a garish fire station.

In 1644 another appealing mannerist façade took its place at one of the outlying points of the village—the pretty **São Francisco Church**, located about 1,320 feet (400 meters) from the Páteo do Colégio. A convent was attached in 1647. The still bustling complex displays colonial-era wood carvings and gold leaf decoration.

Copan Building in downtown São Paulo.

Finally, in 1717, the **Igreja de Santo Antônio** was completed about halfway between the Páteo do Colégio and São Francisco. Recently restored, Santo Antônio's bright yellow-and-white façade is a pleasing contrast to the gray office towers which rise around it.

Until the mid-19th century the quadrilateral of churches, embracing a dozen or so streets of mostly one-story dwellings, was the full extent of the "city" of São Paulo. The 1868 cotton inauguration of the Jundiaí-Santos Railway to transport the crop changed the face of São Paulo forever. Red brick and wrought iron crept into the city's previously rustic architecture. Workshops and warehouses grew up around the train station, near today's Luz commuter rail terminal .

The rise of coffee presaged even more growth. From 1892, when the first iron footbridge was flung across the downtown **Anhangabáu Valley**, through the 1920s, São Paulo added another ring of busy business districts and colorful neighborhoods.

The coffee barons themselves were the first to build on the north side of the Anhangabaú, in a district called **Campos Elíseos**. Some of their Art Nouveau mansions, surrounded by high iron gates and gleaming with bronze and stained-glass finishings, can still be seen, although overall the neighborhood today is a shabby remnant of its glittering past. Later, more mansions were erected in nearby **Higienópolis** and then in an elegant row along Avenida Paulista.

Meanwhile, thousands of immigrants poured into working-class neighborhoods that were sprouting around São Paulo's old downtown. Vila Inglesa, Vila Economizadora and others, their rows of red brick houses and shops still neat and orderly, were civilized efforts to meet the city's critical housing needs. But they didn't work. By the time São Paulo's World War I industrial expansion began, Italian, Japanese and Portuguese immigrants were crowded into cheek-by-jowl tenements in a ring of slums—Bras, Bom Retiro, Bela Vista

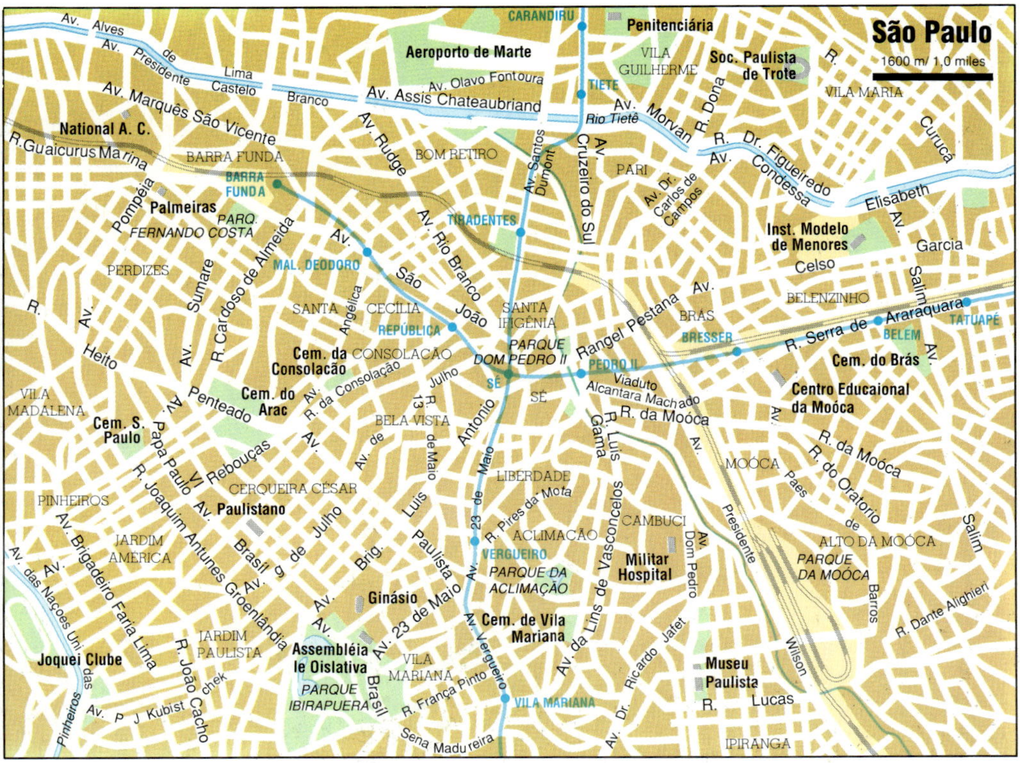

and Liberdade—circling the historic downtown. Even today these same neighborhoods mix shabby tenements with strong ethnic currents.

Today's communities: Liberdade, just behind Praça da Sé, has kept its Japanese origins intact to the point where street signs use Oriental characters and movie houses show Japanese films (see chapter on Liberdade).

Bela Vista (popularly known as Bixiga) is São Paulo's colorful Little Italy. **Rua 13 de Maio**, Bixiga's heart, is a row of green and red *cantinas* and pretty two-story houses. The parish church of **Nossa Senhora Achiropita** is a squat mini-basilica graced by ornate columns and topped by an oversized dome.

Achiropita is the site of an annual festival (every August) celebrating wine, pasta and music. Rua 13 de Maio is roped off as thousands gather for dancing, drinking (5,000 liters of wine) and pastas (three tons of spaghetti and 40,000 pizzas). Bixiga owes its rather unappealing nickname to a turn-of-the-century market which sold tripe (*bixiga* means bladder in Portuguese) to immigrants who could not afford to buy anything else.

Bom Retiro, near the **Luz Train Station**, retains vestiges of its past as São Paulo's Arab and Lebanese Christian neighborhood. Twisting **Rua 25 de Março** packs fabric and rug stores in a noisy bazaar. Jewish, Muslim and Christian merchants sip coffee and chat as if Mid-east tensions never existed.

Beyond Bom Retiro, surrounding cavernous **Roosevelt Commuter Train Terminal**, is **Bras**. Predominantly Italian at the turn-of-the-century, today's Bras is a vast slum, housing thousands of migrants from the impoverished northeast. They are São Paulo's bus drivers, sun-seared road workers and construction laborers with knotty hands and toothless grins.

Their culture, rich with the sap of Brazilian folklore, can be seen on every street corner. *Nordestino* (northeastern) accordion players perform nightly at the shabby north end of Praça da Sé. During

***Paulistanos* enjoy Ibirapuera Park.**

the day *repentistas*, guitar players who make up clever, rhyming lyrics on any subject suggested by on-lookers, hold forth on the breezy **São Bento** esplanade. Bahian *capoeira* performers dance to the eerie sound of the single-string *berimbau* outside the Anhangabaú subway station. At **Praça do Patriarca**, a *nordestino* herb salesman deals in alligator skins, colorless elixirs and Amazon spices sold from burlap sacks spread on the sidewalk.

Nearby, on busy **Avenida São João**, a *nordestino* conman manipulates three tiny cups and a pea atop some wooden fruit crates. Eager bumpkins pay a dollar a throw to play the illegal trick shell game.

Historical downtown: São Paulo's outward thrust also brought a sweeping transformation of the old downtown. The peak coffee year of 1901 coincided with the inauguration of the brick-and-iron Luz train station, marked by an English-style clock tower and expansive gardens. In 1920 the imposing Central Post Office went up on Avenida São João. That same year São Paulo's Roman Catholic Diocese tore down a tottering 18th-century cathedral and began the present **Basilica of Nossa Senhora da Assunção**, whose Gothic façade and 100-meter spires were finally completed in 1954. In 1929 São Paulo's Italian population inaugurated its first great status symbol—the 30-story **Martinelli Building**. Post-war years brought the **Bank of São Paulo**, modeled after New York's Empire State Building and in 1965, Latin America's tallest office building, the 42-story **Edifício Itália**.

The depression year of 1933 saw the completion of the sprawling German Gothic **Municipal Market**, behind Praça da Sé, by noted architect Francisco Ramos de Azevedo. It is still in use, though darkened by pollution and neglect. Ramos de Azevedo was also chiefly responsible for the eclectic (Italian Renaissance and Art Nouveau) **Municipal Theater**, inaugurated in 1911. Isadora Duncan, Ana Pavlova and Enrico Caruso performed under the

Downtown pedestrain street.

LIBERDADE—A TOUCH OF TOKYO

A towering red portico, called a *tori*, straddles the main business street. Next to it is a tiny, expertly manicured garden, lush with dark green shrubs and graced by an arching foot bridge, called a *hashi*. Beyond the portico 450 smaller gateways, each bearing a white strobe light, march toward the urban horizon.

Along the side streets movie theaters advertise in Japanese. Itinerant merchants, with aged Oriental faces wreathed by scores of wrinkles, hawk fresh flowers in carefully tied bunches. Signs on low-rise, concrete buildings announce centers for acupuncture treatment and meditation. Classes in judo, flower arranging and the tea ceremony are also available here.

Welcome to **Liberdade**, São Paulo's lively Japanese neighborhood.

Liberdade residents can choose from three Japanese-language community newspapers and shop for Oriental delicacies at neighborhood grocery stores. Some say Liberdade is more Japanese than Tokyo, which, they claim, has become excessively westernized. Liberdade is lost in both time and space.

The sprawling neighborhood, centered around Rua Galvão Bueno, behind São Paulo's Roman Catholic Cathedral, originated in 1908. On June 18 of that year, the immigrant steamer *Kasato Maru* docked at Santos Harbor with 830 Japanese on board. The immigrants, almost all farmers, were fleeing crop failures and earthquakes in their native islands. Using loans supplied by a Japanese development firm, most of the 165 families set up modest truck-farming operations in the interior of São Paulo. Later, some drifted to Mato Grosso and even to the Amazon jungle, where they successfully introduced production of two unrelated commodities—jute and hot peppers.

Over the next five decades a quarter of a million Japanese followed in their footsteps. The immigrants' story is told in pictures and artifacts, including a

The São Paulo Art Museum (MASP) honoring Japanese immigration.

striking model of the *Kasato Maru*, at Liberdade's **Immigration Museum**, on Rua São Joaquim.

Liberdade became São Paulo's Oriental section in the 1940s, when the sons (*nissei*) and grandsons (*sansei*) of early settlers joined the urban trades and professions. Today, nearly 100 establishments stocking everything from locally-made kimonos to imported Japanese condiments, cater to neighborhood needs and the tourists.

Crowded emporiums like **Casa Mizumoto** and **Minikimono** sell a wide range of artifacts. These range from cheap stone or plastic Buddhas to expensive, delicately carved ivory figures, hand-painted vases and assortments of *furins,* or "Bells of Happiness," which drive away evil spirits whenever they tinkle with a passing breeze.

There is even one store on Rua Galvão Bueno, **O Oratório**, which specializes in laquered wooden altars for Buddhist worshippers. A hushed atmosphere prevails in the shop as salesmen reveal the bronze or gold linings of row upon row of portable altars.

Brazilian semi-precious stones, some mounted on flimsy wooden bases and others superbly embellished by master craftsmen, are another mainstay of the gift and specialty trade.

Sampling the neighborhood cuisine is probably the highlight of any visit to Liberdade. Restaurants like **Hinadé Yamaga** and **Kokeshi** serve Japanese specialties on low wooden tables, with a choice of chopsticks or Western utensils. Larger restaurants normally have their own *sushi* bars, which are a kind of smorgasbord of Japanese delicacies offered to guests seated around a semicircular counter. The most complete *sushi* and restaurant services are at Liberdade's **Banri, Osaka** and **Nikkey Palace Hotels** on Rua Galvão Bueno.

First-time samplers of Japanese cuisine usually stick with conventional choices such as *Okonomi Yaki*, a shrimp, pork or fish pancake; *Sukiyaki,* a meat and vegetable dish soaked in gravy; or *Lobatazaki*, fish or meat broiled on a spit. The more daring might try exotic dishes such as *Unagui*, stewed eel served in sweet sauce, or *Kocarai,* raw carp. Shrimp, raw fish, marine algae patties, mushrooms and salmon are typical appetizers. Main squid or octopus dishes are also featured on most menus.

Although the neighborhood is overwhelmingly Japanese, it is also home to several of São Paulo's best Chinese restaurants. The city does not have a Chinatown and in fact, São Paulo's Chinese population is small, but the quality of Liberdade's Chinese eateries rival that of its Japanese restaurants.

One of the best ways to sample Liberdade's cuisine is one-delicacy-at-a-time at the **Oriental Street Fair** every Sunday morning at **Praça Liberdade** (surrounding the Liberdade subway station). Dozens of wood-and-canvas stalls serve shrimp, fish and meat tidbits from spits that sputter on open grills. Other Japanese and Brazilian appetizers are also sold. The fair sprawls over the plaza and into neighboring streets, where stalls sell most of the products normally on display Monday through Saturday in Liberdade's packed emporiums. Imports, however, are restricted—a measure designed to stimulate local handicraft production.

At first glance, Liberdade nightlife seems surprisingly subdued. Few pedestrians pass beneath the red archways and the traffic is light. The action is all indoors. Some of the larger restaurants feature soothing Japanese music performed by brightly costumed players using acoustic instruments, while multi-course repasts stretch through an entire evening.

Near the subway station a pair of noisy nightclubs, the **Yuri** and the **Tutu**, present striptease acts on tiny, smoke-filled stages. Nearby, on Avenida Liberdade, the plush **Liberty Plaza Club** offers a surprising mix of erotic entertainment, rock-and-roll, a *sushi* bar and billiards.

Day or night, Liberdade is full of life, color and surprises. Visitors typically have only one complaint—they find it hard to believe they're in the heart of South America.

one-and-a-half-ton Swiss crystal chandelier and must have been impressed by the marble, bronze and onyx decor. Perhaps they wouldn't have appeared, though, had they known the theater was haunted. The ghost of an Italian opera singer is said to belt forlorn solos from an upper window as his equally ghostly girlfriend clasps a lily and weeps.

Starting in the 1940s São Paulo added more and more commercial and residential rings as it spiraled outward. Higienópolis and the Jardims, south of Avenida Paulista, became middle- and upper-class high-rise apartment neighborhoods. Later, offices, apartments and shopping centers formed another ring around elegant **Avenida Faria Lima**, a little over a mile (two km) south of Paulista. In the 1970s, São Paulo jumped the Pinheiros River to start an even glitzier ring in hilly **Morumbi**, where strikingly landscaped mansions include the official residence of the state governor.

Parks and museums: While São Paulo's citizens are famed as workaholics, they also find time to relax. During the daytime, prime attractions are the city's excellent museums and parks.

MASP, the **São Paulo Museum of Art**, is the city's cultural pride, with nearly 1,000 pieces from ancient Greece to contemporary Brazil. The unique display arrangement—rows of paintings encased in smoked glass slabs—was designed chiefly as a teaching aid. Detailed explanations on the back of each display put the artist and his work in historical perspective.

The museum is like an art history book—but offering the real thing instead of color plates. Rafael, Bosch, Holbien, Rembrandt, Monet, Van Gogh, Goya, Reynolds and Picasso are only a few of the artists representing major European trends. The museum also includes a survey of Brazilian art from 19th-century court painters, Almeida Júnior and Pedro Américo, to 20th-century modernists Portinari, Di Cavalcanti and Tarsila do Amaral.

Behind the Luz train station and park is **São Paulo's State Art Gallery**, a neo-classical building designed by Ramos de Azevedo. What MASP does for Western art, the state gallery's 3,300-piece collection does for Brazilian art. Highlights include sculptures by Vitor Brecheret, creator of the *Bandeirantes Monument*, and Almeida Júnior's *A Leitura*, a portrait of a young girl reading against a background of palm trees and striped awnings.

Across Avenida Tiradentes from the State Art Gallery is São Paulo's most important collection of colonial-era art and artifacts. The **Sacred Art Museum**'s 11,000 pieces are displayed in the former cloisters and chapel of the labyrinthian Luz Monastery. The main baroque structure was completed in 1774, although portions date to the late 17th century. Oil portraits of São Paulo's first bishops, gold and silver altar accoutrements, carved gold-leaf fragments of churches torn down by the juggernaut of 20th-century progress and rare wood carvings by Brazil's great 18th-century sculptor Antônio Francisco Lisboa (also known as Aleijadinho, "the little cripple") com-

Obelisk, 1932 Civil War Monument.

plete the collection.

Across from the imposing State Governor's Palace in Morumbi, the **Oscar Americano Foundation** is São Paulo's most bucolic setting for art appreciation. Americano was a noted architect and collector who willed his estate to the public as an arts foundation when he died in 1974. The discreet glass-and-stone mansion displays works by Di Cavalcanti, Portinari, Guignard, 17th-century Dutch painter Franz Post and many others against a lush background of broad lawns and landscaped woods. A tea room overlooks the ground floor patio. String quartets and soloists perform in a small auditorium on Sunday afternoons.

Located in a tranquil suburb, the sprawling **Ipiranga Museum** marks the spot where Pedro I declared Brazilian independence in 1822. An equestrian monument stands where the impetuous Pedro shouted "independence or death" before a small entourage. The emperor's remains are buried beneath the bronze and concrete landmark. On a nearby bluff is the massive, neo-classical museum building. Inside is a hodgepodge of historical and scientific exhibits. One wing displays artifacts of Pedro and his family. Another includes furnishings, farm implements and even horse carts from São Paulo's colonial past. Research by the University of São Paulo on Brazil's Indians has yielded material for several galleries, including a display of pre-Colombian pottery from the Amazon island of Marajó. Other exhibits honor aviation pioneer Alberto Santos Dumont and the state militiamen who fought in the 1932 Civil War. A separate gallery displays Pedro Américo's 1888 painting *O Grito do Ipiranga*, a romanticized portrayal of Pedro I's famous "independence or death" pose.

São Paulo's most important park, **Ibirapuera**, is 5.2 million sq feet (1.6 million sq meters) of trees, lawns and handsome pavilions, completed to celebrate São Paulo's 400th anniversary in 1954. Today, a half million *paulistanos* use its playgrounds, picnic areas and ball

Japanese Liberdade district.

fields on sunny weekends. In front of the park are two of São Paulo's most noted monuments: the 72-meter **Obelisk and Mauseleum** honoring heroes of the 1932 Civil War and Brecheret's ***Bandeirantes Monument***. Ibirapuera's low-slung curving pavilions, designed by Oscar Niemeyer, constitute São Paulo's most important cultural center. The main showcase is a three-story rectangle of ramps and glass hosting São Paulo's famed Bienal Art Shows.

Held since 1951, the São Paulo Bienal is the world's largest regularly scheduled arts event, bringing everything that's new, experimental and slightly crazy in the worlds of art and music together for a two-month extravaganza. The pavilion also hosts industrial and cultural fairs. The third floor displays a permanent collection of contemporary Brazilian paintings. Linked to the **Bienal Pavilion** by an undulating breezeway is the **São Paulo Museum of Modern Art**, exhibiting works by 20th-century Brazilian painters and sculptors. A low concrete dome, precursor of Niemeyer's Congress Building in Brasília, houses São Paulo's **Aeronautics Museum**. Replicas of pioneering aircraft designed by Brazil's diminutive aeronautics genius Alberto Santos Dumont are the chief attraction at this museum.

The **Butantã Institute**, founded in 1901, is one of the world's leading centers for the study of poisonous snakes. The slithery reptiles are everywhere—coiled behind glass in ornate kiosks, piled one on top of the other in grassy habitats, stuffed and mounted in display cases next to hairy spiders and scorpions. Altogether, there are some 80,000 live snakes on the premises. Periodically, staff members milk poison from their dangerous fangs as visitors gawk.

São Paulo boasts one of the world's largest zoos—3,500 specimens occupying mainly natural habitats. Noted for its tropical bird collection, the **São Paulo Zoo** annually attracts 2.5 million visitors. Nearby is the **Simba Safari** for the adventurous. An average of 1,000

Shopping at the Ibirapuera Shopping Center.

visitors per day drive along the 2.5-mile (four-km) route, observing the wild African animals that roam freely around the rugged landscape. Staff place metal grids on car windows as visitors enter the park.

Dining out: For most *paulistanos*, as well as foreign visitors, São Paulo is above all else a restaurant city. Food is king in São Paulo—buffet tables burst with it, waiters fuss over it, grills and spits sputter with it, and a priesthood of critics and gourmets argue over it.

Paulistanos love food—in all its flavors, shapes and ethnic varieties—more than any other urban population in Brazil. With more than enough ethnic communities to go around, each with its own national dishes and restaurants, São Paulo has raised food to the level of worship. For the *paulistanos*, the substitute for Rio's beach life is an active nightlife centered around wine and dinner at one of the city's many highly-rated restaurants.

There is no such thing as a definitive São Paulo restaurant guide but many of the city's restaurants have by now been enshrined as world-class eateries.

One of São Paulo's most traditional Italian restaurants is Neapolitan-cuisine **Jardim de Napoli** in Higienópolis. The Buconerba family has been producing its own *calabresa*, *fusilli* and *tartiglione* there since the 1950s. Jardim de Napoli is the kind of Italian restaurant with checkered table cloths, cheeses hanging from the ceiling and elderly waiters who address customers by name. Lamb and eggplant specialties are recommended.

The Italian restaurant winning the broadest kudos in recent years is **Massimo's** in Jardim Paulista. (Massimo is the festive, balding gentleman with the suspenders tirelessly directing employees and greeting customers.)

Bixiga's Rua 13 de Maio is a five-block traffic jam Sunday afternoons, as restaurant-goers line up outside a dozen cantinas. The largest are **Roperto**, **La Tavola**, **Dona Grazia** and **Mexilhão**.

São Paulo's most traditional French restaurant is comfortable, wood-panelled **La Casserole**, near the flower market on **Largo do Arouche**, downtown. Arouche's sculpture garden, highlighting works by Brecheret, embellishes the sense of dining by the Seine. Lamb and bouillabaisse are the restaurant's specialties.

The city's top-rated French restaurant is elegant **La Cuisine Du Soleil** at the Maksoud Plaza Hotel. Duck and lobster are recommended.

Ibirapuera is São Paulo's German restaurant district. Noisy beer halls with names like **Konstanz**, **Windhuk** and **Bismark** serve up heaping platters of *eisbein*, *kassler* and *liberkaese*.

Excellent Chinese restaurants include the **Sino-Brasileiro**, a converted mansion in the suburb of Perdizes and **Genghis Khan**, located at the bustling corner of Avenidas Rebouças and Faria Lima. Japanese restaurants (see chapter on Liberdade), however, tend to overshadow other Oriental choices.

São Paulo also boasts less common ethnic specialties. The **Vikings** restaurant in the Maksoud Plaza offers an overloaded Scandinavian smorgas-

***Orelhão* (Big Ear) pay phones.**

bord. In nearby Jardim Paulista the **Hungaria** serves *gulash* and *galuska* in a spacious dining room where the fireplace roars on chilly winter evenings.

In Itaim, near Ibirapuera, **Brasserie Victoria** holds the title for best Arabic cuisine. *Homus*, *kibe* and *tabule* are among specialties of a multi-course service that never seems to end.

In **Pinheiros**, around the corner from the Genghis Khan, São Paulo's Greek community gathers on Saturday nights to savor *moussaka*, *tavas* and *stifado*, smash hundreds of specially designed plates sold for a dollar-a-dozen and watch a frenetic belly dancer leap from table to table to the accompaniment of a Greek-language band—all at the appropriately named **Zorba**.

For a great sandwich or a truly exquisite espresso, try **Baguette**, on Ruo Consolaçâo at the corner of Av. Paulista. This up-scale fast-food joint is conveniently located across from a bank of cinemas which show the best in foreign films.

Even when it comes to Brazilian cuisine variety is the rule. **O Profeta**, in the **Moema District** near Ibirapuera, specializes in the hearty bean sauces and chicken and pork dishes of Minas Gerais State.

In **Jardim Paulista** two Brazilian beef palaces contend for hegemony over middle-class restaurant-goers. **The Buffalo Grill** weighs in with its famous oyster bar, a Brazilian rarity, and specially prepared *patés*. Nearby, **The Place** counters with a wood-panelled English pub for pre-dinner drinks.

Shopping: When *paulistanos* are not working or dining out, they're shopping. **Rua Augusta**, around **Rua Oscar Freire** in Jardim Paulista, is traditional headquarters for fashionable but pricey men and women's wear. **Dimpus**, **Etcetera** and **Pandemonium** are famous boutiques. **Le Postiche** specializes in fine leather goods. More boutiques can be found in the **Vitrine Gallery** at Augusta 2530.

A narrow gallery of handicraft stores at Augusta 2883 leads to São Paulo's leading arts corner—**Rua Padre João**

Ibirapuera shopping mall.

Manuel and **Rua Barão de Capanema**. A dozen galleries, of which the **Dan** and the **Remet** are the largest, display the best in contemporary Brazilian painting and sculpture.

But the *paulistano's* first love is the shopping center. The priciest is **Morumbi**, featuring top boutiques and designer stores as well as a busy skating rink and an attractive aquarium stocked with everything from the lowly seahorse to the lordly dolphin.

The oldest São Paulo shopping center is **Iguatemi**, on Avenida Faria Lima, noted for its traffic congestion, pedestrian ramps and water clock.

Almost as traditional is **Ibirapuera**, a boxy structure near the park. But the biggest and slickest shopping center is **Eldorado**, a huge glass enclosure of splashing fountains and towering mirrors. Eldorado has its own entertainment plaza on the top floor, featuring live music, movies and an American-style saloon.

Entertainment: São Paulo's nightlife comes alive around midnight. The old money prefers members-only clubs like **The Gallery** and **Regine's** in the Faria Lima area.

When the old money wants to slum, it goes to Bixiga. A hot ticket is the delightfully absurd **Imelda Marcos**, where guests are greeted by an overdressed look-alike of the ex-Philippine dictator's wife (she wears a different pair of shoes every night). Nearby is dank, creepy **Madame Satã**, a hangout for punks, darks and freaks. Less eccentric Bixiga nightlife can be found at a string of animated cantinas, featuring live jazz, folk and Brazilian rock music around Rua 13 de Maio. The **Café do Bixiga**, the **Espaço Off**, which boosts avant garde humor and music, the **Café Piu-Piu** and the **Soçaité** are among well-known spots.

The new money gravitates toward music and dance at extravagant clubs like the **Up and Down** in Jardim Paulista. Five separate bars and disco dance floors for 2,100, with fog machine and a 270-square foot video screen lure São Paulo's monied youth. **The Roof**, a blasting disco near Faria Lima, offers an added attraction—its 22nd-floor view of the city.

São Paulo club crawlers who don't want to go deaf have plenty of options to choose from. A row of bars and restaurants located on **Rua Henrique Schaumann** in Pinheiros lean toward Brazilian pop and folk music, with a preference for *choro*, traditional ballads played with a touch of Tin Pan Alley. Popular spots are the **Clube do Choro** and the **Cathedral do Choro**.

English pubs, complete with darts, taps and wainscotting, are also popular. The **London Tavern**, in the **Hilton Hotel** downtown, was the pioneer. **Clyde's** and **Blend**, in Itaim, quickly followed.

Piano bars are a *paulistano* favorite. The **Baiuca** on Faria Lima is the most popular among singles. One of the prettiest, for its smoked-glass decor and soft lights, is the **San Francisco Bay** in Jardim Paulista. The noisy **Executive Piano Bar**, on the top floor of the Itália Building, is noted mainly for its view.

São Paulo's post-war growth (and money) have made it a magnet for world-class performers. A typical season might bring the Bolshoi Ballet, the New York Philharmonic, Miles Davis, Sting, James Taylor and many other big name stars to a half dozen venues including the **Anhembi Convention Center** (site of an annual Jazz Festival), **Ibirapuera Gymnasium**, the **Municipal Theater** or the cavernous **Palace Night Club** in Moema. More intimate are the **Palladium**, at Eldorado Shopping Center, and the **150 Night Club** at the Maksoud.

São Paulo competes head-to-head with Rio when it comes to X-rated entertainment. Glitzy strip bars featuring unusually bold erotic acts start on Rua Augusta near the **Caesar Park Hotel**, extending all the way to Rua Nestor Pastana downtown. The **Kilt**, **Puma Chalet**, **Vagão** and **Estação** are clubs that offer go-go girls, erotic shows and pseudo-deluxe interior decorating—oak doors, mirrors, glittery strobe lights and fake gilt.

Others are located on **Rua Bento Freitas** near the Hilton. Five blocks from the Hilton, on **Rua Major Sertório**, is venerable **La Licorne**, boasting the flashiest decor and the brassiest erotic numbers.

Mountain resorts: Like *cariocas*, São Paulo residents can vacation at the mountains or the shore without leaving their home state.

At 5,200 feet (1,700 meters), in a lush valley of the Mantiqueira Range, **Campos do Jordão** is São Paulo's chief mountain resort. Tourists like its Alpine chalets, chilly winter weather and **July Music Festival**. The month-long festival, featuring both classical and popular programs, takes place at the modern **Municipal Auditorium**. Next door is the pleasingly landscaped **Felícia Leirner** sculpture garden. Here on display are magnificent bronze and granite works by the Polish-born artist whose name it takes.

The hub of Campos do Jordão's busy downtown is a row of chalet-style restaurants and shops. Local products include metal, wood and leather crafts, woolens and rustic furniture. Primitive arts are on sale.

Nearby is a tranquil lake circled by horse-drawn carriages for hire. Yellow-and-brown trollies carrying tourists occasionally rattle by.

Ringing downtown are 54 hotels and dozens of summer homes belonging to the *paulistano* elite. The largest such abode, bearing the impressive name **Boa Vista Palace**, is the state governor's winter retreat.

A portion of this Tudor-style mansion has been converted into a museum. The attractions include 19th-century furnishings and oil paintings by *paulista* artists. Seven miles (12 km) from downtown, **Itapeva Peak** offers an impressive view of the **Paraíba River Valley**, where São Paulo coffee trees first took root more than a century ago.

The only problem with the state's most bucolic resort, Campos do Jordão, is its distance from São Paulo, which is 90 miles (155 km) away.

Closer to the big-town, 40 miles (60 km) along the São Paulo-Santo André Highway, is a quaint railroad outpost frozen in time—**Paranapiacaba**. Built in 1867 by British railroaders, the brick-and-board station and row houses are a portrait of Victorian England. The tall clock tower recalls Big Ben. At 2,500 feet (800 meters), Paranapiacaba ("Sea View" in Tupi-Guarani) was the last station on the Jundiaí-Santos line before the breathtaking plunge down the Great Escarpment.

A half-hour train ride, on a creaking, huffing engine, will bring tourists through tunnels and across narrow viaducts to the edge of the sheer mountainside for a spectacular view of the Santos lowlands.

Paranapiacaba offers few amenities, however. There are no hotels or restaurants, only a few fruit and soft drink stands. A museum displays 19th-century train cars and memorabilia.

Also close to São Paulo, 40 miles (60 km) on the Fernão Dias Highway, but better organized for visitors, is the mountain resort of **Atibaia**, São Paulo's peach and strawberry capital. A winter festival honors the lowly strawberry, selling everything from strawberry jam to pink strawberry liquors.

At 2,500 feet (820 meters) Atibaia's crisp, clean air contrasts with São Paulo's smog. Brazil's Amateur Astronomers Society, mustering dozens of telescopes including a few installed in mini-observatories complete with domes, has made Atibaia its national headquarters. The society claims the town offers ideal climatic conditions for scanning the heavens.

Atibaia's delightfully landscaped **Municipal Park** features mineral water springs, lakes and a new railway museum. Near the center of town is Atibaia's white-walled **Municipal Museum**, dating from 1836. Sacred art objects are a curious contrast to the erotic pieces displayed by local sculptor Yolanda Mallozzi in a second floor gallery.

Just outside Atibaia are two noted resort hotels, the **Village Eldorado** and the **Park Atibaia**, offering sports and leisure facilities. For São Paulo residents, however, the biggest attraction is the fresh air.

Day trips: Quaint, prosperous **Itu**, 60 miles (100 km) from São Paulo on the Castello Branco Highway, is another fresh air paradise.

In the 1970s Itu's town fathers devised a bizarre campaign to boost tourism. Their slogan was: "Everything is Big in Itu." To prove it they installed an immense public telephone in the town square and an oversized traffic light nearby. Restaurants sold beer in liter mugs and tourist stores hawked huge pencils and other knick-knacks with Itu printed in bold letters.

Fortunately, little remains of the campaign today (although the phone booth still stands), so visitors can appreciate Itu's true delights, which include 18th- and 19th-century row houses on pretty pedestrian streets, a handful of cluttered antique stores and two museums. The **Republican Museum**, just off the main square, displays colonial and imperial-era furnishings and artifacts. The collection of the nearby **Sacred Art Museum** boasts colonial religious art and works by Itu native Almeida Júnior.

Closer to São Paulo, 16 miles (20 km) on the Regis Bittencourt Highway, is the state handicrafts capital of **Embu**. The town's two main squares and a network of pedestrian streets linking them become a vast primitive art, handicrafts and Brazilian food festival every weekend. Wooden stalls sell ceramics, leather and metal-worked handicrafts, woolen goods, lacework, knitted items and colorful batiks.

On **Largo dos Jesuitas**, wood carvers practice their craft in the open air. Rows of quaint 18th-century houses serve as antique and rustic furniture stores. The rude chapel of **Nossa Senhora do Rosário** was built by Indians in 1690. In the annex is a musty Sacred Art Museum.

Visitors can sample Bahian delicacies like *vatapá* or coconut sweets at outdoor stalls or choose from among a dozen interesting restaurants. One, the **Senzala**, occupies the rooftop of a sprawling colonial-era house. Nearby, the **Orixás** serves Bahian delicacies and

Shops and eateries line pedestrian street in Campos do Jordão.

feijoada, Brazil's trademark pork and black bean stew. The **Patação** also specializes in Brazilian cuisine; its long, dark-wood tables and fireplace recall a colonial-era tavern.

Beaches: *Paulistas* criticize *cariocas* for lolling in the sun too much. They forget to mention that São Paulo has beautiful beaches, too. São Paulo's sun coast stretches 240 miles (400 km) from popular Ubatuba in the north to remote Cananéia near the border with Paraná State.

Ubatuba, only 40 miles (70 km) from **Paraty** in southern Rio de Janeiro, is famous for its crystal clear waters, considered ideal for skin diving. A total of 50 miles (85 km) of beaches curl around Ubatuba's inlets and islands. Boat trips take visitors to the **Anchieta Prison** ruins on one of the main islands, then up the coast to the eerie remains of **Lagoinha Sugar Plantation**, which was partially destroyed by fire during the last century.

Caraguatatuba, 30 miles (50 km) south of Ubatuba on State Highway 55, has almost as many beaches as its northern neighbor but fewer historical attractions. A first-class resort hotel, the **Tabatinga**, offers complete sports facilities including golf.

Immigrants Road bridge on the way to the coast.

Caraguatatuba is a springboard for visiting São Paulo's largest off-shore island—**São Sebastião**, 18 miles (30 km) south on Highway 55. Ferry boats take visitors from the quaint town of São Sebastião on the mainland to the village of **Ilhabela** on the island. Ghosts from shipwrecks are said to roam Ilha Bela at night.

Another 60 miles (100 km) down Highway 55 is peaceful **Bertioga**. The **Fortress of São João**, with blazing white walls and miniature turrets, guards a narrow inlet. Its ancient cannons bear down on passing pleasure craft. The fort dates from 1547.

Eighteen miles (30 km) south of Bertioga is São Paulo's elite resort of **Guarujá**. Many of the city's four- and five-star hotels have erected thatch-roofed cabana villages for their guests right on the beach. White-coated waiters serve drinks in the open air.

Enseada is the most popular beach, a horseshoe of spray, sand and gleaming hotels recalling Copacabana. Nearby is more isolated **Pernambuco Beach**. São Paulo's money elite have made this their Malibu.

Mansions of every architectural style—surrounded by broad lawns and closed in by fences, hedges and guards—look out on surf and green and gray off-shore islands.

Like São Paulo, only 54 miles (nearly 90 km) away, Guarujá is a city for restaurant-goers. Highly rated and recommended are **Delphin**, for shrimp, **Il Faro** and **Rufino's** for Italian cuisine, and the bar and restaurant of the **Casa Grande Hotel**, a sprawling colonial inn on Praia da Enseada.

A few blocks from the Casa Grande is the narrow area of **Praia da Pitangueiras**. Streets near the beach have been closed to traffic, permitting pedestrians to browse unhindered among dozens of boutiques, handicraft and jewelry stores.

From downtown visitors can catch

the ferry (it takes cars) across an oily inlet to **Santos**, São Paulo's chief port.

Santistas take little pain to hide the business end of their island—hulking tankers ply the narrow channels spewing oil and refuse; freight containers are piled by the hundreds in ugly pens or next to dilapidated warehouses.

Unfortunately, decay has spread to the city's old downtown. Historic **Igreja do Carmo**, with portions dating to 1589, is a gray façade next to a broken down train station. Nearby, a slum has sprung up around the **São Bento Church** and **Sacred Art Museum**, dating from 1650.

The ocean side of Santos, however, shows the same white-washed face as Guarujá. The **City Aquarium**, on broad **Avenida Bartolomeu de Gusmão**, displays tropical fish, turtles, eels and a playful sea lion.

The **Sea Museum**, on **Rua Equador** near the Guarujá ferry landing, exhibits stuffed sharks killed in nearby waters, an immense 325-pound (148-kg) sea shell and bizarre coral formations. Santos also boasts a lovely orchid garden in the **José Menino District** near São Vicente.

Brazil's oldest settlement, **São Vicente**, retains little of its early history. The main **Gonzaguinha** beach is a row of white and pastel-shaded apartment houses with scattered bars and outdoor restaurants, Copacabana-style.

São Vicente is the gateway to Brazil's most crowded beach—**Praia Grande**, an endless stretch of spray, grayish-brown sand, tourist buses and bobbing human bodies. But another 35 miles (60 km) south on Highway 55 is yet another scene, the slow-moving **Itanhaem**.

One of Brazil's oldest settlements, portions of Itanhaem's gray, spooky **Nossa Senhora da Conceição** chapel go back to 1534.

Other beach towns south of São Vicente include picturesque **Peruibe** (50 miles or 80 km), **Iguape** (120 miles or 200 km), on the quiet inlet formed by **Ilha Comprida**, and remote **Cananéia** (170 miles or 280 km), featuring boat excursions to nearby islands.

The São Paulo coast.

MINAS GERAIS

Bahia may be Brazil's soul, but Minas Gerais is its heart. No other state is as poetic as Minas. Only the Amazon is more isolated and São Paulo more populous. And perhaps only Bahia is the source of as much folklore.

Minas is a Brazilian giant. It covers 352,200 sq miles (587,000 sq km), is the fifth largest state in area and has 15 million inhabitants.

Minas is rugged and isolated. The central plateau rises sharply from an escarpment that rims the entire eastern frontier. The land of this once heavily wooded province is ragged now. *Minas* means mines. Everything from gold and diamonds to iron has flowed from its mineral ore veins to the world. Even today, the streets of its quaint, ancient towns are pink with iron ore dust and the rivers red with it.

The *mineiros* are different; probably more different from other Brazilians than any other regional population. Folklore contrasts the *mineiro* sharply with the extravagant *carioca* and the industrious *paulista*. The *mineiro* is stubborn. He feels a strong sense of duty. He is cautious, mistrustful and shows little emotion. He works hard and he is thrifty.

The *mineiro* is an assiduous preserver. He has kept not only the music box churches of his baroque past, he has also saved family heirlooms and trinkets which clutter his attic rooms. São João del Rei residents have preserved the music and even the musical instruments of the 18th century, performing a liturgy of baroque orchestral pieces every Holy Week.

Yet the *mineiro* is both conservative and progressive. While the *mineiros* boast Brazil's best-preserved colonial towns, they also built the nation's first planned city, Belo Horizonte. And a group of *mineiros,* led by President Juscelino Kubitschek, built Brasília.

Much of *mineiro* traditionalism can be traced to the state's isolation in colonial times. Minas Gerais was established only in 1698, when the gold rush began. The only line of communication between Minas and the rest of the world until the 19th century was by way of mule down the perilous escarpment.

Isolation was so great that the *mineiros* started their own farms and cottage industries. This versatility made the *mineiros* different from other Brazilians. And it also gave them a vocation for democracy. French traveler Saint Hilaire noted, "there were scarcely any absentee landowners in Minas. The landowner worked side by side with his slaves, unlike the aristocratic owners in the rest of Brazil." Famed *mineiro* poet Carlos Drummond de Andrade said, "Minas has never produced a dictator and never will."

Gold and diamond fever: In the 18th century, Minas Gerais' gold was a colossus bestriding the world of commerce. About 1,200 tons of it were mined from 1700 to 1820, which made up 80 percent of all the gold produced throughout the world during that period. So great were the riches that an 18th-century traveler wrote, "at the epicenter of the golden hurricane there was madness. Prospectors and buyers dressed their slaves in gold and drenched them in diamonds. They decorated their homes in lace and silver, their mistresses in gems."

Diamond contractor João Fernandes built an artificial lake and a Portuguese sailing ship for his slave mistress, Xica da Silva, because "Xica had never seen the ocean or sailed the seven seas."

There were even slaves who, clandestinely clawing the earth from underground mines, enriched themselves. Legendary Chico Rei, a tribal king in Africa, vowed he would recover his crown in the New World. That's exactly what he did, earning enough gold to purchase his own freedom and that of his large brotherhood.

The gold rush in Minas had ramifications abroad. Lisbon was flooded by gold coins minted at Ouro Preto's *Casa dos Contos*. But instead of investing their wealth, the kings frittered the fortune away on opulent "improvements."

By the time Brazil's gold rush gave

Left, *Prophet* sculpted by Aleijadinho in Congonhas do Campo.

way to diamonds in 1728, Portugal had learned its lesson. The Tijuco diamond mines were closed to prospectors. A governor was appointed and a garrison sent to back up his decrees. But the plan didn't work. Governors like João Fernandes dealt in contraband, and the diamonds brought renewed wealth for only a short time.

Ouro Preto (black gold): Although the riches disappeared, the art remained. Today, there is no better place to see it than **Ouro Preto**. Located 60 miles (100 km) from the Minas Gerais capital of Belo Horizonte, Ouro Preto was the center of the 18th-century gold rush. First known as Vila Rica, the city was a mountain village when bands of adventurers from the Atlantic coast came in search of slaves and gold. Near Vila Rica they found a strange black stone and sent samples to Portugal. Word came back that they had discovered gold; the black coloring was a result of the iron oxide in the soil. Vila Rica was renamed Ouro Preto (black gold) and the gold rush was underway.

By 1750, the city had a population of 80,000, at that time larger than that of New York City. Jesuit priests also arrived, bringing with them the ideas and aritstic concepts of Europe; they insisted that their churches, financed by the gold from the mines, be built in the baroque style.

Today, Ouro Preto has Brazil's purest collection of baroque art and architecture. Five museums and 13 churches scattered among low hills and picture book cottages make Ouro Preto a Grimm Brothers fairy-tale town. In 1981 UNESCO declared Ouro Preto "a world cultural monument."

At the center of town is spacious **Praça Tiradentes**, fronted by the imposing **Inconfidência Museum**. The cobbled plaza is rich in history. The severed head of patriot Joaquim da Silva Xavier (nicknamed Tiradentes, "the tooth-puller") was displayed on a pole there in 1792. Xavier and six co-conspirators had plotted Brazilian independence. But spies exposed the plan, which led to Xavier's execution.

The museum once served as the town hall. Art and history are its current focuses. A macabre exhibit displays portions of the gallows used for Tiradentes' execution. Nearby is a copy of his death warrant. Some of Tiradentes' co-conspirators are buried beneath masonry slabs on the first floor.

In a separate gallery, the museum displays eccentric, richly-detailed wood carvings by Ouro Preto's other colonial hero—sculptor and architect Antônio Francisco Lisboa (1730s to 1814). He had a nickname, too—Aleijadinho, "the little cripple", because of a debilitating disease contracted in midlife. Of particular note is the moving *Christ at the Pillar*.

More of Aleijadinho's work can be viewed at the impressive **Carmo Church** and at the sacred art collection near the museum. The blocky edifice was designed in 1766 by Aleijadinho's father, engineer Manuel Francisco Lisboa. Aleijadinho altered the plan while work was underway in 1770, incorporating the bell towers into the façade and including an elegant archway over the main door. The changes were a compromise between conservative mannerist traditions and the emerging baroque style which Aleijadinho championed. Especially noteworthy are Aleijadinho's exuberant stone carvings—curlicues and soaring angels—above the main entrance.

Next to the church is Carmo's richly endowed sacred art collection. Aleijadinho's woodcarvings are prominent along with illuminated manuscripts and gleaming gold and silver altar accoutrements. A piece of bone labeled "Saint Clement" floats eerily in a glass and gold reliquary.

Three blocks west of Carmo is the deceptive parish church of **Nossa Senhora do Pilar.** The simple, squarish façade hides Ouro Preto's most extravagent baroque interior. Partly the work of sculptor Francisco Xavier de Brito, Pilar's walls explode with rosy-cheeked saints and angels, their garments fluttering against the gold leaf background. Folklore says 880 pounds

Colonial era house in Ouro Preto.

(400 kg) of gold dust were mixed with paint to adorn Pilar's interior.

Nossa Senhora do Rosário dos Pretos, nearby, produces the opposite effect. Its bold baroque façade houses a nearly bare interior. Rosário was built by slaves, who had just enough gold to erect its stunning shell. But what a shell; its convex walls, curved facade and shapely bell towers make Rosário Brazil's most brashly baroque architectural monument.

Two other museums mark the route along cobbled streets back to Tiradentes Square. The **Casa dos Contos**, at the base of steep Rua Rocha Lagoa, was the tax authority during the gold rush. Gold coins, and the surprisingly sophisticated foundry for minting them, are displayed.

At the high end of the street is Ouro Preto's sprawling **College of Mine Engineering.** The museum's collection of precious stones, ores and crystals is the largest in the world.

Just east of Tiradentes Square is an Aleijadinho architectural masterpiece, the jewel box chapel of **São Francisco.** The church's baroque lines resemble those at Rosário dos Pretos. Extravagant relief work above the main entrance is a continuation of similar labors at Carmo. Inside is a rare collaboration of wood and soapstone carvings by Aleijadinho, which are characterized by the almond eyes, shapely anatomical features and ruffled garments of the high *mineiro* baroque. The wall and ceiling paintings are by Manuel da Costa Ataide (1762-1837). Ataide's works feature slightly distorted human figures and realistic backgrounds. Painted surfaces and architectural features blend at the margins as patches of painted sky seem to open the ceiling to God's austere inspection.

Two blocks east of São Francisco chapel is Ouro Preto's monument to Aleijadinho, the museum church of **Conceicão de Antônio Dias**. Aleijadinho's remains are buried beneath a wooden marker near a side altar. Galleries behind the sacristy display his wood and soapstone carvings, docu-

Colonial churches, Minas Gerais' architectural treasure.

ments relating to his career, and the richly illustrated Bibles and Missals he used to study European artistic models.

Mariana: Seven miles (12 km) from Ouro Preto is the intriguing colonial town of **Mariana**, birthplace of Ataide. The twin chapels of **Carmo** and **São Francisco** and the magnificent **Cathedral of Nossa Senhora da Assuncão** are smothered in the dark colors and mulatto figures of Ataide's opulent art. Especially noteworthy is *The Passion and Death of Saint Francis.*

Ataide is buried under a wooden marker at the rear of Carmo. The cathedral boasts a German-crafted organ, built in 1720 and dragged by mule from Rio de Janeiro. Today, monthly concerts are offered.

Behind the cathedral is Mariana's labyrinthian **Sacred Art Museum,** which contains the largest collection of baroque painting and sculpture in Minas Gerais.

Belo Horizonte: Ouro Preto was Minas Gerais' capital until 1897, when *mineiro* statesmen inaugurated Brazil's first planned city, **Belo Horizonte**. Compared to Ouro Preto the bustling metropolis possesses little for sightseeing, but it is a good base for visiting surrounding historic towns.

In chic **Pampulha**, Brazil's leading 20th-century architect Oscar Niemeyer designed the **São Francisco Chapel**, with its undulating roof and blue tiles, in collaboration with Brazil's greatest modern artist, Cândido Portinari, who is responsible for the starkly painted images of St. Francis and the 14 Stations of the Cross.

In a wooded valley 14 miles (23 km) north of Belo Horizonte is another baroque treasure chest, **Sabará.** A leafy suburb hides the town's bizarre, musty jewel, the oddly shaped chapel of **Nossa Senhora do O**. O's humble exterior belies its exuberant decor; every inch of wall and ceiling space is covered by wood carvings, gold leaf, darkly mysterious paintings which depict Bible stories, and delicate gold-hued designs of Oriental motifs. The Far East figures reflect Portuguese-Jesuits experiences

Ouro Preto, surrounded by green mountains.

in the Orient.

A few blocks from the chapel is Sabará's larger **Nossa Senhora da Conceicão** parish church. Its squarish façade is redeemed by an explosion of rich interior decoration. The Oriental theme is frequently used , especially on the design-crowded sacristy door.

Presiding incongruously over Sabará's main square is the ghostly stone shell of the **Igreja do Rosário dos Pretos**, which was abandoned when the gold mines ran down. A few blocks away is precious **Igreja do Carmo**, a rich treasure-trove of Aleijadinho works, including intricate soapstone pulpits and a bas-relief frontispiece. A pair of muscular male torsos, bulging with wood-carved veins, hold the ornate choir loft in place.

Diamantina: West of Belo Horizonte, on the road stretching toward Brasília, is a rugged hamlet many consider the equal of Ouro Preto in austere beauty and history—**Diamantina**.

Bordering Brazil's semi-arid *sertão*, Diamantina is surrounded by iron-red hills rising to a rocky plain. The town's white-walled cottages and churches cascade down an irregular slope, producing a stark profile of wooden steeples.

Diamantina was headquarters of diamond contractor João Fernandes and his slave mistress Xica da Silva. Her stately home is located on **Praça Lobo Mesquita**. The ornate wood and stone **Igreja do Carmo**, across the square, was another gift from the diamond Czar to his lover. Fernandes ordered the bell tower moved to the rear of the church when his mistress complained its tolling kept her awake. Carmo's ceiling is covered by dark-hued paintings depicting Bible stories, which were favored by 18th-century *mineiro* painters, including José Soares de Araujo, whose work at Carmo and the nearby **Igreja do Amparo** recalls that of Ataide.

Colorful **Nossa Senhora do Rosário**, a block from Carmo, was built entirely by slaves and the woodcarvings of the saints are black. Outside, the roots of a tree nearby have split Rosário's

Pampulha church, designed by Niemeyer.

wooden crucifix, leaving only the bar and tip of the cross visible. Folklore says a slave accused of stealing was executed on the spot while protesting his innocence. He told on-lookers "something extraordinary will occur here to prove my truthfulness." Soon after, buds appeared on the cross, eventually snaking into the ground and producing the sturdy tree.

Across from Diamantina's Cathedral is the informative **Diamond Museum**. Period mining equipment, documents and furnishings are displayed. Grisly implements of torture used against the slaves are kept in a back room.

Also near the square is Diamantina's **public library**, noted for its delicate trellis and *muxarabiê* (a latticework casing covering an entire second-storey balcony). A few blocks away, on **Rua Direita**, is the humble birthplace of one of Brazil's most important presidents—Juscelino Kubitschek, founder of Brasília. Nearby is the **Casa da Glória**, a pair of blue and white masonry structures linked by a wooden footbridge. The site was headquarters of Diamantina's royal governors.

Congonhas do Campo: Eastern Minas Gerais, more economically developed than the bleak *sertão,* offers artistic treasures of the late Mineiro baroque. **Congonhas do Campo**, 48 miles (80 km) from Belo Horizonte, is site of Aleijadinho's two greatest masterworks of sculpture: the 12 lifesize outdoor carvings of *The Prophets,* located on the esplanade of the **Bom Jesus do Matozinhos Sanctuary**; and the 66 painted woodcarvings depicting *The Stations of the Cross,* housed in a series of garden chapels nearby.

Carved entirely from soapstone, *The Prophets* are stolid, gray and severe. In their stylized postures and costumes, they possess a mythic quality, as if sculpted from imagination instead of from real life.

While *The Prophets* seem suitably remote, the carved figures of *The Stations of the Cross* are vibrant and filled with emotion. The Christ statue, with its almond eyes and half-open mouth, skin pale and veined, and muscles as strained as an athlete's, is as haunting as *The Holy Shroud.* The 12 Apostles, with their worried, working-class faces, probably sculpted after local residents, could well be an 18th-century jury.

Another 80 miles (135 km) east of Belo Horizonte is the 1746 birthplace of Joaquim da Silva Xavier. The town, appropriately named **Tiradentes**, preserves the colonial-era feeling better than almost any other in Minas Gerais. Pink slate streets, an occasional horse-drawn cart, lace curtains and brightly painted shutters contribute to a feeling of ineffable tranquility.

The spacious **Padre Toledo Museum** contains period furnishings and sacred art. Nearby is the imposing **Igreja de Santo Antônio**, with its stone frontispiece carved by Aleijadinho. Inside is an 18th-century organ, companion piece to the instrument in Mariana.

São João del Rei: Only eight miles (13 km) from Tiradentes is bustling **São João del Rei.** The best way to get there is by a clattering tourist train, an exhilarating excursion on turn-of-century rolling stock. The **São João Station** has been turned into a gleaming museum. Hulking black-and-red Baldwin locomotives, dating as far back as 1880, are lined up in the roundhouse like oversized toys around a Christmas tree. Wood-paneled excursion cars feature porcelain fixtures and etched windows. The Victorian-style station is clean and authentic, right down to the ear-splitting steam whistle and syncopated huff and puff of the tourist train.

The town has as many churches as it has hotels—seven each. **Igreja do Carmo** recalls the baroque masterpieces of Ouro Preto. Nearby **Pilar Cathedral** presents a blocky façade on the outside, and richly decorated walls and ceilings inside.

But the pleasing proportions and rounded towers of the **Igreja de São Francisco**, which has been rightly called Aleijadinho's most mature architectural triumph, is the town's proudest treasure. Double rows of palm trees lead to a graceful esplanade of curving balustrades and wide steps.

Brazilian Baroque

Brazil's exuberant tradition in baroque art and architecture is one of the wonders of Latin American travel. Unlike the monumental structures which overwhelm the avenues and plazas of many Latin capitals, the rem-nants of Brazil's earliest public works of art are fresh, noble and lively.

The baroque movement had three main centers in 18th-century Brazil, appearing first in Salvador, moving to Rio de Janeiro, then reaching its zenith in Minas Gerais.

The Jesuits, who sponsored the colonial explosion of baroque in Bahia, were noted for their openness to new ideas and local trends, encouraging what many in Europe regarded as "the secular opulence" of the baroque. The missionaries realized that the exuberant qualities of baroque art would both attract and awe the Indian and mixed-blood converts who made up the bulk of the Brazilian faithful.

By the mid-18th century, Brazilian themes began to creep into Bahia's decorative arts. Indian-faced saints, great bunches of tropical fruits and wavy palms formed an incongruous background to the old-fashioned Bible stories depicted in paintings and woodcarvings that grace the great colonial-era churches of Salvador.

In Rio de Janeiro the baroque experience was less intense, as Rio was then secondary to the vice-regal capital of Salvador. Rio's best example of the baroque trend is the small, princely Igreja da Glória do Outeiro.

It is in Minas Gerais that Brazilian baroque reached its apex. In Minas the baroque movement impresses without overwhelming. In Ouro Preto there are no cathedrals, but one can enjoy the sights of this former state capital which has been transformed into a delightful museum town.

The secret of *mineiro* baroque architecture is the substitution of the curve for the line. The purest example, Ouro

Fountain dates from 1752.

Preto's Rosário dos Pretos Chapel, is all curves. The façade is shallowly convex, ending in two delicate bell tower curves. Inside, the nave is an oval. Doors and windows are purposefully framed by archways.

The work of one man: One reason for the striking artistic unity of *mineiro* churches is the dominance of one baroque artisan—Antônio Francisco Lisboa (1730s to 1814). The uneducated, illegitimate son of a Portuguese craftsman and a black slave woman, he became a highly individualistic sculptor and architect.

Undaunted by a crippling disease, probably arthritis, which left his hands paralyzed in middle age, he worked by strapping a hammer and chisel to his wrists.

It was during this period that Lisboa completed the 12 soapstone figures of the *Old Testament Prophets*, and the 66 woodcarvings of the *Stations of the Cross*, at Congonhas do Campo in eastern Minas Gerais.

Lisboa, known as Aleijadinho ("the little cripple"), applied and later extended the principles of European baroque he learned from books and missionaries. His first achievement was Ouro Preto's Igreja de Nossa Senhora do Carmo, marked by two elegant bell towers rising directly out of the smooth brown façade, and by massive, painstakingly carved doorways packed with curlicues and cheerful figures.

Lisboa next attempted an integration of baroque tenets in Ouro Preto's São Francisco Chapel. The chapel, and the larger Igreja de São Francisco in São João del Rei, are Lisboa's masterpieces. Both structures focus on the curved line; even the balustrades on the esplanade of the Igreja de São Francisco are elegant "S" curves. There are circular windows, cross-hatched by fine patterns of woodwork, with meticulously carved curlicues around doors and windows.

The two churches, masterminded by Lisboa, represent the height of baroque art in Brazil and can be considered among the finest in the world.

Our Lady of Mount Carmo church.

BRASILIA

For over two centuries, it has been the aim of Brazilian visionaries to fill the vacuum in the center of their country with a new city. In 1891, Brazil's first republican government sent a scientific team to survey possible sites in Goiás, where the three great rivers of the country—the Amazon, the Paraná and the São Francisco—rise. For this purpose too, a commission was struck later, in 1946, to conduct an aerial survey of the region. Yet until the election of President Juscelino Kubitschek in 1955, Brasília remained as an idea only.

Kubitschek made the development of Brasília the centerpiece of his campaign to modernize the country. The pace of the project was determined by politics; Kubitschek knew that if the city was ever to be completed, it had to be done by the end of his five-year term. He selected as his architect Oscar Niemeyer, a communist and a student of Le Corbusier. Niemeyer chose to confine himself to designing the major public buildings. An international jury selected the city plan which was submitted by a friend of Niemeyer's, Professor Lucío Costa.

Ground breaking: The work began in September 1956 on the highest and flattest of the five sites identified by the aerial survey. The first task was to build a runway, which was used to bring in the initial building materials and heavy equipment. Brasília thus became the world's first major city conceived in terms of air access. Only after construction had begun was a road pushed through from Belo Horizonte, 480 miles (800 km) to the southeast. A dam followed and Lake Paranoa began to emerge. By April 1960, the city housed 100,000 people and was ready for its inauguration.

Most visitors will come to Brasília the way Kubitschek first came—by plane. After flying over the semi-arid and sparsely inhabited Central Plateau, one suddenly sees the city emerge as a

Preceding pages: statue of former president Kubitschek and the Justice Palace. Below, statue honoring workers who built Brasilia and were its first inhabitants.

row of white building blocks curving along a gentle rise above the artificial lake.

Overland, the most spectacular approach is by road from the northeast. After driving through miles of red dust and gnarled scrub, known as *cerrado,* you reach a eucalyptus-lined ridge just beyond Planaltina, the oldest town in this region. Brasília is laid out in a gleaming arc in the valley below.

The first recommended stop not to be missed is the **Television Tower** at the highest point of the **Monumental Axis** which runs through the center of the city. A good map on a billboard at the foot of the Tower explains how the streets are laid out and numbered. An elevator to the top of the tower gives a bird's-eye view of Lucío Costa's plan: two gently curving arcs indicating the residential areas of the city, bisected by the Monumental Axis containing the buildings of government.

Costa's plan has been variously described as a cross, a bow and arrow or an airplane. Costa accepts all these interpretations but claims he did not design Brasília to fit a pre-conceived symbol. Instead he chose its shape to accommodate the curvature of the terrain above the lake, while emphasizing the civic buildings at the center of the city. Costa's design was selected because of its simplicity and suitability for a national capital.

Governmental sector: Heading west from the Television Tower, you come to the **Kubitschek Memorial** built in 1981. It was the first building in Brasília that the military allowed Niemeyer to design after their takeover in 1964. The curious sickle-shaped structure on top of the monument in which the statue of Kubitschek stands seems more like a political gesture by Niemeyer than a symbol of Kubitschek's beliefs. Inside the monument is Kubitschek's tomb and a collection of memorabilia about his life and the construction of Brasília. One showcase contains a summary of the unsuccessful entries in the competition to design the city, including a proposal to house most of its population in

18 enormous tower blocks over 1,000 feet (300 meters) high, each housing 16,000 people. Elevator reliability and other things ruled this plan out.

Heading the other direction, down the hill past the main bus terminal, the Monumental Axis opens onto the **Esplanade of the Ministeries**. A row of 16 pale green identical box-shaped buildings runs down both sides of the vast open boulevard. Each building houses a different government department whose name is emblazoned in gold letters on the front. Since every Ministry has long since outgrown its original quarters, they have sprouted additions out the back, connected in mid-air by concrete tubes to their mother ship. In the late 1960s several buildings were subject to arson attacks, reportedly by disgruntled civil servants protesting their forced move from Rio.

Niemeyer's best: Flanking the end of the Esplanade are Niemeyer's two finest buildings: the **Foreign Ministry**, which floats in splendid isolation in the midst of a reflecting pool, and the **Ministry of Justice**, whose six exterior curtains of falling water echo the countryside waterfalls around Brasília.

Beyond the end of the Monumental Axis is the **Plaza of the Three Powers**—a dense forest of political symbols. Named after the three divisions of powers under the Brazilian constitution, the Executive is represented by the **Planalto Palace** on the left, housing the President's offices, while the judiciary is represented by the **Supreme Court** on the right. Overshadowing both, architecturally if not politically, are the twin towers and off-set domes of the **National Congress**—the building whose silhouette is the signature of Brasília. Even the former monarchy has a place in the Plaza. The rows of imperial palms behind the Congress building were transplanted from Dom João VI's Botanical Garden in Rio.

On the Plaza proper are a number of notable sculptures. The deeply veined basaltic head of Kubitschek protrudes from the marble walls of the small **Museum of Brasília**. Inside are a series

Left, soldier on guard at government building. Right, statue of Justice seated before the Justice Palace.

of panels outlining the history of Brasília and the most memorable sayings of Kubitschek, whose powers of hyperbole must have rivaled his talent for construction.

In front of the Supreme Court is a blindfolded figure of Justice, by the sculptor Alfredo Ceschiatti. Facing the Planaltina Palace are the distended figures of "The Warriors" by Bruno Giorgi, a tribute to the thousands of workers who built Brasília. A note of whimsy is added to the Plaza by Oscar Niemeyer's pigeon house, the **Pombal**, which looks like a giant concrete clothes peg.

The most recent addition to the Plaza is the **Pantheon Tancredo Neves**—a tribute to the founding father of the New Republic, who died in April 1985 before he could be sworn in as President. Inside the darkened interior of the Pantheon is Brasília's most extraordinary and disturbing artwork. The mural, by the painter João Camara, depicts the story of an uprising in the 18th century led by Brazil's most famed revolutionary, Tiradentes. Painted in seven panels entirely in black and white (reminiscent of Picasso's *Guernica*), the mural is heavy with masonic symbolism. In the opening panel, a corpse lies on the floor of a salon, representing infant Brazilian industry murdered by Portuguese and English commerce. In the third panel, Tiradentes rides past a row of toiling gold miners, drawn from 1980s images of the "human ant-hill" at Serra Pelada in the Amazon. In the final panel, the figure of Tiradentes merges into the figure of Christ.

Residential Brasília: To appreciate Brasília as a living city, and not just an architectural theme park, you have to leave the Monumental Axis and its adjacent hotel sectors. The city's residents live in housing centers, known as *quadras*, arrayed along the north and south wings of the city. Each *quadra* is made up of six to eight low-rise residential blocks, grouped around well landscaped lawns and courtyards. The residential blocks are raised on pillars to open the line of sight across the *quad-*

Settling sun gilds Brasília's cathedral.

ras. Short commercial streets, which provide a range of basic services, are evenly interspersed between them. Although the *quadras* differ slightly depending on their developer and their date of construction, they provide an essentially uniform standard of living across the city. For many residents, the orderliness of life in Brasília comes as a welcome respite from the urban jungles of Brazil's coastal cities.

Lucío Costa's original "pilot plan" for Brasília gives the city a rigid shape. Once all the *quadras* planned for the north wing are built, the city proper can grow no further. The great surprise in the evolution of Brasília has been the explosive growth of the "satellite cities" beyond its green belt. These cities were originally settled by the workers who came from the northeast to build Kubitschek's new city and refused to return home once the work was done. Their numbers have swelled with new migrants and lower middle class residents, who have sold the free apartments they were originally awarded in the pilot plan.

Today, Brasília proper accounts for only 22 percent of the population of the Federal District. Despite the egalitarian architecture of the pilot plan, the class barriers in the Federal District are even more rigid than in the rest of the country. The population is zoned by income into completely separate cities.

Visitors staying in the hotel sector in the center of Brasília often get the mistaken impression that the city is completely dead at night. But there is a lively scene in the bars, restaurants and clubs concentrated along certain commercial streets in the residential wings: notably 109/110 South, 405/406 South and 303/304 North. Brasília's very fluid and casual social life is defined by the fact that it is a relatively affluent city with no established upper class. Many young professionals have escaped from their families and peer groups by moving to Brasília. A side effect is that the city has the country's highest divorce rate. Brasília has been described as "a town where people are in bed by ten and home by six o'clock in the morning."

Unconventional spiritualism: Spiritual life in Brasília is as unconventional as its social mores. Established religion is represented by Niemeyer's concrete cathedral along the Monumental Axis, designed to resemble Christ's Crown of Thorns. Closer to the city's true faith is the cult of Dom Bosco, an Italian priest and educator who prophesied in 1883 that a new civilization would arise in a land of milk and honey in the center of South America, between the co-ordinates of present day Brasília.

The first structure built on the city site, overlooking Lake Paranoa, was a small marble pyramid commemorating Bosco's vision. Brasília's most striking church is also named after him, the **Sanctuary of Dom Bosco**, in 702 South. It is a cubical chapel whose walls are entirely built out of blue and violet stained-glass. In effect, Dom Bosco's prophecy has provided spiritual legitimacy for Kubitschek's secular dream of a new capital for Brazil.

Brasília also enjoys a reputation as "The Capital of the Third Millenium",

Federal government headquarters.

by virtue of the more than four hundred contemporary cults that flourish here. Social experimentation seems to encourage religious experimentation and for many, these cults provide a more personal and satisfying alternative to the regimentation of life in the government's "city of the future".

Several "new age" communities have been founded on the outskirts of Brasília. The most accessible is **The Valley of the Dawn**, south of Planaltina. Every Sunday several hundred worshippers come to the Valley to be initiated into the commune established by a retired lady truckdriver. The iconography of the temple draws freely from Brazil's Indian cultures. Its rites of blessing appear heavily influenced by African *macumba*. The weekly parade of initiates, dressed in multicolored cloaks and veils, around a pond adorned with astrological symbols is undoubtedly Brasília's eeriest sight.

Like the United Nations Secretariat in New York, which Brasília closely resembles in the scale of its ambitions and its architectural style, the city is trapped in a 1950s vision of the future. Brasília is a city built around the automobile, and its urban core is a complex of super-highways which creates a hostile environment for pedestrians.

While under construction, Brasília captured the world's imagination. Soon after, the world lost interest and Brasília became synonymous with technocracy run wild, a South American symbol of 20th-century alienation. Yet to this day the building of Brasília remains a point of great pride among Brazilians. It was the only post-war project intended to serve the people, not industry; and it was entirely financed and built at the behest of an elected President, in a time of democracy. Under Brazil's new democratic government, the city has become a political symbol of past accomplishments and future promises.

For all the flaws now evident with hindsight, Brasília's planner Lucío Costa speaks for the majority of Brazilians when he asserts, "The only important thing for me is that Brasília exists".

The ministry buildings.

WILD BUS RIDES

Imagine a week long, buttock-numbing 3,000-mile (5,000-km) bus ride from the borders of Argentina right through to Venezuela, cutting Latin America from South to North, almost from the pampas to the Caribbean.

Brazil's longest bus line stretches from Cascavel in Paraná state to Sta Helena in Venezuela, a journey as long as that between Lisbon and the USSR. The BR 364 highway, built by more than a million migrants seeking a new start in the wild west, cuts through five states and the heartland of Amazonia. Less daunting sections of the line provide the most practical way of glimpsing the western Amazon.

Since 1971, when it began ferrying migrants along the new frontier's mud-bogged roads in buses chopped down like dune-buggies, Eucatur and its 600-strong bus fleet have dominated transportation in Rondônia and Matto Grosso. The 875-mile (1,400-km) Cuiabá-Porta Velho journey once took weeks; comfortable buses now swish easily up the asphalt in 18 hours, charging about US$20. From Porto Velho 560 miles (900 km) northeast to Manaus on the more precarious BR 319 highway, buses cross six rivers by ferry on their 18-hour journey. The fare is about US$18.

At Humaita the highway intersects with the Transamazonia Highway, or BR 230, which was built in the 1970s with World Bank aid. The original intention was to build a road stretching as far east as Marabá near Belém, however, only parts of it are open for traffic today as the advancing forest rebukes man's efforts. From Manaus it's a two-day, 500-mile (820-km) trip to Venezuela via Roraima's capital, Boa Vista. Unscheduled stops on all of these routes, caused by blowouts, engine failures, cattleherds or tropical storms, often provide more intriguing glimpses of Amazon life than the scheduled halts at an homogenized string of gas stations or

Back road in central Brazil.

small-town bus stations (*rodoviarias*), where passengers hurriedly gulp down sandwiches at a *lanchonete*. The succession of bus stations, each crowded with bundle-clutching migrants, reveals Brazil as a nation in movement. And buses are the means by which millions filter into the unoccupied spaces of the wild west.

Traveling by bus is the cultural icebreaker, the quintessential Brazilian experience. Cramped into the same hot space for days on end, no foreign aloofness can resist the unfolding, mobile drama of escaping chickens, family rows or intimate friendships forged around impromptu English lessons that can result in weary travelers being invited into Brazilian homes for a much-needed bath or bed at journey's end.

Medianeira, an Eucatur affiliate, operates on the Cuiabá-Santarém BR 163 highway. This route takes you through the pioneer towns in the heart of the Amazon forest and bisects Brazil north to south.

Those seeking the nostalgic flavor of the 1970s' movie *Bye Bye Brazil* may want to linger along the 1,300-mile (2,118-km) Belém-Brasília highway. Since 1960 it has provided Amazonia's only reliable contact with Brazil. Transbrasiliana and Rapido Marajó buses leave the nation's capital several times daily on the 45-hour run, pausing only once to permit passengers a hotly-contested truckstop shower. The fare is about US$30.

The BR 153 highway running through Goias and Tocantins and Pará's BR 010 give a grandstand view of the climatic transition from dry *cerrado* flatlands around Brasília to the humid density of the Amazon. However, the dreary uniformity of slash-and-burn cattle ranching has forced back the forest, now only a green line on the horizon.

Although dusty and suffocatingly hot, the Belém-Brasília route typifies the country's many highways. The pioneer spirit of the wild west can be best sampled on the buses plying these pot-holed Amazon roads.

Domino players at a road stop.

THE SOUTHERN STATES

The south of Brazil is different. Here palm trees give way to pines, forested mountains are split by tranquil valleys, nature in general is more rugged, with roaring waterfalls and monumental canyons, and the temperate climate provides four seasons with cold weather and even snow in the winter. The people too are different. Blue-eyed blondes replace the dark-featured types of the north and northeast, reflecting the deep European roots of the south.

The traditional breadbasket of Brazil, the south is a region of bounty. The farms and ranches of the states of Paraná, Santa Catarina and Rio Grande do Sul are the leading grain producers of Brazil. Paraná is home to coffee plantations as well as the country's most extensive pine forests. Across the flat pampas of Rio Grande do Sul wander Brazil's largest cattle herds. In recent years the south has drawn from its agricultural wealth to invest in industry and today the region is the center of Brazil's booming textile and footwear industries. Together, the south's rich earth and surging industrial power have given the inhabitants of its three states a standard of living second only to that of those in the state of São Paulo.

Paraná: A mix of pleasing urbanity and the unleashed fury of nature are the trademarks of Paraná. In its capital of **Curitiba**, the state offers one of Brazil's most enjoyable cities, an urban planner's dream, with ample green space, wide avenues, flowered pedestrian malls and a relaxed and comfortable pace of life. Just one hour away by plane is one of South America's most remarkable works of nature, the wildly beautiful Iguaçu Falls.

Founded by gold-seekers in the 17th century, Curitiba today is a bustling metropolis with a population of 1.3 million, located atop an elevated plateau at 2,800 feet (900 meters). In the latter half of the 19th century and the beginning of this century, Curitiba, together with the state as a whole, received an infusion of immigrants from Europe (Poles, Germans, Italians and Russians) which transformed the city into a European outpost in the heart of South America. The profusion of blondes on the city's streets, plus Curitiba's annual ethnic festivals, are proof of the origins of its citizens. The city's best known ethnic neighborhood is **Santa Felicidade**, founded in 1878 by Italian immigrants and today home to Curitiba's finest cantinas.

Preceding pages, magnificent Iguaçu Falls. **Left**, formations at Vila Velha, Paraná.

Walking tour: Aside from its deserved reputation as Brazil's cleanest city, Curitiba is also a pedestrian's delight. A walking tour should begin at the city center, **Rua das Flores**, an extensive pedestrian mall named after its beautiful flower baskets and flanked by stores and boutiques as well as inviting cafés, restaurants and pastry shops. Along the way is the **Boca Maldita**, where in the morning and late afternoon, Curitiba's erstwhile philosophers, politicians and economists discourse at will on the country's latest crises, a Brazilian version of London's Hyde Park.

Nearby is the historical center of Curitiba, concentrated in the blocks around the **Largo da Ordem**, a cobblestoned square dominated by the **Igreja da Ordem Terceira de São Francisco das Chagas** (1737), known popularly as the Ordem Church. Up the hill from the church is the **Garibaldi Mini Shopping**, replete with handicrafts from throughout Brazil, including wood carvings, pottery, leather and straw goods. At night, the Ordem square comes alive with musicians and outdoor cafés. Back down the hill towards the Rua das Flores is the **Praça Tiradentes**, where Curitiba's neogothic cathedral stands, not far from the state historical museum at **Praça Generoso Marques.**

Paranaguá train ride: Although Paraná is not known for its beaches, the trip to them is one of the most breathtaking in Brazil. Each morning at 8:30, the train leaves Curitiba's station for the winding trip down the coastal mountains to the sea port of **Paranaguá**, the state's oldest city. Completed in 1885, the railroad clings to the side of the mountains, at

Southern States
240 km/ 150 miles
Dourados
Ponta Porã
Porto São José
Porto São José
Presidente Prudente
SÃO PAULO
Assis
Botucato
Ourinhos
Maringá
Londrina
Cruzeiro do Oeste
Lima
Saltos de Guaira
Guaira
Itararé
SERRA DO PARANAPIACABA
PARANÁ
San Estanislao
SERRA DO MAR
Cascavel
PARAGUAY
Ponto Grossa
Guarapuava
Vila Velha Park
Curitiba
Foz do Iguaçu
Iguaçu
SERRA
DO
Paranaguá
Villarrica
Pato Branco
GERAL
Boa Vista
Joinvile
São Francisco do Sul
Paraná
Montecarlo
SIERRA
SANTA CATARINA
Itajaí
Blumenau
Uruguay
Uruguai
Encarnación
Posadas
Ita-Ibaté
Florianópolis
Erechim
Bom Retiro
1808
ILHA DE SANTA CATARINA
Passo Fundo
Santa Rosa
Lajes
GERAL
São Luis Gonzaga
Santo Ângelo
Passo Fundo
ARGENTINA
Cruz Alta
Tubarão
Criciuma
São Borja
Jacuí
Uruguai
Bento Goncalves
SERRA
São Francisco de Paula
1250
RIO GRANDE DO SUL
Caxias do Sul
Uruguaiana
Santa Maria
Santa Cruz do Sul
Nôvo Hamburgo
Alegrete
Canoas
Cachoeira do Sul
Porto Alegre
Guaíba
Quarai
São Gabriel
Santana do Livramento
Camaquã
Lagoa
dos
Patos
Bagé
Tacuarembó
Pelotas
Bojuru
Rio Grande
URUGUAY
Melo
Jaguarão
Lagoa Mirim
Paso de los Toros
Artifical Rincón del Bonete
CUCHILLA GRANDE
Treinta y Tres
Atlantic Ocean
Durazno
Santa Vitória do Palmar
Laguna Negra
San José de Mayo
Minas
Laguna de Castillos
Rocha
Rio de la Plata
Montevideo
Punta del Este
La Plata

times threatening to march off into space as it passes over viaducts and through tunnels during the long, slow three-hour descent to the coastal plain (for the best views sit on the left side of the train when going down). The trip offers an unmatched view of the best preserved section of Brazil's Atlantic rain forest, a richly green tangle of trees and undergrowth broken occasionally by waterfalls.

Founded in 1648, Paranaguá is today one of Brazil's leading ports but unfortunately has preserved little of its historical past. What remains is located along **XV de Novembro Street**, where an archaeological musuem features Indian artifacts and items from colonial life. The area's primary attraction is the **Ilha do Mel**, an island paradise that is reached by a 20-minute boat ride from the town of **Pontal do Sul**, an hour's drive from Paranaguá (boats from Paranaguá also make the trip but it takes two hours). The island is a nature preserve with natural pools, grottos and deserted beaches. It is also home to the ruins of an 18th-century fort and a 19th-century lighthouse. There are no cars on the island and transportation is either by foot along the island's many paths or by fisherman's boat. Its primitive, unspoiled nature (there are no hotels) has made the Ilha do Mel a popular spot for campers of late. Visitors may rent tents or a room in a fisherman's hut. For overnight stays, a flashlight and insect repellent are essential.

The best option for the return trip to Curitiba is the **Graciosa Highway**, a winding roadway that cuts through the verdant forest with explosions of wildflowers along the route. From the viewpoints, you can catch glimpses of the old mule trail used by the original Portuguese settlers to climb the mountainside to Curitiba. Real adventurers may still make this trip today.

Vila Velha: Some 50 miles (80 km) west of Curitiba is the area's second great attraction, the **Vila Velha State Park**. Sitting majestically atop the plateau with the wind whipping around are a series of extraordinary rock formations carved over the millennia by the wind and rain. Altogether there are 23 separate formations, each identified by the object, animal or human form that it appears to represent. A mini-train hustles back and forth among the formations, but most visitors will find it hard to resist a long, contemplative walk through the near-mystical site with its sometimes haunting mixture of shadows, rocks and the sound of the wind. Close by is another mystery left by nature, two enormous holes sliced into the rocky ground to a depth of nearly 400 feet (100 meters), half-filled with water. In one of these natural wells an elevator has been installed for visitors to descend to the level of the water.

Iguaçu Falls: Undoubtedly the greatest natural wonder of southern Brazil and perhaps of the entire nation is **Iguaçu**, a mammoth series of waterfalls that plunge through a gorge on the **Iguaçu River** some 390 miles (650 km) from Curitiba on the border with Paraguay and Argentina. A total of 275 falls cascade over a precipice that is 1.8 miles (3 km) wide, sending up an unending wall of spray decorated by omnipresent rainbows. At the heart of this unforgettable scene is the **Devil's Throat**, where fourteen separate falls join forces, pounding down the 350-foot (90-meter) cliffs in a deafening crescendo of sound and spray. A catwalk runs to the base of the first level of the falls where you are surrounded by the roaring water, the mist and white foam shooting up, the green of the jun-gle, uprooted trees and a 180-degree rainbow, an overpowering sensation.

Iguaçu is part of a national park of the same name which is divided between Brazil and Argentina. Visas are not required to visit the Argentine side. For photographers it is best to visit the Brazilian side in the morning and the Argentine side in the afternoon. To see the full force of the falls, visit the park in the months of January and February when the river is high. This is also the period, however, when humidity and heat are nearly unbearable and the park is usually packed with tourists. In September-October, the water level is down but the temperature is pleasant and there are no crowds.

On the Brazilian side, the catwalk leading to the falls can be reached either by a winding trail or an elevator. For another view of the scene, you may take a helicopter ride for $25, however, this option is ecologically unsound as the noise disturbs the park animals. An even better look at the falls and forest is offered by the **Macuco Boat Safari**, run by an American expatriate from Chicago. The one-and-a-half hour journey starts with a trip through the jungle in open wagons pulled by a jeep, slowly descending to the floor of the canyon where you may swim in a natural pool below the falls. A boat trip then takes you to the edge of the crashing water where you have an unmatched view of the water falling from the cliffs above.

Virtually the same view can be had on the Argentine side by walking down lengthy trails that lead to the canyon floor, where a short boat trip takes you to the island of **San Martín**, crowned by an elevated rock formation looking directly at the falling water (some of the falls can only be seen from the island). While beautiful, this option is only for the physically fit. Hiking down to the canyon floor and back is extremely tiring. A less strenuous walk can be had along a concrete catwalk that stretches for over a mile at the top of the falls, affording an excellent view of the water plunging over the top.

Itaipú Hydroelectric: The neighboring city of Foz de Iguaçu has undergone a population and economic boom in recent years due to the construction of the nearby Itaipú hydroelectric plant, which currently stands as the world's largest. The dam has now become a tourist attraction in itself. In addition, visitors to the city can make a shopping a trip to **Puerto Stroessner, Paraguay** (a smuggler's paradise) and **Puerto Iguazú, Argentina.** Resting at a point where the three countries come together, Foz do Iguaçu is a strangely international city, where Argentines, Brazilians and Paraguayans mix freely with travelers from the United States and Europe. The increasing fame of the falls has resulted in the recent addition of several top quality hotels in the area. Only one, the **Hotel das Cataratas**, is located inside the park, with an unobstructed view of the falls. Book well in advance.

Santa Catarina: The smallest of the southern states, Santa Catarina is also the most boisterous. Its German heritage is apparent in the Bavarian architecture of the city of **Blumenau**, which is home to South America's liveliest Oktoberfest, a three-week blowout that attracts nearly a million visitors, making it Brazil's second largest festival after Rio's carnival. Munich itself would be proud.

But the state's real treasure is its coastline, miles of unspoiled white sand beaches stretching north and south of the capital city of **Florianópolis**. An island city, Florianópolis boasts 42 beaches of its own, ranging from quiet coves to roaring surf. **Joaquina beach** is a world-famed surfing center where international competitions are held each year. A few minutes distant is the **Conceição lagoon**, a beautiful fresh-

Alpine-style building in Blumenau.

water lake wedged between the island's mountain spine and the sea. This central area of the island is the most hotly disputed by residents and tourists. Restaurants and bars abound, some of them in the exceptional category such as the unpretentious **Martin Pescador**, a simple wooden structure with a half dozen rustic tables which serves world-class gourmet seafood.

The island's southern beaches are its most unspoiled. Many of them can be reached only by dirt roads. Here are the huts of fishermen whose wives spend the days making lace. **Compeche** and **Armação** beaches are good choices for a day trip. Nearby is the colorful village of **Ribeirão da Ilha**, site of one of the first Portuguese settlements on the island. To the north are the upscale beaches of **Ingleses**, **Canavieiras** and **Jureré**, where new hotels and condominiums are filling up the empty space. Florianópolis is a laid-back city where life centers around basic and simple pleasures: swimming, sunbathing, eating and drinking. Reflecting the relaxed lifestyle of the island's inhabitants, hitchhiking is the favorite mode of transport for the young.

Laguna: To the north of Florianópolis is the resort of **Camboriu**, whose long crescent beach is a near carbon copy of Rio's Copacabana. On the southern coast, the principal beaches are **Garopaba**, **Laguna** and **Morro dos Conventos**. Of these, the acknowledged champion is Laguna, a 17th-century colonial city that has preserved many of its historical structures together with the beauty of its beaches. Considered a jewel of Brazil's southern coast, Laguna is popular among Argentine tourists and the wealthy of São Paulo, thus far virtually the only travelers who have discovered the beauty of Santa Catarina's coastline. Like the major cities and tourism centers of the south, Laguna is affluent, clean and efficient, a far cry from the often depressing poverty and urban decay that has gripped the beach cities of the northeast.

Rio Grande do Sul: The southernmost state of Brazil, Rio Grande do Sul is also

Visiting Vila Velha.

Wine Country

Although it came late to Brazil, wine production has taken a firm hold in the country. Brazil's wine industry is concentrated in the coastal mountains of Rio Grande do Sul, an area that is responsible for 90 percent of national production. Here, vineyards line the slopes and lush green valleys of a region whose principal cities are Caxias do Sul, Bento Gonçalves and Garibaldi.

Italian immigrants: The grapes and resulting wines were first brought to Rio Grande by Italian immigrants who arrived in the 1880s. Since then their descendants have carried on the tradition. Today the cities and small farms of this area still retain an air of Italy about them. Cheeses and salamis hang from the ceilings of the prized wine cellars of the region's small farmers, many of whom make their own wine, cheese and pasta. This culinary combination is also found in the area's restaurants, heavily dominated by Italian cuisine.

The starting point for a visit to Brazil's Wine Country is **Caxias do Sul**, a booming industrial city tucked away in the mountains. Prosperous and middle class, Caxias is home to the region's Grape Festival held every year in March. Festivals are part of the life in Wine Country: in addition to the Caxias grape festival, Garibaldi holds a Champagne Festival and Bento Gonçalves a Wine Festival. All are weeks-long parties with wine flowing freely. The leading vineyard in Caxias is the **Chateau Lacave**, headquartered in a replica of a European castle, complete with drawbridge. In the city proper is the cantina of the **Granja União** vineyard. The cantinas are in effect tasting rooms for the wineries and are found scattered throughout the region's principal cities. The real tasting treats of Wine Country are found in and around **Garibaldi** and **Bento Gonçalves**, the recognized capitals of the wine-growing region.

Along the road, just outside of Garibaldi, is the **Maison Forestier**, which

Descendants of Europeans harvest grapes in Rio Grande.

today is Brazil's top producer of quality table wines. Owned by Seagram's, Forestier represents the trend in Brazilian wine production. Up until the 1970s, national consumption was limited and confined mainly to relatively undistinguished table wines.

In the mid-70s, however, Forestier and other leading vineyards began to invest in quality, because of the growing demand for good wines. Using imported varieties of grapes (mainly from Europe although recently Californian grapes have been added), over the next 10 years, Forestier and the others began to turn out increasingly higher quality products.

While the process is not yet complete, today Brazilian wines, especially the whites, have made a major leap in quality. Several brands are now exported, mainly to the United States, and by the end of the century it is expected that Brazil's wines will be challenging Chile and Argentina for leadership in South America.

Guided tours: At Forestier and the other large wine producers, guided tours are available. Most of the wine makers still cling to the old tradition of oaken barrels but some are stepping into the high tech world of stainless steel vats and tight quality controls. The *piece de resistance* of any vineyard tour is the generous tasting session at the end. For a full-scale introduction to Brazilian wines, begin at Forestier then continue on to Bento Gonçalves for a visit to the **Aurora Cooperative**.

Bento is also home to several smaller producers including **Salton**, **Monaco**, **Riograndense** and **Embrapa**. If you are still on your feet, head back to Garibaldi for a sampling of the best in Brazilian champagnes (while showing marked improvement in recent years, Brazil's champagnes are for the moment trailing the country's white wines in quality. They are, however, ahead of the reds). The most respected champagne producers are **Peterlongo**, French-owned **Moet-Chandon**, **Georges Aubert**, **Chateau d'Argent** and **Vinícola Garibaldi**.

Italian-style wine cellar in Brazil's wine country.

the most distinct. Bordering Uruguay and Argentina, Rio Grande has developed a culture of its own, a mixture of Portuguese and Spanish together with Italian and German. The unique gaucho culture is the trademark of Rio Grande do Sul, where swarthy cowboys roam the southern pampas with their distinctive flat hats and chin straps, their baggy pantaloon trousers, red neckerchiefs and leather boots, securing the symbol of gaucho-land, the *chimarrão*, a gourd of hot "mate" tea. Here machismo runs strong and a man is definitely a man, a heritage of the state's violent history. More than any other state in Brazil, Rio Grande has seen the ravages of war. In the 18th and 19th centuries, it served as a battleground for warring armies, revolutionaries, adventurers and Indians who marched back and forth across its grasslands, leaving a bloody stamp that has today been transformed into legend.

Proud and boastful, the gauchos of today have channeled their warrior's fury into more refined conquests. The state is Brazil's leading manufacturer of leather footwear and of late has gained further fame as the producer of the country's finest wines. In addition, there are the vast herds of cattle and sheep that today graze on Rio Grande's former battlefields, providing the state and the rest of Brazil with beef for the succulent *churrasco* barbecues, a gaucho tradition, and wool for the south's textile factories.

The landscape of Rio Grande do Sul is as rugged and uncompromising as are its inhabitants. The state's 120-mile (200 km) coastline is marked by pounding surf and rocky promontories, the best known of which are located in the resort city of **Torres.** Although the water is colder here, the sun is still warm and the bikinis just as brief as in Rio. **Tramandaí** and **Capão da Canoa** are other top beach resorts, while stretching southward between the bulk of the mainland and the ocean is the **Lagoa dos Patos**, the largest fresh-water lagoon in South America, whose banks offer beaches and camping sites from **Tapes** to **Laranjal.**

Left, rock formation at Vila Velha. Right, waters thunder over Iguaçu Falls.

Serra Gaúcha: A few miles inland is the **Serra Gaúcha**, a coast mountain range that has become the prime attraction for visitors to the state. Pine trees, lush green valleys, solitary waterfalls, shimmering rivers and awesome canyons distract the eyes of visitors winding their way through the *serra*. It was to this idyllic setting that thousands of German and Italian immigrants flocked in the late 19th century, establishing their homesteads along the valley floors where today many of their original stone and wood houses still stand as stolid testimony to the hardy nature of these transplanted gauchos.

Gramado and Canela: The crown jewels of the Serra Gaúcha are the twin cities of Gramado and Canela. Gramado, site of the Brazilian Film Festival held every March, is a tranquil, slow-moving mountain resort where the harried residents of Brazil's non-stop cities escape for the pleasure of doing absolutely nothing. For this, the city and its sister Canela, separated by a sign, offer dozens of small hotels, inns and chalets, all carefully tucked away beneath the pines.

Some 15 minutes away from Gramada and Canela is the small town of **Novo Petrópolis**, where the area's German heritage is on permanent display. In addition to the Bavarian architecture in the community's homes and buildings, Novo Petrópolis' roots are visible in the Immigration Park, highlighted by a reproduction of a German colonial settlement of the 19th century.

The park also contains a band stand and biergarten which are the center of festivities in the months of January, February and July. During these traditional Brazilian vacation periods, the small hotels and inns of Novo Petrópolis, as well as Gramado and Canela, fill up with tourists.

The German influence here is heavy, not only in names and architecture but in the carefully landscaped parks and avenues. Green is the color of Novo Petrópolis, Gramada and Canela and green is everywhere. On the outskirts of Canela is the **Caracol State Park**,

Folk dancing in traditional gaucho costume.

where the **Caracol Falls** plunges 400 feet (130 meters). The area's number one natural attraction, however, is three hours distant. Although the road is potholed and wearisome, the view at its end is well worth the sacrifice. Suddenly in the midst of pasture and forest, the earth seems to open up, revealing the enormous **Itaimbézinho Canyon**, South America's Grand Canyon. Some 2,200 feet (700 meters) deep, four miles (seven km) long and in places over a mile wide, the canyon is the largest in Latin America. So far its difficult access has kept the canyon off the international tourism route, but it seems only a matter of time before Itaimbézinho gets its due. Unlike North America's Grand Canyon, located in the dry southwest, Itaimbézinho impresses not simply because of its extraordinary size but also because of the varied shadings of green that mark it, from the light green pasture to the deep green of its forested cliffs. Waterfalls cascading down the canyon's sides add the final touch to this monument of nature.

The Missions: Due west of the Serra Gaúcha is an area of historical significance known as the Mission Region. Here, in the 17th century, Jesuit priests organized members of the Guaraní Indian tribe into a series of settlements built around missions. The object, according to most historians, was to protect the Indians from slave traders who periodically swept down from São Paulo. Others, however, claim the Jesuits were seeking to create a small fiefdom dominated by them. Whatever their motives, the Jesuit fathers controlled the region for nearly a century, overseeing the construction of Indian cities that reached up to 5,000 inhabitants. Finally, in 1756, after several unsuccessful attempts, the missions were attacked in force and overwhelmed, the Jesuits expelled and the Indians mostly exterminated. Today the solitary ruins of the missions, most notably the mission of **São Miguel**, stand in dramatic solitude on the plain, all that is left of a once thriving Indian community. Visitors to the mission region should stay at the city of **Santo Angelo**, from where day trips may be made to the ruins. The São Miguel mission offers an audiovisual show at night, portraying the history of the area. Other mission ruins may also be visited across the border in Argentina and farther north, near the Iguaçu Falls.

Cowboy country: For gauchos, the soul of their state resides in the **Campanha**, the region on the border with Uruguay and Argentina. Across these windswept prairies, the pampas of legend, the gaucho cowboy still rides herd over the cattle and sheep that first brought wealth to Rio Grande do Sul. The cities of **São Gabriel**, **Rosário do Sul**, **Bagé**, **Lavras do Sul**, **Santana do Livramento** and **Uruguaiana** ring to gauchos with the sound of musketry and cannon fire from the battles of the past. Gaucho tradition and culture are best preserved in these cities and on surrounding *estancias* (ranches) of the Campanha, where Portuguese and Spanish intermix in the colloquial language of the frontier.

Porto Alegre: Although far removed from the Campanha, the state's modern capital city of Porto Alegre provides visitors with a close-up look at the traditional music and dances of the gauchos. These can be seen at a number of popular night spots which feature gauhco folklore shows.

With a population of 1.4 million, Porto Alegre is the largest city of the south. Located near the coast at the northern end of the Lagoa dos Patos, the city is the ideal jumping off point for sojourns into the state's other areas. Gramado and Canela, the wine country plus Rio Grande do Sul's beaches all can be visited in day trips from the capital city. Trips to the mission region and the pampas, however, require two days at least. Porto Alegre is also a stopover on the land route from Brazil to Argentina and Uruguay. Buses head south daily to the border area.

As befits its status as the capital of a beef producing state, Porto Alegre offers excellent leather goods sold in downtown boutiques, plus steak houses where you will be treated to the real mouth-watering Brazilian *churrasco*.

Right, man of the south.

THE WILD WEST

"A land without men for men without land," was how soldier-president Emilio Medici described Brazil's wild western frontier territory in the early 1970s, a land inhabited by rural migrants from the overpopulated south. And wild it was…until well into this century. Overland travel between the western states and the Atlantic coast was one of Brazil's great adventures.

Brazil's western states stand on an immense elevated plateau three times the size of France, from which spring the northern-flowing tributaries of the Amazon, and those draining southward into the rivers Paraná and Paraguay, and thence to the river Plate. Only in the last 20 years have paved roads penetrated the region, bringing with them adventurers and dreamers who have quickly brought modern civilization to Brazil's backlands.

The states of Mato Grosso, Mato Grosso do Sul and Rondônia still embody the elusive myth of the Last Frontier, where virgin land is free and quick riches await the strong and the brave. In truth, however, the frontier of romance has long since moved onward and 100,000 new arrivals a year find the best land settled, and often protected against squatters by *pistoleiros* or hired gunmen. Yet, they continue to come.

Brash, brawling new towns with their unruly main streets choked with red dust sprout almost overnight. The frontier also has its share of losers, who filter back to the shantytowns of São Paulo, defeated by malaria and the labor of hacking down the forest barrier.

This was never a land without men. The first gold-seeking *bandeirantes* (pioneers) who forced their way up the rivers to Cuiabá, capital of Mato Grosso, in the 1720's discovered a forest filled with often hostile Indian tribes. Today the tribes of Mato Grosso and Rondônia form an important part of Brazil's surviving Indians. There are still occasional clashes between settlers and the Indian tribes driven deep into

the forest, where one or two groups untouched by western man still exist. Those inside the National Park of Xingu in northern Mato Grosso, which is closed to outsiders, can adapt at their own pace.

In 1890 Cândido Mariano da Silva Rondon began a military mission to link Cuiabá to the coast by telegraph, a herculean effort that was to revolutionize popular awareness of the forest and its Indian inhabitants. In 1907 he agreed to link Cuiabá with Porto Velho, capital of Rondônia, to the north by cutting across unmapped Indian territory, on condition that Rondon's men would also compile a complete ethnographic, plant and animal survey during the eight-year mission.

Rondon's saddle, riddled with Indian arrows, survives as evidence of his first contact with Indians. His idealism won over hostile Indian tribes and bloodthirsty white woodsmen alike. The telegraph, operated by some of these Indians, became obsolete almost immediately after it was built. But Rondon's thrilling lectures about the forest and the prestige he was later to gain by escorting former U.S. president Theodore Roosevelt on an Amazon expedition, helped him set up the first Indian protection service in 1910.

The state of Rondônia was named after Rondon, himself the grandson of Indians and one of the most striking figures in modern Brazilian history.

In 1935 French anthropologist Claude Lévi-Strauss followed the remains of Rondon's line, establishing camp in tiny settlements like Pimenta, Bueno and Vilhena, where abandoned telegraphists had received no supplies for eight years.

Today these are bustling cities astride the BR 364 highway—which is also the backbone of the New Frontier. Before it was asphalted in 1984 with World Bank financing, buses and trucks sometimes took months to travel the 875 miles (1,400 km) between Cuiabá and Porto Velho.

Cuiabá: Cuiabá was the west's first settlement, founded in 1719 by a group

Preceding pages: jaguar in the Pantanal. Below, Brazil is home to many species of monkeys.

of slave-hunters from São Paulo who struck shallow gold and diamond deposits. The resulting rush of prospectors made Cuiabá colonial Brazil's third most important city. A century ago the city acquired fame as a major supplier of exotic bird feathers to the milliners of Paris.

Today this prosperous, hot city is capital of an immense logging, farming and mining state. Unfortunately, little of colonial Cuiabá survives. The city's cathedral church of **Bom Jesus de Lapa** has a small adjoining museum of religious artifacts. But the old cathedral in the central square was dynamited. The square, **Praça da Republica**, is also the location of Turimat, the state tourism authority, with a very helpful visitor center.

The excellent **Marshal Rondon Indian Museum** shows the artifacts and lifestyle of the Xingu tribes. Some of the items are on sale at the shop run by FUNAI, the government Indian affairs bureau. Other landmarks are the **Governor's Residence** and the **Fundação Cultural de Mato Grosso**.

Fish specialities are Cuiabá's culinary forte. Piranha may be deadly in the water, but legend says that once in the soup they impart aphrodisiac powers—try *caldo de piranha* at the **Beco do Candeiro**, Rua Campo Grande 500, a restaurant whose walls are lined with photographs of old Cuiabá. Another regional speciality is Pôxada—fish char-grilled on a spit.

After the lowland heat, relief is close at hand 45 miles (70 km) from Cuiabá. The **Chapada dos Guimarães** is a rocky outcrop overlooking the flat plain of the Paraguay river and the Pantanal, 2600 feet (800 meters) above sea level. In the misty cool of the Chapada's folded hills and jutting, monolithic rock formations are caves and stunning waterfalls. Local residents attest to the region's mystical qualities and confirm frequent UFO sightings. These uplands provide one of the many water sources for the Pantanal marshlands below.

The **Salgadeiro** tourist center is where several rivers cut through a

marshy plain, providing small waterfalls and pools for bathing. The Salgadeiro center is much frequented by weekenders from Cuiabá.

Farther on, the road curves through the **Portão de Inferno** or Gates of Hell—an unfenced vertical drop that marks the edge of the sandstone escarpment. A policeman is on hand to discourage lovers planning to leap. Overhead tower pencil-like rock formations. Visitors can admire the 200-foot (61 meters) **Véu da Noiva** waterfall from above, or walk for half an hour down the thickly-wooded canyon to reach its base. Further into the Chapada is the **Casa de Pedra**—a natural cave-house capped by an immense stone shelf, and the **Caverna do Francés**, whose walls have primitive paintings. This and other caves reached after several hours' walk may be partly flooded, so guides, lamps and equipment are needed.

The historical town of **Chapada dos Guimarães**, with its 200-year-old church of **Santa Ana,** grew up to provide Cuiabá's hungry miners with food. Just outside the town is a monument to mark the exact geodesic center of South America. There are several hotels, including the modern **Pousada da Chapada**.

Porto Velho: The BR 364 leads north to **Porto Velho,** Rondônia's capital on the Rio Madeira, within striking distance by bus or boat of Manaus and the river Amazon itself. Like Rondônia, Porto Velho has grown too fast for its own good. In the 1950's Rondônia's population was just 37,000, mostly leftovers from the rubber-tapping era. By 1987, the state had almost a million residents. They were attracted by colonization programs which provided patches of fertile soil that gave high yields of coffee and cocoa.

Porto Velho was born a century ago from one of man's tragic attempts to tame the Amazon—the Madeira-Mamoré Railway. A restored steam locomotive still cheerfully plies a tiny section of track, its engineer the last custodian of a territory history.

In the 1860s American and British

Left, the Pantanal is a bird-watcher's paradise. Right, the red-necked "tuiuiu".

engineers began trying to build a railway that would link landlocked Bolivia and its rubber forests to the Amazon, and thence to the ocean. The railway would bypass treacherous rapids on the Madeira river. But for every rail laid, legend held that a man died of fever or malaria. Of the 900 American laborers sent to the Amazon in 1879, 80 drowned, and 141 died of fever, as did 400 Brazilians and 200 Bolivians—all for just four miles (six km) of track. Bankruptcies, mutiny and death dogged the railway. In 1903 Brazil bought rubber-rich Acre from Bolivia in exchange for completing the railway. Ten years and 30,000 diseased workers later, 230 miles (370 km) of track were completed—just in time for the collapse of the Amazon rubber trade.

On Sundays the steam train takes passengers to **Santo Antonio do Rio Madeira**, and sometimes as far as **Teotônio**. Porto Velho also has the **Museu do Rondônia** and **Casa do Artesão**, where relics of the rubber tapping age are on view.

Pantanal caymans.

Wildlife preserve: The highlight of any visit to western Brazil is the **Pantanal**, a vast natural paradise that is Brazil's major ecological attraction: 363,000 sq. miles (140,000 sq. km) of seasonally-flooded swampland offering a density of tropical wildlife unknown outside Africa, and the world's largest concentration of great wading birds. Storks, egrets, ibises, the elegant roseate spoonbill and the stately Tuiuiu or Jaburu birds that stand as tall as an adult; sunbathing alligators, deer, otters, emus, boa constrictors and monkeys. All these can easily be seen by visitors with only a few hours to spare in the Pantanal. The less hurried can visit the Woodstorks' tree-top nesting sites, fish for Dourado or wait for the elusive jaguar or *onça pintada*.

Though the Pantanal offers sanctuary for migratory geese and ducks moving between Argentina and Central America, most of the 600 species of birds found here are residents who follow the changing water levels inside the huge swamp, in pursuit of 350 species of fish that form the basis of the food chain. Rainfall cycles are the key to the Pantanal: from October to April (January and February are months to avoid) the rains flow into the northern part of the Pantanal from the Chapada dos Guimarães and hilly regions, at a time when the southern part is drier. The rivers rise by more than 10 feet (three meters), flooding their banks and spreading into huge *baias* or closed lakes where fish have been breeding. The waters activate ground vegetation and enable the overhanging trees to produce fruit on which the fish gorge themselves, before swimming through open canals to spawn in the rivers—a period known as the *piracema*.

Because the altitude varies only a few feet in the 375-mile (600-km) extension of the Pantanal, the coffee-colored waters drain slowly, producing a tremendous surge in fertility. During high water in the northern part, the southern Pantanal has shallow water, which attracts the wading birds. After April, the situation is reversed and the birds fly northward to nest between June and

September. Here the lakes are once again cut off from the rivers and their fish become captives for predators.

The northern edge of the Pantanal may be reached by car or plane from Cuiabá. From there, visitors must contract a travel agency which will arrange for a guide, transportation (usually by boat) and accommodation in the Pantanal. All of the better travel agencies operate or are associated with hotel *fazendas* (lodges) in the swamp. These hotels supply boats, airplanes, ground transportation and even hot-air balloons to visit the nesting-sites and lakes where the wildlife concentrate—but visitors must be prepared to wake before sunrise and endure the mosquitoes. Care must be taken to choose the right region in the Pantanal, hotel and guide supplied by the travel agency. Samariana and Expeditur agencies in Cuiabá are recommended.

In the Northern Pantanal, in Mato Grosso State, eight hotels are currently operating, plus a number of simpler *Portos de Pesca*—campsites and boat-launching facilities for sport fishermen. Those hotels reached by boat or road cost about US$60 per night, but transport from Cuiabá may be the costliest item. A five-night package at the Pouso da Garça, reachable only by plane, costs US$572 per person.

Santo Antônio de Leverger marks the edge of the swamp, and is just 17 miles (28 km) south of Cuiabá on state highway 040. Here light aircraft take off for the hotels and *fazendas*. Boats may also be hired as far as **Barão de Melgaço**, which was once the region's sugar mill center. Close by is the **Baia Chacororé**, an immense shallow lake filled with alligators, flocks of pink spoonbills and larger mammals around its shore.

This sleepy town is the starting point for the Pantanal's most luxurious option: 10- or 17-day river tours extending as far south as the city of Corumbá down the **Cuiabá**, **São Lourenço** and **Paraguay** rivers. **Cidade Bareo de Melgaço**, a floating hotel with eight double cabins, good cooking and air conditioning, is operated by the Melgatur agency. Director Angelika Juncke, a West German wildlife expert who became a Brazilian citizen after working for years in the Pantanal, provides detailed ecological lectures for passengers, who can bird watch from on deck or venture into the lakes in small motorized canoes.

The boat takes seven days to descend the river and 10 days to return to Cuiabá again. Shorter trips on the CBM, starting at US$395 are also much favored by the European visitors. During the low water season CBM operates in the Southern Pantanal only.

Melgatur also operates in conjunction with the highly-recommended **Passargada Pousada**, reachable only by boat and situated on a small tributary of the Cuiabá river. This 16-bed hotel is run by Marival Sigeault, who takes his visitors out on treks and willingly imparts Pantanal lore.

Due south of Cuiabá on state highway 060 is **Poconé**, where the **Trans-Pantaneira Highway** begins. Poconé itself is a dry area given over to farming and

Bridal Veil Falls, Chapada dos Guimarães.

the swamps nearby have been disturbed by gold-mining, wildlife poaching and excessive fishing. But it is the jumping-off point for some of the best parts of the Pantanal.

Porto Cercado, 125 miles (200 km) from Cuiabá, has three hotels that provide good access to wildlife, with large lakes and a superb nesting-site for woodstorks, ibises and spoonbills nearby. Well-situated beside the river, **Pousada Porto Cercado** sleeps 42 people in reasonable comfort. **Hotel Cabanas do Pantanal** on the **River Piraim** has 11 rooms. Both hotels cost about US$60 per night, plus stiff ground transfer charges. Hiring of boats is expensive too: a canoe with 25 horse power is about US$20 an hour. Upstream is the much simpler **Baias do Pantanal**.

From Poconé the Trans-Pantaneira Highway runs 90 miles (145 km) southward to Porto Joffre over 126 bridges. Begun in the 1970s, the highway was originally intended to link Cuiabá with Corumbá, but local political wrangles and ecologists' pressure cut it short. Because the road runs parallel to the rivers, huge bodies of water collect beside it, ensuring views of alligators and bird life even to those unwilling to get out of their cars. The highway is in a poor state of conservation, but it does permit forest guards to control part of the Pantanal and give visitors access.

Beside the Highway are two hotels, **Pousada das Araras** and **Pousada Pixaim**. At the highway's end is the **Santa Rosa Pantanal Hotel,** which sleeps 46 people.

On the São Lourenço, in the heart of the swamp are reachable only by plane, are the **Pousada Garça** and **Hotel Pirigara**. The Pousada Garça, 112 miles (180 km) south of Cuiabá, is owned by country music singer Sergio Reis, who sometimes provides evening entertainment and is engaged in a wildlife preservation effort with the region's other farmers. A Borôro Indian village is a short distance from the Pousada Garça.

Other hotel-*fazendas* include the **Barranquinho**, 37 miles (60 km) south

Cattle drive slows highway traffic.

of the town of **Cáceres** on the Paraguay river. From this town buses can be caught to Bolivia, or northward to the BR 364. **Pousada Pirigara**, favored by fishermen, is situated close to the **Ilha Camargo** on the São Lourenço—an immense ranch owned by Brazil's wealthiest man, civil construction billionaire Sebastião Camargo.

For the Southern Pantanal in Mato Grosso do Sul, the entry points are Campo Grande and Corumbá. Those with more time can take a train from **São Paulo** to the city of **Bauru**, and then for 27 hours across the Pantanal, arriving at Corumbá in the early morning. Mato Grosso do Sul's state capital, **Campo Grande**, lies 260 miles (420 km) to the east. It began life in 1889 and is still an overgrown cowboy town that has borrowed some habits from Paraguay's Chaco. The **Museu Dom Bosco** has interesting Indian exhibits.

Corumbá, situated on the Bolivian border opposite **Puerto Suarez**, was founded in 1778. The Pantanal laps right into the city and even a brief boat tour gives a vivid impression. Rides can be arranged down at the port, while Safari-Pantanal and the operators of the tourist boat **Perola do Pantanal** offer daylong trips. The more intrepid may be able to arrange rides on slow cement barges, small trading vessels, or cattle barges going as far as Porto Cercado or Barão de Melgaço.

A selection of leatherwork, ceramics, Indian artifacts and other handicrafts are available at the **Casa do Artesão**, once the city's jail. A short drive along the Pantaneira highway back to Campo Grande offers interesting views of the swamps.

Nearby hotel-*fazendas* are **Santa Clara**, **Santa Blanca** and **Cabana do Lontra.** The best option in the southern Pantanal is the 132,500 acre (53,000-ha) **Fazenda Caiman**, close to **Miranda** on the **Campo Grande-Corumbá highway**. Owner Roberto Klabin has established his own wildlife reserve and invited trained guides and naturalists such as American Douglas Trent, who also runs Tropical Tours, a

Gold prospector uses home-made contraption.

travel agency specializing in Brazil's outback, based in Belo Horizonte (MG). University students and professors carrying out research mix with tourists. At the *fazenda* visitors are taken on four separate tours—down the **Aquidauana** river; through the cattle ranch, on horseback to a deer reservation, and to the 17,500 acre (7,000-ha) wildlife reserve. The river-based Camping Club of Brazil has a special arrangement there for campers. Early-morning rides in a hot-air balloon, which floats silently over large animals without startling them, can be arranged.

The Araguaia: "This is the Garden of Eden," declares Durval Rosa Borges, author of *Araguaia, Heart and Soul* — which is a tribute to the 1,700-mile (2,200-km) long river that cuts Brazil in two, from the wetlands of the Pantanal across the *cerrado* or central plains to the Atlantic Ocean at Belém. The mighty river, in which swim over 200 kinds of fish and on whose banks are found many of the Pantanal's bird species, migrant birds from the Andes and the United States, plus Amazonian animals like the tapir, has ceased to be Brazil's best-kept secret.

When the muddy floodwaters shrink in August to reveal immense white sand beaches, 200,000 vacationing Brazilians descend on **Aruanã**, 375 miles (600 km) west of Brasília, and **Barra do Garças** in southern Goias state to establish lavish campsites with freezers, generators, radio-telephones and sound systems for all night parties. Yet their presence, and that of nearby ranches and farms, is dwarfed by the Araguaia's sheer scale and its magnificent sunsets.

The river's source in southern Goias is in the **Parque Nacional das Emas**, from which it flows northward forming a barrier between the states of Mato Grosso, Goiás, Tocantins and Pará, dividing to form the **Ilha do Bananal**—the world's largest fluvial island. To the north of the island is the **Araguaia National Park**. During the low water season, floating hotels operate on these tributaries; it is also favored by sport fishermen.

Passengers and wares on river waterway.

COURO
BAHIA

CASA DE COUROS

BAHIA

Bahia is the soul of Brazil. In this north eastern state, more than anywhere else in Brazil, the country's cultures and races have mixed, producing what is most authentically Brazilian.

It was at Porto Seguro, on the southern coast of Bahia, where Portuguese explorer Pedro Alvares Cabral first discovered this land, in 1500. A year later, on All Saints' Day, a group of settlers sent by the Portuguese Crown arrived at what is now **Salvador**, capital of Bahia. For 233 years until 1763, it also reigned as the capital of Brazil.

Bahia is the site of the country's first medical school, its oldest churches, its most important colonial architecture, and its largest collection of sacred art. Bahia is also the birthplace of many of Brazil's outstanding writers, politicians and composers. Bahia-born novelist Jorge Amado's works have been translated into over 40 languages and several of his books have become major films (including *Dona Flor and Her Two Husbands* and *Gabriela*). The music of Bahians João Gilberto, Baden Powell and Gilberto Gil is enjoyed by aficionados all over the world.

There is another side to Bahia, a side that appeals to the spirit, and the senses. The mysticism of Bahia is so strong that it pervades every aspect of life: it can be perceived in the way people dress, in their speech, their music, their way of relating to each other and even in their food. This mysticism is another reason Brazilians say that in Bahia lies the soul of their country.

The original source of this mysticism was the African slave culture. Today the Pantheist religion of the African Yoruba tribe is still alive and well in Bahia, and many white Bahians who are self-professed Catholics can be seen making their offerings to the deities of the *candomblé* religion. The phenomenon of syncretism, the blending of Catholicism with African religions, resulted when the slaves were forced to worship their deities masked as Catholic saints. Today you can see the devout worshipping the African goddess *Iemanjá* as Our Lady, or the god *Oxumaré* as Saint Anthony.

Preceding pages, colonial Salvador. **Left**, Bahian man wears the colors of his *orixá*, (African god).

The religion and mysticism that are so much a part of Bahian life are reflected in the name of the state's capital city: **Salvador**, meaning Savior. The peninsula where the city was built, first discovered by Amerigo Vespucci in 1501, faces **Todos os Santos Bay** (All Saints' Bay), named in honor of the November 1 discovery. According to legend, Salvador has 365 churches, one for each day of the year.

What is most striking about Salvador is the way it assaults your senses: the sight of gold-encrusted altars and panels of its churches, the exotic taste of the food and drinks with their African influence, the inviting scent of Bahian dishes and condiments, the sounds of the street vendors' cries, the roar of rush-hour traffic, the chant of soccer game fans or political rally enthusiasts and most of all, the distinctive sound of Bahian music.

On almost any street corner in Salvador, certainly on any beach, weekends are a time of music-making. Though much of it today is commercial and almost always takes the lion's share of the Brazilian hit parade, this music has its roots in *candomblé* worship services, where the pulsating, hypnotic rhythm provides a means for contacting the gods. As you walk down Salvador's streets, during the week as well as in summer, you'll see groups of *baianos* gathered at corner bars singing their favorite songs, often with the aid of nothing more than a box of kitchen matches filling in for a simple tambourine. Other clusters of amateur musicians can be seen playing small drums and other percussion instruments, as well as the occasional guitar or *cavaquinho*, a four-string instrument resembling a ukelele.

Music and religion are as much a part of the people's lives as eating and sleeping. The year is organized around religious holidays. Street processions mark the celebrations. The year's religious calendar culminates in Carnival, traditionally the one last fling before the 40-day Lenten period of prayer and penance preceeding Easter.

Officially, Carnival lasts four days, from the Saturday to the Tuesday before Ash Wednesday, but in Salvador, Carnival is practically a summer-long event. Clubs host pre-Carnival balls and on weekends the streets fill with pre-Carnival revelers gearing up for the main event.

If you visit during this time, don't expect to get much sleep during the four days, and don't be surprised at the energy you and everyone else can generate to keep going for 96 hours straight. Salvador's Carnival is not the organized affair of Rio de Janeiro and São Paulo. There are no samba schools competing for government money to keep them going.

In Salvador, the celebration is pure, wild fun: drinking and dancing and a fair amount of promiscuity. Most characteristic of Carnival in Salvador is the *Trio Elétrico*, a band (not necessarily three-piece) perched atop a flatbed truck. The band provides the music for dancing in the streets. These *Trios Elétricos* are often well-equipped with barrels of *cachaça* (sugarcane liquor) to fuel the revelers.

Though Carnival is an outgrowth of Christian religion, in Bahia, mysticism also has its place. During Salvador's carnival, *afoxés*, groups of *candomblé* worshippers, take to the streets with banners and images of their patrons, usually African deities to whom they dedicate their songs and offerings.

One of the most famous *afoxés* differs from the others in its choice of patron. This *afoxé*, based in the center of the historical **Pelourinho** district, is called *Filhos de Gandhi* (Sons of Gandhi), in honor of the great Indian leader.

It is not only at Carnival time, though, that Salvador is home to joyful religious or para-religious celebrations. There is at least one important holiday per month, and if there is no holiday during your stay, you can still arrange to attend a *candomblé* session or a *capoeira* display. Travel agencies and some hotels can make reservations for folklore shows (including *capoeira*) and those *candomblé* sessions that are open to the public. You may also contact Bahiatursa, the state tourism board (phone: 254-7000). Bahiatursa's head offices, as well as its four information centers, always have someone on hand who speaks at least one foreign language (English) and who can assist in making reservations.

While *candomblé* ceremonies are lively, spirited events with much music and dancing, it's good to remember that these are serious religious services and as such, require respectful behavior and conservative dress. It's always safe to wear white, but what's most important is that you be fully clothed—no shorts or halter tops. Also, cameras are strictly forbidden. Ceremonies usually take place at night and can last for two or three hours.

Capoeira, a martial art brought over by the slaves, is a foot-fighting technique disguised as a dance. Forbidden by their owners to fight, the slaves were forced to hide this pastime behind the

Ornamentation reflects a past era.

trappings of a gymnastics display. Today you can see this rhythmic exercise performed on street corners in Salvador to the music of the berimbau, a one-stringed instrument resembling an archer's bow. The music of *capoeira* is directly related to that of *candomblé*, music which paces the ceremony and opens up a channel to the gods.

Another of Salvador's festivals is that of *Boa Viagem*, a New Year's Day procession in honor of *Nossa Senhora dos Navegantes* (Our Lady of the Seafarers). On this day, a procession of boats escorts the image of Our Lady to the **Boa Viagem beach**, where sailors and their families take over and carry the image to its church.

On the third Thursday in January the festival of Bonfim occurs, when *baianas* (Bahian women) in brilliant costumes ritually wash the steps leading to the church of **Nosso Senhor do Bonfim** (Our Lord of Good Ending), the city's most popular house of worship. This festival goes on for four days, with music and feasting.

Iemanjá, the *candomblé* goddess of the sea, is honored on February 2, when *baianas* in white lace blouses and skirts send offerings, such as combs, mirrors and soaps, out to sea on small handmade boats. This *orixá* (goddess), perceived as a vain woman, is placated in this manner to guarantee calm waters for the fishermen.

The saints' days celebrated in June (Anthony, John and Peter) are collectively called *festas juninas* (June parties). On these days, as well as on June weekends, churches sponsor bazaars and neighbors gather together to light bonfires and send up hot-air balloons and fireworks. Street fairs serve corn in every conceivable form and beef chunks on wooden skewers to be washed down with *quentão* (hot spiced *cachaça* or wine).

Nossa Senhora da Conceição da Praia (Our Lady of the Beach) is honored on December 8 with a procession to her church.

The city: Salvador was first settled some 30 years after Brazil was discov-

ered. In 1530 King João III of Portugal sent a group of colonists to stake claim to this new land and strengthened the Portuguese presence against French and Dutch invaders in the area. Salvador became the first capital of Brazil in 1549, when the Portuguese court sent Tomé de Souza as the country's first governor-general.

Perched atop cliffs overlooking Todos os Santos Bay, the tiny settlement was considered an ideal capital because of its natural protection. Since then, Salvador has lost economic and political importance but increased its fame as the center of Brazilian culture, a mixture of black and white races, descending from the Africans and Europeans. With a population of 1.8 million, Salvador is Brazil's fourth largest city. Because Bahian life revolves around Salvador, Brazilians frequently intermix the two, saying Bahia when they mean Salvador.

Today, the best way to orient yourself in this languid, tropical city is to think of it as being divided into four parts: the beaches, the suburbs, the upper city and the lower city. Downtown Salvador encompasses both the historical **Upper City** (*Cidade Alta*) and the newer **Lower City** (*Cidade Baixa*).

A walking tour of the Cidade Alta starts at the **Praça da Sé**, a square that opens out onto **Terreiro de Jesus**, a plaza that is home to three of Salvador's most famed churches.

The largest of the three, the **Cathedral Basilica**, is a 17th-century Jesuit structure largely built of Lioz stone, with beautiful examples of gold leaf work in its main altar. Next to it are the 17th-century **Dominican Church** (O*rdem Terceira de São Domingos*) and the 18th-century **St. Peter's** (*São Pedro dos Clérigos*).

On Sunday mornings, Terreiro de Jesus is the site of a weekly arts and crafts fair where you can buy handmade lace and leather goods and lovely primitive paintings. Visiting hours for the three churches are from 9 to 10:30 a.m. and from 2 to 5 p.m., Tuesday through Saturday. The cathedral is also open

Coconut palms provide shade near the shore.

from 9 to 10 a.m. on Sundays.

Rising majestically from the adjoining square, Praça Anchieta, is one of the world's most opulent baroque churches, paradoxically dedicated to a saint who preached the simple, unencumbered life. The **Church of St. Francis** is an impressive 18th-century structure built of stone imported from Portugal. Its interior, from floor to ceiling, is covered with intricate carvings thickly encrusted with gold leaf. In a side altar is the splendid statue of St. Peter of Alcântara, carved from a single tree trunk by Manoel Inácio da Costa, one of Brazil's most important and famous baroque artists.

The Franciscan monastery, annexed to the church, surrounds a charming courtyard. This monastery can only be visited by men who are accompanied by a church-appointed guide; women must be content to catch a glimpse of the courtyard through a window. Hand-painted blue and white tiles, depicting scenes from the life of St. Francis, were imported from Portugal in the late 18th-century and adorn the church vestibule. Visiting hours are from 8 to 11:30 a.m. and between 2 to 5:30 p.m. Monday through Saturday; Tuesdays the church is open all day. Next door is the smaller **Church of the Third Order of St. Francis**, noted for its Spanish-influenced baroque façade. This church is closed Saturday afternoons.

Crossing again Terreiro de Jesus, walk a short distance down **Rua Alfredo Brito**, and you will reach **Pelourinho** (Pillory), site of Salvador's best preserved colonial buildings, whose colorful façades line the steep, meandering cobblestone streets. The name comes from the colonial period when pillories were set up here to punish slaves and criminals.

Today, Pelourinho is considered by Unesco to be the most important grouping of 17th- and 18th-century colonial architecture in the Americas. Once a fashionable district of Salvador, Pelourinho's fame has deteriorated along with the fortunes of its inhabitants. The area today is favored by pros-

***Capoeira* fighters.**

titutes and petty thieves. Don't be deterred, Pelourinho is charming, attractive and distinct and also well-policed.

The center of the square is now occupied by the **Casa de Jorge Amado**, a museum/library replete with books by the man who is Brazil's most famous living novelist (his works have been translated into nearly 50 languages). The collection also includes photographs, memorabilia and a video on the life of one of Bahia's most beloved sons. Open daily from 9 a.m. to 5 p.m.

Next door is the tiny **Museu da Cidade**, with its collection of Afro-Brazilian folklore. On the top floor are mannequins dressed as the most important *orixás* (gods) of the *candomblé* faith: they are identified by their African names as well as their equivalent Catholic saint's name. The museum is open from 8 to 12 noon and from 2 to 6 p.m. during the week; it is closed on weekend afternoons.

The **Senac restaurant,** on the square, run by a government hotel and restaurant school, is an excellent place to try the local food and see a Bahian folklore show. The self-service restaurant is open daily, except Sunday, for lunch and dinner and also offers a Brazilian-style afternoon tea: coffee served with a variety of Bahian pastries and sweets, from 5 to 8 p.m. The folklore show is presented in the evenings, when Senac is open until 11 p.m. for dinner.

Just down the street from Pelourinho square is the Church of **Nossa Senhora do Rosário dos Pretos** (Our Lady of the Rosary of Black Men). Since the slaves were not permitted inside the churches, they built their own. The protective wall that originally surrounded Salvador ran through Pelourinho. The slaves' church was located outside this wall, the only place they were permitted to build.

At the bottom of Pelourinho square is a flight of steps called the **Ladeira do Carmo** which leads to the **Largo do Carmo** (Carmelite square). Scene of the resistance against the Dutch invaders, this block of buildings is the site of the Dutch surrender. The most interesting building is the **Carmelite church**

Rodeo in Feira de Santana, Bahia.

and convent, dating from 1585. The convent has been partially transformed into a museum and a small hotel, without losing its original characteristics and charm.

Still in the Upper City although in a newer section closer to downtown, are two fascinating museums that can be visited on the same afternoon. **Bahia's Museum of Sacred Art**, located at **Rua do Sodré 25**, is housed in the 17th-century **Church** and **Convent of St. Theresa**. *Baianos* claim that this is the largest collection of sacred art in Latin America. Whether this is true or not, it is easily the most impressive of the city's museums, and one of the most fascinating found in Brazil.

The baroque and rococo art is displayed in large, airy rooms, many of them lined with blue, white and yellow tiles, brought from Portugal in the 1600s. Proving that contraband was a part of secular life in the 17th and 18th centuries, many of the larger images of saints, carved from wood, are intentionally hollowed out to hide smuggled jewels and gold. This type of religious image is called a *santo do pau oco* (a hollow wood saint). Paintings, ivory sculptures and works in earthenware, silver and gold round out this priceless collection. The museum is open Tuesday through Saturday, from 10 to 11:30 a.m. and from 2 to 5:30 p.m.

Going towards the Barra beach area, along **Avenida Sete de Setembro**, one of the city's main thoroughfares, you will find the **Carlos Costa Pinto Museum** at number 2490, in the **Vitória** district. This mansion houses the Costa Pinto family's collection of colonial furnishings, porcelain and jewelry, including baccarat crystal, handpainted Chinese porcelain dishes and opulent silver *balagandans*, clusters of charms which were pinned to the blouses of slave women to indicate their owners personal wealth. Much of the flooring in the main rooms downstairs is pink Carrara marble. At the entrance, uniformed employee's place cloth slippers over your shoes to protect the floor. The museum is open every afternoon (ex-

Donkey rider in the arid *sertão*.

cept Tuesday) from 1 to 7 p.m.

Lower city: The walking tour of the Lower City also starts off at the Praça da Sé: this time, with your back toward Terreiro de Jesus, walk down **Rua da Misericórdia** to the **Santa Casa da Misericórdia**, a late 16th-century church and hospital with 18th-century Portuguese tile panels, open weekdays from 2 to 5 p.m. A short way down the street is the **Praça Municipal**, where the town council and city hall are housed in colonial buildings. The square leads you to Salvador's famous **Lacerda elevator**, a massive blue art-deco -nspired structure built in 1930 to link the Upper and Lower cities. The boxcar-like compartment whisks you down to the **Cidade Baixa**.

Straight ahead is the **Mercado Modelo**, first installed in the old customs house at the city port in 1915. Twice destroyed by fires (latest in 1984) the market has been completely rebuilt in concrete. In this three-storey building you will find stalls selling local handicrafts and souvenirs.

The Mercado Modelo is one of those not-to-be-missed sights in Salvador. Not only is it the best place in town to purchase your souvenirs, it is also a lively microcosm of Bahian life. As you stroll among the stalls, musicians will display their wares by playing them. At one end you might hear a lively percussion ensemble, at the other, a lone man playing the mystical berimbau. It helps to know a little Portuguese or to have a Brazilian friend along to bargain with the vendors. Bartering is part of the market's tradition and you can usually lower the price by 25 percent.

For refreshment, try one of the many types of fresh fruit juices, or if you'e hungry, go upstairs to the Camafeu de Oxossi restaurant, one of the best in the city.

Turn left from the market, keeping the bay to your right, and walk down the street to the Church of Nossa Senhora da Conceição da Praia, the church that houses the image of Bahia's patron saint. This church, planned and built in Portugal in the early 18th century, was brought over piece by piece. It is the site of the annual religious procession held on December 8, one of the most important dates on Salvador's calendar. The church is open daily from 7:00 to 11:00 a.m. and from 3:00 to 5:00 p.m; closed Sunday afternoons.

About six miles (10 km) in the opposite direction stands the famous church of **Nosso Senhor do Bonfim**. On the way to the church, you will pass by the picturesque **São Joaquim Market**, open every day from 6 a.m. to 6 p.m. An interesting stop for visitors, the market is fascinating but it has been neglected over the years and is now dirty and run down. Here you'll find everything from chickens to vegetables and ceramic figurines: if you can stand the smell, make a stop.

Open daily from 6 a.m. to noon and 2:30 to 6:00 p.m., the **Bonfim church** was built in 1754 and is one of the most popular sites for religious pilgrimage in the country. People come from throughout Brazil to pray for jobs or cures or to give thanks for miracles attributed to Our Lord. As you enter the church,

Below, old houses near Pelourinho in Salvador. Right, boy and donkey at work.

you'll be approached by groups of boys and women wanting to sell colorful ribbons printed with the words "*Lembrança do Senhor do Bonfim da Bahia*" (Souvenir of Our Lord of Good Ending). According to legend, a friend should tie the ribbon around your wrist in three knots, representing three wishes: when the ribbon falls off, your wishes will come true.

Lacking the ornateness of Salvador's other churches, Bonfim is still the favorite with both Catholics and practitioners of the *candomblé* faith. Don't miss the **Miracle Room**, filled with photographs of those who have reached a state of grace and the plaster castings of limbs or organs that have been cured through divine intervention.

Farther down this same road is the **Church of Mont'Serrat**, a simple 16th-century chapel with Portuguese titles. Nearby is the **Boa Viagem church**, open everyday from 6:30 to 11 a.m. and from 4 to 8 p.m. This church marks the destination of Salvador's Our Lady of the Seafarers procession held every New Year's day.

The beaches: A series of inter-connecting streets and roads provide a non-stop promenade along Salvador's beaches, from the near-downtown Barra beach to the distant north coast beaches which are considered among Brazil's most beautiful. **Barra**, the city beach, is famed less for its beauty then for the conviviality of its bars and sidewalk cafés.

Here the bars have truly original names: Liver's Bar, Overdose Bar and Bypass Operation Bar, among others. Barra is where office workers spend their happy hour, and beyond. It is also good for shopping and is filled with apart-hotels, renting by the week or month and usually much cheaper then hotels. The beach is protected by the gallant old fort **Santo Antonio da Barra**, with its lighthouse and oceanography museum, open daily except Mondays from 11 a.m. to 7 p.m.

The next beach northward from Barra is called Ondina, home to several top-flight hotels. Inland from the beach, in

Bahian youths in Salvador doorway.

the same neighborhood, is the **Salvador Zoo**. Next is **Rio Vermelho**, an elegant upper-middle class neighborhood where writer Jorge Amado lives six months a year (he summers in Paris). Coconut groves line the beaches as you travel northward, passing by **Mariquita** and **Amaralina**, where several fine restaurants are located. At **Pituba**, you can see a host of *jangadas*, primitive fishing boats made of split logs roped together and propelled by sails. Other beaches along this route include **Jardim de Alá**, **Armação de Iemanjá**, **Boca do Rio**, **Corçãrio** (with one of the city's few bicycle paths), **Pituaçu**, **Patamares** (with good restaurants), and **Piatã**.

Piatã and the last beach before the airport, **Itapuã**, are Salvador's best. Itapuã is slightly less crowded, especially during the week, than Piatã, but in terms of natural beauty, food and drink service, they are at par. The statue of a mermaid *(Iemanjá)* on the Itapuã side of the division between the two beaches is a meeting point for the city's young people. On weekends the two beaches fill with musicians who spend the afternoon singing regional music and playing percussion instruments between beers. One of the most beautiful sights in Salvador is the sunset viewed from Itapuã beach.

Nightlife: Nightlife in Salvador is concentrated in the city's better bars and restaurants, the majority of them located in the Barra neighborhood and along the beach drive. There are a few discos, mostly at the top hotels, where you're more likely to hear Madonna's or Michael Jackson's latest hit than you are to hear Brazilian music.

The **Teatro Castro Alves**, located at the **Campa Grande park** across from the **Hotel da Bahia**, is the place for ballet, theater and musical performances. A huge sign in front of the theater lists the week's events. Occasionally the Castro Alves is host to a Brazilian or foreign symphony orchestra. More often you'll find one of Brazil's top recording artists performing there. Look for names such as Caetano Veloso, Maria Bethania, Gal Costa or Gilberto Gil—these *baianos* are among Brazil's most popular singers and songwriters.

Soccer is a major form of entertainment in Salvador, as it is all over Brazil. Matches, held at the city's **Otávio Mangabeira Stadium**, usually take place on Wednesday nights and Sunday afternoons. Purchase a seat in the reserved section (*cadeiras numeradas*); they are more expensive but it is worth the added cost.

The port area and the Pelourinho district are the venues for the seedier side of Salvador's night life. Avoid these areas at night. In the case of Pelourinho, it's safe to go to the main square, especially to visit the Senac restaurant, but save your exploring of the area for the daylight hours.

For the best in entertainment, day or night, do what the locals do: go to the beach. Choose one of the thatched-roof huts that function as bars on Pituba or Piatã beach, sit on a sawed-off trunk used as a stool, order your batida or *caipirinha* (fruit and sugarcane alcohol drinks) and listen to the music played by

Helping with the laundry.

your neighbors at the next table as you watch the waves roll in.

Day trips: Ilha de Itaparica is a glorious island set in All Saints Bay, a veritable tropical wonderland, where Club Med built its first hotel in Brazil. Some 10,000 people live on the island, divided mainly between fishermen and wealthy weekenders, whose beachfront mansions often can be reached only by boat. For privacy's sake, they resist attempts to build access roads to the highway that runs down the middle of the island.

There are several ways to reach the island. Ferry boats leave Salvador's port at regular intervals for the 45-minute crossing. You can also drive around to the other side of the bay to the bridge that links Itaparica to the mainland, a three-hour trip that may be extended to include stops at the fascinating historical towns of **Santo Amaro** and **Cachoeira**. Once on the island, you can rent a bicycle for some exploring along its many beaches.

If your time is limited, take the daylong bay cruise sold by the top travel agencies in Salvador. The cruise costs under US$20 per person and includes transportation to and from your hotel and free *batidas* and soft drinks aboard. Once aboard the double-masted schooner, you're in for a delightful surprise: the guide and crew are also musicians. As the boat skims the calm waters of the bay between stops, the crew gathers at the prow to sing and play popular songs. Guests aboard join in, and later in the day, after a fair number of *batidas*, nearly everyone is singing and dancing.

After leaving Salvador, most of these boats make two stops. The first, in the late morning, is at **Ilha dos Frades**, an all-but-deserted island inhabited by fishermen who have found a second, more lucrative source of revenue: tourists. The boat anchors offshore and visitors are brought in ten at a time in row boats. Those who are not afraid of the jellyfish ("their sting is just a little nip", the locals say) can swim to shore. After an hour of exploring, drinking or eating something at one of the improvised bars, or purchasing souvenirs, you're taken on to Itaparica Island for lunch and a walking tour. It's then back to the boat for the return trip to Salvador with a splendid view of the sun setting over the city.

The *Estrada de Coco* (**Coconut Road**) leads northward away from Salvador's most distant beach, Itapuã. Along this road, lined with coconut palms, you will pass by virtually unspoiled tropical beaches including **Jaua**, **Arembepe**, **Jucuípe**, **Abaí** and **Itacimirim** before reaching one of the most beautiful regions in Bahia, located some 50 miles (80 km) from Salvador, called **Praia do Forte**.

A hundred thousand coconut palms stand on seven miles (12 km) of white sandy beach protected against the exploitation of tourism and other threats to the environment by a private foundation. The growth of hotels and campsites here is carefully monitored. For every coconut tree cut down, four more have to be planted.

Forte Beach is also the site of a major preservation center for sea turtles. The

One of Salvador's many colonial-era churches.

eggs are collected from "nests" on the beach at night and protected from predators (human and animal) until the babies are old enough to return to the sea and fend for themselves.

Along the road leading south from Salvador to the state of Espirito Santo is the 400-year-old town of **Valença**, where the Una River meets the Atlantic Ocean. The town is the site of Brazil's first textile factory and Bahia's first hydroelectric dam. One of the best beaches in the region, nine miles (15 km) from Valença, is **Guaibim**. The beach features good seafood restaurants and bars.

Morro de São Paulo is a peaceful fishing village that looks out on the 16 islands that are part of the township of Valença, located just 100 miles (170 km) south of Salvador.

Another important city on Bahia's southern coast is **Ilheus**, the cocoa capital of Brazil and one of its major export ports. Just over 240 miles (400 km) from Salvador, Ilheus was founded in 1534 and is today a modern city that has preserved its historical sites. Beaches abound in the region, and the city's Carnival celebration is one of the most lively in Bahia. Local travel agents charter schooners which cruise around the islands. The town has reasonably good hotels and campsites on the beach. **Olivença**, a hydromineral spa 12 miles (20 km) from Ilheus, is an excellent place to camp and "take the waters." Besides Carnival, major festivals in Ilheus include St. Sebastian (January 11-20), the city's birthday (June 28) and the cocoa festival (the entire month of October).

Porto Seguro, in the extreme south of Bahia, nearly halfway to Rio de Janeiro, is where Brazil was discovered by Pedro Alvares Cabral on April 22, 1500. The town has withstood the pressures of progress and has managed to preserve its colonial atmosphere. For a small town (5,000 inhabitants), Porto Seguro has an extraordinarily large number of hotels and inns (called *pousadas*) and an array of beachfront bars and restaurants. Young people flock to

Itapuã beach outside Salvador.

Bahian Cuisine

To the uninitiated stomach, Bahian cooking can be a bit heavy. However, once they've tried it most people agree that this unique Afro-Brazilian cuisine is delicious and satisfying.

Though it contains contributions from the Portuguese colonists and the native Indians, by far the most important influence comes from the African slaves, who not only brought their own style of cooking with them, but also modified certain Portuguese dishes with special African herbs and spices.

Bahian cuisine is characterized by the generous use of *malagueta* chile peppers and *dendê* oil, which is extracted from an African palm that grows well in the northeastern climate. Several Bahian dishes also contain seafood (usually shrimp), coconut milk, banana and okra.

Moqueca, one of the region's most popular dishes, is a mixture of shrimp or other seafood, coconut, garlic, onion, parsley, pepper, tomato paste and the ubiquitous *dendê* oil, sautéed over a low flame and served with rice cooked in coconut milk. In colonial days, this ragout was wrapped in banana leaves and roasted in embers.

Another traditional dish is *vatapá*, which is usually based on seafood but can also be made with chicken. Besides *dendê* and coconut, this stew-like dish also contains ground peanuts and chopped green peppers. *Carurú de Camarão*, another stew, differs from the first two dishes in that it includes both fresh and dried shrimp, as well as sliced okra.

In better restaurants, these dishes are served with a hot *malagueta* sauce. Try the food first before adding any pepper. Sometimes pepper is added directly to the dish and the cook may ask you if you like your food *quente* (hot). Until you get used to the strong flavors of the *dendê* and the *malagueta*, it is best to say no. The word hot, in this land, has nothing to do with temperature.

Bahian meal: seafood, palm oil, coconut milk and pepper.

Experienced Bahian cooks use earthenware pots. This old African tradition is maintained due to the fact that earthenware holds in heat better than other materials. In fact, most Bahian dishes are served in these pots, often the very ones they were cooked in.

The hotels are a good place to kick off your culinary adventure, since they tend to go a little easier on the *dendê*. One of the best places in the city is **Camafeu de Oxossi**, whose cooks manage to maintain the integrity of a dish without overdoing the condiments.

This restaurant, run by an Angolan family, is located on the top floor of the Mercado Modelo and is open daily for lunch, from 11 a.m. to 6 p.m.

Here you can sit out on the terrace overlooking the bay and enjoy *batidas* (fruit drinks made with *cachaça*, a pale liquor distilled from sugarcane), excellent Bahian cuisine and fruit desserts.

Speaking of desserts: The women of Bahia (called *baianas*), are among the world's great confectioners. They concoct sweets from simple ingredients such as coconut, eggs, ginger, milk, cinnamon and lemon.

Cocada, coconut candy boiled in sugar water with a pinch of ginger or lemon, is a favorite. *Ambrosia*, made with egg yolks and vanilla; tapioca; fried croquettes; and *quindim* (little sticky cakes made from eggs and coconut) are other delights. You can buy these from *baianas* in the more sophisticated parts of town, such as Rio Vermelho, and on Piatã and Itapuã beaches.

Baianas, dressed in traditional white off-the-shoulder blouses and generous full skirts, and adorned with colorful bangles and beads (called *balagandãs*), set up shop daily in thatched-roof kiosks or at improvised tables where they serve homemade sweets and the *acarajé*, a Bahian hamburger. Your visit to Bahia is not complete without trying *acarajé*.

But try it on one of the above-mentioned beaches, or at a place that has been recommended to you. That way you're sure of getting a fresh product, and not one that had been fried in last week's oil.

Acarajé is prepared from a batter made of *fradinho* beans (similar to black-eyed peas or navy beans) that have been soaked overnight and then had their skins removed. The beans are mashed together with ground shrimp and onion and plunged by the spoonful into hot *dendê* oil.

The *baiana* splits this bean dumpling to fill it with a sauce resembling *vatapá*, and with the knife in her hand poised over a jar of *malaguetas*, she will smile and ask if you want your *acarajé quente*.

Acarajé is a wonderful treat between meals, have it with a beer at one of the beach-front bars.

Among Salvador's best restaurants for Bahian food are Camafeu de Oxossi, the **Casa da Gamboa**, **Bargaço**, **Agdá**, **Praiano** and **Senac**. Good hotel restaurants are the **Quatro Ro das**, **Bahia Othon Palace** and **Pousada do Carmo**. Some restaurants offer Bahian cuisine together with folklore show. Good bets are **Solar do Unhão**, **Tenda dos Milagres** and **A Moenda**.

Vendor fries *acarajé* bean patties.

the region in the summertime, and Carnival here is famed as one of the best in the country. Indians still live in Porto Seguro, fishing and fashioning handicrafts to sell to tourists.

Inland 120 miles (200 km) from the coast is the Northeast's drought-ridden scrubland region—known as the *sertão*. This area has been the setting for a great deal of Brazil's tragedy. Periodic droughts drive peasants from the *sertão* to the coastal cities in search of food and work. When the rains return, so do the *sertanejos*.

But often the rain does as much damage as good: torrential downpours easily cause massive flooding over this parched earth, which is too dry to absorb the rainwater.

The *sertanejos* are a hardy people, loyal to their birthplace, and their land holds surprises for those willing to discover them.

A good place to start a trip to the *sertão* is in the **Recôncavo da Bahia**, the term used for the region that surrounds Salvador's All Saints Bay. The BR-324 Highway takes you to the colonial town of **Santo Amaro**, located some 50 miles (80 km) from Salvador. The town is revered by Brazilian popular music fans as the home of singers and siblings Caetano Veloso and Maria Bethânia.

Along Santo Amaro's cobblestone streets and tiny *praças*, pink-and-white colonial stucco homes alternate with splendid art deco façades in pastel colors decorated with raised geometric outlines painted in glittering white. These façades, testimony to the area's development in the early part of this century, can be seen in many small, interior towns of the Northeast.

From Santo Amaro, you can either continue along the same highway to **Feira da Santana**, or take the BR-101 Highway south along the Recôncavo to Cachoeira. Feira da Santana, 70 miles (115 km) from Salvador, is known for its cattle and leather goods fair held every Monday. Food and handicrafts are also sold every day except Sunday, open from 7 a.m. to 7 p.m., at the **Cen-**

Transparent ocean pools formed by reefs.

tro de Abastecimento fair. For handicrafts alone, visit the **Mercado de Arte Popular**, open Monday through Saturday from 7 a.m. to 6 p.m. Feira da Santana also has a handful of small hotels and many simple but reasonably good restaurants.

Colonial churches and monuments abound in **Cachoeira**, 72 miles (120 km) from Salvador. Bahiatursa, the state tourism agency, has created a walking tour that will take you past the most important buildings and historical sites in the town. Just follow the blue-and-white numbered signs.

The tour leads you to the church of **Nossa Senhora da Conceição do Monte**, an 18th-century structure with a lovely view of the Paraguaçu River and the village of São Félix on the opposite bank. This and other buildings, many dating from the 16th and 17th centuries, are usually open only in the afternoons, so schedule your visit accordingly. Don't miss the **Correios e Telégrafos**, the post office, with the best example of art deco façade in town. Cachoeira also has little souvenir shops, restaurants and inns. The **Pousada do Convento** is especially interesting: the guest rooms were once nuns' cells, and the mausoleum is now converted to a T.V. room.

Across the bridge is sleepy **São Félix**, which awakens once a week for the Sunday *samba-de-roda* contests. Men and women dance the samba in frenetic circles to a beat usually provided only by hand-clapping. The São Félix cultural center, the **Casa da Cultura Américo Simas**, is located in a fully-restored 19th-century cigar factory. The "culture" taught here ranges from plaster painting to accounting principles to weight-lifting. Aspiring Mr. Universes derive their inspiration from fading photos pinned to the wall clipped from 20-year-old American muscle men magazines.

The *recôncavo* is one of the major centers of Bahia's strong agricultural economy. Grains, sugarcane, coconuts and 95 percent of the country's cocoa output are harvested here. The town of **Camaçari** is now home to one of

Vacation homes in Morro de São Paulo, Bahia.

Brazil's three petrochemical complexes, and industry in the region is rapidly booming.

Once beyond the coastal area, the bleak landscape of the *sertão*, a region of seering heat, cactus and scrubland, fills the horizon. Roads leading west or north from the *recôncavo* head deep into the *sertão*.

This is a land that lionizes its folk heroes, including Lampião, a Robin Hood figure who was killed in 1938 after nearly two decades of riding across the *sertão*, leading a ragged band of outlaws and camp followers called *cangaceiros*.

The *sertão* also has its own music, totally different from the samba or *bossa nova* heard in other parts of Brazil. *Música sertaneja*, in fact, resembles American country music. The two-part harmony is simple and linear, the chords rarely number more than three, and the themes deal with lost love, homesickness, bad weather and death. This music is no longer restricted to the *sertão*: its appeal is universal and today, popular variety shows on Brazilian television are dedicated specially to the genre.

In the middle of Bahia, 255 miles (425 km) from Salvador, is one of Bahia's most distinctive attractions, the city of **Lençóis**. Resting in the foothills of the Sincorá Mountains, on the Diamantina Plateau, the town dates back to 1844, when diamonds were discovered in the region. Hoards of fortune seekers descended on the site, improvising shelters out of large cloth sheets, called *lençóis*, a name that has stuck until today. The diamond rush turned Lençóis into a boom town. Lençóis society wore the latest Parisian fashions and sent their children to study in France. The French government even opened a consulate in Lençóis.

Today, the consular building is one of the city's tourist attractions, as is the municipal market, an Italian-style structure that once served as the diamond miners' trading post.

Though its folklore is unmistakably Bahian, Lençóis has its own peculiarities. Its folk festivals and dances are different from those in the rest of the state. Carnival is not a major event, but the Lamentação das Almas, during the Lenten season, is. Lençóis has its own, unique version of *candomblé*, called **Jarê**. **Jarê** celebrations occur mainly in September, December and January.

The region, known as the **Chapada Diamantina**, is one of the most beautiful in the Bahian countryside. Mountain springs help keep the drought away. The Chapada is a mountain wilderness, best explored with a local guide. Orchids abound near the waterfalls, some of which can only be reached by foot. The **Glass waterfall**, seven miles (12 km) from Lençóis, is 1,300 feet (400 meters) high. It can be reached only after a four mile (seven km) walk. The Lapão Grotto, just over a half-mile (one km) long, is lined with colored sands used by artesans to fill glass bottles to make delightful patterns. A stunning view of the region can be seen from atop the **Pai Inácio mountain**, where a host of exotic plants thrive.

Besides bottles filled with colored

Left, coconut groves on Bahian coastline. Right, Christ image in Igreja Ordem Terceira do Carmo.

sand, local handicrafts include lace, crochet and earthenware. Lençóis has two good campsites and a number of simple inns, headed by the **Pousada de Lençóis**.

Due west of Lençóis, on highway 242, is the city of **Ibotirama**, on the legendary **São Francisco River**. A fisherman's paradise, Ibotirama is 400 miles (650 km) west of Salvador. Its 8,000 inhabitants raise cattle and plant cassava, corn, beans and rice, but when the drought comes, they depend on the river for food. Dozens of species of fish, including the dreaded piranha (seen as a delicacy here), can be had for the taking. Boats and canoes can be rented at the wharf.

Keen photographers can take a canoe out at the end of the day to photograph the spectacular sunset over the river's left bank. From March to October, the dry season, the water level drops, exposing sandy beaches on the river islands of **Gada Bravo** (40 minutes upstream) and **Ilha Grande** (25 minutes downstream).

From Ibotirama, the São Francisco flows northeast to the site of the **Sobradinho Dam** and its massive reservoir, one of the largest artificial lakes in the world, four times the size of Salvador's All Saints Bay. The lake is a magnet for fishing enthusiasts.

Close to the northern edge of the lake is the city of **Juazeiro**, 300 miles (500 km) northwest of Salvador on the border of Bahia and the state of Pernambuco. During the colonial period, Juazeiro was a stopover for travelers and pioneers on their way from the states north of Bahia to Salvador. A township was officially founded in 1706, when Franciscan monks built a mission, complete with chapel and monastery, in a Cariri Indian village. By the end of the 18th century, Juazeiro was the region's most important commercial and social center.

Today, the rich folk heritage of this city of 70,000 includes the legend of Lampião, who refused to invade Juazeiro because he and the town shared the same patron saint. That

Fishermen prepare nets in river boat.

saint's feast day is celebrated the first week of September, with masses and processions. Other holidays include Nossa Senhora do Rosário, the last Sunday in October or the first Sunday in November, and the Divine Holy Spirit, held in May or June, when for one day a boy is made "emperor" of Juazeiro. After a religious ceremony held at the local jail, the boy is allowed to set free the prisoner of his choice.

The **Museu Regional do São Francisco**, located at the **Praça da Imaculada Conceição**, is one of the most important museums in the state. Open daily (except Mondays), the museum displays a visual history of the São Francisco River, with steam whistles, century-old lamps, anchors and buoys, musical instruments and artifacts salvaged from villages that were submerged at the time the Sobradinho Lake was formed.

Folk art of the Juazeiro region is dominated by the *carranca*, the half-man, half-dragon wooden figurehead placed on boats to keep the devil at bay. The *carrancas*, with teeth bared in a permanent silent roar, are carved from tree trunks and painted in bright colors. You may buy them in miniature as souvenirs. The region's accepted master artisan is Xuri, who lives and works in the neighboring town of **Carnaíba**.

Sixty miles (100 km) from **Juazeiro** is the **Convento Grotto**, hidden away in the valley of the Salitre River, one of the São Francisco's most beautiful tributaries. The grotto is over three miles (five km) long and contains two mineral water lakes. It's a good and safe idea to hire a guide in **Abreus**, four miles (seven kilometers) from the site. Only experts should attempt to explore the cave on their own.

For dedicated spelunkers, there is the **Caverna do Padre**, over nine miles (15 km) in extension and considered the largest in South America. The cave, only recently explored, is located near the town of Santana on the far side of the São Francisco River, deep in the Bahian *sertão*, some 120 miles (200 km) southwest of Ibotirama.

Beaches of the northeast have fine, white sand.

NORTHEAST

For Brazilians living in the country's more prosperous southern and southeastern states, the northeast seems like a foreign country. The language accent in Portuguese is decidedly different, the slang and popular expressions are not the same and the people themselves are more mestizo and less mulatto, a different shading of Brazil's parade of colors. The food is also unusual, the culture and history don't seem to belong to the same country and the land, the barren *sertão* of northeastern legends, is more like an African desert than the explosive tropical greenery that is Brazil.

Yet the northeast is clearly Brazil and a major part of it too, covering an area of 600,000 sq miles (1 million sq km), or 12 percent of Brazil's territory. The eight states of the northeast have a combined population totalling 30 million, or 23 percent of the country's population (in terms of geographical divisions, Bahia with its population of 10.5 million is also included in the northeast region but because of its distinctive African cultural roots, not shared by the other states of the region, Bahia is as separate from its neighbors as is the south).

As the early center of Portuguese colonization, the northeast enjoyed a brief spurt of economic growth based on sugar. Its plantations were at one point the pride of the mother country and the principal source of revenue for Portugal. By the 18th century, however, the northeast was already feeling the effects of benign neglect, a malady that has continued to plague the region up to modern times.

Today, the northeast is synonymous with poverty, often the kind of wretched, starvation poverty normally associated with the poorer nations of Africa. For this reason, the northeast is a national embarrassment, especially for the proud Brazilian residents of the southeastern and southern states who see in their modern industrial parks the future of an economically developed and politically important Brazil. There is no room in this image for a region like the northeast.

The problems of the northeast can all be traced to the same source—a land which can not support its people. Except for the 90-mile (150-km) wide strip of arable land along the coastline from Bahia to Rio Grande do Norte, the region is predominantly semi-arid, a vast backlands area of stunted trees and cactus known as the *sertão*. The São Francisco River Valley, running northward from Minas Gerais to Pernambuco, is one of the few fertile areas in the entire northeast.

Subject to periodic and often tragic droughts, the northeast has seen its economic growth brought to a standstill and its population increasingly migrate to the industrial jobs of Rio de Janeiro and São Paulo. Today the region is dependent on government handouts to finance development projects.

Bad as things may seem, however, the northeast is far from a lost cause. Successful irrigation projects in Bahia have demonstrated that it is possible to reclaim the *sertão* and there is still the green coastal strip, home to most of the northeast's major cities, including Recife and Fortaleza, the region's two leading urban centers. In these two cities, and throughout the length of the northeast's coastline, nature has tried to make up for extremes of the *sertão*.

The northeast's warm-water beaches are the most beautiful in Brazil and also the most unspoiled. This has now caught the attention of not only Brazilians but also foreign visitors, turning the northeast coast into a booming center of internationl tourism.

A year-round tropical climate, white sand, blue water and groves of coconut palms along the shoreline make the northeast's beaches a South American version of the South Pacific. Add to this a distinctive regional culture, a relaxed pace of life, a still visible colonial history, a cuisine based on fresh fish, shrimp and lobster plus unbeatable prices and you have what may yet prove

Preceding pages, wattle and daub thatched roof house in the *sertão*.

to be the formula for a prosperous northeast.

The Venice of Brazil: Recife, capital of the state of Pernambuco, is a metropolis of 1.3 million. Its name comes from the Arabic word for "fortified wall," which in Portuguese has acquired the meaning of "reef." Recife's coastline, like much of the northeast, is characterized by barnacle and coral reefs running parallel to the mainland between 100 yards (90 meters) and half a mile (one km) from the shore. The waves break on the far side of the reefs making for bathers the shoal water on the near side a shallow salt-water swimming pool. On **Boa Viagem Beach** in Recife, you can wade out to the reefs at low tide and barely wet your knees.

In 1537, the Portuguese settled the coastal area of Pernambuco. A Dutch invasion a century later, under Prince Maurice of Nassau, brought a new era of art, culture and urbanization to the town. Known as the "Venice of Brazil," Recife was once a maze of swamps and isles that Maurice made habitable through the construction of canals. Today there are 39 bridges spanning the canals and rivers that separate the three main islands of Recife.

A walking tour of Recife's historical district begins at the **Praça da República** with the neo-classical **Santa Isabel Theater** (1850), one of the most beautiful buildings in the city. Visiting hours are Monday through Friday from 2 to 5 p.m. Other 19th-century buildings on this square include the **governor's mansion**, the **palace of justice** and the **law courts**, which double as the Catholic University's law school (the oldest in Brazil).

Across the street from the palace of justice is the **Capela Dourada** (Golden Chapel), which, according to legend, contains more gold than any church in Brazil except Salvador's Church of São Francisco. Built in the late 17th century by laymen of the Franciscan order, this baroque church is one of the most important examples of religious architecture in Brazil. The chapel and its adjoining sacred art museum are open week-

Jenipabu beach in Bahia.

days from 8 to 11:30 a.m. and 2 to 5 p.m. and Saturday mornings.

Eight blocks from the Santa Isabel Theater down Rua do Sol is **Casa da Cultura**, a three-story structure that served as a penitentiary for over 100 years. In 1975 it was remodeled to become Recife's largest handicraft center. The prison cells have been turned into booths displaying handmade articles ranging from leather and straw accessories to clay figurines, silk-screened tee-shirts and fruit liqueurs. The Casa da Cultura is open daily 9 a.m. to 8 p.m.; Sundays from 3 to 8 p.m.

There are a dozen museums in Recife but one stands out: the **Museu do Homen do Nordeste** (Museum of the Northeastern Man). Founded by the late Gilberto Freyre, Brazil's most famed anthropologist, the museum is a tribute to the cultural history of this unique region. The Museum of the Northeastern Man is open Tuesday, Wednesday and Friday from 11 a.m. to 5 p.m., Thursday from 8 a.m. to 5 p.m. and weekends and holidays from 1 p.m. to 5 p.m. It has bilingual guides and is located in the **Casa Forte** district, three miles (six km) from downtown, at Av. 17 de Agosto 2223.

Another fascinating stop is the **Oficina Cerâmica Francisco Brennand**, the workshop and studio of one of the northeast's best known artisans. Located in the working-class district of **Várzea**, this immense atelier was once a brick and tile factory until Francisco Brennand took over the building to use as his workshop.

Brennand is famed in Recife for his beautiful hand-painted tiles, pottery and vaguely erotic statuary, all eagerly bought up by locals and tourists. You can visit the workshop on your own, but if you call ahead for a tour you may be escorted by Mr. Brennand himself (phone: 271-2466). The studio is open on weekdays from 8 to 11 a.m. and from 2 to 5 p.m. and Saturdays from 8 to 11:30 a.m.

Most of the better restaurants and bars and nearly all the city's fine hotels are located on the **Boa Viagem beach**,

Salvador fishermen haul in their net.

Recife's most beautiful beach and also the center of its social life.

The **Praça da Boa Viagem** is the site of the weekend handicraft fair, held in the afternoon. Several excellent seafood restaurants overlook the square, a popular meeting point for tourists and residents. In the evenings, the action is concentrated along the beach and on **Av. Conselheiro Aguiar**, one block inland. The street is home to a number of small bars and sidewalk cafés featuring inexpensive drinks, nibbles and live music. Other good city beaches include **Pina**, **Piedade** and **Candeias**.

Coastal beaches: Outside Recife, the most beautiful beaches lie to the south. One of the best is **Porto de Galinhas**, in the town of **Ipojuca**, 30 miles (50 km) from downtown Recife. Surfing competitions abound in the summer months and the beach's excellent campsite, run by the state tourism board, Empetur, is shaded by coconut palms and cashew trees. The Pernambuco state governor has his summer retreat here.

To the north, the best beaches are found on **Itamaracá Island**, 25 miles (40 km) from Recife. On the way, along highway BR-101, is the historical town of **Iguaçu**, home of the second oldest church in Brazil (1535), dedicated to the twin saints of Cosme and Damião. The adjoining **Franciscan monastery** boasts the largest collection of Baroque religious paintings in the country—over 200. Halfway across the bridge to Itamaracá sits a police checkpoint, a reminder that part of the island serves as an open prison for model inmates serving time at a nearby penitentiary. Married prisoners are allowed to live with their families, and all are engaged in some form of commerce. As you start down the island road, you will see lines of booths and small shops run by prisoners selling postcards and crafts. Each man is identified with a number stencilled on his tee-shirt. The prisoners are not dangerous: they treasure their status and would do nothing to risk it.

Before you reach **Fort Orange**, built by the Dutch invaders in 1631, take the side road to **Vila Velha**, the island's first settlement, founded in 1534. Life in this charming village, tucked away in a coconut grove on the island's southern coast, revolves around the town square where a television set, Vila Velha's first and only, sits perched atop a wooden support, housed in a wooden box under lock and key.

A number of colonial buildings, crowned by the 17th-century **Nossa Senhora da Conceição Church**, line the square. A delightful surprise is the **Port o Brasilis** restaurant, open only for lunch (and not necessarily every day). The meals here are as beautiful as the artwork of its owner, Brazilian painter Luis Jasmim. He can only accommodate four tables at a time, so don't try to go in a group. Splendid beaches line most of the island's shore. Downtown Itamaracá and the historical Fort Orange district have good hotels and restaurants. Fort Orange also offers an organized campsite.

Brazil's cultural wonder: Time has stood still in Olinda, which stretches like an open-air museum across the hills overlooking Recife. The town is a treas-

Sailboat fishermen.

ure trove of Baroque art and architecture, and as such has received the title of World Cultural Monument from UNESCO. The government has taken this title seriously, and today not a single shutter can be painted without prior approval from the commission.

Legend has it that the first Portuguese emissary sent to govern the region was so enthralled by the beauty of these hills that he uttered, "*O Linda situação para uma vila*," or, "what a beautiful site for a settlement." Hence, Olinda's name.

The best way to explore Olinda is on foot. Narrow streets lined with brightly colored colonial homes, serenely beautiful churches, sidewalk cafés and shops displaying ornate signs wind through the 17th-century setting of Olinda's hills.

Starting off at the **Praça do Carmo**, site of Brazil's oldest Carmelite church (1588), continue up **Rua São Francisco** to the **São Roque Chapel and Convent**, with its Baroque frescoes depicting the life of the Virgin Mary. Turn left on **Rua Bispo Coutinho** to visit the **Olinda seminary** and the **Nossa Senhora da Graça church**—well-preserved examples of 16th-century Brazilian baroque architecture. This street opens out onto Alto da Sé, a hilltop square overlooking the Atlantic Ocean and Recife, three miles (six km) in the distance.

The **Igreja da Sé**, the first parish church in the northeast, was built at the time of Olinda's founding in 1537 and is today the Cathedral of the Archdiocese. The sacred art museum, across from the Cathedral, is housed in the **Episcopal Palace** (1696) and contains a collection of panels portraying the history of Olinda. On weekend evenings, Alto da Sé comes alive with outdoor cafes and bars.

As you turn down the **Ladeira da Misericórdia**, on your right is the **Misericórdia Church**, dating from 1540. Its richly detailed wood and gold engravings are reminiscent of the French Boucher school. The **Ribeira Market** on **Rua Bernardo Vieira de Melo** is an excellent place to buy art, and on the corner of **rua 13 de Maio** you'll find the **Contemporary Art Museum**, an 18th-century structure originally designed to house prisoners of the Inquisition. Most of Olinda's historical buildings are open daily for visits, with a two-hour lunch break, generally from noon to 2 p.m. The town has one luxury hotel and many small inns and hotels, some of them run by resident artists and intellectuals.

The *Sertão*: The famed Caruaru fair and the backwoods town of Fazenda Nova are the final destinations of an excellent day trip out of Recife along the BR 232 highway that winds up the coastal mountain range to the resort town of Gravatá and beyond. Halfway to Gravatá, near **Vitória de Santo Antão**, looming on the left, is an enormous bottle with a crayfish on the label: the symbol of the Pitú *cachaça* distillery. The distillery hardly needs its bottle-sign; its product, Brazil's distinctive sugarcane brandy, can be smelled long before the bottle appears. Tours of the plant are available and there's free tasting of the most famous brand of *cachaça* in the northeast.

From here to Gravatá it's 20 miles (32 km) of tortuous mountain road. The air becomes noticeably cooler and the vegetation sparser. **Gravatá** is where Recife's wealthy have summer homes and its fresh mountain air attracts visitors to its hotels and inns for the weekend. This is practically the last you'll see of anything green except for scrubland plants and lizards until you return to the coast.

Ideally, a visit to Fazenda Nova should be made either on a Wednesday or a Saturday. On these two days the next-door city of **Caruaru** turns into one great trading post, with rich and poor rubbing shoulders at the stalls. At one stand a wealthy Recife matron will be choosing her hand-painted earthenware tea set, while at another a toothless old man from the *sertão* will try to exchange a scraggly goat for a few sacks of rice, beans and sugar.

People from outlying villages pay the equivalent of a few cents apiece for a place in a truck or a jeep to come to Caruaru just to do their weekly shop-

Right, the Missões ruins in Rio Grande do Sul.

OLD IAN CHICO— THE SÃO FRANCISCO RIVER

The São Francisco, Brazil's third largest river, has served as one of the most important catalysts that helped to shape the country's economic and cultural development.

In the 19th century, the 1,800-mile (3,000-km) long river played a vital role in the development of the Northeast, through which its reddish-brown waters flow. It served as virtually the only major thoroughfare in the region, which lacked roads and railways.

Its role as primary mover for the northeast's people and products has given the São Francisco a place in Brazilian history and legend equivalent to that of the Mississippi River in the United States. In the last century and well into modern times, riverboats plied the São Francisco, carrying supplies to backwoods towns.

Born from a spring in the hills of Minas Gerais, the São Francisco runs through four other states: Bahia, Pernambuco, Alagoas and Sergipe. It is between these last two states that it empties into the Atlantic Ocean. The villages and settlements that began to spring up along the riverbanks during the colonial period became important trading centers and commercial outposts by the mid-19th century. Today, the river valley still serves as a farming oasis in an otherwise arid terrain.

River spirits: One of Brazil's most curious native art forms has its origins in the São Francisco. Known as Velho Chico (Old Chico) to the local inhabitants, the river is both admired and feared as a breeding ground for evil spirits. In order to protect themselves from these spirits, boatmen in the 19th century designed woodcarved busts of fiercely ugly beasts used as figureheads on their vessels. These figureheads, called *carrancas* (half-man, half-animal), are unique to Brazil.

Today only the older boatmen still use and cling to their belief in the pow-

Doing the laundry along the São Francisco river.

ers of *carrancas*. The figures have no place on modern boats except as curiosities for tourists.

Not only does their mere presence scare off evil spirits (and alligators), but they are also attributed with powers of communication; if they sense that the boat is in danger of sinking, they will emit three low moans to alert the crew.

Though much of the superstition has disappeared, the *carrancas* live on in native Brazilian folk art. Two of the best places to purchase authentic sculptures, carved from cedar wood, are Petrolina, Pernambuco (460 miles or 770 km from Recife) and Juazeiro, Bahia (300 miles or 500 km from Salvador). Smaller versions, in the form of table decorations or key chains, can be found in all the main handicraft fairs around the country. The best sculptors in the São Francisco Valley region are Mestre Guarany and his student Afrânio, as well as Sebastião Branco and Moreira do Prado.

Many of the boatmen who live in the towns along the river offer day-long cruises at low prices. Some of the towns where tourists can take boat rides include Penedo, Alagoas; Paulo Afonso, Bahia; Juazeiro, Bahia and directly across the river in Petrolina, Pernambuco (these towns lie at the spot where the river widens into lake-like proportions); Ibotirama, Bahia; Januária and Pirapora, both in Minas Gerais.

One gallant old steamboat, built in the United States in 1913 for use on the Mississippi River, makes weekly jaunts down the São Francisco. For many years the boat made the 820-mile (1,370-km) trip from Pirapora to Juazeiro, serving both tourists and the people who live along the route.

Today, the boat is exclusively for tourists. It departs from Pirapora on Sundays for a five-day trip, 190 miles (320 km) downstream to Januária. The steamboat can accommodate 24 people in 12 twin-sharing cabins equipped with bunk beds. Reservations can be made at the tour operator Unitur in Belo Horizonte, capital of Minas Gerais (phone: 031-201-7144).

Left, São Francisco river boat figurehead. Right, carved wooden figures and *carrancas*.

ping. Others come from distant states or foreign countries to purchase some of Brazil's most beautiful and artistic handicrafts.

The gaily painted figurines, first created by the late Mestre (master) Vitalino, are among the most popular items, but beware of vendors who try to charge high prices alleging that their figurines were made by the Mestre himself. Vitalino wasn't that prolific. What's on display here and in Recife's **Casa da Cultura** (where many of the same items are sold, but with less variety) was made by students of Vitalino. Caruaru's twice-weekly handicrafts fair opens at 5 in the morning and goes on until 7 p.m. and is considered the best of its kind in South America.

Fazenda Nova, a sleepy village that survived for years on what it could scratch out of the parched earth, took its place on the map in 1968 when the Pacheco family, with support from the state government, inaugurated **Nova Jerusalem**. This open-air theater, designed to resemble the Jerusalem of A.D. 33, comes to life once a year, during Holy Week, when the Passion of Christ is reenacted before tens of thousands of spectators.

The setting is perfect: huge stages, each depicting a station of the cross, rise out of the sandy soil, looming over actors and spectators. The audience follows the players (500 in all, most of them village residents) from scene to scene and they become part of the Passion Play. Audience participation is at its height when Pontius Pilate asks the crowd, "Who shall it be—the King of the Jews or Barabbas?" The actors do not speak. Instead they mouth the recorded dialogue.

Just a short walk from the theater is the no less impressive **Parque das Esculturas**, a mammoth tribute to the northeast. There you'll find 38 immense stone statues, some weighing as much as 20 metric tons (when finished, the park will have 100 statues), representing both folk heroes and everyday people of the northeast. In one section there is the washerwoman, the cotton

Recife, with its canals.

picker, the sugarcane cutter, the lace maker—all 10 to 13 feet tall (three to four meters). In another section, *Lampião*, the legendary Robin Hood of the northeast, and his beloved, Maria Bonita, stand tall.

Sector Four of the park is a collection of figures taken from Pernambuco's unique folk dances and celebrations. There you'll see the immense sea horse and his rider; the *jaraguá*, half-man, half-monster; and the *frevo* dancer.

Frevo is the centerpiece of Pernambuco's Carnival. In this Carnival there are no samba schools as in the south and no electric instruments as found in Salvador. People dance in the streets holding up parasols to help keep their balance. Groups portray *maracatu*, a typical northeastern legend mixing religious figures with circus characters. The center of Northeast Carnival is **Olinda**, whose narrow streets are packed with delirious celebrants during the four-day blowout.

The tropical northern coastline: Just over 60 miles (100 km) north of Recife on the Atlantic coast lies **João Pessoa** (population 400,000), the easternmost point of the hemisphere. The dozens of beaches in this region share two characteristics: they are protected from the pounding surf by rows of reefs and they are protected from the tropical sun by rows of coconut palms. Capital of the state of **Paraíba**, João Pessoa is the third oldest city in Brazil; it celebrated its 400th anniversary in 1985. Tropical greenery is abundant in the city: palm trees, bougainvillaeas, flamboyants and other flowering trees. The lake in **Solon de Lucena Park** downtown is ringed with majestic royal palms.

The lovely Baroque architecture exemplified by the **São Francisco church** contrasts with the futuristic design of the **Tambaú Hotel**, an immense flying saucer set halfway into the Atlantic Ocean. All guest rooms look out onto the sea. At high tide, the waves nearly reach the windowsills.

If you make a pre-dawn trek out to **Cabo Branco** (White Cape), eight miles (14 km) from the city, you can

Boa Viagem, district of Recife.

enjoy the unique sensation of being the first person in all the Americas to see the sun rise.

One of the best beaches in the region is **Praia do Poço**, just six miles (10 km) north of the Tambaú Hotel. Go there at low tide, when the ocean recedes to reveal the island of **Areia Vermelha** (Red Sand). Rows of *jangadas*, the fishermen's primitive rafts that are an integral part of the coastal scenery, are always ready to take visitors out to the island. Since there is no vegetation on Areia Vermelha, it's good to bring along a hat and sunscreen. Reflected off the sand, the sun can burn your skin in a matter of minutes. Sea algae and schools of colorful fish glitter in the transparent water.

Left, coconut water vendor on the beach. **Below**, colonial village of Olinda, with Recife in the background.

Rio Grande do Norte, which borders Paraíba to the north, lies on the northeastern curve of the continent. Its capital, **Natal**, 110 miles (185 km) from João Pessoa, is another of the region's popular beach resorts. Natal's enormous sand dunes, especially at **Genipabu beach**, 18 miles (30 km) north, attract visitors from all over the country, who rent buggies to do their beach exploring.

The name Natal is Portuguese for Christmas, the day in 1599 when the city was officially founded. Its most famous monument, the star-shaped **Forte dos Reis Magos** (Three Kings Fort) was so named because construction on it began on the Epiphany, January 6, 1599. Natal (population 510,000) has a number of good museums. The best is the **Museu Câmara Cascudo**, a catch-all of displays ranging from Amazonian Indian artifacts and fossils to sacred art and objects used in *candomblé* rites. Located at **Avenida Hermes da Fonseca 1398**, the museum is open Tuesdays through Fridays from 8 to 11 a.m. and from 2 to 4 p.m.

Some 12 miles (20 km) south of Natal is the town of **Eduardo Gomes**, home to **Barreira do Inferno**, the country's rocket launching center. It is open to the public (reservations needed) only 12 times a year, on the first Wednesday of each month. A view of Barreira can be had from nearby **Cotovelo Beach**, one of the most beautiful on the state's southern coast.

The 60-mile (100-km) drive from Natal northwards to **Touros Beach** is an adventure, following a succession of semi-deserted beaches marked by sand dunes and coconut palms. You'll pass by **Genipabu**, **Maxaranguape**, and **Ponta Gorda**, the site of **São Roque Cape**, where, on August 16, 1501, the first Portuguese expedition arrived, one year after the discovery of Brazil. Other beaches discovered include **Caraúbas**, **Maracajaú**, **Pititinga**, **Zumbi**, **Rio do Fogo**, **Peroba** and **Carnaubinha**. Fishermen's huts dot the landscape.

Touros, a town of 20,000, gets its name from the bulls that once wandered freely here. There are two small inns and a handful of bars and restaurants (the locals recommend **Castelo**) where you can enjoy shrimp roasted in garlic butter or fresh broiled lobster.

At night, go to the **Calcanhar Cape**, five miles (eight km) away, to watch the sunset and the lighting of the Touros lighthouse.

An island wildlife preserve: For years a military outpost off limits to visitors, the island of **Fernando de Noronha** has recently been opened to the public. Its population of about 1,300 is almost entirely descended from soldiers and prisoners, dating from the time the island was a correctional institute and, during the Second World War, a political prison.

Today, Fernando de Noronha serves as a wildlife preserve. It is the largest of the twenty islands in an archipelago created over 10 million years ago by a volcanic eruption. Thousands of dolphins and giant sea turtles live here and the sea is perfect for scuba diving.

The only way to visit the island is by booking with a group that departs Saturdays from Recife for a week-long stay. The package tour, sold by only one agency (Bancor, based in São Paulo), includes round-trip air fare, hotel and all meals. The one hotel on Fernando de Noronha is adapted from housing built in the 1960s by NASA for the crew at a now-defunct satellite tracking station. The food served is simple: the only local ingredient is fish. Everything else, including water, has to be flown in from the mainland.

Emerald green waters: Between Recife and Salvador, the two most important cities in the northeast, are 500 miles (840 km) of beautiful coastline. Bordering Bahia to the north is the state of **Alagoas**, whose capital, **Maceió**, is rapidly developing into a major tourist destination. With a total population of 400,000, the city, founded in 1815, grew out of a sugar plantation established there in the 18th century.

Maceió beaches are famed for the transparent bright emerald green of the water, especially at low tide on downtown **Pajuçara Beach**. Trapped between the beach and offshore sand bars, the water becomes an enormous wading pool. Local fishermen will take you out to the sand bars in their *jangadas* for the equivalent of a dollar.

The city is struggling to keep up with the flow of tourists who descend on it every summer. December is an espe-

Left, harvesting sugarcane. Right, homemade surboard in Maceió.

cially busy month, when Maceió holds its *Festival do Mar* (Festival of the Sea) at Pajuçara. It is celebrated with a giant street and beach party which includes sporting events, folk dancing and booths selling native handicrafts.

One of the most popular beaches outside the city limits is **Praia do Francês**, near the historical town of **Marechal Deodoro**, the first capital of Alagoas.

The town itself is home to some lovely examples of colonial Brazilian architecture, among which are the **Monastery of St. Francis** (1684) and the **Church of Nossa Senhora da Conceição** (1755). Originally called Alagoas, the town was renamed after its most famous son, Field Marshall Manuel Deodoro da Fonseca, the first president of Brazil (1891).

Moving south along the BR 101 highway from Maceió is the state border between **Alagoas** and **Sergipe**, delineated by the immense São Francisco River. Here, the historical town of **Penedo**, built in the 17th and 18th centuries, is a good place to stop on your way to the beaches of **Aracaju**, capital of the state of Sergipe, Brazil's smallest state. The town's Baroque and Rococo churches are its main attractions; in particular, **Nossa Senhora dos Anjos** (1759) and **Nossa Senhora da Corrente** (1764). River trips downstream to the mouth of the São Francisco at **Brejo Grande** can be arranged at the town's port. Or take the ferry across the river to **Carrapicho** to buy handmade articles of earthenware and porcelain. Food and lodgings in this region are very simple.

Festivals galore: Aracaju, 120 miles (200 km) from the border, lies in the middle of the Sergipe coastline. Founded in 1855, Aracaju (population 360,000) is noted for the beauty of its beaches and the hospitality of its people, whose festival calendar is one of the fullest in the northeast.

These festivals, nearly always based on religious holidays (though they may often appear more secular then sacred), include: Bom Jesus dos Navegantes, a maritime procession of gaily decorated

St. Peter Cleric church in Recife.

boats (January 1); St. Benedict, folk dances and mock battles (the first weekend in January); Festas Juninas—a harvest festival in honor of three saints: John, Anthony and Peter (the month of June); Expoarte, a handicraft fair (the month of July); *Iemanjá*, a religious procession in honor of the *candomblé* goddess (December 8).

Delicious seafood abounds here but Aracaju's main claim to fame is its freshwater shrimp (similar to crayfish in appearance), caught in the Sergipe River. Crab is another of this city's specialties, and for dessert, breadfruit compote or stewed coconut.

The obligatory appetite-opener is the *batida*, made from sugarcane liquor (*cachaça*) and any of a variety of local fruits (the best are mango, cashew, coconut and mangaba).

The **Santo Antonio Hill**, site of the city's founding, offers an excellent panoramic view of the region, including the Sergipe River and Atalaia Beach. Motorboats take visitors to **Santa Luzia Island**, a tropical paradise of coconut palms and sand dunes. Other good beach areas include **Abaís**, **Caueira** and **Pirambu**.

A few miles to the south of the Santo Antonio is the historical town of **São Cristóvão**, founded in 1590. One of the oldest cities in Brazil, it has a number of well-preserved colonial structures, including the **São Francisco monastery** (1693), the **Carmo Church and Convent** (1743/1766) and the **Nossa Senhora da Vitória Church** (late 17th century), as well as the **Sacred Art** and the **Sergipe Museums**.

Nearby **Laranjeiras** is another town that has preserved its heritage, notably the **Sant'Aninha Church** (1875) and the **Comendaroba Church** (1734).

Portuguese architecture: On the northern end of the region, between the Amazon basin and the *sertão*, is **São Luís**, capital of the state of **Maranhão**. Perched on the bayside of São Luís Island (population 400,000), the city was founded in 1612 by French colonists, who were driven out by the Portuguese three years later. In 1641, the

Colorful fruit stand in Salvador.

Dutch invaded the island, but like the French, were able to maintain their dominion for only three years.

The city's most striking feature is the colorful sight of brightly tiled two-story homes that line its narrow, sloping streets. These blue, yellow, white and green azulejos were originally imported from Portugal and today have become the city's trademark.

Major points of interest include the **Sé Cathedral** (1763), **Remédios Square** (1860), **Santo Antonio Chapel** (1624) and the **Maranhão Art and History Museum**, housed in an early 19th-century villa. The best beaches are **Ponta d'Areia**, with its **Santo Antonio Fort** (1691) to the north and **Calhau**, to the east. The undercurrent can be strong at these and other beaches; swimmers should inquire first before diving in.

Across São Marcos Bay, 13 miles (22 km) from São Luís, is the historical town of **Alcântara**, originally a Tupinambá Indian village, which in the 17th century became the favored retreat for the landed gentry of Maranhão.

A walking tour begins at the **Praça da Matriz** (site of the towns only hotel), and includes the **Alcântara Museum** (open daily), the **Trojan Horse Villa**, on Rua Grande, the **Nossa Senhora do Carmo Church** (1663) and the ruins of the **São Sebastião Fort**.

The boat trip to Alcântara takes 80 minutes, over choppy waters. Air taxis are also available.

The state of Ceara's coastline has 350 miles (560 km) of exuberant beaches backed by palms, sand dunes and freshwater lagoons, where state capital **Fortaleza's** favored sons spend strenuous weekends drinking beer, and cracking open crabs and lobsters while watching the *jangadas* bring the day's catch through the rollers.

In the coastal villages, where offshore breezes blow constantly, lacemakers and embroiderers still ply their trade. But tourism and the weekend homes of city dwellers are rapidly changing the coastal area. Even remote **Jericoaquara**, a paradisal fishing village cut off behind the dunes, is now

Boys prepare to slide down dune in Natal.

linked by four-wheel drive service to the city.

In gritty contrast, the hinterland of Ceará is periodically wracked by droughts that have made the state the most tenacious pocket of backwardness and poverty in the hemisphere. When the crops are ruined, and the landlords dismiss their *vaqueiros* or cowboys these *flagelados* or tortured ones pack their belongings and head for the swollen cities in search of survival.

The People: Many leave to look for a better life in the coastal cities or the factories of São Paulo, but those who remain keep alive a strong oral culture derived from the troubadours. Village poets or *repentistas* duel for hours to cap each other's rhymes with more extravagant verbal conceits. Traditions are also recorded in the *cordel* pamphlets (chapbooks) illustrated with woodcuts, and whose humorous rhymes recount deeds of the anarchic *cangaceiros* or cowboy-warriors, local politics and religious miracles.

The toughness of existence has produced a succession of religious movements rejecting any outside control, and thousands of pilgrims still do homage to Padre Cícero, who if not yet officially a saint, is undoubtedly the northeast's patron.

Early History: The first attempt to colonize the arid *sertão* of Cearã, which separated the colonies of Rio Grande and Maranhão was in 1603. The Indian-fighter Pero Coelho de Souza led a mob of Portuguese soldiers and Indian warriors on a raid for slaves. He returned again in 1606 but was driven off by a terrible drought.

Martim Soares Moreno was on the first expedition and was ordered by the governor-general of Brazil to open up the region by befriending the Indians. By 1611 he was promoted to captain of Ceará and founded Fortaleza by building the first fortress of São Paulo and a chapel by the Ceará River's mouth.

The fortress stood Soares Moreno in good stead when the French attacked that year—and so did the Tapuia and Tupinambá tribes with whom he had made friends. Fighting alongside the

Indians stark naked, his body smeared with vegetable dye, he drove off the French, but then succumbed to the charms of Iracema, a seductive Indian princess who is still the city's muse and patron saint. Brazilian literati, led by José Alencar, rediscovered Indian history in a romantic movement that flowered a century ago with the novel *O Guaraní*, and a short story retelling Iracema's story.

Dutch invaders in 1649 built the foundations to the Schoonenborch fort in what is now the center of Fortaleza. The Dutch fort is still used today as a garrison. By 1654 the Dutch were driven out by the Portuguese, who rechristened the fort Nossa Senhora de Assuncão. Fortaleza consolidated itself as a trading center for the arid cattle country of the interior.

Many of the Indian-fighting *bandeirantes* from São Paulo stayed behind, to establish immense cattle ranches that still exist today. In contrast to the sugar plantations of Pernambuco, Ceará's ranches required almost no African slaves, and the region's culture is more influenced by its Indian-Portuguese *mestiço* past than African roots.

The Seafront: Today, nothing remains of the original fortress that gave Ceará's seaside capital its name. With a population of over 1.5 million, the ungraceful city instead looks forward, as the aptly-named Praia do Futuro indicates. Here, beachfront condominiums and bars are sprouting up, pushing visitors in search of unspoilt coastline away to beaches outside the sprawling city.

Fortaleza's seafront hotels are situated on **Avenida President Kennedy**, which runs along the **Praia do Meirelles**, the city's principal meeting-place. At night the noisy bars and the broad sidewalks below the **Othon Palace Hotel** are packed with strollers drawn by the handicraft market, offering lace or embroidery, turtleshell bracelets, ceramics, leather goods, colored sand packed into bottles, and articles of more dubious origin.

Fortaleza is now a major exporter of lobster. Seafood restaurants along the

Preceding pages, fishermen haul their boat onto the beach near Fortaleza. Below, salt extracted from seawater near Fortaleza.

ocean front, such as **Trapiche** and **Peixada do Meio**, offer crab, shrimp, lobster or *peixada*—the local seafood speciality. Northeasterners round off the night at hot, crowded dance halls like **Clube do Vaqueiro**, where couples clinch for the *forró*, a lively but seductive jig accompanied by accordion music.

The city beach: The Meirelles beach stretches from **Mucuripe** near the docks, where there's a lighthouse dating from 1840, to the breakwater at **Volta de Jurema**. The central section, **Praia de Iracema**, is marked by a modern sculpture designed by Fortaleza's founder, Soares Morena, and his native princess.

One look at the trash hauled up every morning in the fishermens' nets confirms the beach is too polluted for discerning swimmers. Another deterrent are the assiduous salesmen from the *barracas* or beach bars who give the sunbather little peace.

City tour: Handicrafts for sale on the sidewalk by night are better purchased at the **Tourist Center** (Rua Senador Pompeu 550), the tastefully converted old city jail. The state tourism authority, **Emcetur**, has an information center here. There are over 200 boutiques installed in the old cells and visitors can test, try on or examine handicraft goods by daylight. Some of these items may be sold more cheaply at the **Mercado Central**, which has more than 1,000 close-packed booths near the newly-built cathedral and the central Post Office. The **Luisa Travora Handicraft Center** (Avenue Santos Dumont 1500, Aldeota) provides a third alternative.

Fortaleza's **historical** and **anthropological museum** (Av. Barão de Studart) has relics of the Indian tribes which were obliterated by the cattlemen, and of the evolution of the city. It also shows the remains of a 1967 plane crash that killed President Humberto Castelo Branco, the army officer who took power after the 1964 coup. Many Brazilians remain convinced his death was not an accident; across the street his remains are housed in a modern mausoleum. A visit to the **José Alencar Theatre**, whose cast-iron structure was imported from Britain in 1910, or a boat ride across the harbor to see the sunset, completes a city tour.

The southeastern beaches: Fortaleza's real *forte* is its selection of out-of-town beaches. Heading southeastward past the **Praia do Futuro**, the first halt is the still-urban and sophisticated resort of **Porto das Dunas**.

A 17-mile (27-km) drive from Fortaleza is **Aquiraz**, which in the 17th century was Ceará's first capital, and contains the ruins of a Jesuit mission. There's an 18th-century church with the image of São José do Ribamar, the state's patron saint. The historic church ruins may be reached by way of a rum distillery.

Close by, **Prainha** offers the closest authentic slice of beach to the city. There are several seafood restaurants and bars stretching across the sand.

The local fishermen here will take tourists for *jangada* rides. The flat rafts with lateen sails are as decked with advertising as racing cars. In July, pro-

"Maternity," wood carving by R.P. Athyde in Ceará Museum of Folk Art and Culture, Fortaleza.

fessionals compete in the "Dragon of the Sea" regatta.

Iguape is famous for its lacemakers (ask to look at the Renaissance pattern) and for the artificially-colored sands packed into bottles which depict landscapes. The eroded sandstone cliffs of **Morro Branco**, 53 miles (85 km) from Fortaleza, provide the raw material for these craftsmen while the less-crowded beach here provides a welcome relief from Fortaleza's urban sprawl. During the 1970s the lunar dunescape of **Canoa Quebrada**, 105 miles (170 km) south of Fortaleza, attracted a lingering generation of hippies from Brazil and abroad. They settled down in the fish-ermen's primitive houses, blending natural fruit juices, *forró* and free love with a village lifestyle that had changed little in 300 years. Development and its accompanying ills have inevitably followed the influx. Fortunately, Canoa Quebrada's broad expanse of beach, the dunes behind and its crumbling red sandstone cliffs still retain something of the original magic.

The Northwestern beaches: To the northwest of Fortaleza, the beaches begin at **Barra do Ceará**—the river's mouth where the city was established—but **Cumbuco** is the first port of call, 15 miles (24 km) from the city. The attractions are its surfing beach and the dunes stretching inland as far back as the black surface of the **Parnamirim** freshwater lagoon.

At the beach bars, rides are available on the sailing rafts that regularly set out through the surf. Onshore, dune-buggy owners offer exhilarating rides up to the lagoon, where for a small tip village kids teach visitors to slither on sand "skateboards" down the dunes and into the cool water.

There is no coastal road running north, but 53 miles (85 km) from the city is **Paracuru**, reached inland on the BR 222 federal highway. A lively community that enjoys a week-long carnival and regular surf or sailing regattas, the town is a favorite weekend beach spot. A few miles further on is the less sophisticated **Lagoinha**, where rooms

Pilgrims touch image of Padre Cicero.

are available to rent in local village houses.

An intersection on the highway leading from BR 222 to Paracuru leads to **Trairi**, where the beaches of **Freixeiras, Guajiru** and **Mundáu** are reached.

Icarai is 87 miles (140 km) from Fortaleza, via the BR 222 intersection leading past **Itapipoca**, behind the Mundáu dunes and across the Trairi River. Beaches here include the **Praia do Pesqueiro**, **Praia do Inferno** and **Praia da Baleia.**

Acaraú, 144 miles (231 km) from Fortaleza, is one of the most popular beach centers. **Almofala** has a fine unspoilt beach and an early 18th-century church which for years was covered by shifting sands.

The finest of Ceará's beaches is **Jericoaquara**, which is the picture postcard of Brazil's northeast. One hopes it will stay that way because an alliance of ecologists and local fishermen has succeeded in banning new construction or tourist development. The pure horizontals of sea, dunes and sky are cut by coconut palms, and in the village the fishing folk are content without electric lights or motorcars. The preservation effort also means that rare and endangered species are protected in the dunes and lagoons. Sea turtles come up the beach to lay their eggs, and the village has taken on much of the mystique that Canoa Quebrada enjoyed a decade ago, its simplicity attracting foreigners and Brazilians from the south. Accommodation means slinging a hammock and nightlife, the local *forró* .

Reaching Jericoacoara, about 150 miles (240 km) from Fortaleza, is difficult because it is still cut off by the dunes. The trip can be made by bus and then four-wheel drive jeep. **Casa do Turismo** runs short excursions using a four-wheel drive bus that leaves the city early every Tuesday, Thursday and Saturday morning.

The Arid interior: Heading southward into Ceará's arid interior or *sertão*, it seems impossible that the scrubland or *caatinga* could sustain human life during the periods of drought, when locals refer to blue skies as "terrible weather" and clouds on the horizon as signalling "a lovely day." Yet almost one third of Ceará's 6 million people scratch out a living here, with the help of irrigation systems like the one on the huge Oros reservoir.

Icó, 226 miles (362 km) south of Fortaleza on the BR 116 highway, is an interesting historical monument. It is also the turnoff for **Orós**, the northeast's biggest reservoir, built in the 1950s, and has a hotel and local handicraft center. Icó's town hall and other buildings date from the 18th century, and its theater from 1860.

Juazeiro do Norte, 300 miles (480 km) south of Fortaleza and reachable by plane, is a religious center where pilgrims come to make their promises to Padre Cícero Romão Batista, who in 1889 wrought a miracle that earned him excommunication from the Catholic Church in 1894. Padre Cícero then consolidated his temporal powers and in 1911 became a political leader whose rabble army of *cangaceiros* defeated federal troops sent to arrest him. He died in 1934 but the Vatican has yet to pronounce his beatitude.

Nevertheless, pilgrims or *romeiros* come to visit the 75-foot (25 meter) high statue of the austere Padre Cícero with his characteristic hat and stick. The devotional tour begins in the **Capela de Socorro** where he lies buried, and passes through churches and the **House of Miracles**. High points in Juazeiro's devotional year are July 1 and November 20.

The **Cariri Valley**'s other townships are **Crato**, noted for its university, museums and active cultural life, and **Barbalho**, whose hot springs offer more secular pleasures.

The hilly **Chapada do Araripe**, due west of Juazeiro, 2000 feet (700 meters) above sea level, provides welcome relief with waterfalls and natural pools inside a national park.

Due west of Fortaleza, in the Ibiapaba hills, is the **Ubajara National Park**, with caves containing interesting stalagmite formations and a cable car to take visitors up to waterfalls and green vegetation.

The Amazon

Though it is not the longest, there is no rival to the claim that the Amazon is the world's greatest river. At the end of a 4,000 mile (6,700 km) journey that begins at the Andean Lake Lauricocha, near the Pacific Ocean, the river's 200 mile (330 km) wide mouth discharges a quarter of all the world's fresh water into the Atlantic, coloring the ocean over 60 miles (100 km) from the shore. Amazonia is a vast greenhouse of global evolution; a tenth of the world's 10 million species of living things breed there—2,500 kinds of fish, 50,000 higher plant species and untold numbers of insects. A river of 1,000 tributaries, draining an immense basin that covers 4.7 million sq miles (7.9 million sq km) and sprawls across eight Latin nations, the Amazon dominates Brazil, yet Brazilians are only just beginning to discover it.

Two million years ago the river was born. The waters of a huge Amazonian sea imprisoned by the Andes burst their way eastward through the Obidos narrows near modern Santarém, chiselling their way along the dividing line between the two ancient geological "shields" that form Brazil's surface. Tributaries to the north and south draining the flat, ancient soils of the former seabed are poor in nutrients and organic life. These are the "black" rivers like the Rio Negro. The **Marañón**, which carries the melted snow and rich sediment off the geologically-young Andes, becomes the **Solimões** at the Brazilian border—a "white" river. These nutrients enrich the 30- mile (50- km) wide *varzea* or flood-plain of the lower Amazon, which supported an indigenous population of about four million.

Amerigo Vespucci, an engaging Italian adventurer much given to exaggeration, and after whom the American continents were named, claimed to have sailed up the Amazon in 1499. He was followed a year later by the Spaniard Vicente Pinzon, but the credit for the first voyage of discovery down the river goes to Francisco de Orellana. He set out by boat in 1542 on a short reconnaissance to find some food for Gonzalo Pizarro, the conquistador of Peru who was hunting for El Dorado. For six months his boat was swept downriver through "the excellent land and dominion of the Amazons," where his startled scribe Friar Carvajal had a vision of classical antiquity that gave the river its name: bare-breasted warrior women "doing as much fighting as ten Indian men."

Preceding pages, young Carajás Indian of the Amazon. **Left**, highway cuts through Amazon forest.

Amazonia begin to excite scientific interest all over the world a century after its discovery, when in 1641 the Spanish Jesuit Cristóbal de Acuña published *A New Discovery of the Great River of the Amazons,* carefully recording Indian customs, farming methods and herbal medicine and concluding that—mosquitoes apart—it was "one vast paradise."

Bedrock scientific research about the Amazon was carried out by a trio of long-suffering English collectors led by Alfred Russell Wallace, whose work on the diversity of Amazonian flora and fauna influenced Darwin's *Origin of the Species*. Together with Henry Walter Bates and Richard Spruce, he set out in 1848 to discover over 15,000 species new to science.

Another Englishman used his botanical skills to provoke the region's economic undoing when he broke Brazil's extravagant rubber monopoly. For a modest fee of 1,000 pounds, adventurer Henry Wickham in 1876 loaded 70,000 seeds of *hevea brasiliensis* aboard a chartered steamer and slipped them past Brazilian customs in Belém, pretending they were rare plant samples for Queen Victoria. Weeks later the seedlings sprouted under glass in London's Kew Gardens; by 1912 they had grown into Malaya's ordered, disease-free rubber plantations and Brazil's rubber boom went forever bust.

With its public parks, wrought-iron bandstands, Beaux Arts buildings and mango tree-lined avenues, **Belém** retains more elegance of the bygone rubber era than its rival Manaus. During its "*belle epoque*" French visitors compared the city favorably with Marseilles or Bordeaux. A city of a million set on the river's southern bank just one degree south of the Equator and 90 miles (145 km) from the open sea, Belém is the gateway to the Amazon.

Between November and April it rains constantly, but a breeze generally makes the humid climate tolerable. Belém is the capital of **Pará**, a state covering almost the area of Western Europe. It was properly linked to southern Brazil by the **Belém-Brasília Highway** only in 1960, and is still chiefly a port city for export of tropical hardwoods, Brazil nuts, jute and other primary products.

A tour of the old city, whose narrow streets still contain old houses fronted with Portuguese tiles, begins at the **Forte Castelo**, the nucleus of the original settlement of **Santa Maria do Belém do Grão Pará**. The Fortress also contains the **Circulo Militar** restaurant, which serves regional specialties including the powerful *pato no tucupi*—duck stewed with poisonous manioc leaves. The Cathedral church of **Nossa Senhora da Graça**, opposite the fort, contains artworks in Carrara Marble and paintings by the Italian artist De Angelis. The 18th-century **Santo Alexandre church** is now a museum of religious art.

Belém's most important church is the **Nazaré Basilica**, built in 1909, with impressive marble work and stained glass. It is the center of the **Cirio de Nazaré** religious procession that was instituted by the Jesuits as a means of catechizing Indians, and still draws over a million faithful on the second Sunday of every October—a period for which visitors need to make advance hotel reservations. The venerated image of the Virgin was found in the forest near Belém in 1700.

Close to the customs house on **Praça Kennedy** the state tourism authority, **Paratur**, operates a visitor center with a small zoo, containing toucans, parrots and waterbirds. Inside are displays of local pottery.

If less famous than the Teatro Ama-

Life along the Amazon River.

zonas in Manaus, Belém's theater, built in 1874, rivals it in elegance. The **Teatro da Paz** is close to the **Praça da República**, the **Hilton Hotel** and **Avenida Presidente Vargas**, the main shopping street leading down to the port. The restored theater is set in a green area complete with bandstand and the **Bar do parque**—an agreeable stop for a *Cerpa*, the city's local beer.

The **Ver-O-Peso**, Belém's vast dockside market, is a store window of Amazonia's prodigious variety of fish and tropical fruit. Fishing boats bring in their catches, which may include 200-pound (90-kilogram) monsters. There are few souvenirs to buy inside the two food pavilions, but alongside is a fascinating covered area of booths selling herbal medicines and charms used in Afro-Brazilian *umbanda* rituals. Seahorses, armadillo's tails, the sex organs of freshwater dolphins, tortoise shells and tiny pineapples used for birth control are piled up beside herbs which locals swear by for rheumatism and heart problems. On sale are perfumes guaranteed to attract men, women, money and good fortune.

The **Emílio Goeldi Museum**, on Av. Magalhães Barata, includes a fine zoological garden with manatees, jaguars and forest birds. The museum, founded in 1866, has a superb anthropological collection and its staff continue to produce temporary exhibitions about Amazon life that are of international standard. Also worth a visit are the **Bosque Gardens** (open from 8 to 11 a.m. and 2 to 5 p.m.), which enclose a preserved area of almost-natural forest and a small zoo.

Paratur runs a **Handicraft Fair—Feira do Artesanato**, useful for souvenirs. **Icoaraci**, less than an hour from the city, is a center for modern ceramic ware that follows the pre-Columbian Indian maroajara pottery tradition whose elaborate motifs are believed to have been borrowed from Inca culture.

Several tour agencies, including **Ciatur** and **Neytur**, operate one-day river trips which usually go up the

Left, river reflects jungle vegetation. Right, a golden sunset.

Guajará river to visit some well-prepared *caboclo* dwellings. A better option is the **Acará Lodge**, two hours up the river, which offers two-day stays in very modest accommodations.

Marajó Island, at the river's open mouth, is larger than Switzerland yet has a population of 200,000 people—far outnumbered by the herds of buffalo that wallow in the flat, swampy northern part. It has fine beaches and rare traces of colonial history.

Every night a government-owned ENASA ferryboat makes the five-hour trip to **Soure** on the island's eastern tip. Air taxis from the Belém Aeroclub charge about US$50 per person for the 40-minute trip. The **Marajoara Hotel** in Soure can arrange trips to the **Praia do Pesqueiro** and **Araruna beaches** washed by water that is part river, part ocean, or the **Santa Caterina buffalo ranch**. A ferry crosses the river to **Salvaterra**, where a battered taxi continues to **Joanes**. First called the Ilha Grande do Joanes, Marajó was settled in 1617 by Capuchin monks who built a stone church here in 1665, the ruins survive by the lighthouse. At nearby **Monserrat** there is another stone-built church with baroque images.

Bank housed in old building in Manaus.

From Soure, day trips can be arranged to the **Providencia buffalo farm**. But buffalo ranches in the island's interior, reachable only by boat, horse or tractor, have much more wildlife than the populated coastal region. **Fazendas Laranjeira** and **Tapeira** both have private museums containing archaeological relics from ancient Indian sites.

Macapá, at the Amazon's northern mouth, stands on the equator, a popular spot where visitors can pose for photographs straddling the marker line or *marca zero*. It has a large fort built of Lisbon brick by the Portuguese in 1764 and a thriving economy based on shrimp fishing and manganese mining. Planes leave Macapá for **Monte Dourado** and the **Jari Project**, U.S. billionaire Daniel K. Ludwig's ill-fated attempt to substitute the natural forest with plantations to produce pulp and paper on a massive scale.

The southeastern Amazon occupies a special place in the perennial dreams of economic greatness that haunt Brasília's government planners—dreams that have become nightmares for conservationists. Development mega-projects that have consumed billions of dollars sprout across the region under the umbrella of the Carajás project. Conceived around an 18 billion ton iron-ore mine in the Carajás hills some 340 miles (550 km) south of Belém, Brazil's "moonshot" in the Amazon already includes the Tucuruí hydroelectric dam, a 560 mile (890 km) railroad through the forest, an immense aluminium smelter and deepwater port complex—and plans for cities, highways, steelworks, agribusinesses and colonization programs.

Those interested in Brazil's development bravura can reach both Tucuruí and the Carajás mine at **Serra Norte** by plane from Belém. More primitive mining takes place at **Serra Pelada**—the naked mountain—which resembles a Babylonian nightmare produced by D.W. Griffith. During the dry season, an antlike army of 60,000 gold prospectors in search of fortune dig, drag and sift some 25 tons of gold from an immense man-made crater.

Santarém stands exactly halfway between Belém and Manaus, at the junction of the **Tapajós** and **Solimões** rivers. Founded in 1661 as a fort to keep foreign interests out of the mid-Amazon before the arrival of the Portuguese, Santarém was the center of a thriving Indian culture. Today Santarém is a center for gold-prospecting *garimpeiros* and lumber companies.

It is well worth a stopover to take on the flavor of this mid-Amazon town, which has a comfortable **Tropical Hotel** operated by the Varig airline. Riverboats bring in their produce for the busy daily market along the waterfront. Most one-day boat tours travel up the Tapajós as far as **Alter do Chão**, site of the original settlement and a superb beach some 23 miles (38 km) from Santarém. The white sand beach forms a long curving spit that almost closes the **Lago Verde** lagoon off from the river. Also reachable by car, the village has a simple but satisfying fish restaurant, a *pousada* and a number of weekend homes for Santarém's wealthy. The dark clear water and wide beaches of the Tapajós during the dry season make for perfect swimming or fishing for the sporty tucunaré.

Manaus is an oddity, an urban extravagance that turns its back on the rich surrounding forest and survives instead on federal subsidies, and on its exotic past—and, increasingly, on tourism. Its moving spirit has always been quick riches. Once it had art nouveau grandeur; today its image is that of a tawdry electronics bazaar justified by its status as a free port. The port city's strategic position, close to the point where the three greatest tributaries form the Amazon river, means it has long been the collecting-point for forest produce from a vast area.

The force that propelled Manaus to become one of the world's most glamorous cities was rubber, whose properties had been discovered by the Omagua

Medicinal plants and extracts for sale at street market.

Indians and which fascinated French travelers in the 18th century. Charles Goodyear's 1844 discovery of vulcanization and Dunlop's 1888 invention of the pneumatic tire caused a commercial explosion: as the price of rubber soared, production rose from 156 metric tons in 1830 to 21,000 metric tons in 1897. The cities were emptied of labor and thousands migrated from the northeast to become rubber tappers or *seringeiros*.

Such wealth flowed into the city that rubber men dispatched their dirty laundry to Paris for washing, drank Vichy water when they tired of drinking champagne—or when their horses did. Their mansions were littered with unused grand pianos and crystal chandeliers, while eggs cost a dollar each. Manaus had electricity and the continent's first tramway. British engineers in 1906 built the **Customs House** out of Scottish bricks in the style of imperial India, and to accommodate the Rio Negro's 40-foot (14-meter) rise and fall they assembled foreign-made sections of the floating dock.

The Teatro Amazonas was begun in 1881, after numerous complaints from European touring companies forced to play in smaller halls. Invited to sing there during a cholera scare, the Italian singer Caruso returned to Europe without disembarking. After the inaugural performance of *La Gioconda* there are scant records of other operas before the boom collapsed. The theater's columns and banisters are of English cast-iron, the stage curtains were painted in France, which supplied the chandeliers and mirrors. The marble came from Italy and the porcelain from Venice. Decorative motifs show the meeting of the waters and scenes from romantic literature about the Indians.

A monumental sculpture outside depicts trading vessels, presumably laden with rubber, departing for the four continents. The theater has been restored several times and the huge dome of yellow and green tiles refurbished. It is open Tuesday to Saturday from 11 a.m. to 5 p.m. Also worth taking a look is the wedding cake-like **Palácio Rio Negro**, a former rubber palace that is now seat of the state government, on **Av. Sete de Setembro**.

Though its rubber industry enjoyed a brief wartime recovery, Manaus was not rescued from lingering decay until 1967, when it was declared a free trade zone. To take advantage of tax breaks, hundreds of factories have installed themselves in the industrial zone. **A Zona Franca** selling electronic consumer goods has also sprung up in the city center. Prices will hardly excite foreigners. The narrow streets of the port district are lined with stores selling goods to those who live on outlying tributaries. There is busy trade in some of the 1,500 different varieties of river fish and, in a separate section, Indian artifacts, basketware, *umbanda* items and *guarana*—a popular ginseng-like herbal energy preparation.

The **Salesian Indian Museum**, **Rua Duque De Caxias**, and the **Northern Man Museum**, **Av. Sete de Setembro**, give a good idea of traditional lifestyles. A 20-minute ride out of the city along the **Estrada Ponta Negra** leads to

Catching up on news at the butcher shop.

CIGS, the army's jungle warfare training school. There is an excellent zoo stocked with jaguars, constrictors and other animals recently captured in the forest by trainee officers (Open Monday-Saturday 8 a.m. - 5 p.m.) INPA, the **National Amazonian Research Institute** carries out advanced studies with the help of many top foreign scientists. The aquatic mammals division has a collection of manatees, freshwater dolphins and others (about 25 minutes by taxi along the **Estrada do Aleixo**, open Monday to Friday from 8 a.m. to noon and from 2 to 6 p.m.). INPA scientists can also provide information for dedicated ecologists wishing to visit a long-term survey into deforestation close to the city, being carried out by the World Wildlife Fund.

The **Tropical Hotel**, situated on the **Praia da Ponta Negra**, 12 miles (20 km) outside the city, has become the social center of Manaus. Its architecture is hardly tropical, but the gardens, the parrots, the circular swimming pool and above all the excellent swimming in the Rio Negro during the low-water season, make it a major attraction in a city starved for options. The hotel operates daily boat tours five miles (nine km) up the Rio Negro to **Lago Salvador** and the **Guedes Igarapé** (a forest backwater or creek). Visitors may fish, swim, walk the forest paths and eat at a floating restaurant which belongs to the hotel. An overnight stay at the lake allows visitors time to travel up the Igarapé by motorized canoe and go flashlighting for alligators.

Several tour companies operate day-long river trips that follow a well-beaten track toward the **January Lake** ecological park to examine the Victoria Regia giant waterlilies (best in April-September). The boats then turn toward the *encontro das aguas*—the confluence of the Rio Negro and Solimões just below Manaus where the banks are some five miles (eight km) apart. The dark, warm clear waters of the Negro collide with the silty Solimões and without mixing run side-by-side for 12 miles (20 km) in a great churning pat-

Mermaid adorns façade of bar.

RIVERBOAT

The River trip from **Belém** to **Manaus**—or vice versa— can be made comfortably aboard two passenger cruisers or catamarans operated by the government ENASA line. Both ships accommodate 138 passengers in double or four berth cabins and offer reasonable comfort including a swimming pool, nightclub, restaurant and observation deck. Ships leave Belém at night, passing above Marajó and into the clustered islands of the river the following morning. On the third day, after passing close to the forested shores, the ship enters the **Tapajós River** to pause for passengers to bathe, explore beaches and visit **Santarém**. Before arriving in Manaus, the ship passes the **Rio Negro** and the **Rio Solimões**. The reverse five-day journey includes a stop at **Souré**, on **Marajó Island**. A cabin for two costs about US$570, but passengers on shorter trips may disembark at Santarém. The same trip can be made by a non-tourist ENASA boat for about US$100, first class.

Discovering the true pace of the Amazon means traveling by smaller motor launches or *gaiolas*, that operate regular lines between river towns. The three-decker passenger-cum-cargo launches, seldom more than 75-foot (25-meters) long, are built neither for comfort nor speed.

Gaiola means birdcage—a fitting term for the area between decks where passengers sling their hammocks above one another. Larger boats have first class accommodation in the form of small, airless cabins, but they offer more deckspace and better food. The price difference is small, and passengers who opt for second class must arrive early to stake out space and avoid spending the voyage sandwiched between blaring radios, swinging above a hold filled with unsavory-smelling dried pirarucu fish.

Eating on board is a dreary business—passengers are regaled twice

Amazon River passenger boats.

daily with tasteless plates of rice, beans, spaghetti and manioc flour, topped with bony fish or gristly meat. Drinking water comes from the river, so most travelers are obliged to bring their supply in bottles, along with fruits and biscuits. Visitors to the Amazon are advised to get yellow fever injections (free at Brazilian airports) but the threat of malaria is often exaggerated.

Delays are frequent because of fuel shortages, breakdowns and navigation difficulties caused by shifting channels. Boats have noisy engines that often break down, while sailing at night is made dangerous by huge submerged treetrunks that occasionally split hulls with fatal results. Small trading vessels that obey no fixed schedule but may accept a few passengers are the best—they pause at river inlets to buy cheeses, dried fish or turtles. The smallest launches—which Amazonians treat almost like bus or horse transport—are called *montarias*, and can easily be hired for a few hours. Canoes with outboard motors can be hired in Manaus for short trips up the Rio Negro, but are much costlier than slower diesel craft. Boats heading upstream stick closer to the shoreline to avoid the current, therefore providing better views of flora and fauna on the banks. Downstream, passengers may only see the forest as a green line on the horizon.

Boats leave from the crowded *cais do porto* near the municipal market in Manaus nightly for Santarém (about US$35, for two-and-a-half-days), and once a week for Belém (ENASA first class about US$95, for five days). Upstream on the Solimões, past **Teffé** (three days, US$25) to **Tabatinga** and Peru, is a US$40, six to 14 day run. From Belém, ENASA car ferries leave for Manaus three times a month, about US$100 for first class.

More wearying journeys such as the four-day 500 mile (800 km) descent of the **Rio Madeira** from **Porto Velho** to Manaus, during which passengers change boats at Manicoré, provide natural opportunities for stopping. But beware: the next boat may be full.

Accommodations on board a river boat.

tern through which the boat passes. Some trips pause at the island of **Terra Nova**, where riverine dwellers show their rubber-tapping skills—and their souvenirs. Leading operators are **Amazon Explorers** and **Selvatur**, both charging about $35 with lunch.

Among jungle lodges found here, the most luxurious is the **Pousada dos Guanavenas** on **Silves Island**, reached after a five hour bus and boatride—or by plane from Manaus. Designed as an immense but comfortable Indian hut, it has a panoramic view over the **Canacari Lake**, near **Itacoatiara**. With 15 air-conditioned rooms, swimming pool and telephone link, the *pousada* is staffed by Indians and offers two, four, or six night packages with boat rides for fishing and alligator spotting. A three night stay for two people costs about US$680.

The **Amazon Lodge**, 50 miles (80 kms) south of Manaus on the **Mamori River**, near the town of **Careiro**, offers the visitor something more modest. A three-day trip allows visitors to fish for piranha, watch birds leaving their roosts at sunrise and, during the March-August highwater season, explore the *igapos* or flooded woodland by canoe.

Also to the south of the Solimões is the **Janauaca Jungle Lodge**, set on a placid but reportedly mosquito-angry lake. Because of its muddy waters and insect population, the Solimões is less of a tourist river than the Negro.

The **Anavilhanas Archipelogo**, on the Rio Negro, is one of the most attractive options for a longer river cruise. **Ecological Safari** offers a six-night trip (US$805 per person or US$435 for three nights) aboard a comfortable French-owned boat with trained naturalist guides and video presentations. The journey through the 400 islands to **Nova Airao** allows time for birdwatching and fishing. Also included is a trip up the **Apuau** tributary. Longer trips on the Solimões, Negro and Branco rivers can also be arranged. A briefer glimpse of the archipelago is offered on a three-day **Expeditours** trip.

But a better and cheaper option is to form a small group and hire a guide to plan a trip off the beaten track: Ruben Silva at **Wagon Lits Tur**, **Av. Eduardo Ribeiro**, arranges canoe trips for those willing to sling their hammocks in river-dwellers' huts. Portuguese speakers can arrange with the IBDF forestry institute in Manaus a trip to the **Jaú National Park**, close to Novo Airão. Due north of **São Gabriel de Cachoeira**, reachable by boat or plane from Manaus, is the **Pico de Neblina**, at 6,630 ft (3,014 m) Brazil's highest mountain.

Those with real time to spare can ride the Solimões as far as **Letícia** on the Peru-Columbian border, where it becomes the **Marañón River**. Launches from Manaus—subject to frequent delays—take about eight days and first class fare is around US$50. The shores are lined with small homesteads, where *caboclos* scratch a living from a few cultivated acres, and fish and sell palm-hearts or turtles to passing boats.

The **Rio Branco** drains Brazil's northernmost territory of **Roraima**, whose dense forests and unmapped borders divide the Amazon and Orinoco river basins. Roraima is the last truly undiscovered fragment of Latin America and by legend the location of the mythical El Dorado. The mysterious, flat-topped **Mount Roraima** is believed to have inspired Sir Arthur Conan Doyle's novel *The Lost World*.

Until a highway was built in 1977 from Manaus, at considerable loss of life from hostile Indian tribes, its capital **Boa Vista**, was isolated from Brazil. The lawless territory is still administered from Brasília, where travelers determined to visit the territory's Indian reserves must seek permission. The 18,000-strong Yanomami Indian tribe—the continent's largest and least acculturated—live straddling the Brazil-Venezuela border in the Parima mountains—a region of jagged, forested peaks and chasms that even US aviation maps warn is largely unknown. The Indians' misfortune is also similar to a modern El Dorado, with rare minerals that businessmen and *garimpeiros* are now determined to exploit, bringing their "progress" to Brazil's last frontier.

Right, Manaus Opera House.

PEPSI

EAT, DRINK AND BE MERRY

Brazilians are among the world's most musical, fun-loving people. This image has for decades drawn tourists; the first wave hit after Fred Astaire and Ginger Rogers danced *The Carioca* in a breezy 1933 Hollywood musical titled *Flying Down to Rio*.

Brazil's many attractions, including Carnival, "The Biggest Party on Earth," are deeply rooted in the nation's ethnic and racial heritage. Carnival's roots are European, although experts disagree over the origin of the word. According to one school of thought, "Carnival" comes from the Latin expression *Carrum Novalis,* a Roman festival float. Another says it comes from the Italian *Carne Vale*, "good-bye to meat," since Carnival marks the last days before Lenten abstinence.

The Romans had more than 100 festivals during their year, of which the most famous was the December *Saturnalia*, marked by the temporary disappearance of class distinctions. Slaves and masters dined at the same table, drank the same wine and slept with the same women.

Carnival disappeared during the Dark Ages. When it came back, it was better than ever. Again, it was with the sexual license and the inversion of social roles that typified Carnival.

In Brazil, pre-Lenten observances have existed since colonial days. But, until the 20th century, they emphasized pranksterism rather than celebration. This aspect of Carnival was called *entrudo* and featured stink bombs, water balloons and even arson.

Entrudo was so bad that decent citizens spent Carnival locked in their homes. One of those who didn't was architect Grandjean-de Montigny, who died of pneumonia in 1850 after being doused with water balloons during Carnival.

It wasn't until the early 1900s that an enforcement campaign finally ended *entrudo*. The indiscriminate tossing of confetti and streamers, still a part of Carnival, is a throwback to the days of violence against strangers.

The fancy dress ball was part of European Carnival as early as the 18th century. Paris and Venice had the best masked Carnival balls. Masked balls hit Rio in 1840 with a *chic* event at the Hotel Itália on Praça Tiradentes, but that ball lost money and it wasn't until 1846 that a second one was held, this time in the uppercrust district of São Cristóvão. The balls continued and royalty was added to the guest lists. Emperor Pedro II, known throughout his 58-year reign as a dedicated reveler, was pushed into a fountain at one São Cristóvão ball in the 1850s.

The first modern Carnival ball was the High Life, at a Copacabana hotel in 1908; guests danced the polka and Viennese waltzes. The formal City Ball was inaugurated in 1932 at the Teatro Municipal. By then there were a hundred fancy dress balls in Rio at Carnival time.

For Rio's working class, music, dance and drink were, and still are, the main Carnival diversions. A Portuguese immigrant, José Nogueira Paredes (nicknamed Zé Pereira), is credited with originating the first Carnival club. One of his ideas was to get everybody in the club to play the same kind of drum, creating a powerful, unified sound. This technique became the basis for the modern samba school *bateria* or percussion section.

The working and middle class clubs were called *blocos*, *ranchos* or *cordões*, and played European-origin ballads known as *choros*, some of which are still popular. In the 19th century, such clubs often had charitable or, as in the case of the Clube dos Socialistas, frank political aims, and were active in the off-season. Many of these predominantly white clubs still exist, including the Clube dos Democráticos, which annually kicks off the downtown street Carnival with a Friday night parade.

Carnival parade: One of the main contributions of the clubs to modern Carnival was the parade, complete with elaborate costumes, wheeled floats and appropriate musical accompaniment. Parade themes stressed Bible stories, mythology and literature. The first parade was organized in 1855 by a group

Preceding pages: "Amazons" samba atop Carnival float; Rio men dolled up for Carnival capers; New Year's fireworks in Copacabana. Left, the Red and Black ball.

grandly named *O Congresso das Sumidades Carnavalescas*. They marched before an elite audience which included the emperor. The presentation saw overdressed Cossacks and tableaux depicting scenes from French history and *Don Quixote*. By 1900 the annual downtown parade of such groups, called *Grandes Sociedades*, had become the highlight of Carnival.

Late in the 19th century, blacks became involved in Carnival for the first time. This was partly due to the northeast drought of 1877, which sent many freed slaves to Rio. They brought their music and dance traditions to Carnival in the 1890s.

Rio's Carnival celebration: Today's celebration of Carnival in Rio has three main features: frenzied street events, traditional club balls and the samba parade.

Street events begin on Carnival Friday, when Rio's mayor, during a hectic ceremony on downtown Avenida Rio Branco, the official headquarters of street Carnival, delivers an oversized "Key to the City" to Rei Momo. Momo is the rolly-polly King, symbol of polygamy and indulgence, who presides over Rio until Ash Wednesday.

Street Carnival draws thousands of revelers, many dressed as clowns, TV personalities or animals. The most common sight is men dressed as women; the *Bloco das Piranhas*, for example, is a group of men elaborately dressed as prostitutes. Another popular presence is the *Bloco dos Sujos*: members smear themselves with cheap paint and, dressed as Indians or vagrants, parade through the streets.

In addition, a number of special events are featured every year. One is awarding of the street Carnival costume prize. Recently, a group of men calling themselves *The Young Widows* won. They were splendidly dressed as middle-class women and worked out an elaborate dance routine to please the judges.

Carnival nights belong to the club balls. Among events attracting both *cariocas* and tourists are nightly bashes at the Sírio-Libanés, Flamengo, Fluminense and Monte-Líbano clubs. Monte-Líbano boasts the hottest of the balls, especially its "Night in Baghdad" held on Carnival Tuesday. The "Night" is so popular, sometimes Middle-Eastern sheiks attend.

Another Carnival highlight is the contest for best costumes, held at several balls and featuring outrageous get-ups which depict everything from Medieval troubadours to Roman Catholic archbishops.

But the most colorful and undisputed centerpiece of any Rio de Janeiro Carnival is the main Samba School Parade. The samba parade is the most African of the Carnival events due mainly to the samba, a composite of European folk influences and African techniques. The parade is a 20th-century innovation. The first samba school was called *Deixa Falar* (Let 'Em Talk), organized by the black residents of Rio's Estácio District in 1928.

Deixa Falar paraded for the first time in 1929. Paraders followed no fixed route and were poorly organized, but their very size made them different. Unlike other parading groups, *Deixa Falar* presented clever dance routines. It wasn't long before other black neighborboods set up rival organizations. By 1930 there were five groups and so many spectators, police had to clear a special area around Praça Onze for their parade. (By then the Praça Onze groups had acquired the name school, because they practiced on school grounds.)

Modern samba music dates from the 19th century, when the crude tones of the former slaves met the stylized European sound of Rio. The word "samba" is believed to derive from the Angolese *semba* describing a ceremony in which tribesmen were allowed to select female partners from a circle of dancers. In Brazil during colonial times, the rhythmic music of *semba* and the accompanying dance were prohibited by the Jesuits as excessively erotic.

Today the 14 samba schools which parade down Avenida Marques de Sapucai are judged by a government appointed jury. Each school's presentation must have a central theme, such as an historical event or personality, or a Brazilian Indian legend. The theme embraces every aspect of the school's effort. Costumes must accord with historic time and place. The samba song must recount or develop the theme and the huge floats that push ponderously down the avenue must detail it through the media of papier-mâché figures and paintings.

Left, sea of colorfully costumed Carnival dancers at the Rio parade. Above, luxurious feathered costumes move past the packed grandstand.

Each school's presentation includes the *Abre-Alas*, "the opening wing," consisting of a group of colorfully costumed *sambistas* marching next to a large float. The float depicts an open book or scroll and is, in effect, the title page of the school's theme. Behind the *Abre-Alas* is a line of formally dressed men, the *Comissão de Frente*, or "Board of Directors," who are chosen for their dignified air.

The real event begins when the *Porta Bandeira* (Flag Bearer) and the *Mestre Sala* (Dance Master) appear. They dress in lavish 18th-century formal wear. The *Porta*

Bandeira is a woman dancer who holds the school's flag during an elaborate dance routine with her consort. The bulk of the samba school follows, including the small army of percussion enthusiasts known as the *bateria*. They maintain a constant rhythm, so other members of the school may keep up with the tempo of the samba song.

Behind the *bateria* are the major samba school *alas*. These groups of *sambistas* show different aspects of the school's theme through their costumes. If the school's theme is based on an Amazon myth, one of its main *Alas* might be *sambistas* dressed as Indians; another could have its members dressed as Amazon animals.

dance routines.

Finally there are the giant Carnival floats called *Carros Alegôricos*, created from papier-mâché and styrofoam, which present the major motifs of the school's theme. Using the Amazon example again, floats might depict incidents or characters from a mythological Amazon story. The impact of the floats is primarily visual. Critics argue that the papier-mâché extravaganzas detract from the music which, they say, should be the mainstay of the parade.

The man who practically invented the contemporary samba parade "look," Joãozinho Trinta of the Beija-Flor School, attacked the "folkloric" view a few years ago

There are some *alas*, like the *ala das Baianas*, which must be part of every samba school presentation. This group consists of dozens of elderly women dressed in the flowing attire of Bahia. They honor the earliest history of samba.

In between the major *alas* are lavishly costumed individuals depicting the main characters of the school's theme. They are *Figuras de Destaque* ("Prominent Figures"), and often include local celebrities. The preference is for voluptuous actresses. There are also groups of dancers known as *passistas*. These agile young men and women often stop to perform complicated

in a famous comment: "Intellectuals want poverty, but the public doesn't. It wants luxury." Later, he pointed out that strong visual elements were needed to make the parade appeal to foreign tourists and, especially, television viewers. Besides the glitter of the floats, Joãozinho Trinta has invented another popular aspect of today's parade, the presence of beautiful, topless young women on the floats.

The announcement of the winning schools is made on the Thursday after Carnival and is one of the big events of the year in Rio. Losing schools are rarely satisfied with the results and cries of fraud are common.

The two Class 1-A schools earning the fewest points drop to Class 1-B and the two Class 1-B Schools which earn the most points (in a separate competition) move up to Class 1-A in the subsequent year's parade.

And where do the Class 1-A winners go? Back to the club house for a celebration that lasts until the following Sunday. Indeed, all the way to the following year, when there is another Carnival and another samba parade.

Carnival in the northeast: Rio is not the only Brazilian city with a tradition of fervent Carnival revelry. Many experienced travelers prefer Carnival in the northeast coastal cities of Salvador and Recife, where non-stop street action is the highlight.

The centerpiece of Carnival in Salvador (capital of Bahia State; pop. 1.8 million) is a glittering music festival on wheels called *Trio Elétrico*. The celebration started in 1950 when a hillbilly singing act called *Dodô and Osmar* drove a beat-up Chevy convertible through the city playing pop and folk tunes during Carnival week for anyone who would stop to listen.

In subsequent Carnivals the concept was perfected. Instead of convertibles, Bahian

Left, samba school rehearses for the parade. Above, children dress as country bumpkins for Saint John's Day party.

musicians used flat-bed trucks decorated with flashing lights and streamers. They installed elaborate sound systems and added a third performer. But the basic idea remained—performers circulate triumphantly through the city followed by a sweating, frenzied throng.

Today, there are dozens of *Trio Elétrico* groups, with carefully planned but rarely respected schedules and routes. However, they all pause religiously at Praça Castro Alves, the traditional headquarters of Bahian Carnival.

Samba, a hopped-up northeast dance music called *frevo*, and a new style called *deboche*, which blends traditional Carnival sounds with rock-and-roll; dominate the *Trio Elétrico* repertoire.

Bahian Carnival also has another, more folkloric facet known as the *afoxé*. Dressed in flowing satin robes and carrying banners and canopies, the followers of Bahia's African-origin religions conduct subdued, reverent processions during the four days of Carnival. *Afoxé's* monotonous music, often sung in African languages, provides the eerie accompaniment.

The preeminent Carnival music of Recife (capital of Pernambuco; pop. 1.2 million) is *frevo*. Described by folklorists as recent, *frevo* is a corruption of the Portuguese word for "boiling" (*fervura*). *Frevo*, in other words, ignites the passions of its listeners.

While Carnival in Bahia moves horizontally, as fans follow their favorite musicians through the city streets, in Pernambuco the movement is vertical—dancers seem to leap up and down like ballerinas in double time.

Frevo may have evolved as musical accompaniment to *capoeira*, the devilishly complex northeast dance style which is also a form of the martial arts. Except that modern *frevo* has been simplified musically and its listeners freed to invent their own dance routines. The result is that Recife Carnival revelers dance a myriad of tortured styles, some of which have gained fame and peculiar nicknames such as "The Crab" and "The Screwdriver."

Skilled *frevo* dancers are called *passistas*, and although their dance steps may differ, they share a common costume—knee britches, stockings, a floppy shirt and a colorful umbrella. The attire is a throwback to colonial days, when African cultural elements combined to create *capoeira*. The umbrellas are probably the ornate canopies used by African kings then.

As in Salvador, Recife's African-origin religions maintain their own Carnival activities parallel to the main celebration. *Maracatu*, like *afoxé*, is a procession mixing theatrical and musical elements. The central figure is a queen protected by a canopy and surrounded by elaborately costumed consorts. In Recife, a native Indian element is also present—many paraders use body paint and feathered headdresses.

Christmas in Brazil: Although Carnival is probably the world's most exhausting holiday, Brazilians do muster enough energy for the other major dates on the Roman Catholic calendar. Befitting the world's largest Catholic country, Christmas is Brazil's chief religious and family observance.

Most Brazilian children believe Santa Claus (*Papai Noel*) distributes gifts to families around the world on Christmas Eve. He enters each home through an open window, leaving presents in shoes which have been placed on the floor or the window sill. He wears his familiar red suit and travels in an enormous sled drawn by reindeer.

The Brazilian belief in Santa Claus is remarkably similar to that of the Europeans and the North Americans because of relatively recent influences.

Brazilian Christmas in the 19th century, for example, was a more religious and family oriented celebration than it is today. The custom was to serve a lavish Christmas Eve supper, then attend midnight mass followed by a procession. Instead of a Christmas tree, most families displayed a Nativity scene, called a *presépio*.

The contemporary celebration of Christmas in Brazil had its origin in the turn-of-the-century influence of German immigrants, who introduced the Christmas tree, gift-giving and Santa Claus. The usual commercialism, including the department-store Santa Claus, pushed the trend.

One aspect of Christmas which hasn't changed, however, is the Christmas Eve supper. Brazilian families typically consume a variety of nuts and dried fruits including figs, chestnuts, almonds, hazel nuts, raisins and dates. Turkey, *rabanada* (a kind of French toast) and ham still adorn many dinner tables as main courses.

As in many countries, Christmas eating stiffens the spirit for New Year's drinking. Brazil's most popular New Year's Eve celebration happens in Rio de Janeiro. Crowded club balls, brought to a boil by samba and the summer heat, are a rehearsal for Carnival. An elaborate fireworks splashes brilliant hues across the velvet sky at midnight.

The best place to observe the New Year's celebration is on the beach. Hundreds of *Filhas-de-Santo*, white-robed priestesses of Rio's African religions, burn candles on the Copacabana sands and launch make-shift wooden vessels on the waters. The tiny boats are filled with flowers and gifts for Iemanjá, the Queen of the Seas. When the tide carries one of the gift-laden boats to sea it means Iemanjá will grant the gift-giver's wish. If the vessel washes the gifts back, the wish has been rejected. (Salvador honors Iemanjá on February 2.)

On January 1, Salvador celebrates the colorful festival of *Bom Jesus dos Navegantes*, during which a procession of small craft burdened with streamers and flags carry a statue of the Lord Jesus of Seafarers from the main harbor to the outlying beach of Boa Viagem. Thousands line Salvador's beaches to witness the spectacle. According to legend, sailors participating in the stately event will never die by drowning. (A similar procession takes place on the same day in the resort of Angra dos Reis, 90 miles or 150 km south of Rio.)

In mid-January, Salvador girds for another spectacle unique to the pageantry-loving former Brazilian capital—the *Festa do Bonfim*. Central to the event, which takes place in a Salvador suburb, is "Washing of the Steps" at the famed Bonfim Church. Scores of Bahian women, dressed in their traditional flowing garments, scour the stairs of the church until they are sparkling white. Thousands crowd the tree-shaded church square to witness the toilsome labor.

Visitors should be sure to obtain colorful Bonfim ribbons sold by hawkers in the church square. Then do as the Bahians do: tie the ribbon in knots (each knot is a wish), then fasten it to your wrist. When the ribbon breaks (from normal wear and tear) the wishes will be granted. However, for wishes to come true, the ribbons must be received as a gift, not purchased, so visitors should buy and then exchange them.

Another colorful event from the Roman Catholic calendar is the *Festa do Divino*, just before Pentecost Sunday. Two of Brazil's most strikingly beautiful colonial-era towns—Alcântara in the northeast state of Maranhão and Paraty, 150 miles (250 km) south of Rio—feature classic *Festa do Divino* celebrations.

Townspeople dress in colonial attire, with many playing roles of prominent figures

Left, exclusive Carnival ball at a social club. Above, *Trio Eléctrico* provides music for dancing in the streets.

from Brazilian history. The climax is a visit from the Emperor, who arrives attended by servants for a procession and mass at the church square. In a gesture of royal magnanimity, he frees prisoners from the town jail. Strolling musicians, called *Folias do Divino*, serenade the townsfolk day and night.

The June Festivals: Soon after Pentecost begins one of Brazil's most interesting celebration cycles, the June Festivals. Feasts of Saints John, Anthony and Peter all fall in June—a good excuse for an entire month of festivities.

The feast of St. Anthony, patron of lost possessions and of maidens in search of a husband, begins June 12. Strictly religious observances dominate this saint's day.

But feast days for Saints John and Peter are festive. St. John's days are June 23 and 24, and are characterized by brightly illuminated balloons filling the skies and bonfires blazing through the night.

St. Peter's feast days are last, June 28 and 29. Fireworks, ample food and drink and folk music are the elements for celebrating this occasion. The saint is especially honored by widows, who place lighted candles on their doorsteps during the festival.

Most June festivities take place outdoors. Participants, including those in big cities, dress up like country people, or *caipiras*. Country music, square dancing and mock wedding ceremonies (at which the bride may appear pregnant) are featured at the most authentic June Festival parties.

In the sprawling São Paulo suburb of Osasco, Brazil's largest bonfire, measuring 70 feet (22 meters) high, is lit the last week of every June. Consisting entirely of long-burning eucalyptus logs, the fire takes a week to burn itself out.

October celebrations: October hosts a month-long cycle of religiously-inspired celebrations. Three of Brazil's most characteristic festivals are celebrated all month long, one of which, *Nossa Senhora de Aparecida*, is also highlighted by a national holiday on October 12.

In October 1717, "the Miracle of Aparecida" occurred in Guaratingueta, situated about halfway between Rio and São Paulo. The colonial governor of São Paulo was passing through the town at lunchtime when he stopped at a fisherman's cottage demanding a meal for his party. The fisherman and two friends hurried to their boats on the Paraíba River but had no luck in the normally fish-crowded waters.

So they prayed. When they cast their nets again, they pulled a black, two-foot-high statue of the Blessed Virgin Mary out of the river. With the image safely aboard their craft, they landed a catch that nearly burst their nets.

The story quickly spread to the surrounding countryside and in 1745 a rustic chapel was built to house the statue. Mainly because of the shrine's strategic location on the Rio-São Paulo Highway, the cult of Our Lady of Aparecida grew and, in the mid-19th century, a church more grand than the first was built.

That structure still stands on a low hill overlooking the new basilica. Coronation of the original statue, in 1931, as Vatican-anointed patron saint of Brazil made Aparecida the country's chief religious shrine.

The idea of building a third church was suggested as early as 1900, when a Vatican-decreed Holy Year brought 150,000 pilgrims to Aparecida. The first stone of the new basilica was laid in 1955 and, although a great deal of finishing work remained, the main outlines of the cathedral were finally completed in 1978.

The basilica is a massive structure. It is out of proportion with its surroundings, and its modest 19th-century shrine could be stored easily in the vast box of the new church. The cathedral's enormous nave and network of chapels and galleries annually host about 8 million pilgrims. About 1 million visit Aparecida in October alone.

In comparison, the picturesque Igreja de Nossa Senhora da Penha in Rio de Janeiro is less imposing in size, but almost as unusual as its surroundings. Located atop a 300-foot cone-shaped hill, Penha represents one of Brazil's oldest lay religious organizations.

The order of Penha was founded in the 17th century by Portuguese landowner Baltazar Cardoso, who believed he had been saved from death in a hunting accident by divine intervention.

The incident occurred near a mountain called Penha in Portugal. The lay order which Cardoso founded transferred its activities to Brazil later in the century, finding in the rocky cone of Penha in Rio a small-scale copy of Cardoso's Penha in Europe.

The first church was built on the rock in 1635 and the second in 1728. That year members of the order began carving 365 steps, directly into the rock face, which have made the church famous. (Before the steps, worshipers simply clammered up the side of the mountain).

Left, "Children of Gandhi" *afoxé* group in Salvador.

The most extraordinary aspect of Penha's annual month-long celebration is the ordeal of climbing the steps on hands and knees. Thousands of penitents perform the arduous task every October. Given the increasing number of worshipers, a third church was built in 1871. That edifice now plays host every year to the Penha October festivities.

Penha festivities are unique for Rio's religious calendar. Not only do worshipers participate in religious ceremonies every Sunday of October, they also enjoy a "lay festival" on the esplanade at the base of the hill. The secular festivities are known for their good food, abundant beer and reliance on live music to animate the crowds.

Festivals in the Amazon: October also marks the chief religious observance of the Brazilian Amazon—the fervent procession and festival of Círio de Nazaré in Belém. A city of 1 million at the mouth of the Amazon, Belém annually attracts tens of thousands of penitents and tourists for the remarkable procession, a four-hour cortege along four miles of downtown streets on the second Sunday of October.

A thick rope, several blocks long, is used to drag a colorfully decorated carriage bearing the image of Our Lady of Nazareth. Pilgrims who succeed at grabbing hold of the rope are granted favors by the saint. When the image reaches the basilica, a 15-day festival, similar to Penha festivities in Rio, begins.

The Círio de Nazaré story tells of a mulatto hunter named José de Sousa who found the foot-high image lying in the forest. Sousa felt the image brought him luck, and later it was placed in a makeshift chapel where it was said to bring miraculous cures for his ailing neighbors. The first procession displaying the image took place in 1763. The rope was only added in the 19th century.

Festivals like Círio de Nazaré, Bom Jesus dos Navegantes, and even Carnival have common aspects: they are all observed on important dates on the Roman Catholic liturgical calendar; they all possess central themes with traditional and folkloric elements; and perhaps what makes them most typically Brazilian, their participants have a rollicking good time.

SONG AND DANCE

On a Saturday night in any sizeable Brazilian city, a vast musical choice presents itself. Will you follow the beat of the drums in a samba school rehearsal? Or tap cutlery to a samba *pagode* in a tile-floored bar? Dance hip-to-hip to the deceptively simple rhythm of the *forró*, pumped out by a four-piece band—accordion, bass drum, guitar and triangle—in a dance hall filled with Northeasterners? Try the tango-like ballroom virtuosity of the *gafiera*? Converse over the twinkling swirls of the *choro* played on mandolins and violas? Or risk the decibels of one of Brazil's new generation rock groups?

In the nightclubs, jazz takes its turn with the melancholy of the Portuguese *fado*, or any one of several generations and genres of Brazilian torch singers, from *samba-canção* to *bossa nova*.

Discotheques juxtapose Madonna, The Smiths and Bob Marley with the Brazilian singer of the moment. In the working men's clubs and suburban dance halls, there is the nostalgia of *duplas sertanejas*, country duos.

The first *duplas* were a product of turn-of-the-century music halls; today they are the fastest growing segment of popular music, selling more records than any other. Sentimental verses of uncomplicated romance and tearful farewells keep the city dweller's yearning for lost country simplicity alive. The message seems universal; a popular duo, Millionário e José Rico, sell large quantities of records—in Portuguese—to mainland China.

Outside the urban centers, regional music is still very much alive. In Rio Grande do Sul, *gauchos* listen to accordion music much as their German forebears did 70 years ago. In Mato Grosso do Sul, bordering on Paraguay, *boleros* blend with country music.

Northeastern rhythms like *baião*, *forró* and *maracatu* in the interior and the faster *frevo* on the coast, especially Recife, dominate not only in their region of origin but wherever northeasterners have migrated in search of work and a better life.

Musical history: The heterogeneity of the nation itself explains why so many genres of popular music co-exist with equal vigor. Successive waves of immigration left their imprint, beginning with the Portuguese colonials, the Jesuit missions, and the forced immigration of the slaves, to the economic and political refugees from 19th- and 20th-century Europe: Italian anarchists, Polish Catholics, German Jews, and, more recently, Palestinians, Japanese, Koreans, and new Christians from the Middle East.

Culturally mixed, socially hierarchical, Brazil has one foot in the computer age and another in the 17th century. It is 70 percent urban, but so newly urban that large sectors of the city population retain the cultural habits of the *sertão*; still a predominantly oral culture, yet one exposed to the rest of the world through transistors and TV.

Folksongs still survive alongside the latest releases on international compact discs. The sound of the city—jazz, pop, rock—is newly imposed on rural roots. A generation from now, the homogenizing power of the electronic media will undoubtedly take its toll, but for now, Brazil is one of the most fertile musical terrains in the world for traditional ethnic music.

Rhythm makers: It is a tired old cliché that Brazil has rhythm. What it actually has is *rhythms*, in the very definite plural. Brazilian music is also marked by fusions.

Indeed the history of Brazilian music is the history of fusions.

The first was Amerindian-Jesuit. At the time of contact, in 1500, there were an estimated 5 million native Indians in Brazil. The Jesuits soon perceived the Indians' response to music and its importance in ritual. They adapted Catholic liturgy to Amerindian ritual song and choreography as an instrument of preaching the good news. Gradually, the Gregorian chant was absorbed by the Indian population.

Four centuries later—with the total Indian population reduced to 250,000—the same process can still be witnessed in certain regions. Although the orientation of the Catholic church in recent years has been to respect Indian culture, in the more traditional orders, the dissemination of sacred music continues. In the northwest of Amazonas state, near the

Left, dancers attract a crowd.

Venezuelan border, Indians of the Tucano tribe still sing Gregorian Credos and Glorias, taught by the Salesian missions.

Amerindian music is complex rhythmically but poor melodically. Principal instruments are maracas, various types of rattles and, in some Indian nations, primitive flutes and pan pipes. Song was such a sacred element that, for some nations, it was restricted to ritual.

Over the years, the words of ritual song lost their meaning, becoming mere magic sounds. The principal exception to song-as-ritual appears to have been in lullabies, sung softly and sweetly by the women.

Certain animist ceremonies practiced by non-Indians today, such as the *Catimbo* in the interior of the northeast of Brazil and the *Pajelança* in the northern Amazon, owe more to Indian ritual, especially in their choreography, than to the musically and visually richer Afro-ceremonies of the coast. And some surviving country folkdances, such as *Caiapos* and *Cabochlinhos*, are of direct Amerindian inspiration.

The heritage of the Brazilian Indian in popular music includes percussion instruments, a nasal tone in song, the one-word chorus and the habit of ending a verse on a lower note.

Mário de Andrade also credits the Brazilian Indian for incorporating the Portuguese tendency for song to revolve around lost love. "...it seems incontestable to me that Amerindian themes, owing almost nothing to love songs...have brought us to a more complete lyrical contemplation of life."

But for four centuries the dominant influence was that of the colonizers of Brazil, the Portuguese.

They defined Brazilian harmonic tonalism, established the four beat bar and the syncopation which would later blend so well with African rhythms.

They brought the *cavaquinho* (similar to the ukelele, today steel stringed) the *bandolin* (mandolin), the Portuguese guitar (ten strings, arranged in five pairs, more like a large mandolin or a sitar or Greek bazuki), the Portuguese bagpipes and other instruments disseminated over Europe such as the flute, piano, viola and harp.

It was not, however, the Portuguese guitar which was destined to become the backbone of Brazilian popular music, but the Spanish guitar. The same happened with the Italian mandolin, preferred to the Portuguese. The Italian accordion was also to be incorporated into popular music, especially country music. In the northeast, the accordion player is still the mainstay of country parties, traveling around from village to village and in huge demand during the month of June for the traditional feasts of São João (St. John). In recent years, *festas juninas* have enjoyed an extraordinary revival throughout Brazil, even in the cities, where accordion players are suddenly too few to go around and have to be substituted by records.

Over the years the northeasterners developed a style of accordion playing far re-

moved from the wailing tones of the Europeans. Bahian Pedro Sertanejo, who owns a *forró* dance hall in São Paulo, recently toured Europe with his all-musician family, "They stared at us open-mouthed, wondering how we got all that rhythm into the accordion".

The undisputed king of the accordion is Luis Gonzaga, inventor of the rhythm *baião*, still playing in his late 70s. Nearly all of Gonzaga's songs recount the hardships of life in the northeast.

Asa Branca (after a bird, the whitewing), the haunting lament of a peasant farmer driven off his land by draught, has become virtually an unofficial anthem. Paradoxically, it is sung to a cheerful rhythmic backing.

The Portuguese provided the basis of Brazilian folkdance, from children's rings and maypole dances to the dramatized dances, although the ones which have survived are those which best incorporated African rhythm.

Most dramatized dances are linked to the Catholic religious calendar, such as the *reisados* (performed on the sixth day after Christmas to celebrate the visit of the Magi to the infant Jesus), *pastoris* (sung and danced nativity plays) and *Festa do Divino* (performed at Pentecost).

Yet the liveliest are profane: the *Congadas* (sometimes known as *embaixadas*), a dramatization of the battles between Moors and Christians, and *Bumba meu Boi*, generally presumed to be a comic representation of the *tourinhos*—Portugal's non-lethal, playful bull-fights.

Today, *Bumba meu Boi* is colorful, rhythmic and essentially black, performed in its most authentic form in the states of Pernambuco, Maranhão and Bahia.

If the Portuguese provided the lyrical-poetical framework, and, to an extent, the range of themes and emotions present in Brazilian popular music, we must look to Africa for its life-force and energy.

The majority of Brazil's slaves came from Africa's west coast, principally Angola, followed by the Congos and Sudan, to the north. There were Nagos, Jejes, Fantis, Axantis, Gas, Txis, Fulos, Mandingos, Haussas, Tapas, Bornus, Grumans, Calabars and the elite, Mohammedan Malés.

Unlike the protestant United States, where virtually all trace of African religious ritual was wiped out, Brazil's colonial slave owners did not systematically repress animist ritual among the slaves.

As long as religious rituals and parties were held out of earshot of the mansion, they were largely tolerated. It was later, when blacks tried to organize their religion in the cities, that police repression was unleashed against them and they had to resort to the subterfuge of blending their own natural, forest gods with Catholic saints.

The musical instruments for both religious and pagan festivals were the precursors of those used in every samba band today: *atabaque* (drums), *ganza* (a type of metal rattle), *cúica* (a skin fastened within a small drum and pulled to make a hoarse rasping noise), *agogo* (a single or double conical bell, beaten with a stick or metal rod).

Left, Gilberto Gil. Above, Caetano Veloso.

In informal dances such as *umbigadas* (literally, belly button thrusts) the blacks formed a circle, clapping, singing, beating percussion instruments while one dancer at a time twirled and gyrated in the middle. When his (or her) time was up, the dancer would place himself in front of someone in the circle and, with an *umbigada*—a forwards thrust of the hips—elect that person to take his place.

Versions of *umbigadas* survive today in black communities all over Brazil, known variously as *samba de roda, jongo, tambor-de-crioulo, batuque, caxambu.* It is thought that the word *samba* comes from the Angolan *semba*, a synonym for *umbigada*.

lundus but of *modinha*, a musical form which was to last into this century (indeed, in 1967 popular composer Chico Buarque composed and recorded the *modinha, Até Pensei*). Originally ostracized for their capacity to "corrupt women of fine morals" Caldas Barbosa's romantic *modinhas* soon became so popular that, in 1775, he was invited to Portugal.

By the mid-19th century, *modinhas* had become the favorite of the court, rarified to a unique form of near-classical chamber music, with opera-like arias. Yet, at the end of that century they had descended again to street level, to the gaslight *serenatos* of wandering guitarists.

Long rejected by the Portuguese elites for its "lascivity", the *umbigada* was eventually to enter the living rooms of white urban society, in the form of the *lundu* in the late 18th century. Toned down by "a certain civilized polish which transforms the harsh primitive sensuality of the *batuque* into a langurous hip-sway" (Oneyda Alvarenga), the *lundu* was danced in pairs and with the addition of viola and sitar.

Domingos Caldas Barbosa, born in Rio de Janeiro around 1740, of a black mother and white father, educated in a Jesuit college before joining the army, became the most renowned and prolific composer not only of

Anyone familiar with the theme song of the Ali McGraw-Ryan O'Neil film *Love Story*, has tasted the flavor of the *modinha*. Its melody is virtually identical to a 1907 composition by Pedro de Alcantaram entitled *Dores de Coração* (Heartache), later popular throughout Brazil as *Ontem, Ao Luar* ("Yesterday When the Moon Shone"), sung by Catulo da Paixão Cearense.

In the second half of the 19th century, the slave bands of the country plantations and city ballrooms were required to copy fashionable dance rhythms imported from Europe such as polka and mazurka.

When playing for themselves, however,

these bands let rip, endowing polka's lively jig with their own sensuous thrusts and swings. The result was *maxixe,* an extravagant, rhythmic form of tango. As with *lundu, maxixe* was first condemned and then began a gradual ascension to high society.

It suffered a setback in 1907, in a comic but very telling incident when, at a ball in honor of a German military delegation, the Prussian official in charge asked the band to play a popular *maxixe*. Shocked by the gusto with which his military band launched into the number, Brazilian army minister, Marshal Hermes da Fonseca, banned the dance from the repertory of all military bands.

Five years later he was forced to admit defeat in his own household when his wife delivered a spirited rendering of a *maxixe* at an official party.

A failed Brazilian dentist, Lopes de Amorin Diniz, known as Duque, became a huge success in Paris in the early 20th century as dancer and teacher of *le vrai tango bresilien.* In 1913 he danced for Pope Pious X, who remarked indulgently that it reminded him of an Italian dance of his youth, the *furlana*. Back in Brazil, however, the *maxixe* was still being combatted tooth and nail by church leaders.

Left, spontaneous dancing in the street. Above, Milton Nascimento.

By the time Fred Astaire danced a version of the *maxixe* in the 1934 Hollywood film *Flying Down to Rio*, the dance was dying out in Brazil as the more aggressive, simpler *sambas* popularized by the carnival parades took over.

Today there are still dance halls, usually known as *gafieras*, where one can watch open-mouthed as couples, glued together, dance *maxixes, choros* and *sambas*, with all the extravagant virtuosity of the 'Duque' in his day.

Two other musical forms were to develop almost simultaneously to the *maxixe*—the more elitist *tango brasileiro* with its influences of Cuban *Habanera*, eternalized by pianist Ernesto Nazaré, and *choro*, a fast-moving instrumental rhythm played on flute, guitar and *cavaquinho*.

Samba was born in the *umbigadas* of the slaves, but the first *samba* to receive the name, to launch the genre, was the famous "Pelo Telefone", registered in a Rio notary public's office by a lower-middle class *carioca* composer, Donga, in 1916. The following year, "Pelo Telefone" was the success of the carnival, and in successive years the new genre put an end to the rag-bag of different rhythms that had characterized Rio carnival up until then—polka and stately *marcha-ranchos* for the classes, rhythmic *afoxé* and *lundu* for the blacks.

Over the next half century *samba* sprouted variations, from the purest *samba do morro*—with its percussion instruments only, to the *samba enredo*—the epic samba of the carnival parade, with lead singer and chorus, reminiscent of the call and response songs of U.S. blacks; *samba do breque*—a samba which stops abruptly, usually for some wry intermission, before picking up again; and the *samba-canção*—a ballad-version, the Frank Sinatra of sambas.

Today, with musical frontiers blown wide open, and musical fashions flashing by at increasing speed, the fusions seem virtually limitless—samba-rock, samba-jazz-funk and even samba-reggae.

Bossa nova met the world on November 22, 1962, when pianist and composer Tom Jobim gave his famous concert at Carnegie Hall, New York, playing classics such as *The Girl from Ipanema*, and *Samba de uma nota só*.

Five years earlier *bossa nova* was born in Brazil; precisely, in Copacabana, Rio de Janeiro. Its precursors were the jazzified sambas, or 'samba sessions' then popular in Rio's nightclubs, and the U.S. cool jazz, themselves outgrowths of the bebop sambas of the 1940's.

The key figure in the birth of *bossa nova* was not the classically trained Tom Jobim, but a young guitarist from the interior of Bahia—João Gilberto. Gilberto's unique contribution was a style of guitar playing that combined jazz harmonies with a chunky, persistent, offbeat rhythm extracted from the guitar itself.

João Gilberto was discovered playing in a Copacabana nightclub by a group of youngsters, mostly university students, who were themselves experimenting with a cooler form of *samba*.

Bossa nova thus took shape in the apartments and bars of Rio's chic Zona Sul rather than in the hillside shacks and suburbs. Poet and former diplomat, Vinicius de Moraes, an inveterate bohemian, was to become the movement's high priest, writing lyrics such as the exquisite *Eu sei que vou te amar* (I know that I will love you).

Often, though, *bossa nova*'s lyrics were reduced to a sonorous "Pam, bim-bam, bim-bam". Minimalism was the essence.

Although João Gilberto's style of guitar playing was to influence a generation of Brazilian musicians, *bossa nova* itself always remained an elitist taste in Brazil, like cool jazz in the United States, never filtering down to mass consumption.

It requires considerable skill to play the *bossa nova* guitar. One musician compared it to "talking in a long sentence, but one in which you switch language every two words". The melody flows on, but changes scale every few notes.

The next important movement in Brazilian popular music was *tropicalismo*, a reaction against the cool of *bossa nova* and the socially committed 'protest sambas' which succeeded *bossa nova* in the 60s.

The latter were aptly defined by literature professor Walnice Nogueira Galvão as the songs of *o dia que virá* —the day that will come. It was the period of the military regime, of increasing censorship and repression. In 1968, Geraldo Vandré, composer of the anti-military protest song *Pra não dizer que não falei de flores* (So as not to say I didn't speak of flowers) was arrested, tortured and exiled.

Tropicalismo exploded onto the scene in 1967, when *baianos* Gilberto Gil and Caetano Veloso, presented, respectively, the songs, *Domingo no Parque* (Sunday in the Park) and *Alegria, Alegria* (Joy, Joy) at a São Paulo music festival.

Tropicalismo shocked the purists in much the same way as Bob Dylan did the day he appeared on stage with an electric guitar. The *baianos* used all the resources of pop-rock—electric guitars and a backing group called the Beat-boys (the Beatles were then the idols of the university class).

It was loud, anarchic and irreverent, mixing concrete images of Brazil with international junk culture in striking juxtapositions. Once they got over the shock, Brazilian audiences were, for the first time, driven to delirium.

In 1969, the alarmed military government arrested Caestano and Gil, eventually forcing them into exile in London.

By the time they returned, in 1972, the breakthroughs of *tropicalismo* had become the norm and every Brazilian group included electric instruments.

Twenty years after the advent of *tropicalism*, three singer-songwriters of that generation still dominate the more sophiscated reaches of the Brazilian musical scene: Caetano Veloso, with his sinuous, poetic imagery, is always one step ahead of the collective consciousness; Gilberto Gil, who is more direct, more African, more rhythmic; and Chico Buarque, a composer and an intellectual.

Many of today's talents have made inroads on the international scene: Milton Nascimento (recording with Wayne Shorter and Gil Evans), Hermeto Paschoal and Egberto Gismonti in jazz, singers Gal Costa, Maria Bethania (Caetano Veloso's sister), the effervescent northeasterner, Elba Ramalho, Jorge Ben with his eternal, eminently danceable sambas, one of which was 'borrowed' by Rod Stewart for his hit song *D'ya Think I'm Sexy* and resulted in an international law suit.

In the early 80s, *rock brasileiro* hit the Brazilian music scene with a whole new cast of young singers and groups. Musically, *rock brasileiro* is largely a second-hand incorporation of international trends. The innovative element is its contemporary language—direct, urban, often humorous, mocking, or ironic, dealing with sex and emotions openly, rather than through the veils of romanticism and suggestion so dear to Brazil's Catholic-lyrical tradition.

For real musical innovation in the mid-80s one must look to the city of Salvador, State of Bahia, where an unprecedented 're-Africanization' is currently taking place.

It began in the late 1970s when *afoxés,* groups of dancers linked to the city's *candomblé* African religion, began to make their presence felt during Salvador's Carnival. Dressed in flowing white robes, they paraded, not to the frenetic *trio elétrico* or to samba, but to the African rhythms of the same *agogos* and drums commonly used in religious ritual.

Left, open-air concert in Rio park. Above, Chico Buarque.

The *afoxés* proliferated, their influence spreading outside carnival. They became the nerve centers of a growing black consciousness movement. Simultaneously, imported L.P.'s of Bob Marley, not available then in record shops, found their way to Bahia.

Identification with reggae was immediate. Gilberto Gil gave a spine-tingling concert with Jamaican Jimmy Cliff. Soon *baianos* discovered other Caribbean rhythms and the whole of Africa.

The result is an unparalleled cultural effervescence. Each Carnival brings a new Afro-Baiano-Caribbean rhythm, a new dance, a new local idol.

Let's

SOCCER

Brazilians didn't invent the game of soccer. They just perfected it. Brazil is probably as well known around the world today for its unique brand of soccer play as it is for its coffee or Carnival.

The game arrived in Brazil just before the turn of the 20th century, brought to São Paulo by a young Brazilian-born Englishman named Charles Miller, who learned it while studying in Great Britain. His parents were part of the vanguard of British technicians who were building railways, ports and power facilities in Brazil late in the 19th century.

Miller learned the game well, and upon his return to Brazil in 1895, he taught the fundamentals to his friends at the São Paulo Athletic Club (SPAC), a British community club. By 1901, a citywide soccer league was formed and SPAC became the first Brazilian champion team, winning the soccer cup three times in a row in 1902, 1903 and 1904.

But 1904 was the last time the soccer trophy in Brazil was won by British descendants. Brazilians were quick to learn the game, and beat the British at their own sport as soccer spread across the nation like a wild prairie fire.

A passion for soccer: Today, some 80 years later, soccer is much more than just a "national pastime" of Brazil. It is an all-consuming passion for millions of fans. A frenzied peak is reached every four years when the World Soccer Cup is played.

There are millions of players and thousands of teams. Every town, school and neighborhood has its own soccer field, ranging from a humble vacant lot to the mighty, multi-thousand-seat stadiums. Even remote Indian villages in the Amazon Basin boast soccer fields and their soccer balls are ingeniously improvised from local materials such as coconuts.

When the Brazilian national squad plays a World Cup match, the country is shut down more completely than it is during a general strike. In fact, many factory managers now install television sets on the production lines in a mostly futile effort to keep absenteeism

Left, ecstatic soccer fans cheer their team on.

to a minimum on World Cup game days. Most businesses, however, simply close down for the duration of the match and for the subsequent celebration, if Brazil wins.

Known as *futebol*, soccer has become as firmly entrenched as samba in Brazil. The game is so immensely popular that some of the world's largest stadiums have been erected in Brazil.

Rio de Janeiro's gigantic oval Maracanã can seat (or, better, stand and cram) 180,000 persons. Morumbi Stadium in São Paulo can hold up to 120,000 onlookers and five other Brazilian stadiums can easily handle 80,000-100,000 spectators.

Probably one of the reasons *futebol* has become so popular in Brazil is that it is a sport readily accessible to youths of all social classes. The game has attracted many young players from Brazil's slums, who see the sport as a ticket out of poverty and who are encouraged by the many rags-to-riches stories of poor kids who became rich and famous through their talents on the field.

The king of soccer: The richest and the most famous is Edson Arantes do Nascimento, better known to the world as Pele, the king of soccer. A frail-looking slum boy from a small city in the state of São Paulo, Pele had never even owned a pair of shoes when he was contracted at the age of 15 to play for the Santos Soccer Club. One year later, in 1958, he led the national team to Brazil's first World Cup championship. Four years later Pele together with another Brazilian soccer legend, Garrincha, propelled Brazil to its second consecutive world championship.

The Brazilian dynamo was injured in 1966 when opposing teams at the World Cup competition in London discovered that by confining Pele on the field they could neutralize the Brazilian team. A victim of tight defense and foul play, Pele was forced out of the championship.

Four years later, he was back and led Brazil to a record third World Cup title. He was named the tournament's most valuable player. In 1977, Pele retired, having scored an extraordinary 1,300 goals. No other player has even reached 1,000.

The dream of millions of youths is to follow Pele's example and play for one of the major metropolitan clubs, such as Flamengo, Vasco, Botafogo or Fluminense in Rio de Janeiro; São Paulo Futebol Club, Santos, Corinthians or Palmeiras in São Paulo; Gremio or Internacional in Porto Alegre; Atletico Mineiro and Cruzeiro in Belo Horizonte; and Bahia in Salvador, all keen contenders for the national title.

The ultimate honor for any player is to be picked for the national team, formed from the total professional player pool. The fortunes of this team—and its players—are followed with passion by the fans. Instant fame or national shame can ride on a few seconds' action during an important match.

The World Cup: In fact, the entire mood of the country can be altered by the success or failure of the national team in an important tournament. In 1970, for instance, the winning of the national squad's third World Cup gave a tremendous shot of popularity to the dictatorial military government headed by President Emilio Garrastazu Medici. At the time the government was bogged down in a messy internal war against urban guerrillas. To this day, General Medici's term in office is remembered more for the victories of the national soccer squad than for his action in office.

Many distinguished soccer commentators consider the 1970 squad to have been the best. Soccer fans around the world were enthralled by the fluid attacking, marvelous ball handling and malicious play-making of the Brazilians during the Mexico City tournament. The names of many great players on the team are still invoked nostalgically today—Pele, Tostão, Gerson, Carlos Alberto and Jairzinho, among the most remembered. The win was certainly the zenith of Brazilian soccer and culminated in the retiring of the prestigious Jules Rimet Cup for having won the third world title.

Left, professional soccer game in Rio's giant Maracanã stadium. Above, "sand lot" soccer players begin young.

Since the memorable 1970 World Cup, however, no Brazilian squad has made the finals of the World Cups in 1974, 1978, 1982 or 1986. Yet it is also true that Brazil is the only country that has always made it into the World Cup tournament. According to die-hard Brazilian fans, Brazil's World Cup drought is not due to a decline in the level of Brazilian play but to keener competition and the domestic squabbling among club owners and politicians who want to take part in the selection process for the national team. No matter. The Brazilian style of play, with its superb dribbling and incredible virtuosity, continues to amaze the world.

The fans: Brazilian fans are eternally hopeful and are, in fact, an unbelievable breed unto themselves. While Brazil's players are considered the top talent in the world, their fans are also considered some of the most enthusiastic in the world.

One of the "you-can't-miss-it" attractions of a visit to Brazil is a soccer league classic match, such as Rio's Flamengo versus Fluminense in Maracanã Stadium (a match traditionally known as "Fla-Flu").

Even if the game is dull, the spectacle of the fans is worth the price of admission. At a Fla-Flu, the rooting sections are as much a part of the action as are the players. Organized into fanatical sub-groups, they wave gigantic banners, sing and dance with unmatched energy and let loose barrage after barrage of fireworks before, during and after the game—and especially when one of the teams scores a goal, making the whole experience exhilarating.

At the finish of the Brazilian national championship, which takes six months and involves up to 44 teams, the final game day becomes a virtual national holiday. If you are visiting the hometown of the national champion on the evening the title is won, prepare yourself for an unforgettable experience. Hundreds of thousands of fans will emerge into the streets for a night of carousing and merry making, a celebration that can make even a Brazilian Carnival look dull by comparison.

NORBIM

ART AND ARTISTS

Brazilian art is intricately linked to Brazilian light. The hot, heavy tropical sun creates a visual ambience in which colors are more intense, and light and dark are more distinct. It has even been said that Impressionism began in Brazil when Manet, suffering from a tropical disease aboard a French frigate in the Rio de Janeiro harbor, captured the luminous sky vibrating off Guanabara Bay and the rainforest mountains.

Where does Brazilian art fit into the international art world? Brazilian art is not an island unto itself. It is intimately linked with the trends and fashions from abroad. However, leading artists are unique in their own right, creating personalized styles that manifest their vision of art and the world.

Just as light is one characteristic of Brazilian art, the originality of its leading artists is another. This originality has been particularly evident in the country's art since 1922. That year, the artists broke away from the European Academic tradition after the Week of Modern Art in São Paulo, which was considered a watershed in the country's cultural history.

Native art themes were given precedence over European molds in a movement called "Anthropophagy," alluding to a Brazilian Indian habit of eating one's enemies. Tarsila do Amaral was at the forefront of this movement, which is considered parallel to the Modernist movement led by Vicente do Rego Monteiro, Segall and Di Cavalcanti. Cavalcanti glorified the seductive *mulatta* women in his work for more than half a century because, like most Brazilian men, he considered the *mulatta* to be the epitome of erotic beauty.

The European Art Deco movement influenced Monteiro and the sculptor Brecheret, whose *Face of Christ* shows a marked inner tension, and whose earlier work of *Eve* reveals the influences of Rodin and Michelangelo.

This *gesso* sculpture of the symbol of womanhood has the muscles of a man pumping iron. The Art Deco style blended with the Mussolini style in Brecheret's giant *Monument to the Bandeirantes* (Pioneers) in São Paulo's Ibirapuera Park.

Impressionism: When Brazilian artists borrow from Europe they often do so a generation or two later. Impressionism, which began in France in the last quarter of the 19th century, became important in Brazil in the second quarter of the 20th century with artists such as Manuel Santiago, who till today interprets impressionism in his own manner with heavy masses, thick brush strokes and volumes of color.

Another artist, impressionist José Pancetti, was a tubercular ex-sailor whose moody landscapes and seascapes reflected more the state of his mind than the bright scenery about him.

Brazilian originality, however, was expressed most clearly in the work of Candido Portinari, a painter of Italian origin, whose family came to work in the coffee fields in the state of São Paulo.

Portinari, considered Brazil's greatest 20th-century artist, painted so intensely he got cancer from his highly toxic paints and died early. His *War and Peace* fresco adorns the United Nations Building in New York and his *Discovery and Colonization* painting is hung in the Library of Congress in Washington.

Concerned with the plight of Brazilian farm workers, he intentionally exaggerated their hands and feet in his paintings, as if to say, "These are the only assets I have. When my hands and feet are no longer any good I'm tossed away like a squeezed orange". The presence of hunger is characterized in *Dead Child*, in which a skeletal family weeps over the body of an infant in a wasteland. Whether the land is dry or fertile, Portinari's rural inhabitants reflect the pain and suffering of the landless workers and *retirantes*, or migrants.

In contrast, Orlando Terluz's countryside is a rich loamy brown and the rural inhabitants of his paintings are full of a beatific innocence, like the figures in Fulvio Pennacchi's rural canvases. Pennacchi dwells on country pleasures, like church fairs and parties. His migrants look more like happy families on a pilgrimage compared to

Left, primitive painting by Norbim.

Portinari's starving people. Pennacchi's farm families seem to be moving from one village to another, where the houses are sometimes built in the Brazilian style and at other times in the style of his native Tuscany.

Another Tuscan export to Brazil, Alfred Volpi, changed his early figurative paintings of church kermises to the geometrical banners which festoon rural church fairs, obeying a logical pattern which some call minimalism, for minimizing lines, colors and decorative elements.

Volpi's paintings only became highly regarded when he started to paint in the geometrical style which caught the attention of art dealers. In his latter years, Volpi signed many serigraphs based on his earlier geometrical oils. There are thousands of serigraphs of Volpi's banners on the market. He has been lionized as one of the great masters of Brazilian art and the dealers who have a corner on his paintings have made astronomical profits. Volpi's popularity rose when social realism declined.

Social influences: Social realism was a significant movement in the 1940s and early 50s. Although Brazil was only marginally involved in World War II, the conflict changed artistic and cultural values radically. The left promoted social realism, in the fashion of the Mexican artists, Diego Rivera and Orozco. Portinari's frescoes and oils with social themes belong to this movement. Carlos Scliar painted in this fashion for some time, reflecting the conditions of the rural workers in Rio Grande do Sul. Gradually, however, he eliminated all social elements in his paintings and concentrated on landscapes with geometrical forms and planes, including towns and seascapes, still-lives of flowers and his trademark—a squarish teapot in a two-dimensional perspective with a minimal use of light and shade and marked pastel tones.

While social realism was still popular, there was a parallel movement in abstract art. The First Bienal of São Paulo in 1951 helped spread this tendency. And over the years, the Bienal promoted vanguard art movements, from Picasso's famous Guernica panel to constructivism, happenings and "installations".

It was during the 1950s that Volpi's figurative paintings gave way to geometrical colonial arched windows and banners. Milton da Costa used geometrical elements for his symbolism, while Bahian-born Rubem Valentim played with semi-abstract signs and symbols of Afro-Brazilian *macumba* and *candomblé* rituals, the Brazilian versions of voodoo.The leading exponents of abstract art from the 1960s through the 80s include the Ianelli brothers: Thomaz, who used subtle *degrade* tones of brown, blue and pink, as though he were blurring Volpi's little banners; and Arcangelo, who was noted for his stunning use of brilliant yellow squares and rectangles one inside another.

In another geometrical context, Arthur Piza created texture and elevations in his engravings, applying a logical, cerebral approach also shared by Sacilotto, Fernando Lemos and Ferrari. The Brazilian expatriate in Paris, Cicero Dias, on the contrary, evoked his country's lush colors and brightly colored houses in a form of magical surrealism, adding here and there a few levitating figures.

"Group of 19": Some of Brazil's leading artists today participated in a heterogeneous movement classified loosely as the "Group of 19". These artists first exhibited in São Paulo's Galeria Prestes Maia in the late 1940s. Magical surrealism was also a characteristic of two leading exponents of this group, Mario Gruber and Otavio Araujo.

Mario Gruber is fascinated by the soulful facial features from all over Brazil, including those of blacks and northeasterners, wearing leather hats typical of the cowboy of the arid *sertão* of Brazil's backward northeast. Otavio Araujo might be called Brazil's foremost surrealist. First promoted by the U.S. bi-national center in São Paulo, he was later given grants to travel in China and the Soviet Union. He spent ten years in Russia where he met his wife Clara, who has served as a model for many of his oils and engravings, which show her surrounded by esoteric emblems, signs, snakes and Greek herms with rabbit ears.

A third member of the "Group of 19," Marcelo Grassman, has made hundreds of engravings of medieval knights mounted and unmounted, bearing lances. Another surrealist of the group, Lena Milliet, was one of the first Brazilian women to gain recognition in the art world.

A more recent surrealist is Carlos Araujo, whose father wanted him to take over his construction company, but when it collapsed, he was freed to dedicate himself to painting. His immense oils of human forms are richly textured cloud-like patterns which the artist spreads with his hands or spatulas on wood panels, using nine layers to create a rich glow, or *velatura*. Nora Beltran might also be classified as a magical surrealist. Her fat tango dancers, frivolous women and bemedaled generals ridicule the social and political mores of Latin America. Also

Left, A Portinari fresco in Pampulha church. Above, *Fishermen*, by Di Calvacanti, 1951.

MODERN ARCHITECTURE

A select group of Brazilian architects—creators of a fresh "tropical" aesthetic and new techniques—are among the most honored leaders of their profession today.

Urban planner Lúcio Costa, tropical landscape magician Roberto Burle-Marx and architect Oscar Niemeyer have left dozens of monuments in Brazil's major cities. Niemeyer counts, among his achievements, the sweeping French Communist Party Headquarters in Paris, the National University Campus in Algeria and the United Nations Building façade in New York.

But the high point of modern Brazilian architecture is the gleaming capital of Brasília, founded in 1960.

The first seeds were sown, however, in 1931: the year Rio's newly appointed Fine Arts Academy Director Lúcio Costa invited legendary French architect Le Corbusier for a lecture series.

The French master imparted his functionalist views to eager students, including Niemeyer. He urged simplicity in design, economy in materials, and open spaces. His ideas were accepted for a project which was viewed as the first great monument to modern Brazilian architecture—the Education Ministry Building in Rio.

Many of the themes which dominate Brazilian architecture made their appearance in the ministry building. One is the use of open spaces, including a breezy patio which was made possible by raising the main structure 30 feet (nine meters) on concrete pillars called *pilotis*. Interior spaces were protected from glare by sleek outdoor shutters called *bries soleil*.

Inside, the building's floor spaces were left entirely open, so future administrations could alter the space by removing room dividers. A sense of open space and a magnificent view of Guanabara Bay were achieved by nearly doubling the normal size windows.

Outside, the broad esplanade was landscaped by designer, Roberto Burle-Marx, who was fresh from Germany where he had been tutored by Walter Gropius.

Juscelino Kubitschek, Mayor of Belo Horizonte, was impressed by their work and brought the Costa-Niemeyer-Marx team together again in the 1940s, to create Brazil's most pleasing park—Pampulha.

An expansive recreational area built around an artificial lake, Pampulha is a unique combination of the landscaper's art and the discreet placement of public buildings, which include an art museum, a dance pavilion and the Roman Catholic Chapel of São Francisco.

Fascinated by the "plasticity" of concrete, Niemeyer erected elegant monuments using curves, ramps and undulating roofs. The low-rise, sub-tropical constructions included great stretches of ground floor patios and breezy esplanades.

The overall effect is an architecture of fresh, light structures which seem to hover over the green parkland and the blue waters of Lake Pampulha.

At Pampulha which was laid out by Lúcio Costa, landscaped by Burle-Marx and designed by Niemeyer, the first fruits of Brazil's modern architectural development were gathered. Kubitschek was delighted and critics stood in awe.

Brasília: In 1956 Kubitschek became Brazil's president. One of his first acts was to reunite the Pampulha team for an even bolder project—a new capital city. Among other things, Brasília was an expression of Kubitschek's immense confidence in Costa and Niemeyer.

An international competition was held to select the best urban plan for Brazil's new capital. However, according to Burle-Marx, "everybody knew in advance who was going to win". In fact, Lúcio Costa's submission to the jury consisted of only a few pen and pencil sketches scratched on the back of notepaper. The crude effort was enough to win him the contract.

Kubitschek himself recruited Niemeyer to design the main public buildings and within weeks Brasília was on the drawing boards.

The new capital represented the last stage in Niemeyer's march toward spare construction and austere design. The searing white walls of the main buildings on the Plaza of Three Powers are the same texture as the clouds which fill the Brasília sky. Great fields of glass create a similar effect. The city and the sky seem to be one.

"I sought forms distinctly characterizing the buildings, giving them lightness, as if they were only tentatively attached to the ground," said Niemeyer years later. "People had not seen anything like it before."

Niemeyer today continues to be Brazil's premier architect, most recently responsible for Rio's Sambodrome, site of the city's famed samba school parade.

Left, Itamaraty Palace in Brasília. Above, near the port in Salvador, with elevator behind.

painting in a humorous vein, with no surrealist overtones, is Gustavo Rosa. His art is expressed in thematic cycles: boys flying kites, then cats, horses, bathers, ice-cream and fruit carts and human forms with triangulated eyes, hats or pipes.

The Bienal: The Bienal placed São Paulo in the center of the Latin American art world. Every two years hundreds of artists exhibit their work in a three-month extravaganza which includes art and sculpture exhibits, video shows, installations, lectures, films and plays.

Founded by the patron of the arts Cicillo Matarazzo, the Bienal has had a marked impact on international art, and has included major shows by artists such as Picasso, Delvaux, Tamayo and others. Oddly enough, the international artists receive more promotion than the Brazilians, even when the quality of the Brazilian art may be at times equal or superior. Brazilian art suffers from a lack of international promotion and marketing.

There seems to be a generalized belief that only artists from Europe, Japan or the United States can be marketed. Many international art brokers regard the São Paulo Bienal more as an opportunity to push their own favorite artists than to disseminate the art of the host country.

One major exception is the Japanese-Brazilian Manabu Mabe, who represents not only a stunning achievement, but a striking cultural interchange between Brazil and the country of his birth.

Mabe is the one artist in Brazil who has an international market. First contracted to work as a field hand, Mabe came to São Paulo, where later his reputation grew steadily and his art became more abstract. Today his stunning colors and forms mingle Oriental harmony with bold Brazilian chromatic tones and light. Every painting of Mabe's is a sheer visual delight, with brush strokes of white daringly exploding in a field of stark reds, blues and greens.

Far more cerebral and geometrical, using only two or three colors, is Tomie Ohtake. Ohtake began painting professionally after her family, also contracted as farm workers in the interior (like Mabe and Portinari), moved to São Paulo. A member of São Paulo's talented Japanese community, Ohtake began painting professionally relatively late in life. Her settings for *Madame Butterfly* at Rio's Municipal Theatre are a landmark in Latin American scenography.

Tikashi Fukushima's son, Takashi, is more cerebral in style, and his earlier landscapes have yielded to wilder brush strokes—in the horizontal-vertical dichotomy of Oriental tradition.

Mabe's son, Hugo Mabe, began painting figurative landscapes with an expressionist vigor, but his canvasses are becoming more abstract. Likewise, Taro Kaneko is reaching the limit where landscape painting fuses into abstract art. Rio's Corcovado, Sugarloaf, the curve of Guanabara Bay, and São Paulo's Jaragua Peak are barely perceptible in his intense, thick-massed oils with explosive, unexpected colors. Kaneko's seas are gold or red, his skies, green or orange, his mountains yellow or black. He uses masses to create textures and often leaves lunar-like craters on his canvases.

Another example of the artistic energy of the Orientals in Brazil is the Chinese painter, Fang, who was forced to leave mainland China shortly after the Communist Revolution. His father had been a colleague of Sun Yat-Sen and Fang was educated in a Buddhist monastery in China, where he learned the traditions of the martial arts and painting. His still lifes of lilies in a vase on a two-dimensional table are a *tour de force* of *ton-sur-ton* shades of gray, white and off-white, with muted harmonies reminiscent of the Italian Morandi.

Art centers: São Paulo and Rio, although the most important art centers of the country, have no monopoly on creativity. German and American art dealers have been flocking to Goiás, near Brasília, to snap up the paintings of Siron Franco who, obsessed by wild animals, portrays them with magical energy and blazing color. Snakes and the *capivara*, a native animal with a round snout, are among his favorites. Some liken his style to that of Francis Bacon, but his colors and figures are more arresting. His human and animal faces have bold white, yellow or flourescent lines about the eyes. (Siron's father, who had been a small landholder, was so distraught when he lost his land that he lay down on the ground and stared into the sun until he went blind.)

Recife is solidly represented by João Camara and Gilvan Samico. Camara first achieved fame protesting against the oppression of the military government, painting figures with tortured, non-anatomical limbs in *A Confession*. His later works, without any social protest, show figures with heads and limbs attached to their bodies with a surprising contortionism, at times sexual.

His neighbor in Olinda, Gilvan Samico, draws on the chapbook or *literatura de cordel* tradition of woodcut engravers. He illustrated the crudely-printed ballads of Charlemagne and his *Twelve Peers of France* and legendary local figures such as the charismatic Padre Cicero and bandit heroes, Lampiao and Maria Bonita. Samico's engravings are highly prized by museums and are several cuts above the folk art of the northeastern wood engravers. Reynaldo Fonseca paints in a hieratic neo-Renaissance style, with human forms in rigid poses, individualized, like his cats, only by their exaggeratedly large and sad eyes.

Minas Gerais is represented by Brazil's most original and creative wood sculptor, Maurino Araujo, who follows the tradition of the nation's greatest sculptor, the 18th-century Aleijadinho. Maurino Araujo specializes in wall-eyed, myopic, crooked-eyed and one-eyed angels, archangels, cherubim and seraphim. From the same central plateau region is GTO, whose mandala-like primitive woodcarvings exemplify the best in folk art sculpture. Guignard, the Polish-born Babinski, Iara Tupinamba and Chico Ferreira of Lagoa Santa have also enriched Minas' artistic traditions.

Aldemir Martins, born in Ceará, paints flora and fauna of his native northeast. Subjects include such exotic fruits as *jenipapo*, jack fruit, *jabuticaba*, cashew and the wrinkled *maracujá* (passionfruit). Also from Ceará, Servulo Esmeraldo works in a completely different, abstract vein. He designed the *Monument to the Ocean Sewer* (it supposedly spews Fortaleza's sewage out to sea rather than on the beaches), which is formed by two black-and-white sewer pipes shaped like a "V," presumably for the Victory over the sewage, although sometimes the smell from the beach indicates that the battle is not won.

Brasília has attracted artists from many states for the decorative elements of Oscar Niemeyer's superb architecture. Bruno Giorgi's meteors have been used to adorn the reflecting pool of the Palacio dos Arcos. Ceschiatti's bronze sculpture of two seated female forms combing their hair adorns the reflecting pool of the President's Palace.

Above, *Idíllo na Noite*, 1963 painting by Mario Gruber.

Ceschiatti's mobile of dangling angels hangs from the soaring ceiling of the Cathedral of Brasília with its boomerang-shaped columns designed by Niemeyer.

Bahian Art: From the Amazon, Rita Loureiro paints the Indian legends as well as flood scenes, with cattle half disappearing in the water.

Rio Grande do Sul is noted for its sculptors, particularly Vasco Prado, who is fascinated by pregnant stallions. Francisco Stockinger's warriors of bronze and metal have an ominous air, with limbs and faces merely suggested, while his nude male and female figures are sculpted separately with an overt erotic force. Likewise, Beth Turkeniez's aluminium sculptures pay homage to the force of love.

The best of Bahian art can be found in the remarkable sculptures of Mario Cravo Junior, who experiments in wood and pigmented polyester resin for such creations as *Germination I, II and III.*

His son, Mario Cravo, creates wrinkled untitled forms out of polyester resin and fiberglass. Emanoel Araujo's abstract wood and iron sculptures have a marked minimalist effect.

In complete contrast, however, are the paintings and engravings of Raimundo de Oliveira, whose tortured life contrasted sharply with his geometrical angles and biblical scenes. Oliveira killed himself in 1966.

One of the leading artists of Paraná is Rubens Esmanhotto, strongly influenced by Scliar, but who broke away early in his career and now paints houses in the chilly, moody light of southern Brazil in works, reminiscent of Andrew Wyeth.

Today's artists: Artists now living in Brazil but born abroad have had a great influence on the nation's cultural scene. The sculpture of Japanese-born Toyota creates a brilliant statement with polished stainless steel rods cut in the form of a chandelier at the entrance of the Hotel Mofarrej Sheraton in São Paulo. Almost as stunning in effect is his mobile in the twenty-story atrium of the Maksoud Plaza Hotel.

Domenico Calabrone, an Italo-Brazilian, creates granite, stainless steel, bronze and rock sculptures for public spaces, which include the Praça dos Franceses in São Paulo and St. Peter's in Rome.

The Italian Beccheroni creates banana plant sculptures in bronze multiples, while Egyptian-born Dolly Moreno dresses in the height of fashion at night, but during the day she puts on an asbestos uniform and goggles and cuts her steel sculptures with an acetyline torch in her São Paulo atelier. Her carved, polished steel forms are on display in a place of honor on the ground floor of the São Paulo Art Museum.

Next to it is a sensual ceramic sculpture of a nude couple by the remarkable Czech, Jan Trmaal, of Rio, who first studied filmmaking in Italy before moving into jewels and sculpture.

Franco de Renzis got his training, interestingly, by sculpting monuments for the World War II dead in the Allied Cemetery in Lucca, Italy. In Brazil, he created *Impossible Equilibrium*, with horses, ballet dancers, and gymnasts defying the laws of gravity. His work has made him one of the most highly praised sculptors of the 1980s.

A fellow Italian, Renato Brunello, carves winged and meteoric sculptures in white marble and wood.

The Tangiers-born Madeleine Colaco and her daughter, Concessa, use flora and fauna motifs in their tapestry. Madeleine invented a special form of tapestry registered at the international Tapestry Museum in Lausanne as the "Brazilian Stitch."

French-born Jacques Douchez, along with the São Paulo artist Norberto Nicola, modernized Brazilian tapestry with their abstract designs and the use of non-embroidered elements, including hemp and other native plant fibers.

Left, ***Equador No 2*****, 1973 painting by Manabu Mabe. Above,** ***São Paulo*****, 1975 painting by Lena Milliet.**

Primitive art: In primitive art, however, Brazil has shown its greatest originality and vigor, through bold colors and mythical themes. Chico da Silva's monsters, often created with ample use of *pinga*, or sugarcane brandy, are painted in psychodelic colors, while Francisco Severino Dila and Eduardo Calhado portray farm workers in the field or at play.

Rodolfo Tamanini is noted for capturing city scenes, such as a photographer at a church wedding and bathers on balconies at seaside apartment buildings. He paints Indians on fragments of paper as a protest against the official view that the Indians are not total human beings.

Iracema Arditi, Nunciata and Madalena depict the paradisiacal vegetation of Brazil, while Waldomiro de Deus portrays angels, lambs and country scenes. He painted *Jacob Wrestling with the Angel* in a Brazilian country setting with the angel's robes in a blue violet.

Waldomiro's portrayal of angels and biblical scenes reflects his "conversion" to religion, which he experienced during a visit to Israel. Ivonaldo portrays cross-eyed zebu cattle, cross-eyed sugarcane cutters and cross-eyed couples in canoes. Oddly enough, Ivonaldo's vision is perfect.

For those interested in purchasing primitive art, the Jacques Ardies Gallery in São Paulo and the Jean-Jacques Gallery in Rio, both run by a Belgian with a Dali moustache and Dali eyes, are a must.

Modern Art: In 1922, Paulo Prado organized the Week of Modern Art, which revolutionized art in Brazil. His grandson, also called Paulo Prado, runs Brazil's most important gallery, Galeria Paulo Prado in São Paulo. The gallery promotes new artists until they reach fame. It is then that Paulo Prado lets them go on to other galleries while he searches for good new artists.

São Paulo also boasts other important galleries such as *Arte Aplicada*, run by Sabina Libman and *Galeria Sadala*, *Andre* and *Documenta*. Leading galleries in Rio include *Ipanema* and *Bonino*, and the galleries in the Gavea and Cassino Atlantico shopping centers.

AMAZON DREAMS

The Amazon, immense and mysterious, speaks a universal language. Its vocabulary is scientific knowledge, business profits and pure adventure. The Amazon is sexy, lawless and seemingly without end. A man can escape into its network of jungles, the Green Hell of legend, and be safe forever. He can make his fortune or vanish in the tropical wilderness. The call of the wild has sounded to generations of Amazon dreamers and schemers alike.

Today in cities and towns along the Amazon's multitude of rivers you see prospectors, geologists and jungle project managers. Each has his own story to tell and all play a part in a legend that began four centuries ago.

Sixteenth-century explorers such as Francisco de Orellana, the first European to traverse the entire Amazon Basin, were less interested in national glory or the conversion of souls than in the gold of El Dorado. Orellana didn't find gold but reported finding a matriarchal mini-state in the middle of the jungle run by Indian women.

A man of commanding presence, Orellana was captain-general of western Ecuador. He governed his province in an uneasy partnership with Gonçalo Pizarro, the brash younger brother of Andean conquistador, Francisco Pizarro.

Both men were ambitious. Their dreams were fed by rumors of the fabled "Kingdom of Manoa" which was ruled by a king who daily encrusted his large naked body in gold dust. The Spanish dubbed him El Dorado, the golden one.

Separate expeditions in search of Manoa left Ecuador in 1540. Pizarro traveled with 220 armored soldiers, dozens of Indian guides, 2,000 hunting dogs and 5,000 pigs. Orellana left with only 23 soldiers and a handful of guides. The expeditions joined forces at a remote mountain site.

The combined force ran into trouble as soon as its absurdly attired knights-in-armor, trailed by clamorous packs of dogs and pigs, began their descent of the eastern slope of the Andes. Indians attacked and killed the ill-prepared knights.

After the attacks many guides deserted, leaving the Spaniards to go hungry. Orellana left to lead a hunting party into jungle terrain to the east. He reappeared one year later after traversing the entire Amazon River Basin. Pizarro eventually broke camp and returned ignominiously to Quito with only 80 ragged soldiers.

On his trek, Orellana traveled light and ordered his men to make swift, arrow-shaped canoes like those of the river Indians, from trees. Orellana never found gold, only the unending jungle, wild animals and hostile Indians.

The Amazons: The Indians fascinated him, especially the tribe he called "the women who live alone". Later, these remarkable warriors would be dubbed "Amazons", after the women of Greek mythology who removed their right breast to facilitate using a bow and arrow.

Near the Nhamunda River, Orellana's men tangled with the fierce Amazons. Orellana described the Amazons as "very white and tall and (they) had their hair braided and wrapped around their heads and they were muscular and wore skins to cover their shameful parts and with their bows and arrows they made as much war as ten men".

Orellana took a male prisoner, an Indian named Couynco. He spoke a dialect understood by some of Orellana's companions and described the warrior women's world, which included the forceful domination of outlying tribes. Couynco said the women lived in a stone and thatch village surrounded by a high stone wall. Indian families were permitted to live in another village but were servants of the warrior women, who retreated at night to their private enclosure.

Once a year the women invited male adults from surrounding tribes to a mating festival. The male offspring of these unions were returned to the tribes of their fathers, but the females were raised by the Amazons inside the mysterious enclosure.

Orellana faithfully reported Couynco's story after his return to Spain in 1543. But neither Orellana nor any other European explorer was able to rediscover the Ama-

Left, Sera Pelada gold prospector.

zons. Spanish scholars who studied Orellana's account of the female tribe gave the name Amazon to the world's greatest rain forest and to the mighty river.

Lost Manoa: Portuguese explorer Francisco Raposo may have discovered the remains of Manoa two centuries later. His 1754 report describes "a rock-built city over which brooded a feeling of vast age," the fabulous relic of a lost civilization. Raposo and his men found stone-paved streets, elaborate plazas and stately architecture which, like that of the Incas, used no mortar between blocks.

Wrote the explorer, "We entered fearfully through the gateways to find ourselves within the ruins of a city", in places well-preserved and places apparently "devastated by earthquake."

Raposo continued, "We came upon a great plaza and, in the middle of the plaza, a column of black stone and, on top of it, the figure of a youth was carved over what seemed to be a great doorway. It portrayed a beardless figure, naked from the waist up with shield in hand, a band across one shoulder and pointing with his index finger to the North".

Around the plaza Raposo discovered more walls and buildings. Some were carved with hieroglyphics, others with bas-relief, including repeated renderings of a kneeling youth bearing a shield. Inside, Raposo found "rats jumping like fleas" and "tons of bat droppings". He also found colorful frescoes and a handful of gold coins.

Raposo's fascinating city of stone was never rediscovered. It continues, nevertheless, to lure 20th-century explorers. British adventurer Colonel Percy Fawcett wrote in 1925, "It is certain that amazing ruins of ancient cities, ruins incomparably older than those of Egypt, exist in the far interior of Mato Grosso".

Fawcett was one of the great eccentrics of Amazon exploration and spent his life traveling. Army assignments took him to Hong Kong, Ceylon, Boliva, Peru and Brazil. Yet he wrote, "I loathed army life". Military discipline must have conflicted with his interest in the occult, which included telepathy, Buddhism, reincarnation and ancient civilizations.

It was these interests which first attracted Fawcett to "The Lost City", especially after he obtained, by means he never made clear, a ten-inch black stone image allegedly taken from the city by explorer Francisco Raposo.

Fawcett wrote of the relic, "There is a peculiar property in this stone image to be felt by all who hold it in their hands. It is as though an electric current were flowing up one's arm and so strong is it that some people have been forced to lay it down". Fawcett's irresistible fascination with the stone led him into the deep interior of Brazil.

Fawcett, 60, began his last journey on April 20, 1925, leaving the Mato Grosso capital of Cuiabá accompanied by his 25-year-old son Jack, his son's friend Raleigh Rimell and a number of Indian guides. The trip was financed by the North American Newspaper Alliance, which distributed dispatches sent by Fawcett to Cuiabá via Indian guides during his journey.

The last of the guides arrived in Cuiabá in mid-June carrying what was Fawcett's final dispatch, dated May 30, 1925. Along with the dispatch, Fawcett included a letter to his son Brian, then living in Peru. He told the younger Fawcett, "I am not giving you any closer information as to location because I don't want to encourage any tragedy for an expedition inspired to follow our footsteps... For the present no one else can venture it without encountering certain catastrophe". But he added, "As for me, you need have no fear of any failure". Those were Colonel Fawcett's last recorded words.

For more than a decade after his disappearance, he was the subject of stories told by missionaries and adventurers. They told about a hobbled, white-bearded caucasian living among the Indians and even claimed to have found a pale, blond-headed Indian boy—allegedly Jack Fawcett's son—in a Mato Grosso Indian village in the 1930s. However, no Fawcett sighting has ever been authenticated.

Rubber riches: The actual riches of the Amazon are even grander than the gold of El Dorado or the "ruins of ancient cities" described by Raposo and Fawcett. For 25 years around the turn of the century, the Amazon port of Manaus, a thousand miles from the Atlantic, was one of the richest cities in the world. Its wealth was based on the black gold of Amazon rubber and the system of debt slavery used to harvest it over a vast area of Amazon jungle.

During the first decade of the century Brazil sold 88 percent of all exported rubber in the world. The hundred or so rubber barons who controlled Manaus sent their laundry to Lisbon and their wives and children to Paris. They lit their cigars with 50 pound treasury notes and would spend a thousand pounds sterling "for a night with an Indian princess". The fountains in front of Manaus' historic Amazon Opera House ran with champagne on opening nights.

Left, ore is hauled out of the pit manually. Above, the human ant hill of Serra Pelada.

The grand Opera House was assembled in 1896 from panels shipped from overseas. The iron frame was built in Glasgow; 66,000 colored tiles came from France and frescoes were painted by Italy's Domenico de Angelis. The project cost an astounding $10 million. The boom ended when British-controlled plantations in Asia undercut Amazon rubber prices just before World War I. Within a decade Manaus was a jungle backwater again.

American industrialist Henry Ford, dreaming of a vertical integration of the auto industry, attempted to compete with the British by organizing his own Amazon rubber plantation in 1927. He failed, mainly due to poor disease control over his crops, and lost $80 million over 19 years. Ford's two plantation sites, Fordlandia and Belterra, near the Amazon River 500 miles (825 km) from Belém, can still be seen. Pre-war trucks and electric generators sit rusting in the tropic air behind rows of white, Dearborn houses with screened-in porches: another shattered Amazon dream.

Two decades later, another American industrialist, billionaire Daniel Ludwig, tested his wits against the Amazon at a sprawling forestry and farm project. Ludwig's experience, as it turned out, was eerily similar to Ford's.

In 1967, Ludwig, then 70, paid $3 million for a Connecticut-sized chunk of jungle along the Jarí River in the eastern Amazon. Chiefly known as the inventor of the supertanker, Ludwig was the owner of Universal Tankship Company.

Mastering the jungle: His dream was to create an integrated forestry and paper operation. Ludwig chose Jarí for its year-round growing season and seemingly endless land for timber planting.

But Ludwig never mastered the jungle, even after investing $900 million. The thin Amazon topsoil proved inadequate for massive plantings. Weeds, fungus and ants further cut productivity. Without government support, Ludwig was forced to build his own roads, schools and power plants. He eventually sold out to Brazilian interests in 1982 for $440 million.

Nature may be subtly vengeful in the Amazon, but man is crudely so. "There's only one constitution in the Amazon. It's called a Winchester 44", said a turn-of-the-century rubber baron.

Julio Cesar Arana, one of the most notorious of the barons, is said to have murdered 40,000 Indians during his 20-year reign as "King of the Putumaya River".

Another baron, Nicholas Suarez, reportedly killed 300 Indians during a single day's "hunting expedition".

The single example which probably best illustrates the collision of Amazon myth with lethal Amazon reality is the Madeira-Mamore Railroad, 225 miles (362 km) of standard gauge track in what is still a remote region of Rondonia state.

The Madeira-Mamore, completed in 1913, was born of a typical Amazon dream—that of continental unification and vast profits from the deep jungle rubber trade. In execution, however, it proved fantastically expensive, costing its backers $30 million and the deaths of 1,500 laborers. Once again, nature and man conspired brutally against an Amazon enterprise: nature, in the form of beri-beri, heat exhaustion and malaria; man, in the form of hostile Indians and negligent managers, including American entrepreneur Percival Farquhar, owner of the railbed rights.

Farquhar, 48 in 1913, was a classic industrial age empire builder. He owned trolley lines and utilities in southern Brazil and built ports, bridges and railroads in Guatemala, Cuba and Panama during more than a quarter century of intense business activities. His slogan was "think in continents". In the end, his scheme failed.

The Madeira-Mamore Railroad's inauguration coincided with the collapse of the Rubber Boom.

Today, all but nine of the original 232 miles (375 km) of track lie in ruins. As in Fordlandia there are still reminders of the doomed exploit—rusted hulks of locomotive engines, the boarded-up shacks of railroad workers and rows of headstones at Candelaria Cemetery, which one Madeira-Mamore veteran compared to a vast plantation of the dead. Another Amazon dream that lay in ruins.

Perhaps the greatest irony is that Amazon reality is as fantastic as its myths. Amazonia is the world's largest rain forest, covering about 2.5 million sq miles in nine countries. The river system is the globe's largest body of fresh water. Besides the Amazon River itself, there are 1,100 tributaries, including 17 which are more than 1,000 miles (1,612 km) long. At places the Amazon is seven miles (11 km) wide. Ship-board travelers are often unable to see either bank, which creates the sense of a vast "inland sea" which so impressed Amazon River discoverer Vicente Yanez Pinson in 1500.

Left, iron mining at Carajás. Above, boatman paddles through reflection at sunset.

Roosevelt-Rondon Mission: The Amazon has not yet been thoroughly explored by land. In 1913 former American President

Theodore Roosevelt explored a region penetrated by a river whose existence was purely conjectural. He discovered an Amazon tributary nearly a thousand miles long. That river, previously called the River of Doubt, was rechristened the Roosevelt River.

The ex-president and his co-leader, famed Brazilian explorer Candido Rondon, set out with two dozen companions on their journey from northern Mato Grosso in December 1913.

Rondon, a veteran Indian agent, surveyor and builder of telegraph lines, was 48 at the time. Roosevelt was 55. In all, the 59-day expedition covered 900 miles (1,451 km) of open *cerrado* and dense rain forest. The first eleven days were spent in sparsely populated sugarcane country. During the following 48 days, the party traveled through an unrecorded track of Amazon rain forest.

Roosevelt wrote of this region, "We were about to go into the unknown and no one could say what it held. No civilized man, no white man, had ever gone down or up this river or seen the country through which we were passing. Anything might happen". And something did.

The former president wrote in his diary a few days later, "Mosquitos hummed about us, the venomous fire-ants stung us, the sharp spines of the small palms tore our hands. Afterwards, some of the wounds festered".

The worst horror was the river itself. Roosevelt wrote, "When a rushing river canyons and the mountains are very steep, it becomes almost impossible to bring the canoes down the river itself and utterly impossible to portage them along the cliff sides...shooting the rapids is fraught with the possibility of the gravest disaster, and yet it is imperatively necessary to attempt it".

Within days all the party's original canoes, which were dragged across the *cerrado* and pushed and pulled through the Amazonian rain forest, were smashed against the canyon cliffs. Rondon ordered

crude new canoes honed out of tree trunks. Some were smashed by the wild river and a Brazilian porter, named Simplicio, drowned when his canoe turned over in white water.

Two and a half weeks from Manaus, the former president suffered a sharp attack of fever. But he reported that, thanks to the excellent care of the doctor, he was over it in just about 48 hours.

However, others believe Roosevelt suffered a serious bout of malaria. At times he was delirious and for two weeks he couldn't walk. At one point Roosevelt told Rondon to leave him behind, to which Rondon reportedly replied, "Do you think you are still president and can order everybody around? Permit me to remind you that the expedition is called Roosevelt-Rondon and it is for this reason, and this reason alone, that I cannot go off and let you die.".

Rondon ordered a make-shift stretcher with a palm-frond canopy. The stretcher was dragged through the jungle during the portages and loaded onto a canoe for travel down the smoother stretches of the river. Roosevelt suffered for two weeks.

By the time the party reached the confluence of the River of Doubt and the Madeira, he was able to dress himself and walk. There was a ceremony at the site and Rondon dedicated a plaque with the two simple words "Rio Roosevelt".

The former president was justifiably proud. He wrote, "We were putting on the map a river running through between 5 and 6 degrees of latitude of which no geographer in any map published in Europe or the U.S. or Brazil had ever admitted the possibility of the existence".

"The Great, Green Hell": But even expeditions as heroic as the Roosevelt-Rondon Mission have proven inadequate to the task of thorough Amazon exploration. The geography of the region is constantly, often rapidly, changing. In 1836, five Portuguese trading vessels anchored off Santarém were washed away by an unstable "grass" island uprooted by the powerful Amazon current. Even today these "ghost islands" can rapidly alter the Amazon's geography to the point where navigational charts are only valid for about 20 years.

And then there is the jungle itself, described by earlier travelers as "The Great, Green Hell", a vast heart of darkness so overgrown and dim that, during rubber boom days, collectors of the precious latex often used lanterns while tramping through the forest during the day.

While the obstacles remain, so do the dreams. In the early 1980s, gold was discovered in an Amazon mountain range, the Serra Pelada.

By 1985, over 50,000 prospectors were toiling up and down vast pits dug into the mountainsides in search of their fortunes. The gold strike sparked a new rush of adventurers, all in search of the same yellow metal that first brought the white man to the Amazon over 400 years ago, taking the Amazon's eternal boom-bust cycle back to its origins in the El Dorado legend of the conquistadors.

Left, weighing gold at Serra Pelade. Above, nuggets from the world's largest gold mine. Following page, lineman at work.

TRAVEL TIPS

GETTING THERE

BY AIR

A total of 28 airlines offer international service to and from Brazil with a variety of routes (see list under Domestic Travel, GETTING AROUND section). Although most incoming flights head for Rio de Janeiro, depending on where you are coming from, there are also direct flights to São Paulo and Brasília, Salvador and Recife on the northeastern coast, and to the northern cities of Belém and Manaus on the Amazon River. Direct international flights link Brazil with both the east and west coast of the United States, as well as with Florida and Canada, major cities in Europe and South America, Japan and several African cities. Flight time is nine hours from New York, slightly less from Miami, and 13 hours from Los Angeles; flights from Europe average 11-12 hours. Almost all international flights are overnight, so that you arrive conveniently in the early morning.

There are a variety of special low-cost package deals, some of them real bargains. A travel agent will be able to find out what is available and make arrangements at no extra cost to you. (See Domestic Travel, under GETTING AROUND section for details on Brazilian air passes which must be bought outside Brazil).

Upon arrival, the airports have facilities for exchanging currency and information posts to help you find transportation or make a connecting flight.

BY SEA

Although there is no regular ocean passenger service to Brazil, it is possible to come by boat. Both Oremar and Linea C, which operate cruises up and down the Atlantic coast of South America during the European winter, will take on transatlantic passengers when the ships come over the return. One of Linea C's cruises out of Rio visits Miami. Several round-the-world cruise ships call at Brazilian ports and it is possible to book a seat for just the trip to Brazil.

Special cruises are also organized to travel up the Amazon River or to visit Rio at Carnival. The Blue Star Line, headquartered in London, carries a limited number of passengers on its cargo boats.

BY ROAD

There are bus services between a few of the larger Brazilian cities and major cities in neighboring South American countries, including Asuncion (Paraguay), Buenos Aires (Argentina), Montevideo (Uruguay) and Santiago (Chile). While undoubtedly a good way to see a lot of the countryside, remember that distances are great and you will be sitting in a bus for several days and nights.

TRAVEL ESSENTIALS

VISAS & PASSPORTS

Until just a few years ago, tourist visas were issued routinely to all visitors upon arrival. Brazil has now adopted a reciprocity policy: citizens from countries which require Brazilians to hold a visa to visit, now need an entry visa, which must be obtained before arriving in Brazil. U.S. and French citizens are required to arrive with such a visa; Britons and Germans are not. The airline you are flying or your travel agent should be able to tell you whether you need to apply for a visa before traveling. If not, contact the nearest Brazilian consulate or embassy.

If your passport was issued by one of the countries whose citizens are not required to arrive with an entry visa, it will be stamped with a tourist visa upon entry. The tourist visa permits you to remain in the country for 90 consecutive days. If you apply for a visa abroad, it will permit entry into Brazil for 90 days following the issue date. Upon entry you will receive the same tourist visa, valid for 90 days beginning with the entry date stamped in your passport.

If, however, you are traveling to several countries and not straight to Brazil, the entry visa needn't be issued in your home country. But it's still a good idea to allow for enough time so as to avoid surprises and hassles. The 90-day tourist visa can be renewed once only for another 90 days, so that you can stay a maximum of 180 days as a tourist in Brazil. To obtain such an extension, you must go to the immigration section of the federal police. Your country's consulate may be helpful here and will be able to furnish some addresses.

Temporary visas are issued to foreigners who will be working or doing any business in Brazil. These allow a longer stay than a tourist visa would. If you are a student, journalist or researcher, or someone in the employment of a multinational company, contact a Brazilian consulate or embassy well before you plan to travel, as it is usually difficult or even impossible to change the status of your visa once you are in the country. If you come with a tourist visa, you will probably have to leave the country to obtain and return on another type of visa.

Permanent visas which allow foreigners to reside and work in Brazil without giving up their own nationality are more difficult to obtain. Once again, it's best to contact a Brazilian consulate or embassy for more specific information you need.

MONEY MATTERS

Brazil's currency was changed in 1990 to the *cruzeiro* (abbreviated Cz$). As the two previous currencies that existed from 1986 to March 1990, the *cruzado* and the *cruzado novo*, are still in circulation (along with remnants of the old *cruzeiro* used prior to 1986), it can be confusing at times for the visitor to sort things out.

The bills are supposed to bear a stamp with their new name and value, but not all bills have been stamped. To understand the bills, use the following guidelines:

One *cruzado novo* is equal to one *cruzeiro*.

One thousand *cruzados* are equal to one *cruzeiro* (simply lop off three zeroes from the *cruzados*).

One million old *cruzeiros* equal one *cruzeiro* (this conversion will rarely be necessary as so few old *cruzeiros* are still used).

Thus, the purple-and-tan 1,000 *cruzado* bill is worth 1 *cruzeiro*, and the green-and-red 100 *cruzeiros*. A general rule to help sort out the confusion: the smaller (in size of paper) bills are actually worth more than the seemingly more important bigger notes.

One *cruzeiro* is made up of one hundred *centavos*, or cents. Following the same rules of conversion, green 500 *cruzado* bills are worth fifty *centavos* or half a *cruzeiro*.

Because of rampant inflation, coins have not been greatly in use.

The use of commas and decimal points in Portuguese is the opposite of what you are probably used to, so that 1,000 *cruzeiros* is written Cr$ 1.000,00.

Unfortunately, the exchange rate fluctuates so often that even an idea of what it might be cannot be given here. Leading newspapers list the U.S. dollar-*cruzeiro* exchange values daily, with a higher rate for "buying" (*compra*) than for "selling" (*venda*) dollars. There is a special rate for tourists, called the *turismo* rate, which closely follows the "parallel" (*paralelo*), or black market rate but is perfectly legal. (Both of these rates are, naturally, higher than the "official" government-set exchange rate). You can exchange your dollars, as well as yen, pounds and other currencies, at the *turismo* rate at accredited banks, hotels and tourist agencies. If you can't find one of these, just about any old travel agency will exchange your currency at the black market rate, although this is, strictly speaking, an illegal transaction.

Hotels do not exchange traveler's checks or they give a worse rate for these bills. They cannot change any leftover *cruzeiros* back into your currency at the end of your stay.

Banks will not exchange *cruzeiros* or traveler's checks into into foreign currency. The only exception is the Banco do Brasil branches located at international airports. As you are leaving the country, they will exchange back, at the official rate, 30 percent of the amount of currency that you exchanged at a similar airport branch bank on your way into Brazil (you must show the receipt of the initial exchange). You can't get your traveler's checks cashed into dollars anywhere at all.

Most hotels will accept payment in traveler's checks or with almost any major credit card. Many restaurants and shops also take credit cards and will usually display those which they accept at the entrance—most frequently Diners Club, American Express, Mastercard and Visa—which all have offices in Brazil. Back home, your bill will be calculated using the *turismo* exchange rate. The exception to this is for airline tickets purchased on credit in Brazil (including tickets for travel just within Brazil). These will be calculated at the less favorable official rate.

Of course, you can also pay with dollars. Hotels, restaurants, stores, taxis, etc. will usually quote an exchange rate that falls somwhere between the official and the parallel. Just try to keep up to date with the rates so that you will know what is fair.

HEALTH

Brazil does not normally require any health or inoculation certificates for entry, nor will you be required to have one to enter another country from Brazil. If you plan to travel in areas outside of cities in the Amazon region or in the Pantanal in Mato Grosso, however, it is recommended for your own comfort and safety—that you have a yellow fever shot (protects you for 10 years, but is effective only after 10 days, so plan ahead). It is also a good idea to protect yourself against malaria in these same jungle areas and although there is no vaccine against malaria, there are drugs that will provide immunity while you are taking them. Consult your local public health service and be sure to get a certificate for any vaccination.

WHAT TO WEAR

Brazilians are very fashion conscious but are actually quite casual dressers. What you bring along, of course, will depend on where you will be visiting and your holiday schedule. São Paulo tends to be more dressy; small inland towns are more conservative. If you are going to a jungle lodge, you will want sturdy clothing and perhaps boots. However, if you come on business, a suit and tie for men, and suits, skirts or dresses for women are the office standard.

Although some restaurants in the downtown business districts of the larger cities require a tie at lunch, other restaurants have no such regulations—although obviously in a posh establishment you are expected to dress appropriately and you yourself will feel better if you blend in. Still, a suit and tie are rarely called for when you go out. Generally speaking, suits and ties are used less the farther north you go in Brazil, even by businessmen, and the opposite holds true as you go farther south. Bring a summer-weight suit for office calls—linen is smart and cool.

If you do like to dress up, there are plenty of places to go out to in the evening in the big cities. But avoid ostentation and using jewelry that will attract more attention to yourself than you may want. There are many desperately poor people in Brazil and unwitting foreign tourists make attractive targets for pickpockets and purse-snatchers.

Shorts are acceptable for both men and women in most areas, especially near the beach or in resort towns, but are not usually worn downtown. Loose bermudas are comfortable for the hot weather.

Most churches and some museums do not admit visitors dressed in shorts and the traditional *gafieira* dance halls will not admit those, especially men, dressed in shorts. Jeans are also acceptable dress for men and women and are worn a great deal in Brazil—but they can be hot.

Don't forget to pack your swimsuit! Or buy a tiny local version of the string bikini, called a tanga, for yourself or someone back home—there are stores that sell nothing but beachwear. New styles emerge each year, in different fabrics and colors, exposing this part or that. They seem to get smaller every year, but somehow they never disappear completely.

Although there have been a few timid—or rather brave—attempts at topless sunbathing on Brazil's beaches, it has never really caught on. Women exposing their breasts on the beach have often been hassled and sometimes even attacked, which is really rather ironic because the skimpy bikinis that Brazilians wear are actually much more provocative than if everyone were quite naturally naked.

Another contradiction is that while everyone can walk around with practically nothing on at the beach—indeed the bikini bottoms are small—decently dressed women get ogled too. While Brazilian men don't go in for catcalls, they draw their breath in sharply between clenched teeth and murmur comments as the women pass by...just as well you don't understand what they're saying. Brazilian women certainly don't let this cramp their style.

In Rio and São Paulo nothing will be considered too trendy or outlandish. In smaller towns, although the locals may dress more conservatively, they are used to outsiders, including Brazilian tourists from the big cities. Somehow, no matter how foreign tourists are dressed, Brazilians seem able to spot most of them a mile away.

If you come during Carnival, remember that it will be very hot to begin with and you will probably be in a crowd and dancing nonstop. Anything colorful is appropriate. If you plan to go to any of the balls, you will find plenty of costumes in the shops—you might want to buy just a feathered hair ornament, flowered lei or sequined accessory to complete your outfit. Many women wear no more than a bikini and makeup and sometimes even less. Most men wear shorts—with or without a shirt—or sometimes a sarong. There are also fancy-dress balls with themes such as "Hawaii" or "Arabian Nights."

If you are traveling in the south or in the mountains or even to São Paulo in winter, it can be quite chilly. Even in the areas where it is hot all year round, you may need a light sweater, jacket or sweatshirt, if not for the cooler evenings, then for the air conditioning in hotels, restaurants and offices!

Rain gear is always handy to have along—Brazilians tend to use umbrellas more than raincoats. Something that folds up small and can be slipped into your bag is best. Sunglasses are also a good idea, especially for the beach. Seaside hotels will provide you with sun umbrellas and beach towels.

As on any trip, it is sensible to bring a pair of comfortable walking shoes—there is no better way to explore than on foot. Sandals are comfortable in the heat and either sandals or beach thongs, even if you don't plan to wear them for walking around the streets, are very convenient for getting across the hot sand from your hotel to the water's edge. If there's one thing that gives Brazilians the giggles, it's the sight of a "gringo" going to the beach in shoes and socks. Brazilians often wear high-heeled shoes and show special agility on the sidewalks which can be veritable obstacle courses—with holes, puddles, beggars, vendors, garbage cans and cobblestones—and are frequently completely taken over by parked cars. Or you may want to buy shoes or sandals while in Brazil—leather goods are a steal.

A sturdy shoulder bag is a practical item—use it to carry your camera discreetly. Toss in a foldable umbrella, guidebook and map and you're ready for a day's outing. But in the big-city streets, don't wear it slung around behind you.

Clothing made of synthetic fibers may be handy—easy to wash and doesn't need ironing. But in the tropics these fabrics do not breathe, absorb perspiration as natural fibers do and will make you feel twice as hot. Bring washable clothes instead, or if you have anything that needs special cleaning, have it washed when you return from your trip. While laundry service in the hotels is usually excellent, dry cleaning in Brazil is generally not very reliable.

There is nothing better for the heat than cotton and since Brazil produces linen and exports cotton, you might want to pack the bare essentials and acquire a new wardrobe; clothes are a great bargain. When buying clothes, remember that although most material is sanforized, some natural fabrics will shrink. *Pequeno* = Small; *Médio* = Medium; and *Grande* = Large (often marked "P," "M" and "G"). *Maior* means larger; *menor* means smaller.

CUSTOMS

You will be given a declaration form to fill out in the airplane before arrival. At the airport, customs officials spot check 50 percent of incoming "nothing to declare" travelers. If you are coming as a tourist and bringing articles obviously for your personal use, you will have no problem. As with most countries, food products of animal origin, plants, fruit and seeds may be confiscated.

You can bring in $300 worth of anything bought at the airport duty free shop—with no restriction as to quantity, type of goods or age—and $300 worth of anything brought from abroad, except liquor, which is limited to one bottle (each) of wine and spirits.

If you are coming on business, it's best to check with the consulate as to what limitations or obligations you are subject to. Brazil has very strict regulations limiting the entrance of computers into the country. If you must bring specialized equipment, especially computers, into the country, apply for written authorization through a Brazilian consulate before traveling and then register with customs for temporary entrance—you must take it out of the country with you.

Electronic devices worth no more than $300 can be brought in on a tourist visa and need not leave the country with you. You do not need to seal such items while visiting as a tourist and they can be left in the country as gifts. Professional samples may be brought in if the quantity does not lead customs inspectors to suspect that they are, in fact, for sale.

Such items that may not be allowed into the country, although they won't be confiscated, may be detained by the customs service and returned to you as you leave the country. Once again, if in doubt, consult the nearest consulate and bring their written reply with you.

Baggage of outgoing travelers is usually never checked, except for a security check of hand luggage. If you have purchased what could be considered a reasonal amount for a tourist of anything—including semi-precious stones—you have nothing to worry about. Be wary of buying and bringing out wild animal skins, including alligator, as hunting of these species is strictly prohibited. It's a good idea to find out what you can or cannot bring back into your own country.

GETTING ACQUAINTED

GOVERNMENT & ECONOMY

Brazil is a federal republic with 26 states and one federal district. Each state has its own legislature. Since the federal government exercises enormous control over the economy, the political autonomy of the states is restricted. The overwhelming majority of government tax receipts are collected by the federal government and then distributed to the states and cities. The head of government is the president who has large powers and, in fact, exercises more control over the nation than the American president does over the United States. The legislative branch of the federal government is composed of a Congress divided into a lower house, the Chamber of Deputies, and an upper house, the Senate.

In February 1987, however, the Federal Congress was sworn in as a Constituent Assembly to draft a new Constitution for Brazil. The result of their work, promulgated the following year, produced some alterations in the balance of power. Moves towards decentralization boosted the state and municipal authorities, and Congress' hand was significantly strengthened against the presidency. However, in 1990, the early months in government of President Fernando Collor de Mello proved that a strong head of state backed by the popular vote could still ride roughshod over Congress and disregard some of the constitutional restrictions on his authority. The Constituent Assembly fixed 1993 as the date for a plebiscite to determine whether the country's government will remain essentially presidential or move towards a parliamentary system; Brazilians will even have the option of voting for a return to monarchy.

Brazil's main problem throughout this century has been political instability. The

1988 constitution is the country's fifth since 1930. During this period, Brazil has suffered frequent intervention by the military leading to a situation where brief attempts at democratic civilian rule have been substituted by either increased military influence or a direct military takeover. The last military regime began with a coup in 1964 and extended until 1985 when a civilian president, chosen by an electoral college, took office. The transition to full democracy was completed at the end of 1989 with Brazil's first direct presidential elections in almost three decades.

Despite its political problems, Brazil has enjoyed excellent economic growth rates for most of the past 30 years. Though growth faltered with the high inflation of the 1980s and the 1990 austerity package brought the country face to face with recession, Brazil has held on to its position as the economic leader among Third World nations. Thanks to massive investments from abroad through foreign loans and direct investments by multinational companies, Brazil in the 1960s and 1970s underwent a rapid phase of industrialization, emerging as the tenth largest economy in the world in terms of gross national product. Brazil is also the leading exporter in Latin America. Today 70 percent of its exports are composed of manufactured goods.

TIME ZONES

Despite the fact that Brazil covers such a vast area, over 50 percent of the country is in the same time zone and it is in this area, which includes the entire coastline, that most of the major cities are located. The western extension of this zone is a north-south line from the mouth of the Amazon River, going west to include the northern state of Amapá, east around the states of Mato Grosso and Mato Grosso do Sul and back west to include the south. This time zone, where Rio de Janeiro, São Paulo, Belém and Brasília are located, is three hours behind Greenwich Mean Time (GMT). Another large zone encompassing the Pantanal states of Mato Grosso and Mato Grosso do Sul, and most of Brazil's north is four hours behind GMT. The far western state of Acre and the westernmost part of Amazonas state are in a time zone five hours behind GMT. This compares as follows to standard times in other parts of the world:

7:00 a.m.- San Francisco
9:00 a.m.- Mexico City
10:00 a.m.- Bogota, Montreal, New York
10:30 a.m.- Caracas
11:00 a.m.- Manaus, Santiago
12:00 p.m.- Buenos Aires
12:00 p.m.-Belém, Brasília, Recife, Rio de Janeiro, Salvador, São Paulo
3:00 p.m.- London
4:00 p.m.- Berlin, Geneva, Paris
5:00 p.m.- Capetown, Helsinki
6:00 p.m.- Moscow
11:00 p.m.- Hong Kong
12:00 a.m. - Tokyo
1:00 a.m.- Melbourne

Daylight-saving time has been used in recent years, with clocks being set ahead in October and back to standard time in March or April.

CLIMATE

Almost all of Brazil's 5.3 million square miles (8.5 million sq. km) of territory lie between the Equator and the Tropic of Capricorn. Within this tropical zone, temperatures and rainfall vary from north to south, from the coast inland, and from low areas (Amazon River Basin, Pantanal as well as along the coast) to higher altitudes. If you're coming from the Northern Hemisphere, remember that seasons are inverted, although at this latitude seasons are less distinct than in temperate zones.

In Brazil's north, in the Amazon River Basin jungle region, the climate is humid equatorial, characterized by high temperatures and humidity, with heavy rainfall all year round. Although some areas have no dry season, most places have a short respite occurring some time between July and November so that the rivers are highest from December through June. Average temperature is 75°-80°F (24°-27°C).

The eastern Atlantic coast from Rio Grande do Norte to the state of São Paulo has a humid tropical climate, also hot, but with slightly less rainfall than in the north and with summer and winter seasons. The northeastern coast, nearer to the equator, experiences little difference in summer/winter temperatures, but more rain fall—in winter, especially April-June. The coastal southeast receives more rain in summer (December-March). Average temperature is 70°-75°F (21°-24°C), being consistently warm in the northeast, but fluctuating in Rio de Janeiro from summer highs of 104°F (40°C) down to 65°F (18°C), with winter temperatures usually in the 70 degrees bracket.

Most of Brazil's interior has a semi-humid tropical climate, with a hot, rainy summer from December through March and a dryer, cooler winter (June-August). Year-round average temperature is 68°-82°F (20°-28°C). São Paulo, at an altitude of 2,600 feet (800 meters) above sealevel, and Brasília, 3,500 feet (over 1,000 meters) above sealevel on the central plateau, as well as mountainous Minas Gerais, can get quite cool—although the thermometer may read a mild 50°F (10°C), it will not feel so balmy indoors if there is no heating.

Mountainous areas in the Southeast have a high-altitude tropical climate, similar to the semi-humid tropical climate, but rainy and dry seasons are more pronounced and temperatures are cooler, averaging from 64°-73°F (18°-23°C).

Part of the interior of the Northeast has a tropical semi-arid climate—hot with sparse rainfall. Most of the rain falls during three months, usually March-May, but sometimes the season is shorter and in some years there is no rainfall at all. Average temperature is 75°-80°F (24°-27°C).

Brazil's South, below the Tropic of Capricorn, has a humid subtropical climate. Rainfall is distributed regularly throughout the year and temperatures vary from 30° and 40°F (0°-10°C) in winter, with occasional frosts and snowfall (but the latter is rare) to 70°-80°F (21°-32°C) in summer.

CULTURE & CUSTOMS

Social customs here are not vastly different from what you will find in other "western" countries.

Brazilians can be both awkwardly formal and disarmingly informal.

Surnames are little used. Yet even though people start out on a first name basis, titles of respect—*senhor* for men and most frequently *dona* for women—are used to be polite to strangers but also to show respect to someone of a different age group or social class. In some families, for example, children address their parents as *o senhor* and *a senhora* instead of what would be the equivalent of "you."

While handshaking is a common practice when people are introduced, it is customary to greet not only friends and relatives but also complete strangers to whom you are being introduced with hugs and kisses. The "social" form of kissing consists usually of a kiss on each cheek. While men and women greet each other with kisses, as do women among themselves, in most circles men do not kiss each other, rather shaking hands while giving a pat on the shoulder with the other hand. Or if they are more intimate, men will embrace, thumping each other on the back. Although this is the general custom, there are subtleties about who kisses whom governed by social position.

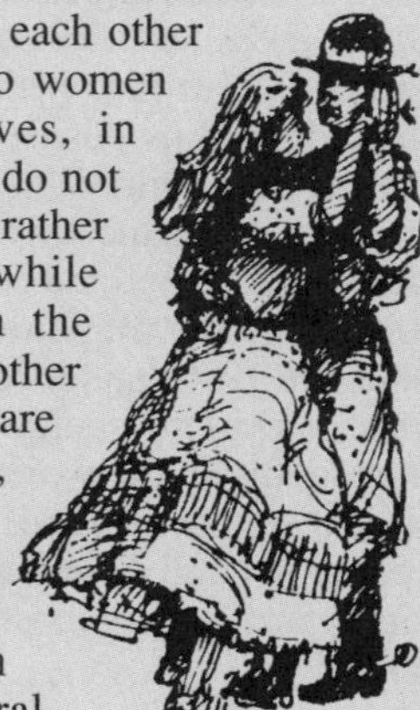

Besides the more formal forms of hugging and kissing, visitors from some cultures remark that Brazilians seem to be quite unabashed about expressing affection in public.

Brazilians are generous hosts, seeing to it that guests' glasses, plates or coffee cups are never empty. Besides the genuine pleasure of being a gracious host, there is the question of honor. The "pot luck" or "bring-your-own-bottle" party is not popular in Brazil—people like to give a party, even the poor.

Although Brazil's is definitely a male-dominated society, machismo here takes a milder and more subtle form than it is generally found in neighboring Hispanic America.

While they are at all other times a polite, decent people, something happens when Brazilians get behind the steering wheel. Be cautious when driving or crossing streets and be prepared to make a dash. Drivers expect pedestrians to watch out for themselves and get out of the way.

Unless you're here on business, expect schedules to be more flexible than you may be used to. It's not considered rude to show up half an hour to an hour late for a social engagement.

TIPPING

Most restaurants will usually add a 10 percent service charge onto your bill. If you are in doubt as to whether it has been included, it's best to ask (*O serviço está incluido*?). Give the waiter a bigger tip if you feel the service was special. Although many waiters will don a sour face if you don't tip above the 10 percent included in the bill, you have no obligation to do so. Tipping at a lunch counter is optional, but people often leave the change from their bill—even a sum as little as U.S.10 cents is appreciated.

Hotels will also add a 10 percent service charge to your bill, but this doesn't necessarily go to the individuals who were helpful to you. Don't be afraid that you are overtipping—if you tip as much as you would at home, it will be considered very generous indeed; if you tip too little in hotels, however, it could be insulting and it would have been better not to tip at all.

Tipping taxi drivers is optional, most Brazilians don't. Again, if your driver has been especially helpful or waited for you, reward him appropriately. Drivers should be tipped if they help with the luggage—some will charge from US 35 to 50 cents per bag. Tip the airport porter about this rate (or he may tell you how much it is) and tip the last porter to help you. What you pay goes into a pool.

A 10-20 percent tip is expected in barbershops and beauty salons; shoeshine boys, gas station attendants, etc. should be paid about a third to half of what you would expect to tip at home. Boys offering to watch your car on the street expect to get about U.S. 45 to 50 cents when you return to collect the car. If they try to charge you as much as U.S.$1 or U.S.$1.50 in advance outside a busy nightclub or theater, it's best to pay or you may find the car scratched when you return.

If you are a houseguest, leave a tip for any household help (who cooked or laundered for you while you were there). Ask your hosts how much would be appropriate; you can always tip in dollars if you want to. This will be especially appreciated.

WEIGHTS & MEASURES

The metric system is used throughout Brazil and temperature is measured on the centigrade or Celsius scale. Other measuring units are sometimes used in rural areas, but people are generally familiar with the metric system. But if you are not, here's how to convert to and from the imperial system:

TEMPERATURE

degrees Celsius x 9/5 + 32 = degrees Fahrenheit
degrees Fahrenheit - 32 x 5/9 = degrees Celsius
(degree = *grau*)

CAPACITY/LIQUIDS

liter x 1.06 = quart
liter x .26 = gallon
liter x 2.11 = pint
(liter = *litro*)
quart x .95 = liter
gallon x 3.79 = liter
pint x .47 = liter

WEIGHT

gram x .04 = ounce
kilogram x 2.20 = pound
metric ton x .98 = ton
ounce x 28.35 = gram
pound x .45 = kilogram
ton x 1.11 = metric ton
(gram = *grama*, kilogram = *quilograma* or more often *quilo* or kilo and ton = *tonelada*)

LENGTH

millimeters x .039 = inch
meter x 3.28 = foot
meter x 1.09 = yard
kilometer x .62 = mile
inch x 25.40 = millimeter
foot x .30 = meter
yard x .91 = meter

mile x 1.61 = kilometer
(millimeter = *milímetro*, centimeter = *centímetro*, meter = *metro* and kilometer = *quilômetro*)

AREA

hectare x 2.47 = acre
acre x .40 = hectare

ELECTRICITY

Electric voltage is not standardized throughout Brazil, but most cities have a 127-volt current, as is the case of Rio de Janeiro and São Paulo, Belém, Belo Horizonte, Corumbá and Cuiabá, Curitiba, Foz do Iguaçu, Porto Alegre and Salvador. The electric current usage is 220 volts in Brasília, Florianópolis, Fortaleza, Recife and São Luis. Manaus uses 110-volt electricity.

If you can't do without your electric shaver, hair dryer or personal computer, enquire about the voltage when making hotel reservations. If you plug an appliance into a lower voltage than it was made for, it will function poorly, but if you plug it into a much stronger current it can overheat and short-circuit. Double check at the front desk when you check into your hotel. Adapters are cumbersome, but many appliances have a switch so that they can be used with either a 110- or 220-volt current (110-volt appliances work normally on a 127-volt current). Many hotels have adapters and some even have more than one voltage available.

BUSINESS HOURS

Business hours for offices in most cities are 9:00 a.m. to 6:00 p.m. Monday through Friday. Lunch "hours" may last literally hours.

Banks open from 10:00 a.m. to 4:30 p.m. Monday through Friday. The *casas de câmbio* currency exchanges operate usually from 9:00 a.m. to 5:00 or 5:30 p.m.

Most stores are open from 9:00 a.m. to 6:30 or 7:00 p.m., but may stay open much later, depending on their location. The shopping centers are open Monday through Saturday from 10:00 a.m. to 10:00 p.m., as a rule, although not all the shops inside keep the same hours. Large department stores are usually open from 9:00 a.m. to 10:00 p.m. Monday through Friday and from 9:00 a.m. to 6:30 p.m. on Saturdays. Most supermarkets are open from 8:00 a.m. to 8:00 p.m.; some stay open even later.

Service station hours vary, but they now have the option of staying open 24 hours a day seven days a week.

Post offices are open to the public from 8:00 a.m. to 6:00 p.m. on weekdays and from 8:00 a.m. to noon on Saturdays. Some of the larger cities have one branch that stays open 24 hours a day. (See Postal Services).

Many pharmacies stay open until 10:00 p.m. and larger cities will have 24-hour drug stores.

Hours of the day are numbered straight through from "zero hour" to 24, but can also be referred to as being in the morning (*da manhã*), in the afternoon (*da tarde*) or at night (*da noite*), so that 8:00 p.m. could either be referred to as vinte horas (literally 20 hours, written 20:00) or as *oito* (8) *horas da noite*, eight at night.

HOLIDAYS

National holidays in Brazil are now moved to the nearest Monday, with the exception of New Year's Day, Carnival, Easter and Christmas. Besides national holidays, there are many dates on which religious or historical events are commemorated locally. Each city celebrates the day of its patron saint and the date on which it was founded. Some regional folk celebrations do not have a set date, but take place in a given month, with each village and neighbourhood staging their own party—usually festivals with music, dancing (sometimes in costumes) and stalls hawking food and drinks traditionally prepared for the event. There are simply too many to mention here. The following calendar includes national holidays and just a few of the most important local fests.

January 1
—New Year's Day
(national holiday)
—Good Lord Jesus of the Seafarers (four-day celebration in Salvador; starts off with a boat parade)

January 6
—**Epiphany** (regional celebrations, mostly in the Northeast)

January (3rd Sunday)
—Festa do Bonfim (one of the largest celebrations in Salvador)

February 2
—**Iemanjá Festival** in Salvador (the Afro- Brazilian goddess of the sea in syncretism with Catholicism corresponds with the Virgin Mary)

February/March (moveable)
—**Carnival** (national holiday; celebrated all over Brazil on the four days leading up to Ash Wednesday. Most spectacular in Rio, Salvador and Recife/Olinda)

March/April (moveable)
—**Easter** (Good Friday is a national holiday; Colonial Ouro Preto puts on a colorful procession; passion play staged at Nova Jerusalem)

April 21
—**Tiradentes Day** (national holiday; in honor of the martyred hero of Brazil's independence—celebrations in his native Minas Gerais, especially Ouro Preto)

May 1
—**Labor Day** (national holiday)

May/June (moveable)
—**Corpus Christi** (national holiday)

June/July
—**Festas Juninas** (a series of street festivals held in June and early July in honor of Saints John, Peter and Anthony, featuring bonfires, dancing and mock marriages)

June 15-30
—**Amazon Folk Festival** held in Manaus

June/July
—**Bumba-Meu-Boi** (processions and street dancing in Maranhão are held in the second half of June and beginning of July)

September 7
—**Independence Day** (national holiday)

October
—**Oktoberfest** in Blumenau (put on by descendents of German immigrants)

October 12
—**Nossa Senhora de Aparecida** (national holiday honoring Brazil's patron saint)

November 2
—**All Souls Day** (national holiday)

November 15
—**Proclamation of the Republic** (national holiday, also election day)

December 25
—**Christmas** (national holiday)

December 31
—**New Year's Eve** (on Rio de Janeiro beaches, gifts are offered to Iemanjá).

RELIGIOUS SERVICES

Catholicism is the official and dominant religion in Brazil, but many people are followers of religions of African origin. Of these *Candomblé* is the purer form, with deities (the *orixás*), rituals, music, dance and even language very similar to what is practised in the parts of Africa from which it was brought. *Umbanda* involves a syncretism with Catholicism in which each orixá has a corresponding Catholic saint. Spiritualism, also widely practised in Brazil, contains both African and European influences. Many Brazilians who are nominally Catholic attend both Afro-Brazilian and/or spiritual and Christian rites.

Candomblé is practised most in Bahia, while *Umbanda* and Spiritualism seem to have more mass appeal. You can arrange through your hotel to see a ceremony—visitors are welcome so long as they show respect for the belief of others. Ask permission before taking any photographs.

If you wish to attend a service at a church of your faith while in Brazil, many religious groups can be found in the larger cities and, besides the ever-present Catholic churches, there are many Protestant churches throughout Brazil. Because of the diplomatic personnel in Brasília, there is a large variety of churches and temples. Rio de Janeiro and São Paulo both have several synagogues, as well as churches with services in foreign languages, including English. Your hotel or your country's consulate should be able to help you find a suitable place of worship.

COMMUNICATIONS

MEDIA

Newspapers and Magazines: The *Miami Herald*, the Latin America edition of the *International Herald Tribune* and the *Wall Street Journal* are available on many newsstands in the big cities, as are such news magazines as *Time* and *Newsweek*. At larger newsstands and airport bookshops are other foreign newspapers and a large selection of international publications, including German, French and English magazines.

You may want to buy a local paper to find out what's on in town (besides the musical shows, there are always many foreign movies showing in the original language with Portuguese subtitles) or to check the exchange rate. You don't need to be proficient in Portuguese to read the entertainment listings under the headings *cinema*, *show*, *dança*, *música*, *teatro*, *televisão*, *exposicões*. *Crianças* means "children," and exchange rates are listed under *câmbio*.

If you do know some Portuguese and want to read the Brazilian newspapers, the most authoritative and respected include: São Paulo's *Folha de São Paulo*, *Estado de São Paulo* and *Gazeta Mercantil* and *Rio's Jornal do Brasil* and *O Globo*. There is no nationwide paper, but these wide-circulation dailies reach a good part of the country. The colorful weekly magazine *Manchete*, along with *Veja* and *Isto E*, are also good sources of information

Television and Radio: Brazilian television is very sophisticated—so much so that Brazil successfully exports programs, not just to Third World nations, but to Europe as well. There are five national and three regional networks, which along with independent stations bring television service to nearly all parts of Brazil.

Only one network, the educational television, is government-controlled. Brazil's giant *T.V., Globo* is the fourth largest commercial network in the world. With over 40 stations in a country with a high illiteracy rate, it has great influence over the information many people have access to.

The Brazilian soap opera or *telenovela* is a unique feature. They're shown on prime time and just about everybody watches, getting so caught up in the continuing drama that they schedule social and even professional activities so as not to clash with the crucial chapters. The well-made soaps both reflect customs and set trends in fashion, speech and social habits. You might find it interesting to watch a few simply because of the fact that they are considered a true mirror of Brazilian urban middle-class society.

Only about a third of all television programs are imports—mostly from the United States. Foreign series, specials, sports coverage and movies are dubbed in Portuguese, except for some of the late-night movies and musical shows. Some of the top hotels have satellite dishes and receive the English-language *Armed Forces Radio and Television Service* with a selection of news and sports from American networks.

There are close to 2,000 radio stations around Brazil which play international and Brazilian pop hits, as well as a variety of Brazil's rich musical offerings, reflecting regional tastes. A good deal of American music is played; classical music airing is also strong including Sunday afternoon operas in some areas. The Culture Ministry station often has some very interesting musical programs. All broadcasts are in Portuguese. But if you have a radio that picks up short-wave transmissions, the *Voice of America and BBC World Service* broadcast English-language programs to Brazil.

POSTAL SERVICES

Post offices generally are open from 8:00 a.m. to 6:00 p.m. Monday-Friday, 8:00 a.m. to noon on Saturdays and are closed on Sundays and holidays. In large cities, some branch offices stay open until later. (The post office in the Rio de Janeiro International Airport is open 24 hours a day.) Post offices are usually designated with a sign reading correios or sometimes "ECT" (for *Empresa de Correios e Telégrafos* = Postal and Telegraph Company).

An airmail letter to or from the United States takes about a week. Domestic post is usually delivered a day or two after it is mailed. National and international rapid mail service is available, as well as registered post and parcel service (the post office has special boxes for these). Stamps for collectors can be also be purchased at the post office.

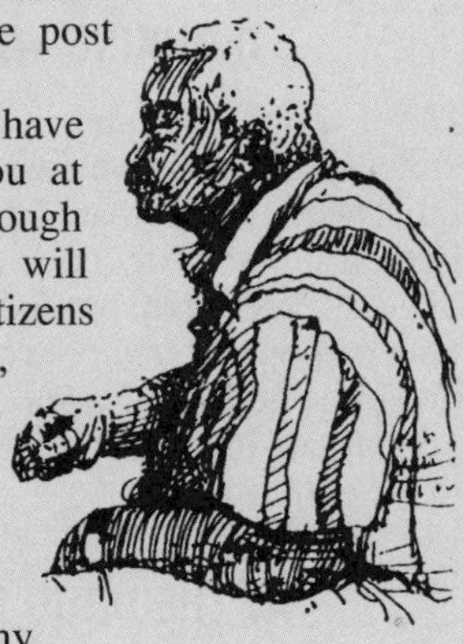

You can also have mail sent to you at your hotel. Although some consulates will hold mail for citizens of their country, they tend to discourage this practice.

Telegrams: You can send telegrams from any post office or by telephone (dial 135). This is easily arranged through your hotel. If you are a houseguest, the operator will be able to tell you how much will be charged to your host's phone bill.

TELEPHONE & TELEX

Pay phones in Brazil use tokens which are sold at newsstands, bars or shops, usually located near the phones. Ask for *fichas de telefone* (the "i" is pronounced like a long "e" and the "ch" has an "sh" sound). Each ficha is good for three minutes, after which your call will be cut off. To avoid being cut off in the middle of a call, insert several tokens into the slot—unused tokens will be returned when you hang up. The sidewalk *telefone público* is also called an *orelhão* (big ear) because of the protective shell which takes the place of a booth—yellow for local or collect calls, blue for direct-dial long-distance calls within Brazil. The latter requires a special, more expensive token. You can also call from a *posto telefônico*, a telephone company station (most bus stations and airports have such facilities), where you can either buy tokens, use a phone and pay the cashier afterward, or make a credit card or collect call.

International Calls to almost any country can be made from Brazil. Country codes are listed at the front of telephone directories. To place a call:

Direct dialing—00 + country code + area code + phone number; **000333**—information regarding long distance calls (area codes, directory assistance, complaint s);

000111—international operator. Go through operator to place person-to-person, collect and credit card calls. Operators and interpreters who speak several languages are available;

107—collect or telecard calls from a pay phone (no token needed);

000334—information regarding rates—international rates go down 20 percent between 8:00 p.m. and 5:00 a.m. (Brasília time) Monday-Saturday and all day Sunday.

Long Distance Domestic Calls: Area codes within Brazil are also listed on the first few pages of directories.

Direct dialing (IDD)—0 + area code + the phone number;

Direct-dial collect call—9 + area code + phone number. A recorded message will tell you to identify yourself and the city from which you are calling after the beep. If the party you are calling does not accept your call, they simply hang up;

107—operator-assisted collect call from pay phone (no token needed).

Domestic long-distance rates go down 75 percent every day between 11:00 p.m. and 6:00 a.m. and are 50 percent less expensive between 6:00 and 8:00 a.m. and 8:00 and 11:00 p.m. on weekdays, between 2:00 and

11:00 p.m. on Saturdays and between 6:00 a.m. and 11:00 p.m. on Sundays and on holidays.

Other service telephone numbers:

100—local operator

101—domestic long-distance operator

102—local directory assistance

area code + 102—directory assistance in that area.

108—information regarding rates

135—telegrams (local, national and international)

134—wake-up service

130—correct time

A telex can be sent from certain post offices and most hotels have telex service for their in-house guests.

Some of the top hotels have facsimile service: in Rio, the Rio Palace and Caesar Park hotels, in São Paulo, the Maksoud Plaza. You needn't be a guest to use this facility. (See addresses under WHERE TO STAY section).

EMERGENCIES

MEDICAL SERVICES

Should you need a doctor while in Brazil, the hotel you are staying at will be able to recommend reliable professionals who often speak several languages. Many of the better hotels even have a doctor on duty. Your consulate will also be able to supply you with a list of physicians who speak your language. In Rio de Janeiro, the Rio Health Collective (English-speaking) runs a 24-hour referral service. Tel: (021) 325-9300, ramal (or extension) 44 for the Rio area only.

Check with your health insurance company before traveling—some insurance plans cover any medical service that you may require while abroad.

DRINKING WATER

Don't drink tap water in Brazil. Although water in the cities is treated and is sometimes quite heavily chlorinated, people filter water in their homes. Any hotel or restaurant will have inexpensive bottled mineral water, both carbonated (*com gas* or "with gas") and uncarbonated (*sem gas* or "without gas"). If you are out in the hot sun, make an effort to drink extra fluids.

AT THE DRUG STORE

Prescription drugs are available in abundance—frequently without a prescription—and you may even find old favorites that have been banned for years in your country. Bring a supply of any prescription drugs that you take regularly but simple things like aspirin, antacids, bandaids, sunscreen, etc. are easy to obtain. Drug stores offer a variety of cosmetics, including many familiar brands. Sanitary napkins can be found in any drugstore or supermarket, but tampons are not always available.

SUNBURN PREVENTIVES

Don't underestimate the tropical sun! Often there is a pleasant sea breeze and as you loll on the beach, you are not aware of how the sun is baking you, until it's too late. Especially if you come from a cold northern winter, when your skin has not been exposed to the sun for months, it's a good idea to be cautious. Use an appropriate sunscreen or filtro solar (there are several excellent brands on sale in Brazil). Start out with short sessions and avoid the hottest part of the day. It's silly to be too eager and end up with a painful sunburn that will cause peeling. Take care of your skin after a tanning by using a moisture cream. Remember to drink enough—coconut and other fruit juice or mineral water are excellent for replacing lost fluids.

GETTING AROUND

FROM THE AIRPORT

Until you get your bearings, you are best off taking a special airport taxi for which you pay in advance at the airport at a fixed rate set according to your destination. There will be less of a communication problem, no misunderstanding about the fare and even if the driver takes you around by the "scenic route," you won't be charged extra for it. If you should decide to take a regular taxi, check out the fares posted for the official taxis so that you will have an idea of what is a normal rate.

A special airport bus service will take you into town and in some cases the route includes stops at the larger hotels. Enquire at the airport information desk.

Some of the top class hotels will send a driver to pick you up—it's best to arrange for this service when you are making your room reservations.

PUBLIC TRANSPORT

Taxis are probably the best way for visitors to get around in the cities. Of course, it's easy to get "taken for a ride" in a strange city. Whenever possible, take a taxi from your hotel where someone can inform the driver where you want to go.

Radio taxis are slightly more expensive, but safer and more comfortable. Although the drivers of the yellow cabs you flag down on the street won't actually rob you, some occasionally try to overcharge or take you the long way around. Try to find out the normal fare for a given destination—most trips will be just a few dollars. Airport taxis charge exorbitant rates by Brazilian terms—U.S.$10 to U.S.$20 in Rio, depending on the distance—but you will still probably find fares relatively low compared to North America or Europe.

Because of inflation and consequent frequent fuel price increases, it is impossible to keep all meters regulated at the latest authorized fare. Drivers are required to post a chart on the inside of the left rear window so the passenger can calculate the fare based on what the meter reads.

Radio taxis calculate a certain percentage above the meter rate. If you hail a taxi at the curbside, be sure the driver raises the no. 1 tag when he resets the meter for your run. The black no. 2 tag indicates that the meter is set at a 20 percent higher rate—chargeable after 11:00 p.m., on Sundays and holidays, when going beyond certain specified city bounds or up steep areas. Cab drivers can also use the no. 2 rate during the month of December to earn the "13th month salary" that Brazilian workers receive as a sort of a Christmas bonus.

BUSES

Comfortable, on-schedule bus service is available between all major cities, and even to several other South American countries. Remember that distances are big and bus rides can be long, i.e., a few days. But you could break the long journey with a stop along the way.

For the six-hour ride between Rio and São Paulo, you can either take a regular bus, with upholstered, reclining seats, or the more expensive sleeper bus, which has wider and fully reclining seats with footrest, as well as coffee and soft drinks aboard. At busy times like holidays, buses on the Rio-São Paulo line depart at the rate of one per minute.

On other routes, there may be just one bus per day (such as the Rio-Belém route, a 52-hour trip) or just one or two per week. Try to buy your ticket in advance through a travel agent or at the bus station.

There is a local bus service to the smaller, more isolated towns. This is quite a different experience and will leave you with no doubts that you are in a still developing country.

Almost always overcrowded, buses bump along dirt roads, picking up passengers who wait along the roadside, often with large bundles they are taking to market. Those who travel standing up—often for three to four hours or more—are charged the same as those who paid for a numbered seat.

For the visitor, it may be a new and unique experience, but you certainly have to admire the endurance and patience of the people for whom this precarious system is the only form of getting around.

CITY BUSES

Since just a small percentage of Brazilians can afford cars, public transportation is used a great deal. The larger cities have special air-conditioned buses connecting residential areas to the central business district, including routes from airports and bus stations that swing by many of the larger hotels. You will be handed a ticket as you get on. Take a seat and an attendant will come around to collect your fare—U.S. 75 cents to just over U.S.$1, depending on the route. Your hotel can be helpful in providing information about bus routes, but most hotels discourage tourists from riding anything but the special buses.

The regular city buses cost around U.S. 15 cents. Get on through the back door (often quite a high step up) and after paying the trocador, who will give you change, move through the turnstile. It's a good idea to have your money handy—several people may board at your stop and all have to get through the turnstile before they can sit down.

This is also a favorite bottleneck for pickpockets who can jump out the back door as the bus takes off. If you travel standing up, be sure to hold on tight. Some bus drivers (especially in Rio) can be very inconsiderate, jamming on the brakes suddenly, careening around corners at full tilt, etc. Signal when you want to get off by pulling the cord (some buses have buttons) and alight via the front door.

Robberies are committed on crowded buses, even in broad daylight. If you are bent on riding the regular city buses, try to avoid the rush hour when passengers on certain lines are packed tighter than the proverbial sardines in a can.

Don't carry valuables, keep that shoulderbag in front of you and your camera inside a bag. Avoid calling attention to yourself by speaking loudly in a foreign language. In other words, be discreet.

THE METRÔ

Rio de Janeiro and São Paulo have excellent, though not extensive, subway service with bright, clean, air-conditioned cars. The *metrô* is one of the easiest ways for a foreign tourist to get around without getting lost. Maps in the stations and in each car help you find your way without having to communicate in Portuguese. Lines radiate from the city center and service is further extended by bus links, often with train-bus combination tickets. Subway extension bus lines are marked *integração*.

São Paulo's two lines cross underneath the Praça da Sé square at the city's heart and run from 5:00 a.m. to 12:00 midnight. The north-south line connects Santana and Jabaquara, and the east-west line runs from Barra Funda to Penha. There are stops at the inter-city bus stations and bus link-ups to the Guarulhos International Airport.

Rio's two lines reach out from downtown only as far south as Botafogo, and on the other side as far as the northern suburb of Irajá, with stops near the Sambadrome and Maracanã soccer stadium. Bus link-ups extend service on either end. The Rio subway is closed on Sundays and operates from 6:00 a.m. to 11:00 p.m. Monday-Saturday.

There is just one price for a single (*unitário*) ticket, even if you transfer from one line to another. There are round-trip (*ida e volta*) and multi-fare tickets as well as different combination tickets with the buses (*metrô—ônibus*). Tickets are sold in the stations and on the *integração* buses and prices are clearly posted. (*Entrada* = entrance; *saída* = exit).

BOATS

Local boat tours and excursions are available in coastal and riverside cities. There are also options for longer trips.

There are Amazon River boat trips lasting a day or two to up to a week or more. These range from luxury floating hotels to more rustic accommodations. Boat trips can be taken on the São Francisco River in the Northeast and in the Pantanal marshlands of Mato Grosso, where many visitors go for the fishing. The Blue Star Line will take passengers on its freighters which call at several Atlantic coast ports. Linea C and Oremar have cruises out of Rio which stop along the Brazilian coast on the way down to Buenos Aires or up to the Caribbean. Book well in advance for the longer trips .

Cities along the coast (and along major rivers) offer short sight-seeing or day-long boat tours. Many towns have local ferry service across bays and rivers and to islands. And schooners and yachts, complete with crew, may be rented for an outing.

TRAINS

Except for crowded urban commuter railways, trains are not considered a major form of transportation in Brazil and rail links are not extensive. There are a few train trips, however, which are tourist attractions in themselves, either because they are so scenic or because they run on antique steam-powered equipment.

— In the southern state of **Paraná**, the 66-mile (110-km) Curitiba-Paranaguá railroad is famous for spectacular mountain scenery.

— The train to Corumbá, in the state of Mato Grosso do Sul, near the Bolivian border, crosses the southern tip of the **Pantanal** marshlands. There are train links all the way to São Paulo, over 840 miles (1,400 km) away—a long ride. The most scenic part is the 240-mile (400-km) stretch between Campo Grande (you can also fly there) and Corumbá.

— In the **Amazon** region, you can ride what is left of the historic Madeira-Mamoré Railway—the 16 miles (27 km) of track between Porto Velho and Cachoeira de Teotônio in the state of Rondônia. The Madeira-Mamoré runs on Sundays only and strictly as a tourist attraction.

— In the state of **Minas Gerais**, antique steam locomotives haul passengers seven miles (12 km) between São João del Rei and Tiradentes and between Ouro Preto and Mariana, 12 miles (20 km) on Saturdays and Sundays.

— In the state of **São Paulo**, the Paranapiacaba steam train climbs 29 miles (48 km) through mountains, part of the way pulled by a funicular system;

— In the state of **Rio de Janeiro**, the Mountain Steam Train runs 17 miles (28 km) between Miguel Pereira and Conrado every Sunday.

— The night train between **Rio de Janeiro** and **São Paulo** offers pleasant service, with a diner car and "room service" in the sleeper compartments. Departs at 11:00 p.m., arrives at 8:00 a.m. Reserve in advance, tel: (021) 263-9856 (Rio) or (011) 991-3212 (São Paulo).

PRIVATE TRANSPORT

Rental car services are available in the larger cities. Both Avis and Hertz operate in Brazil and the two largest Brazilian national chains are Localiza and Nobre. There are also good local companies. Rates will vary from around $30 a day up to $85-$90 (including insurance and taxes), depending on the type of the car. Some companies charge a flat daily rate, while others charge by mileage. Major international credit cards are accepted by these rental companies. Some companies will charge extra if you rent a car in one city and hand it back in another. If you plan to drive one way only between cities, it's best to rent from one of the two largest chains with more branches.

Arrangements can be made right at the airport as you arrive, through your hotel or at the agencies. An international driving license is helpful, but you can also rent a car with your country's driving license. For another U.S.$20 or so you can hire a driver along with the car for eight hours plus about U.S. $4 for each extra hour.

Driving in Brazil will be chaotic compared to what you are used to. Rio drivers are especially notorious for their erratic lane changing, in-town speeding and disregard for pedestrians and other drivers on the road. Be on the defensive and expect the unexpected. In the big cities, parking can be a difficult business downtown. A good solution in Rio is to park your car at the Botafogo subway station and take the underground into town.

It seems wherever you park in the cities, within seconds a freelance car "guard" will appear, either offering to keep an eye on your car in the hopes of receiving a tip or even demanding that you pay him in advance for his (dubious) vigilance. The equivalent of U.S. 40 or 50 cents is sufficient. It's best to pay or risk finding some slight damage to the car upon your return.

The highways, especially the interstates, are generally quite good but are crowded with more trucks than you will have ever seen. These huge vehicles bog down traffic on winding, climbing stretches in the mountains. If you plan to travel much by road in Brazil, buy the *Quatro Rodas* (Four Wheels) road guide, complete with road maps and itineraries, which is available at most of the newsstands.

DOMESTIC TRAVEL

For travel within Brazil, the major airlines are Trans-brasil, Varig/Cruzeiro and Vasp with several other regional carriers which service the smaller cities. All three of the larger lines fly extensive routes throughout the country and have ticket counters at the airports and ticket offices in most cities. Tickets can also be purchased at travel agencies, often at hotels, and reservations can be made by phone or telex. Unless you want to play things by ear, it is easiest to make reservations at home through your travel agent, before traveling.

Different lines have similar prices for some the same routes, although it's hard to say what these are, as prices are always changing.

There is a 20 percent discount for night flights (*vôo econômico* or *vôo noturno*) with departures between midnight and 6:00 a.m. Sometimes 50 percent discounts are offered for women on these night flights. Most routes will have a night flight by one or another of the major airlines.

Transbrasil and Varig also offer an air pass, which must be purchased outside Brazil. It costs U.S.$440 (mid-1990 price), is valid for 21 days and allows you to visit four cities (not including your starting point in Brazil). Extra stops are U.S. $100 each. Ask your travel agent about this option—it is a good deal if you plan to travel extensively within Brazil.

The large airlines also cooperate in a shuttle service between Rio and São Paulo (with flights every half hour), Rio and Brasília (flights every hour) and Rio and Belo Horizonte (usually about 10 flights per day). Although you may be lucky, a reservation is a good idea.

On domestic flights checked baggage is limited to 20 kg (44 lb) and internationally accepted norms apply for hand luggage.

Air taxi service is also available to fly anywhere in the world. Enquire at the airport or make arrangements through a travel agent or your hotel.

Be sure to verify from which airport your flight leaves, if the city has more than one. Your hotel will be able to help you with such arrangements and provide transportation to the airport.

BRAZILIAN AIRLINES

Transbrasil (Domestic)
Belém:
Reservations—Tel: (091) 224-3677/6711
Airport—Tel: (091) 233-3941/2674
Brasília:
Reservations—Tel: (061) 248-6433
Airport—Tel: (061) 248-5152
Manaus:
Reservations—Tel: (092) 234-9229
Airport—Tel: (092) 212-1356
Recife:
Reservations—Tel: (081) 224-7711/6166
Rio de Janeiro:
Reservations—Tel: (021) 297-4422
International Airport—Tel: (021) 398-5985.
Santos Dumont Airport—Tel: (021) 220-

9278/262-6061
Salvador:
Reservations—Tel: (071) 241-1044
International Airport—Tel: (071) 249-2467/204-1100
São Paulo:
Reservations—Tel: (011) 228-2022
Congonhas Airport—Tel:(011) 240-2652/533-7111
Guarulhos Airport—Tel:(011) 945-2253/2702

Varig/Cruzeiro (International and domestic)
Belém:
Reservations—Tel: (091) 224-3344/223-5269
Airport—Tel: (091) 233-3541
Brasília:
Reservations—Tel: (061) 242-4111
Airport—Tel: (061) 248-4497/222-7267/232-7275
Manaus:
Reservations—Tel: (092) 232-8198/8293/234-0251
Airport—Tel: (092) 232-8112/234-3397
Recife:
Reservations—Tel: (081) 231-2037
Airport—Tel: (081) 231-2037/326-1019/326-1040
Rio de Janeiro:
Reservations—Tel: (021) 220-3821
Salvador:
Reservations—Tel: (071) 243-7811/2142
Airport—Tel: (071) 249-2586/2811
São Paulo:
Reservations—Tel: (011) 240-3922
Guarulhos Airport—Tel: (011) 945-2195/2295

Vasp (Domestic)
Belém:
Reservations—Tel: (091) 222-9611/224-5588
Airport—Tel: (091) 233-0941/1152/1814/224-5588
Brasília:
Reservations—Tel: (061) 244-2020
Airport—Tel: (061) 226-4115/248-5187/5245
Manaus:
Reservations—Tel: (092) 234-1266/0349/0576/0886
Airport—Tel: (092) 212-1355/1437/1252
Recife:
Reservations—Tel: (081) 231-3048/222-3611
Airport—Tel: (081) 222-3611/326-1699/341-7772
Rio de Janeiro:
Reservations—Tel: (021) 292-2112
International Airport—Tel: (021) 398-5989
Santos Dumont Airport—Tel: (021) 292-2112
Salvador:
Reservations—Tel: (071) 243-7277/7044
Airport—Tel: (071) 243-7044/249-2495/2464
São Paulo:
Reservations—Tel: (011) 533-2211
Congonhas Airport—Tel: (011) 533-7011
Guarulhos Airport—Tel: (011) 945-2962/2424

REGIONAL DOMESTIC AIRLINES

Nordeste
Brasília:
Airport—Tel: (061) 248-6918/5348
Recife:
Airport—Tel: (081) 341-4222/3187
Rio de Janeiro:
Reservations—Tel: (021) 220-4366/9652/262-2237
Santos Dumont Airport—Tel: (021) 262-3580
Salvador:
Reservations—Tel: (071) 224-7755
Airport—Tel: (071) 249-2630
São Paulo:
Reservations/Congonhas Airport—Tel: (011) 241-8397/542-2591

Rio-Sul
Rio de Janeiro:
Reservations/Santos Dumont Airport—Tel: (021) 262-6911
São Paulo:
Reservations—Tel: (011) 543-7261/240-3044/3267/61-6518

Taba
Belém:
Reservations—Tel: (091) 223-3111
Rio de Janeiro:
Tel: (021) 220-2529/2649

Tam
Brasília:
Airport—Tel: (061) 248-5961
Rio de Janeiro:
Santos Dumont Airport—Tel: (021) 262-6311
International Airport—Tel: (021) 398-3271
São Paulo:
Reservations—Tel: (011) 578-8155
Congonhas Airport—Tel: (011) 240-5404

INTERNATIONAL AIRLINES

Aerolineas Argentinas
Rio de Janeiro:
Reservations—Tel: (021) 224-9242
International Airport—Tel: (021) 398-3520/3737/3375
São Paulo:
Reservations—Tel: (011) 255-6022
Brasília:
Tel: (061) 224-0461/9724/226-7796

Aeroperu
Rio de Janeiro:
Reservations—Tel: (021) 240-0722
International Airport—Tel: (021) 398-9585
São Paulo:
Reservations—Tel: (011) 257-4866
Guarulhos Airport—Tel: (011) 945-2928
Brasília:
Tel: (061) 225-0889/224-3125

Air France
Rio de Janeiro:
Reservations—Tel: (021) 220-3666
International Airport—Tel: (021) 398-3311
São Paulo:
Reservations—Tel: (011) 255-2111
Guarulhos Airport—Tel: (011) 945-2211
Viracopos Airport—Tel: (0192) 47-7778
Brasília:
Tel: (061) 223-4152/4299/4355/4575
Recife:
Tel: (081) 224-7944
Guararapes Airport—Tel: (081) 341-0670

Alitalia
Rio de Janeiro:
Reservations—Tel: (021) 262-5088
International Airport—Tel: (021) 398-3663/3143
São Paulo:
Viracopos Airport—Tel: (0192) 47-0016/0067
Brasília:
Tel: (061) 225-4331

Avianca
Rio de Janeiro:
International Airport—Tel: (021) 398-3775/3778
São Paulo:
Tel: (011) 259-8455
Brasília:
Tel: (061) 224-3236/3108/3306/3307

British Airways
Rio de Janeiro:
Reservations—Tel: (021) 242-6020/
Toll Free: 021-800-6926
International Airport—Tel: (021) 398-3888
São Paulo:
Information—Tel: (011) 259-6144/6354
Guarulhos Airport—Tel: (011) 945-2021/2142
Brasília:
Tel: (061) 224-3236/3108/3306

Canadian Pacific—C P Air
Rio de Janeiro:
Tel: (021) 220-5343
São Paulo:
Tel: (011) 259-9066/9603

Iberia
Rio de Janeiro
Reservations—282-1336
São Paulo:
Reservations—Tel: (011) 258-5333
Guarulhos Airport—Tel: (011) 945-4726
Brasília:
Tel: (061) 226-0456

Iraqi Airways
Rio de Janeiro:
International Airport—Tel: (011) 398-3541/3448/3349
São Paulo:
Tel: (011) 227-1544
Brasília:
Tel: (061) 226-6076/6004/6503

Japan Air Lines
Rio de Janeiro:
Reservations—Tel: (021) 221-9663
São Paulo:
Tel: (011) 259-5244/5445/5845
Brasília:
Tel: (061) 226-2458/2530

KLM
Rio de Janeiro:
Reservations—Tel: 292-7747
São Paulo:
Congonhas Airport—Tel: (011) 61-8266
Viracopos Airport—Tel: (0192) 47-0423/0056
Guarulhos Airport—Tel: (011) 945-2887/2636
Brasília:
Tel: (061) 225-5513/224-5397

Ladeco
Rio de Janeiro:
International Airport—Tel: (021) 398-3601
São Paulo:
Guarulhos Airport—Tel: (011) 945-2080
Brasília:
Tel: (061) 226-2458/224-3306

Lan Chile
Rio de Janeiro:
Reservations—Tel: (021) 221-2882
Toll Free: 021-800-6110
International Airport—Tel: (021) 398-3799/3797/3529
São Paulo:
Viracopos Airport—Tel: (0192) 47-0774
Brasília:
Tel: (061) 226-0318

Lineas Aereas Paraguayas
Rio de Janeiro:
International Airport—Tel: (021) 398-3950/383-7395
São Paulo:
Reservations—Tel: (011) 259-2477
Airport—Tel: (011) 531-8425

Lloyd Aereo Boliviano
Rio de Janeiro:
Tel: (021) 220-9548
São Paulo:
Guarulhos Airport—Tel: (011) 945-2425
Brasília:
Tel: (061) 225-3118

Lufthansa
Rio de Janeiro:
Reservations—Tel: (021) 282-1253
International Airport—Tel: (021) 398-3620
São Paulo:
Av. São Luis, 59
Tel: (011) 256-9833
Brasília:
Tel: (061) 223-8202

Pan American
Rio de Janeiro:
Tel: (021) 210-3214
São Paulo:
Reservations—Tel: (011) 257-6655
Brasília:
Tel: (061) 23-2000

Pluna
Rio de Janeiro:
Reservations—Tel: 262-4466
São Paulo:
Guarulhos Airport—Tel: (011) 945-2130
Brasília:
Tel: (061) 256-0274

Royal Air Maroc
Rio de Janeiro:
International Airport—Tel: (021) 398-3766
São Paulo:
Tel: (011) 231-4999

SAA—South African
Rio de Janeiro:
Reservations—Tel: (021) 262-6252
International Airport—Tel: (021) 398-3767/3365/3366
São Paulo:
Tel: (011) 257-2914/259-1522

SAS
Rio de Janeiro:
Reservations—Tel: 210-1222
São Paulo:
Guarulhos Airport—Tel: (011) 945-2002
Brasília:
Tel: (061) 225-0889

Swissair
Rio de Janeiro:
Reservations—Tel: (021) 203-2152
International Airport—Tel:(021) 398-3304/3547

São Paulo:
Reservations—Tel: (011) 258-6211
Guarulhos Airport—Tel: (011) 945-2010
Viracopos Airport—Tel: (0192) 47-1722
Congonhas Airport—Tel: (011) 241-2915
Brasília:
Tel: (061) 223-4005/4382

TAG—Angolan Airlines
Rio de Janeiro:
Tel: (021) 263-4911

TAP Air Portugal
Rio de Janeiro:
International Airport—Tel: (021) 398-3565/3455
São Paulo:
Tel: (011) 255-5366
Brasília:
Tel: (061) 23-7138

Viasa
Rio de Janeiro:
Reservations—Tel: (021) 224-5345
International Airport—Tel: (021) 398-3808
São Paulo:
Reservations—Tel: (011) 257-9122
Brasília:
Tel: (061) 226-1514

WHERE TO STAY

HOTELS & CAMPGROUNDS

There is no shortage of excellent hotels in Brazil. The larger cities and resort areas especially have high quality international standard hotels, with multi-lingual staff prepared to help you find what you want and need. Many even have their own travel agencies. The following list includes just a few of the top hotels in the major tourism areas.

Rooms are usually clean and the staff are polite, but you most likely will have to communicate in Portuguese. It's a good idea to ask to see the room before deciding to take it. A continental breakfast is usually included in the price.

It is always best to make reservations well in advance, especially if you are visiting during Carnival or on a major holiday. Hotels then are full of Brazilian tourists as well as visiting foreigners. Travelers from colder climates often come to get away from the Northern Hemisphere winter and Brazilians also travel more during the school holidays in the summer months of January and February and in July. Even if you are traveling to an area that you think is off the usual tourist route, local facilities may be saturated with Brazilian vacationers during these peak months.

If you are venturing away from tourist spots for which no hotels are included in our listing, you will find the *Guia Brasil* road guide useful. Available on newsstands, it has road maps and lists hotels, restaurants and local attractions for 715 Brazilian cities. Although available only in Portuguese, it uses a system of symbols with explanations in English and Spanish.

If traveling by car, you should be aware that motels may not be what you're used to at home: rooms, often garishly decorated and outfitted with mirrors, private pools and round beds, are rented out by the hour for amorous trysts.

Contact the Camping Clube do Brasil, if you are interested in camping. Their national headquarters is located at Rua Senador Dantas, 75, 29th floor, Rio de Janeiro, RJ, tel: (021) 262-7172. The Casa do Estudante do Brasil, located at Praça Ana Amelia, 9, 8th floor, Castelo, Rio de Janeiro, RJ, tel: (021) 220-7223, has a list of hostels in 10 Brazilian states which are registered with the International Youth Hostel Federation and charge just a few dollars. Despite the name, there is no age restriction.

RIO DE JANEIRO (STATE)

Rio de Janeiro (city)

California
Av. Atlântica, 2616
Copacabana
Tel: (021) 257-1900
Telex: (021) 22655

Caesar Park (luxury)
Av. Vieira Souto, 460
Ipanema
Tel: (021) 287-3122
Telex: (021) 21204

Copacabana Palace (luxury)
Av. Atlântica, 1702
Copacabana
Tel: (021) 255-7070
Telex: (021) 21482

Everest-Rio (luxury)
Rua Prudente de Morais, 1117
Ipanema
Tel: (021) 287-8282
Telex: (021) 22254

Gloria
Rua do Russel, 632
Gloria
Tel: (021) 205-7272
Telex: (021) 23623

Inter-Continental Rio (luxury)
Rua Prefeito Mendes de Morais, 222
São Conrado
Tel: (021) 322-2200
Telex: (021) 21790

Leme Palace
Av. Atlântica, 656
Leme
Tel: (021) 275-8080
Telex: (021) 23265

Luxor Copacabana (luxury)
Av. Atlântica, 2554
Copacabana
Tel: (021) 257-1940
Telex: (021) 23971

Luxor Continental (luxury)
Rua Gustavo Sampaio, 320
Leme
Tel: (021) 275-5252
Telex: (021) 21469

Luxor Regente (luxury)
Av. Atlântica, 3716
Copacabana
Tel: (021) 287-4212
Telex: (021) 23887

Marina Palace (luxury)
Av. Delfim Moreira, 630
Leblon
Tel: (021) 259-5212
Telex: (021) 30224

Marina Rio (luxury)
Av. Delfim Moreira, 696
Leblon
Tel: (021) 239-8844
Telex: (021) 30224

Meridien-Rio (luxury)
Av. Atlântica, 1020
Leme
Tel: (021) 275-9922
Telex: (021) 23183

Miramar Palace
Av. Atlântica, 3668
Copacabana
Tel: (021) 247-6070
Telex: (021) 21508

Nacional-Rio (luxury)
Av. Niemeyer, 769
São Conrado
Tel: (021) 322-1000
Telex: (021) 23615
Ouro Verde
Av. Atlântica, 1456
Copacabana
Tel: (021) 542-1887
Telex: (021) 23848

Praia Ipanema (luxury)
Av. Vieira Souto, 706
Ipanema
Tel: (021) 239-9932
Telex: (021) 31280

Rio Othon Palace (luxury)
Av. Atlântica, 3264
Copacabana
Tel: (021) 255-8812
Telex: (021) 22655

Rio Palace (luxury)
Av. Atlântica, 4240
Copacabana
Tel: (021) 521-3132
Telex: (021) 21803

Rio-Sheraton (luxury)
Av. Neimeyer, 121
Vidigal
Tel: (021) 274-1122
Telex: (021) 21206

Sol Ipanema (luxury)
Av. Vieira Souto, 320
Ipanema
Tel: (021) 227-0060
Telex: (021) 21979

Trocadero
Av. Atlântica, 2064
Copacabana.
Tel: (021) 257-1834
Telex: (021) 22655

Angra dos Reis

Hotel do Frade/Portogalo
(Reservations for both hotels in Rio at)
Rua Joaquim Nabuco, 161 Copacabana
Tel: (021) 267-7375
Telex: (021) 31034

Buzios

Pousada Casas Brancas
Morro Humaitá, 712
Tel: (0246) 23-1458

Pousada La Chimere
Praça Eugenio Honold, 36
Praia dos Ossos
Tel: (0246) 23-1460
Reservations in Rio
Tel: (021) 220-2129

Pousada nas Rocas
Ilha Rasa
Marina Porto Buzios
Tel: (0246) 23-1303
Telex: (021) 31356
Reservations in Rio
Tel: (021) 253-0001

Cabo Frio

Ponta de Areia
Av. Espadarte,184
Caminho Verde, Ogiva
Tel: (0246) 43-2053

Pousada Porto Pero
Av. dos Pescadores, 2002
Tel: (0246) 43-1395
Telex: (021) 34343

Pousada Portoveleiro
Av. dos Espardartes, 129
Caminho Verde, Ogiva
Tel: (0246) 43-3081

Itacurucá

Aguas Lindas
Itacurucá Island
Reservations in Rio-
Tel: (021) 220-0007

Hotel do Pierre
Itacurucá Island
Tel: (021) 788-1016

Jaguanum
Jaguanum Island
Reservations in Rio-
Tel: (021) 237-5119

Itatiaia

Cabanas de Itatiaia
Parque Nacional 6 km
Tel: (0243) 52-1328

Hotel do Ypê
Parque Nacional 13 km
Tel: (0243) 52-1453

Simon
Parque Nacional 13 km
Tel: (0243) 52-1122

Nova Friburgo

Bucsky
Estrada Niteroi-Nova Friburgo, km. 76.5
Mury
Tel: (0245) 22-5052

Fazenda Garlipp
Estrada Niteroi-Nova Friburgo, km. 70.5
Mury
Tel: (0245) 42-1330

Mury Graden
Estrada Niteroi-Nova Friburgo, km. 70
Mury

Tel: (0245) 42-1176

Park Hotel
Al. Princesa Isabel
Parque São Clemente
Tel: (0245) 22-0825

Sans Souci
Rua Itajaí
Sans Souci
Tel: (0245) 22-7752
Telex: (0245) 34348

Parati

Pousada do Ouro
Rua Dr. Pereira, 145
Tel: (0243) 71-1311
Reservations in Rio
Tel: (021) 221-2022

Petrópolis

Casa do Sol
Estr. Rio-Petrópolis, km. 115
Quitandinha
Tel: (0242) 43-5062

Riverside Parque
Rua Hermogêneo Silva, 522
Retiro
Tel: (0242) 42-3704

Resende

Espigão Palace
Rua Sebastião José Rodrigues, 255
Tel: (0243) 54-1855

Teresópolis

Alpina Estr. Teresópolis-Petrópolis
Vila Imbui
Tel: (021) 742-5252
Telex: (021) 34587

Rosa dos Ventos, Estr. Teresópolis-
Nova-Friburgo, km. 22.6
Tel: (021) 742-8833
Telex: (021) 34958

São Moritz, Estr. Teresópolis-
Nova- Friburgo, km. 36
Tel: 742-4360

SÃO PAULO (STATE)

São Paulo (city)

Augusta Boulevard (luxury)
Rua Augusta, 843
Cerqueira Cesar
Tel: (011) 257-7844
Telex: (011) 21552

Bourdon Hotel (luxury)
Av. Vieira de Carvalho, 99
Centro
Tel: (011) 223-224
Telex: (011) 32781

Bristol (luxury)
Rua Martins Fontes, 277
Centro
Tel: (011) 258-0011
Telex: (011) 24734

Caesar Park (luxury)
Rua Augusta, 1508/20
Cerqueira Cesar
Tel: (011) 285-6622
Telex: (011) 22539

Comodoro
Av. Duque de Caxias, 525
Centro
Tel: (011) 220-1211
Telex: (011) 36261

Eldourado Boulevard (luxury)
Av. São Luis, 234
Centro
Tel: (011) 256-8833
Telex: (011) 22490

Eldourado Higienópolis (luxury)
Rua Marquês de Itu, 836
Higienópolis
Tel: (011) 222-3422
Telex: (011) 30546

Grand Hotel Ca'D'Oro (luxury)
Rua Augusta, 129
Centro
Tel: (011) 256-8011
Telex: (011) 21765

Maksoud Plaza (luxury)
Alameda Campinas, 150
Bela Vista

Tel: (011) 251-2233
Telex: (011) 30026

Moferrej Sheraton (luxury)
Alameda Santos, 1437
Cerqueira Cesar
Tel: (011) 284-5544
Telex: (011) 34170

Novotel São Paulo (luxury)
Rua Min. Nelson Hungria, 450
Morumbi
Tel: (011) 542-1244
Telex: (011) 25662

Samambaia
Rua 7 de Abril, 422
Praça da Republica
Centro
Tel: (011) 231-1333
Telex: (011) 30441
São Paulo Center
Largo Santa Ifigênia, 40
Centro
Tel: (011) 228-6033
Telex: (011) 22441

São Paulo Hilton
Av. Ipiranga, 165
Centro
Tel: (011) 256-0033
Telex: (011) 21981

Transamerica (luxury)
Av. Nações Unidos, 18591
Santo Amaro
Tel: (011) 523-4511
Telex: (011) 31761

Aguas da Prata

Ideal
Rua Gabriel Rabelo de Andrade, 79
Tel: (0196) 42-1011

Panorama
Rua Dr. Hernani G. Correa, 45
Tel: (0196) 42-1511

Parque Paineiras
Estr. Aguas da Prata-São João da Boa Vista
Tel: (0916) 42-1411

Aguas de Lindóia

Hotel das Fontes
Rua Rio de Janeiro, 267
Tel: (0192) 94-1511

Nova Lindóia Vacance
Av. das Nações, 1374
Tel: (0192) 94-1193

Tamoyo
Rua São Paulo, 622
Tel: (0192) 94-1212

Atibaia

Park Atibaia
Rod. Fernão Dias, km. 37
Tel: (011) 484-3423

Recanto da Paz
Av. Jerônimo de Camargo
Tel: (011) 487-1369

Village Eldorado
Rod. Dom Pedro I
km. 70.5
Tel: (011) 2533
Telex: (011) 33341

Campos do Jordão

Orotour Garden Hotel
Rua 3, Vila Natal
Jaguaribe
Tel: (0122) 62-2833
Telex: (0122) 329

Toriba (luxury)
Av. Ernesto Diederichsen
Tel: (0122) 62-1566
Telex: (0122) 378

Vila Inglesa
Rua Senador Roberto Simonsen, 3500
Tel: (0122) 63-1955
Telex: (0122) 399

Caraguatatuba

Guanabara
Rua Santo Antonia, 75
Tel: (0124) 22-2533

Pousada Tabatinga (luxury)
Estr. Caraguatatuba-
Ubatuba. Praia Tabatinga
Tel: (0124) 24-1411
Telex: (0122) 390

Guarujá

Casa Grande (luxury)
Av. Miguel Stedano, 999
Praia da Enseada
Tel: (0132) 86-2223
Telex: (013) 1746

Delphin Hotel
Av. Miguel Stefano, 1295
Praia da Enseada
Tel: (0132) 86-2111
Telex: (013) 1738

Ferrareto Guaruja Hotel
Rua Mário Ribero, 564
Tel: (0132) 86-2111
Telex: (0132) 1938

Gávea Hotel
Alameda Floriano Peixoto, 311
Pitangueiras
Tel: (0132) 86-2212

Guarujá Inn
Av. da Saudade, 170
Praia da Enseada
Tel: (0132) 87-2332
Telex: (013) 1500

Jequiti-Mar
Av. Marjory Prado, 1100
Praia de Pernambuco
Tel: (0132) 53-3111
Telex: (013) 1683

Ilhabela

Devisse
Av. Almirante Tamandaré, 343
Tel: (0214) 72-1385

Ilhabela
Av. Pedro Paula de
Morais, 151
Tel: (0124) 72-1083

Mercedes
Prainha Mercedes
Tel: (0124) 72-1071

Pousada do Capital
Av. Almirante Tamandaré, 272
Tel: (0124) 72-1037

Santos

Avenida Palace
Av. Presidente Wilson, 10
Gonzaga
Tel: (0132) 4-1166
Telex: (013) 2209

Fenícia Praia
Av. Presidente Wilson, 184
José Menino
Tel: (0132) 37-1955

Indaiá
Av. Ana Costa, 431
Gonzaga
Tel: (0132) 4-1134
Telex: (013) 1521

Deville Colonial
Rua Com. Araújo, 99
Centro
Tel: (041) 222-4777
Telex: (041) 5894

Iguaçu Campestre
BR-116, km. 92
Alto
Tel: (041) 262-5313
Telex: (041) 5943

Mabu
Praça Santos Andrade, 830
Centro
Tel: (041) 222-7040
Telex: (041) 5125

Foz do Iguaçu

Bourbon
Rod. das Cataratas,
km. 6.5
Tel: (0455) 75-1313
Telex: (0452) 247

Carimã
Rod. das Cataratas, km. 10
Tel: (0455) 74-3377
Telex: (0452) 256

Hotel das Cataratas
Rod. das Cataratas, km. 28
Tel: (0455) 74-2666
Telex: (0452) 113

Internacional Foz
Rua Almirante Barroso, 345
Tel: (0455) 73-4240
Telex: (0452) 574

Panorama
Rod. das Cataratas, km. 12
Tel: (0455) 74-1200
Telex: (0452) 257

Salvatti
Rua Rio Branco, 577
Tel: (0455) 74-2727
Telex: (0452) 237

Parque Balneário
Av. Ana Costa, 555
Gonzaga
Tel: (0132) 34-7211
Telex: (013) 1241

Praiano
Av. Barão de Penedo, 39
José Menino
Tel: (0132) 37-4033
Telex: (013) 1575

Ubatuba

Mediterrâneo
Praia da Enseada
Tel: (0124) 42-0112
Telex: (0122) 396

Sol e Vida
Praia da Enseada
Tel: (0124) 42-0188

Solar das Aguas Cantantes
Praia do Lázaro
Tel: (0124) 42-0178

Wembley Inn
Estr. Ubatuba-Caraguatatuba
Praia das Toninhas
Tel: (0124) 42-0198
Telex: (011) 31499

SOUTH

•Paraná

Curitiba

Araucária Palace
Rua Amintas de Barros, 73
Centro
Tel: (041) 224-2822
Telex: (041) 5548

Caravelle Palace
Rua Cruz Machado, 282
Centro
Tel: (041) 223-4323
Telex: (041) 5085

Del Rey
Rua Ermelino de Leão, 18
Centro
Tel: (041) 224-3033
Telex: (041) 5031

San Martin
Rod. das Cataratas, km. 17
Tel: (0455) 74-3030
Telex: (0452) 248

•Rio Grande do Sul

Caxias do Sul

Alfred
Rua Sinimbu, 2266
Tel: (054) 221-2111
Telex: (054) 2441

Alfred Palace
Rua Sinimbu, 2302
Tel: (054) 221-8655
Telex: (054) 2441

Alfred Volpiano
Rua Ernesto Alves, 1462
Tel: (054) 221-4744

Cosmos
Rua 20 de Setembro, 11563
Tel: (054) 221-4688

Samuara
Estr. Caxias do Sul-
Farroupilha
Tel: (054) 221-7733
Telex: (054) 2409

Canela

Grande Hotel
Rua Getulio Vargas, 300
Tel: (054) 282-1285

Laje de Pedras
Av. Presidente Kennedy
Tel: (054) 282-1530
Telex (054) 2226

Gramado

Canto Verde
Av. Coronel Diniz, 5660
Tel: (054) 286-1961

Gramado Palace Hotel
Rua D'Artagnon de
Oliveira, 237
Tel: (054) 286-2021

Hotel das Hortênsias
Rua Bela Vista, 83
Tel: (054) 286-1057

Ritta Höppner
Rua Pedro Candiago, 305
Tel: (054) 286-1334

Serrano
Av. Presidente Costa e Silva, 1112
Tel: (054) 286-1332

Nova Petrópolis

Recanto Suiço
Av. 15 de Novembro, 2195
Tel: (054) 281-1229

Veraneio Schoeller
RS-235, Estr. Nova Petrópolis-Gramado,
km. 8.5
Linha Imperial
Tel: (054) 28-1229

Porto Alegre

Alfred Porto Alegre
Rua Senhor dos Passos, 105
Centro
Tel: (0512) 26-2555
Telex: (051) 2761
Center Park
Rua Frederico Link, 25
Moinhos de Vento
Tel: (0512) 21-5388
Telex: (051) 2737

Continental
Largo Vespasiano Júlio Veppo, 77
Centro
Tel: (0512) 25-3233
Telex: (051) 2038

Embaixador
Rua Jerônimo Coelho, 354
Centro
Tel: (0512) 26-5622
Telex: (051) 1527

Plaza Sao Rafael
Av. Alberto Bins, 514
Centro
Tel: (0512) 21-6100
Telex: (051) 1339

Santo Angelo

Avenida II
Av. Venâncio Aires, 1671
Tel: (055) 312-3011

Maerkli
Av. Brasil, 1000
Tel: (055) 312-2127

Santo Angelo Turis
Rua Antônio Manoel, 726
Tel: (055) 312-4055

•Santa Catarina

Blumenau

Garden Terrace
Rua Padre Jacobs, 45
Tel: (0473) 22-3544
Telex: (0473) 224

Grande Hotel Blumenau
Alameda Rio Branco, 21
Tel: (0473) 22-0366
Telex: (0473) 220

Plaza Hering
Rua 7 de Setembro, 818
Tel: (0473) 22-1277

Florianópolis

Canajurê Club, Estr. Geral de
Canasvieiras
Praia de Jurerê
Tel: (0482) 66-0175

Faial Palace
Rua Felipe Schmidt, 87
Centro
Tel: (0482) 23-2766
Telex: (0482) 487

Florianópolis Palace
Rua Artista Bittencourt, 2
Centro
Tel: (0482) 22-9633
Telex: (0482) 191

Jurerê Praia
Alameda 1
Praia de Jurerê
Tel: (0482) 66-0108

Maria do Mar
Rod. Virgílio Várzea
Saco Grande
Tel: (0482) 33-3009
Telex: (0482) 319

Joinville

Anthurium Parque
Rua São José, 226
Tel: (0474) 22-6299
Telex: (0474) 414

Joinville Tourist
Rua 7 de Setembro, 40
Tel: (0474) 22-1288
Telex: (0474) 470

Tannenhof
Rua Visconde de Taunay, 340
Tel: (0474) 22-2311
Telex: (0474) 439

Laguna

Itapirubá
Praia de Itapirubá
BR-101 Norte
Tel: (0486) 44-0294
Telex: (0482) 423

Lagoa
Trevo BR-101 Sul
km. 313
Cabeçudas
Tel: (0486) 44-0135

Laguna Tourist (luxury)
Praia do Gi
Tel: (0486) 44-0022
Telex: (0482) 598

CENTRAL

Brasília

Carlton
Setor Hoteleiro Sul
Quadra 5, Bloco G
Tel: (061) 224-8819
Telex: (061) 1981

Eron Brasília
Setor Hoteleiro Norte
Quadra 5, Lote A
Tel: (061) 226-2125
Telex: (061) 1422

Garvey Park Hotel
Setor Hoteleiro Norte
Quatra 2, Bloco J
Tel: (061) 223-9800
Telex: (061) 2199

Nacional
Setor Hoteleiro Sul
Lote 1
Tel: (061) 226-8180
Telex (061) 1062

Phenícia
Setor Hoteleiro Sul
Quadra 5, Bloco J
Tel: (061) 224-3125
Telex: (061) 2254

•Mato Grosso/Pantanal

Corumbá

Nacional, Rua América, 936
Tel: (067) 231-6868
Telex: (067) 3205

Pousada do Cachimbo
Rua Alan Kardec, 4
Dom Bosco
Tel: (067) 231-4833

Santa Mônica
Rua Antônio Maria Coelho, 345
Tel: (067) 231-3001
Telex: (067) 3205

Cuiabá

Aurea Palace
Av. General Mello, 63
Centro
Tel: (065) 322-3377
Telex: (065) 2476

Excelsior
Av. Getúlio Vargas, 264
Centro
Tel: (065) 322-6322
Telex: (065) 2183

Las Velas
Av. Filinto Müller, 62
Aeroporto
Tel: (065) 381-1422
Telex: (065) 2354

Pantanal

Botel Amazonas/Botel Corumbá (boat hotels)
Information in Corumba
Tel: (067) 231-3016
Telex: (065) 3146

Cabana do Lontra
Estr. Miranda-Corumbá
Information in
Aquidauana
Tel: (067) 241-2406

Hotel Cabanas do
Pantanal
Rio Piraim
Information in São Paulo
Tel: (011) 34-4245

Hotel dos Camalotes
Fazenda Três Barras
Porto Murtinho
Information in Campo Grande
Tel: (067) 382-5361
Telex: (067) 2258

Hotel Fazenda Barranquinho
Rio Jauru, Caceres
Information in Cuiabá
Tel: (065) 322-0513

Santa Rosa Pantanal
Rod. Transpantaneira
Rio Cuiabá, Porto Jofre
Information in Cuiabá
Tel: (065) 321-5514

•Minas Gerais

Araxá

Grande Hotel
Estância do Barreiro
Tel: (034) 661-2011
Telex: (034) 3347

Belo Horizonte

Belo Horizonte Othon Palace
Av. Afonso Pena, 1050
Centro
Tel: (031) 226-7844
Telex: (031) 2052

Brasilton
BR-381, km. 423.5
Contagem
Tel: (031) 351-0900
Telex: (031) 1860

Hotel Del Rey
Praça Afonso Arinos, 60
Centro
Tel: (031) 222-2211
Telex: (031) 1033

Wembley Palace
Rua Espírito Santo, 201
Centro
Tel (031) 201-6966
Telex: (031) 3019

Caxambu

Gloria
Av. Camilo Soares, 590
Tel: (035) 341-1233
Telex: (031) 5011

Grande Hotel
Rua Dr. Viotti, 438
Tel: (035) 341-1099
Palace Hotel
Rua Dr. Viotti, 567
Tel: (035) 341-1044

Diamantina

Tijuco Hotel
Rua Macau do Meio, 211
Tel: (037) 931-1022

Ouro Preto

Estrada Real
Road. Dos Inconfidentes km. 87
Tel: (031) 551-2122
Telex: (031) 6133

Grande Hotel Ouro Preto
Rua Senador Rocha Lagoa, 164
Tel: (031) 551-1488

Luxor Pousada
Rua Dr. Alfredo Baeta, 16
Tel: (031) 551-2244
Telex: (031) 2948

Poços de Caldas

Minas Gerais
Rua Pernambuco, 615
Tel: (035) 721-8686

Palace
Praça Pedro Sanches
Tel: (035) 721-3392
Telex: (031) 2332

São Lourenço

Brasil
Praça João Lage, 87
Tel: (035) 331-1422

Primus
Rua Coronel José Justino, 681
Tel: (035) 331-1244
Telex: (031) 3561

NORTHEAST

•Alagoas

Maceió

Beira Mar
Av. Duque de Caxias, 1994
Praia da Avenida
Tel: (082) 223-8022
Telex: (082) 2202

Enseada
Av. Dr. Antônio Gouveia, 171
Pajucara
Tel: (082) 231-4726
Telex: (082) 2295

Jatiúca
Rua Lagoa da Anta, 220
Lagoa da Anta
Tel: (082) 231-2555
Telex: (082) 2302

Luxor
Av. Duque de Caxias, 2076
Praia da Avenida
Tel: (082) 223-7075
Telex: (082) 2179

Pajuaçara Othon
Rua Jangadeiros Alagoanos, 1292
Pajucara
Tel: (082) 231-2200
Telex: (082) 2392

Ponta Verde Praia
Av. Alvaro Octacílio, 2933
Praia Ponta Verde
Tel: (082) 231-4040
Telex: (082) 2368

•Bahia

Salvador

Bahia Othon Palace (luxury)
Av. Presidente Vargas, 2456
Ondina
Tel: (071) 247-1044

Telex: (071) 1217

Club Mediterranee (luxury)
Estr. Itaparica-Nazaré
km. 13

Itaparica
Tel: (071) 833-1141
Telex: (071) 2143
Reservations in Salvador
Tel: (071) 247-3488

Enseada das Lajes
Av. Presidente Vargas 511
Morro da Paciencia
Rio Vermelho
Tel: (071) 237-1027

Grande Hotel da Barra
Av. 7 de Setembro, 3564
Porto da Barra
Tel: (071) 247-6011
Telex: (071) 2300

Grande Hotel Itaparica
Av. Beira Mar, Centro
Itaparica
Tel: (071) 831-1120
Telex: (071) 1874

Luxor Convento do Carmo
Largo do Carmo, 1
Santo Antonio
Tel: (071) 242-3111
Telex: (071) 1513

Marazul
Av. 7 de Setembro, 3937
Barra
Tel: (071) 235-2110
Telex: (071) 2296

Meridien Bahia (luxury)
Rua Fonte do Boi, 216
Rio Vermelho
Tel: (071) 249-8011
Telex: (071) 1029

Quatro Rodas Salvador (luxury)
Rua Pasárgada
Farol de Itapoã
Tel: (071) 249-9611
Telex: (071) 2449

Salvador Praia
Av. Presidente Vargas, 2338
Ondina
Tel: (071) 245-5033
Telex: (071) 1430

Ilhéus

Britânia
Rua 28 de Junho, 16
Centro
Tel: (073) 231-1722

Ilhéus Praia
Praça Dom Eduardo
Tel: (073) 231-2533
Telex: (073) 2180

Pontal Praia
Av. Lomanto Jr. 1358
Pontal
Tel: (073) 231-3033
Telex: (073) 2169

Lençóis

Pousanda de Lençóis
Rua Altina Alves, 747
Reservations Salvador
Tel: (071) 233-9395
Telex: (071) 1896

Paulo Afonso

Grande Hotel de Paulo Afonso
Acampamento da Chesf
Vila Nobre
Tel: (075) 281-1914

•Ceará

Fortaleza

Beira Mar
Av. Presidente Kennedy, 3130
Praia de Meireles
Tel: (085) 224-4744
Telex: (085) 1852

Colonial Praia
Rua Barão de Aracati, 145
Iracema
Tel: (085) 211-9644
Telex: (085) 1200

Esplanada Praia
Av. Presidente Kennedy, 2000
Praia de Meireles
Tel: (085) 224-855
Telex: (085) 1103

Imperial Othon Palace
Av. Presidente Kennedy, 2500
Praia de Meireles
Tel: (085) 224-777
Telex: (085) 1569

Praiano Palace
Av. Presidente Kennedy, 2800
Praia de Meireles
Tel: (085) 244-3333
Telex: (085) 2464

San Pedro
Rua Castro e Silva, 81
Centro
Tel: (085) 211-9911
Telex: (085) 1391

Savanah
Trav. Para, 20
Praça do Ferreira
Centro
Tel: (085) 211-9966

•Maranhão

São Luis

Panorama Palace
Rua dos Pinheiros, Q-16
15, São Francisco
Tel: (098) 227-0067
Telex: (098) 2564

São Francisco
Conjunto São Francisco
São Francisco
Tel: (098) 227-1155
Telex: (098) 2301

São Luis Quatro Rodas (luxury)
Praia do Calhau
Tel: (098) 227-0244
Telex: (098) 2123

Vila Rica
Praça Dom Pedro II, 299
Centro
Tel: (098) 222-4455
Telex: (098) 2169

•Paraíba

João Pessoa

Manaíra Praia
Av. Flávio Ribeiro, 115
Manaíra
Tel: (083) 226-1550
Telex: (083) 2178

Nazareno
Altiplano do Cabo Branco
Cabo Branco
Tel: (083) 226-1183

Tambaú
Av. Almirante Tamandaré, 229
Tambau
Tel: (083) 226-3660
Telex: (083) 2158

•Pernambuco

Olinda

Marolinda
Av. Beira-Mar, 1615
Tel: (081) 429-1699
Telex: (081) 3249

Quatro Rodas Olinda (luxury)
Av. José Augusto Moreira, 2200
Casa Caiada
Tel: (081) 431-2955
Telex: (081) 1324

14-Bis
Av. Beira-Mar, 1414
Tel: (081) 429-0409

Recife

Boa Viagem
Av. Boa Viagem, 5000
Boa Viagem
Tel: (081) 341-4144
Telex: (081) 2072

Hotel do Sol
Av. Boa Viagem, 978
Boa Viagem
Tel: (081) 326-7644
Telex: (081) 1337

International Othon
Palace
Av. Boa Viagem, 3722
Boa Viagem
Tel: (081) 326-7225
Telex: (081) 2141

Jangadeiro
Av. Boa Viagem, 3114
Boa Viagem
Tel: (081) 326-6777
Telex: (081) 1502

Miramar (luxury)
Rua dos Navegantes, 363
Boa Viagem
Tel: (081) 326-7422
Telex: (081) 2139

Park
Rua dos Navegantes, 9
Boa Viagem
Tel: (081) 325-4666
Telex: (081) 1903

Recife Palace (luxury)
Av. Boa Viagem, 4070
Boa Viagem
Tel: (081) 325-4044
Telex: (081) 4258

Savaroni
Av. Boa Viagem, 3772
Nos Viagem
Tel: (081) 325-5077
Telex: (081) 1428

Vila Rica
Av. Boa Viagem, 4308
Boa Viagem
Tel: (081) 326-5111
Telex: (081) 1903

•Rio Grande do Norte

Natal

Jaraguá Center
Rua Santo Antônio, 655
Centro
Tel: (084) 221-2355
Telex: (084) 2246

Luxor
Av. Rio Branco, 634
Centro
Tel: (084) 221-2721
Telex: (084) 2175

Natal Mar
Via Costeira, 8101
Ponta Negra.
Tel: (084) 236-2121
Telex: (084) 2449

Reis Magos
Av. Café Filho, 822
Praia do Meio
Tel: (084) 222-2055
Telex: (084) 2102

Vila do Mar
Via Costeira
Tel: (084) 222-3755
Telex: (084) 2749

NORTH

•Amapá

Macapá

Amapaense
Av. Tirandentes
Centro
Tel: (096) 222-3366

Novotel
Av. Amazons, 17
Centro
Tel: (096) 222-1144
Telex: (091) 1480

•Amazonas

Manaus

Amazonas
Praça Adalberto Vale
Centro
Tel: (092) 234-7679
Telex: (092) 2277

Ana Cassia
Rua dos Andradas, 14
Centro
Tel: (092) 232-6201
Telex: (092) 2713

Da Vinci
Rua Belo Horizonte,
240-A
Adrianopolis
Tel: (092) 233-6800
Telex: (092) 1024

Imperial
Av. Getúlio Vargas, 227
Centro
Tel: (092) 233-8711
Telex: (092) 2231

Lord
Rua Marcílio Dias, 217/2, 217/225
Centro
Tel: (092) 234-9741
Telex: (092) 2278

Novotel
Av. Mandii, 4
Grande Rótula
Distrito Industrial
Tel: (092) 237-1211
Telex: (092) 2429

Tropical Manaus (luxury)
Praia da Ponta Negra
Tel: (092) 238-5757
Telex: (092) 2173

•Pará

Belém

Equitorial Palace
Av. Braz de Aguiar, 612
Nazaré
Tel: (091) 224-8855
Telex: (091) 1605

Excelsior Grão Pará
Av. Presidente Vargas, 718
Centro
Tel: (091) 222-3255
Telex: (091) 1171

Hilton International Belém (luxury)
Av. Presidente Vargas, 882
Praça da República
Tel: (091) 223-6500
Telex: (091) 2024

Novotel
Av. Bernardo Sayão, 4804
Guamá
Tel: (091) 229-8011
Telex: (091) 1241

Regente
Av. Governador José Malcher, 485
Centro
Tel: (091) 224-0755
Telex: (091) 1796

Sagres
Av. Governador José Malcher, 2927
Sao Bras
Tel: (091) 228-3999
Telex: (091) 1662

Selton Belém
Av. Júlio César, 1777
Val-de-Cans
Tel: (091) 233-4222
Telex: (091) 1585

Vanja
Rua Benjamin Constant, 1164
Centro
Tel: (091) 222-6457
Telex: (091) 1343

Marajó Island

Pousada Marajoara
4a. Rua, Soure
Tel: (091) 741-1472
Reservations in Belém
Tel: (091) 223-2128

Santarém

Santerém Palace
Av. Rui Barbosa, 726
Tel: (091) 522-1285

Tropical
Av. Mendonça Furtado, 4120
Tel: (091) 522-1583

Uiapuru
Av. Adriano Pimentel, 140
Tel: (091) 522-1531

Food Digest

WHAT TO EAT

A country as large and diverse as Brazil naturally has regional specialities when it comes to food. Immigrants, too, influence Brazilian cuisine. In some parts of the south, the cuisine reflects a German influence; Italian and Japanese immigrants brought their cooking skills to São Paulo. Some of the most traditional Brazilian dishes are adaptations of Portuguese or African foods. But the staples for many Brazilians are rice, beans and manioc.

Lunch is the heaviest meal of the day and you might find it very heavy indeed for the hot climate. Breakfast is most commonly *café com leite* (hot milk with coffee) with bread and sometimes fruit. Supper is often taken quite late.

Although not a great variety of herbs is used, Brazilian food is tastily seasoned, not usually peppery—with the exception of some very spicy dishes from Bahia. Many Brazilians do enjoy hot pepper (*pimenta*) and the local *malagueta* chilis can be infernally fiery or pleasantly nippy, depending on how they're prepared. But the pepper sauce (most restaurants prepare their own, sometimes jealously guarding the recipe) is almost always served separately so the option is yours.

Considered Brazil's national dish (although not found in all parts of the country), *feijoada* consists of black beans simmered with a variety of dried, salted and smoked meats. Originally made out of odds and ends to feed the slaves, nowadays the tail, ears, feet, etc. of a pig are thrown in. *Feijoada* for lunch on Saturday has become somewhat of an institution in Rio de Janeiro, where it is served *completa* with white rice, finely shredded kale (*couve*), *farofa* (manioc root meal toasted with butter) and sliced oranges.

The most unusual Brazilian food is found in Bahia, where a distinct African influence can be tasted in the *dendê* palm oil and coconut milk. The Bahianos are fond of pepper and many dishes call for ground raw peanuts or cashew nuts and dried shrimp. Some of the most famous Bahian dishes are *Vatapá* (fresh and dried shrimp, fish, ground raw peanuts, coconut milk, *dendê* oil and seasonings thickened with bread into a creamy mush); *moqueca* (fish, shrimp, crab or a mixture of seafood in a *dendê* oil and coconut milk sauce); *xinxim de galinha* (a chicken *fricasse* with *dendê* oil, dried shrimp and ground raw peanuts); *caruru* (a shrimp-okra gumbo with *dendê* oil); *bobó de camarão* (cooked and mashed manioc root with shrimp, *dendê* oil and coconut milk); and *acarajé* (a patty made of ground beans fried in *dendê* oil and filled with *vatapá*, dried shrimp and *pimenta*). Although delicious, beware of the fact that the palm oil and coconut milk can be too rich for some digestive tracts.

Seafood is plentiful all along the coast, but the Northeast is particularly famed for its fish, shrimp, crabs and lobster. Sometimes cooked with coconut milk, other ingredients that add a nice touch to Brazilian seafood dishes are coriander, lemon juice and garlic. Try *peixe a Brasileiro*, a fish stew served with prião (manioc root meal cooked with broth from the stew to the consistency of porridge) and a traditional dish made all along the coast. One of the tastiest varieties of fish is *badejo*, a sea bass with firm white meat.

A favorite with foreign visitors and very popular all over Brazil is the *churrasco* or barbecue, which originated with the southern gaucho cowboys who roasted meat over an open fire. Some of the finest *churrasco* can be eaten in the South. Most *churrascarias* offer a *rodizio* option: for a set price diners eat all they can of a variety of meats. Waiters bring spits of barbecued beef, pork, chicken and sausage to your table and slice off the piece you select right onto your plate.

The cooler climate in Minas Gerais will whet your appetite for the state's hearty pork-and-bean cuisine. Try *tutu* (mashed black beans thickened with manioc meal into a mush) or *feijão tropeiro* (literally, mule skinner beans: *fradinho* beans, bacon and manioc meal). Mineiros eat a lot of pork and produce some very tasty pork sausage called *linguiça*. Minas is also corn country and a dairy state, lending its name to Brazil's fresh, bland, white *queijo minas* cheese.

A few exotic dishes can be found in the Amazon region, including those prepared with *tucupi* (made from manioc leaves and having a slightly numbing effect on the tongue), especially *pato no tucupi* (duck) and *tacacá* broth with manioc starch. There are also many varieties of fruit that are found nowhere else. The rivers produce a great variety of fish, including piranha and the giant *pirarucu*. River fish is also the staple in the Pantanal.

In the arid inland areas of the Northeast, life is frugal, but there are some tasty specialities, like *carne seca or carne de sol* (dried salted beef, often served with squash) and roast kid. Bananas (especially certain varieties that are only eaten cooked) are often served together with other food. Tapioca (the starch leached out of the manioc root when it is ground into meal) is popular all over the Northeast in the form of *beijus* (like a snowy white tortilla, usually stuffed with shredded coconut) and *cuscuz* (a stiff pudding made of tapioca, shredded coconut and coconut milk).

Two Portuguese dishes that are popular in Brazil are *bacalhau* (imported dried salted codfish) and *cosido*, a glorified "boiled dinner" of meats and vegetables (usually several root vegetables, squash and cabbage and/or kale) served with *pirão* made out of broth. Also try delicate *palmito* palm heart, served as a salad, soup or pastry filling.

Salgadinhos are a Brazilian style of finger food, served as appetizers, canapés, ordered with a round of beer or as a quick snack at a lunch counter—a native alternative to U.S.-style fast food chains that are also very evident in the country. *Salgadinhos* are usually small pastries stuffed with cheese, ham, shrimp, chicken, ground beef, palmito, etc. There are also fish balls and meat croquettes, breaded shrimp and miniature quiches. Some of the bakeries have excellent *salgadinhos* which you can either take home or eat at the counter with a fruit juice or soft drink. Other tasty snack foods include *pão de queijo* (a cheesy quick bread), and *pastel* (two layers of a thinly rolled pasta-like dough with a filling sealed between, deep-fried). Instead of French-fried potatoes, try *aipim frito* (deep-fried manioc root).

Many Brazilian desserts are made out of fruit, coconut, egg yolk or milk. Compotes and thick jams, often served with mild cheese, are made out of many fruits and also out of squash and sweet potatoes. Avocado is also used as a dessert, mashed or whipped up in the blender with sugar and lemon juice. Fruit mousses are light when the weather's hot—passion fruit mousse is especially nice. And there are wonderful tropical fruit sherbets and ice creams. Coconut appears in many types of desserts and candies—sidewalk vendors sell molasses-colored and white *cocadas*. Portuguese-style egg yolk desserts are delicious, especially *quindim* (a rich sweet egg yolk-coconut custard). *Doce de leite* is a Brazilian version of caramel, made by boiling milk with sugar, sometimes stopping at a consistency for eating with a spoon (often served with cheese). *Pudim de leite* is a very common dessert, a sweet pudding made with sweetened condensed milk and caramel syrup. Manioc also returns to the table for dessert in the form of *bolo de aipim*, despite the name, more of a pudding than a cake, made with the grated root and coconut. Special sweet shops sell *docinhos* (home-made bonbons) and a variety of sweet snacks. One of the most special desserts (and after a large meal on a hot day perhaps the most appropriate) is the wonderful tropical fruit—there's always something exotic and delicious in season.

DRINKING NOTES

Brazilians are great social drinkers and love to sit for hours talking and often singing with friends over drinks. During the hottest months, this will usually be in open air restaurants where most of the people will be ordering *chope*, cold draft beer, perfect for the hot weather. Brazilian beers are really very good. Take note that although *cerveja* means beer, it is usually used to refer to bottled beer only.

Brazil's own unique brew is *cachaça*, a strong liquor distilled from sugar cane, a type of rum, but with its own distinct flavor. Usually colorless, it can also be amber. Each region boasts of its locally produced *cachaça*, also called *pinga*, *cana* or *aguardente*, but traditional producers include the states of Minas Gerais, Rio de Janeiro, São Paulo and the northeastern states where sugar cane has long been a cash crop.

Out of *cachaça*, some of the most delightful mixed drinks are concocted. Tops is the popular *caipirinha*, also considered the national drink. It's really a simple concoction of crushed lime—peel included—and sugar topped with plenty of ice. Variations on this drink are made using vodka or rum, but you should try the real thing. Some bars and restaurants mix their *caipirinhas* sweeter than you may want—order yours *com pouco açucar* (with a small amount of sugar) or even *sem açucar* (without sugar). *Batidas* are beaten in the blender or shaken and come in as many varieties as there are types of fruit in the tropics. Basically fruit juice with *cachaça*, some are also prepared with sweetened condensed milk. Favorites are *batida de maracujá* (passion fruit) and *batida de coco* (coconut milk), exotic flavors for visitors from cooler climates. When sipping *batidas*, don't forget that the *cachaça* makes them a potent drink, even though they taste like fruit juice.

Straight *cachaça* or beer is what the working class Brazilian will drink in the neighborhood *botequim*, little bars where you drink standing up at the counter. Some of these will serve *cachaça* steeped with herbs—considered to be "good for whatever ails you." The *botequins* are male-dominated; while women are not barred and won't usually be hassled, you may not feel comfortable being the only female in this male stronghold. And you will be more obvious as a foreigner.

Try the Brazilian wines. Produced in the cooler southern states, they are quite good. Restaurants offer a selection of the best—ask the maitre d' for help in ordering what you like. *Tinto* is red, *branco* is white and *rosé* is the same; *seco* is dry and *suave*, which actually means soft, refers to the sweetness of the wine. Excellent wines imported from Argentina and Chile are not expensive in Brazil, so you may want to take advantage of this.

The usual variety of spirits are available, both *importado* (imported) and *nacional* (domestic). There are no really good Brazilian whiskeys and imports are very expensive. Some of the brands you may be familiar with are produced locally—you will know by the price.

Among the non-alcoholic beverages, a real treat are the fresh fruit juices. Any hotel or restaurant will have three or four types but the snack bars specializing in *suco de fruta* have an amazing variety. The fruit is on display—guavas, mangoes, pineapples, passion fruit, persimmons, tamarind, as well as more familiar apples, melons, bananas and strawberries—all as tasty as they are colorful. They will also whip up a glass of lemonade for you or squeeze a plain old orange. All juices are made fresh for each order. Delicious fruit milkshakes called *vitaminas* make a nutritious snack. Most common are the *mista* or mixed fruit—usually papaya and banana with a touch of beet root to give it a pretty color; *banana com aveia*, which is banana and raw oatmeal; and *abacate* which is made of avocado. These are great for breakfast.

If you've never tasted coconut juice—the colorless liquid contained in the shell—you can stop at a street vendor, often a trailer near the beach. Restaurants or bars that serve *água de coco* will usually hang the cocos near the door (pronounced similar to cocoa, so if you want hot chocolate, ask for *chocolate quente*, otherwise you'll probably get a coconut). The top is lopped off and you drink the juice through a straw. After drinking your fill, ask to have the *coco* split open to sample the soft, gelatin-like 'flesh' that is beginning to form inside the shell.

Another tropical treat is sugarcane juice, served at snack bars that advertise *caldo de cana*. Street vendors use a crank wringer to squeeze the juice. Naturally, the juice is sweet with a pleasant, subtle flavor.

Among the soft drinks, you will find the familiar Coca-Cola and Pepsi products as well as domestic brands. A uniquely Brazilian soft drink is *guaraná*, flavored with a small Amazon fruit. Quite sweet, but good, it is a favorite with children.

Bottled mineral water (*água mineral*) is available everywhere, both carbonated (*com gás*) and plain (*sem gás*), and its best for visitors to stick to it. Although water in the cities is treated, people further filter it in their homes and if you are a houseguest, you will no doubt be served *água filtrada*. It's common sense not to drink unfiltered tap water.

If you are terribly traditional and can't do without your morning tea, never fear. Tea is grown in Brazil and many of the fancier hotels and restaurants can even offer you an English brand. Try the indigenous South American *mate* (pronounced ma-tchee) tea. The black tea is usually drunk as a refreshing iced tea; the green tea, called *chimarrão*, is sipped through a silver straw with a strainer at the lower end, in Brazil's far south—a gaucho tradition.

Finally there is wonderful Brazilian coffee. *Café* is roasted dark, ground fine, prepared strong and taken with plenty of sugar. Coffee mixed with hot milk (*café com leite*) is the traditional breakfast beverage throughout Brazil. Other than at breakfast, it is served black in tiny demitasse cups, never with a meal. These *cafezinhos* or "little coffees", offered the visitor to any home or office, are served piping hot at any *botequim* (there are even little stand-up bars that serve only *cafezinho*). However you like it, Brazilian coffee makes the perfect ending to every meal. Note: While decaffeinated coffee (*café descafeinado*) is now available on supermarket shelves, it is not yet a public hit; finding it in restaurants may be difficult, but it won't hurt to ask.

THINGS TO DO

TRAVEL PACKAGES

A variety of individual and group tours to Brazil are available. Some are all-inclusive packages with transportation, food and lodgings, excursions and entertainment all arranged for you; some include only air transportation and hotel accommodations. A travel agent will be able to supply you with information about different options being offered. There are also special interest tours which include international travel to and from Brazil, such as boat trips on the Amazon river, fishing and wildlife (including bird watching) tours to the Pantanal Matogrossense in the Central-West, and Carnival tours to Rio, Salvador or Recife, to mention just a few.

If you aren't on a tour where everything is planned, check at your hotel or a local travel agency to find out about readily available city sight-seeing tours, boat outings to nearby islands, day trips to mountain and beach resort areas and evening entertainment tour groups that take in a show.

Longer excursions can also be quite easily arranged once you are in Brazil—from Rio or São Paulo, for example, it is easy to get on a tour to the Amazon or Pantanal, take a day trip by plane to Brasília or the Iguaçu falls, or join a tour of the Northeast or the colonial towns of Minas Gerais. However, in the peak season there may be a wait, as these excursions do get fully booked. If your stay is short, it would be best to make reservations beforehand.

Ocean cruises up and down the coast usually need to be booked well in advance and this is best done through your travel agent back home.

CULTURE PLUS

MUSEUMS

Brazil's historical museums are unlikely to be the highlight of your visit. With rare exceptions, there are just not enough resources available for proper upkeep and acquisitions. Below is a partial listing. Temporary exhibits are announced in the newspapers under *Exposições*.

•Rio de Janeiro

Carmen Miranda Museum
(Museu Carmen Miranda)
Parque do Flamengo
(across from Av. Ruy Barbosa no. 560)
Tel: (021) 551-2597
Tues-Fri 11 a.m.-5 p.m.
Sat/Sun/holidays 1-5 p.m.

Chacara do Céu Art Museum
(Museu Chacara do Céu)
Rua Murtinho Nobre
93, Santa Teresa
Tel: (021) 232-1386/ 224-8981
Tues-Sat 2-5 p.m
Sun 1-5 p.m.

City Museum
(Museu da Cidade)
Estrada de Santa Marinha
Parque da Cidade, Gávea
Tel: (021) 322-1328
Tues-Sun 12-4.30 p.m.

Folk Art Museum
(Museu do Folclore Edison Carneiro)
Rua do Catete.
Tel: (021) 285-0891
Tues-Fri 11 a.m.-6 p.m.
Sat/Sun/holidays 3-6 p.m.

Indian Museum
(Museu do Indio)
Rua das Palmeiras, 55 Botafogo
Tel: (021) 286-8799
Tues-Fri 10 a.m.-5 p.m.
Sat/Sun 1-5 p.m.

H. Stern Museum
(Museu H. Stern)
Rua Visconde de Pirajá, 490
3° andar
Ipanema
Tel: (021) 259-7442
Mon-Fri 8.30 a.m.-6 p.m.
Sat 8.30 a.m.-12 p.m.

Itamaraty Palace Museum of History and Diplomacy
(Museu Histório e Diplomático do Palácio do Itamarati),
Av. Marechal Floriano, 196
Centro
Tel: (021) 291-4411 ramal 6

Museum of Image and Sound - (Cinema)
(Museu da Umagem e do Som)
Praça Rui Barbosa, 1
(near Praça 15 de Novembro)
Centro
Tel: (021) 262-0309, 210-2463
Mon-Fri 1-6 p.m.

Museum of Modern Art
(Museu de Arte Moderna)
Av. Infante D. Henrique, 85
Parque do Flamengo
Tel: (021) 210-2188
Tues-Sun 12-6 p.m.

National History Museum
(Museu Histórico Nacional)
Praça Marechal Ancora
(near Praça 15 de Novembro)
Centro
Tel: (021) 240-7978/ 220-2628
Tues-Fri 10 a.m.-5.30 p.m.
Sat/Sun/holidays 2.30-5.30 p.m.

National Museum
(Museu Nacional)
Quinta da Boa Vista
São Cristóvão
Tel: (021) 264-8262
Tues-Sun 10 a.m.-4.45 p.m.

National Museum of Fine Arts
(Museu Nacional de Belas Artes)
Av. Rio Branco, 199
Centro
Tel: (021) 20-0160/
240-0068
Tues/Thurs
10 a.m.-6.30 p.m.
Wed/Fri 12-6.30 p.m.
Sat/Sun/holidays 3-6 p.m.

•São Paulo

Anchieta Museum of History
(Casa de Anchieta)
Pátio do Colégio
Centro
Tel: (011) 239-5722
Tues-Sat 1-5 p.m.
Sun 10 a.m.-5 p.m.

Bandeirante (Pioneer) Museum of History
(Casa do Bandeirante)
Praça Monteiro Lobato, Butantã
Tel: (011) 211-0920
Tues-Fri
10.30 a.m.-5 p.m.
Sat/Sun 12-5 p.m.

Folk Art Museum
(Museu de Folclore)
Parque do Ibirapuera
Pavilhão Lucas Nogueira Garcez
Tel: (011) 544-4212
Tues-Sun 2-5 p.m.

Museum of Brazilian Art
(Museu de Arte Brasileira)
Rua Alagoas, 903
Higienópolis
Tel: (011) 826-4233
Tues-Fri 2-10 p.m.
Sat/Sun/holidays 1-6 p.m.

Museum of Contemporary Art
(Museu de Arte Contemporânea)
Parque do Ibirapuera
Pavilhão da Bienal
3° andar
Tel: (011) 571-9610
Tues-Sun 1-6 p.m.

Museum of Image and Sound - (Cinema)
(Museu da Imagem e do Som)
Av. Europa, 158
Jardim Europa
Tel: (011) 852-9197
Tues/Sun/holidays 2-10 p.m.

Museum of Modern Art
(Museu de Arte Moderna)
Parque do Ibirapuera
Grande Marquise
Tel: (011) 549-9688
Tues-Fri 1-7 p.m.
Sat/Sun 11 a.m.-7 p.m.

Museum of Nativity Scenes
(Museu de Presépios)
Parque do Ibirpuera
Grande Marquise
Tel: (011) 544-1329

Paulista Museum of History
(Museu Paulista/Museu do Ipiranga)
Parque da Independência
Ipiranga
Tel: (011) 215-4588
9.30 a.m.-5 p.m.

Sacred Art Museum
(Museu de Arte Sacra)
Av. Tiradentes, 676
Luz
Tel: (011) 227-7694
Tues-Sun 1-5 p.m.

São Paulo Museum of Art
(Museu de Arte de São Paulo - MASP)
Av. Paulista, 1758
Cerqueira César
Tel: (011) 251-5644
Tues-Fri 1-5 p.m.
Sat/Sun 2-6 p.m.

•Belém

Emilio Goeldi Museum
Av. Magalhães Barata, 376
Tel: (091) 224-9233
ramal 223
Tues-Fri 8-12/2-6 p.m.
Sat 8 a.m.-1 p.m./3-6 p.m.
Sun 8 a.m.-6 p.m.

•Belo Horizonte

Abilio Barreto History Museum
(Museu Histórico Abílio Barreto)
Rua Bernardo
Mascarenhos
Cidade Jardim
Tel: (031) 212-1400 ramal 372
Wed-Mon 10 a.m.-5 p.m.

Belo Horizonte Museum of Art
(Museu de Arte de Belo Horizonte)
Av. Otacílio Negrão de Lima, 16585
Pampulha
Tel: (031) 443-4533
8 a.m.-12 p.m.

Mineiro State Museum
(Museu Mineiro)
Av. João Pinheiro, 342
Centro
Tel: (031) 201-6777 ramal 175
Tues/Wed/Fri
12-6.30 p.m.
Thurs 12-9 p.m.
Sat/Sun 10 a.m.-4 p.m.

Museum of Mineralogy
(Museu de Mineralogia)
Rua da Bahia, 1149
Tel: (031) 212-1400 ramal 359
8 a.m.-5 p.m.

Natural History Museum
(Museu de História Natural)
Rua Gustavo da Silveira, 1035
(Instituto Agronômico)
Tel: (031) 461-7666
8 a.m.-4.30 p.m.

•Brasília

Brasília Museum of Art
(Museu de Arte de Brasília - MAB)
SHTS (near the Brasília Palace hotel)
Tel: (061) 224-6277
Tues-Sun 10 a.m.-5 p.m.

Brasília Museum of History
(Museu Histórico de Brasília)
Praça dos Três Poderes
8 a.m.-12 p.m./1-6 p.m.

•Curitiba

City Museum
(Casa da Memória)
Rua 13 de Maio, 571
Tues-Fri 8 a.m.-12 p.m./2-6 p.m.

David Carneiro Museum of History
(Museu David Carneiro)
Rua Com. Araújo, 531
Tel: (041) 222-9358
Sat 2-4 p.m.

Immigrant Museum
(Museu da Habitação do Imigrante)
Bosque João Paulo II
Wed-Mon 7 a.m.-7 p.m.

Museum of Contemporary Art
(Museu de Arte Contemporânea)
Rua Des. Westphalen, 16
Tel: (041) 222-5172
Mon-Fri 9.30 a.m.-6 p.m.
Sun 1-5 p.m.

Paranaense Museum of History
(Museu Paranaense)
Pça Generoso Marques
Tel: (041) 234-3611
Mon-Fri 9 a.m.-6 p.m.
Sat/Sun 1-6 p.m.

Sacred Art Museum
(Museu de Arte Sacra)
Lgo. Cel. Eneas
Tues-Fri 9 a.m.-12 p.m/1.30-6.30 p.m.
Sat/Sun 9 a.m.-12 p.m.

•Diamantina

Diamond Museum
(Museu do Diamante)
Rue Direita
Tues-Sun 12-5.30 p.m.

•Manaus

Amazon Geographic and Historical Institute Museum
(Museu do Instituto Geográfico e
Histórico do Amazonas)
Rua Bernardo Ramos, 117
Tel: (092) 232-7077
Mon-Fri 9 a.m.-1p.m.

Indian Museum
(Museu do Indio)
Rua Duque de Caxias/Av. 7 de Setembro
Tel: (092) 234-1422
Mon-Sat 8-11 a.m./2-5 p.m.

Man of the North Museum
(Museu do Homem do Norte)
Av. 7 de Setembro, 1385
Centro
Tel: (092) 232-5373
Tues-Fri 9 a.m.-12 p.m./2-6 p.m.

Museum of Mineralogy
(Museu de Mineralogia)
Estr. do Aleixo, 2150
Mon-Fri 8 a.m.-12 p.m./2-6 p.m.
Tel: (092) 236-13344

Museum of the Port of Manaus
(Museu do Porto de Manaus)
Boulevard Vivaldo Lima
Centro
Tel: (092) 232-4250
Tues-Sun 8 -11 a.m./2-5 p.m.

•Ouro Preto

Aleijadinho Museum
(Museu Aleijadinho)
Pça de São Francisco
Tues-Sun 8-11.30 a.m./1-5 p.m.

Inconfidencia Historial Museum
(Museu da Inconfidência)
Pça Tiradentes
Tues-Sun 12-5.30 p.m.

Mineralogy Museum
(Museu de Mineralogia)
Pça Tiradentes, 20
12-5 p.m.

Silver Museum
(Museu da Prata),
Pça Mons. João Castilho Barbosa.
Tues-Sun 12-5 p.m.

•Petrópolis

Imperial Museum
(Museu Imperial)
Av. 7 de Setembro,220
Tues-Sun 12-5 p.m.
Santos Dumont House
(Casa de Santos Dumont)
Rua do Encanto, 124
Tues-Sun 9 a.m.-5 p.m.

•Porto Alegre

Julio de Castilhos Museum
(Museu Júlio de Castilho)
Rua Duque de Caxias, 1231
Tel: (0512) 21-3959
Tues-Sun 9 a.m.-5 p.m.

Porto Alegre Museum
(Museu de Porto Alegre)
Rua João Alfredo, 582
Tel: (0512) 21-6622
Mon-Fri 8-11.30 a.m./2-5:30 p.m.
Sat 8-11.30 a.m.

Rio Grande do Sul Museum of Art
(Museu de Arte do Rio Grande do Sul)
Pça Barão do Rio Branco
Tel: (0512) 21-8456
Tues-Sun 10 a.m.-6 p.m.

•Recife/Olinda

Abolition Museum
(Museu da Abolição)
Rua Benfica, 1150
Madalena
Tel: (081) 228-3011
Mon-Fri 8 a.m.-12 p.m./2-5 p.m.

Brennand Plantation Museum
(Museu Brennand)
Engenho São João (Vaz)
Mon-Fri 8-11.30 a.m./2-5 p.m.
Sat 8-11.30 a.m.

Ceramic Museum
(Museu do Barro)
Rua Floriano Peixoto
Raio Oeste, 3° andar
Tel: (081) 224-2084
Mon-Fri 9 a.m.-12 p.m./2-6 p.m.
Sat 9 a.m.-12 p.m.

Franciscan Museum of Sacred Art
(Museu Franciscano de Arte Sacra)
Rua do Imperador (Santo Antônio)
Tel: (081) 224-0530
Mon-Fri 8 -11.30 a.m./2-5 p.m.
Sat 8-11.30 a.m.

Museum of Contemporary Art
(Museu de Arte Contemporânea)
Rua 13 de Maio, Olinda
Mon-Thurs
8 a.m.-5.30 p.m.
Sat/Sun 2-5.30 p.m.

Museum of the Northeasterner
(Museu do Homem do Nordeste)
Av. 17 de Agosto, 2187
(Casa Forte)
Tel: (081) 268-2000
Tues/Wed/Fri
11 a.m.-5 p.m.
Thurs 8 a.m.-5 p.m.
Sat/Sun/holidays
1-5 p.m.

Pernambuco Archaeological and Geographical Museum
(Museu Arqueológico e Geográfico de Pernambuco)
Rua do Hospício, 130
(Boa Vista)
Tel: (081) 222-4952
Mon-Fri 10 a.m.-12 p.m./3-5 p.m.

Pernambuco Museum of Sacred Art
(Museu de Arte Sacra de Pernambuco)
Rua Bispo Coutinho, 726
Alto da Sé
Tues-Fri 8 a.m.-12 p.m./2-6 p.m.
Sat/Sun 2-6 p.m.

Pernambuco State Museum
(Museu do Estado de Pernambuco)
Av. Rui Barbosa, 960
Graças
Tel: (081) 222-6694
Tues-Fri 8 a.m.-5 p.m.
Sat/Sun 2-5 p.m.

Recife City Museum
(Museu da Cidade de Recife)
Forte das Cinco Pontas
São José
Tel: (081) 224-8492
Mon-Fri 8 a.m.-6 p.m.
Sat/Sun 2-6 p.m.

Train Museum
(Museu do Trem)
Pça Visc. de Mauá
(Estação Ferroviária - train station)
Santo Antônio
Tel: (081) 231-2022
Tues-Fri 9 a.m.-12 p.m./1-5 p.m.
Sat 8 a.m.-12 p.m./2-6 p.m.
Sun 2-6 p.m.

•Salvador

Abelardo Rodrigues Art Museum
(Museu Abelardo Rodrigues)
Rua Gregório de Mattos, 45
Pelourinho
Tel: (071) 242-6155
Mon-Fri 10-11.30 a.m./2-5 p.m.
Sat/Sun 2-5 p.m.

Afro-Brazilian Museum
(Museu Afro-Brasileiro)
(old medical school/Faculdade de Medicina building)
Terreiro de Jesus
Tel: (071) 243-0384
Tues-Sat 9 -11.30 a.m./2-5.30 p.m.

Archaeological and Ethnological Museum
(Museu Arqueológico e Etnológico)
(old medical school/Faculdade de Medicina)
Terreiro de Jesus
Tel: (071) 243-0384
Tues-Fri 9-11.30 a.m./
2-5.30 p.m.
Sat 9-11.30 a.m.

Bahia Museum of Art
(Museu de Arte da Bahia)
Av. 7 de Setembre, 2340
Vitória
Tel: (071) 235-9492
Tues-Sun 2-6 p.m.

Carlos Costa Pinto Museum
(Museu Carlos Costa Pinto)
Av. 7 de Setembro, 2490
Vitória
Tel: (071) 243-0983
Tues-Sat 9 a.m.-12/2-5.30 p.m.

Carmelite Door Museum
(Museu das Portas do Carmo)
Lgo do Peloutinho
Senac
Tel: 242-5503
Mon-Sat 11 a.m.-6 p.m.

Carmelite Convent Museum
(Museu do Carmo)
Lgo Carmo
Carmo
Tel: (071) 242-0182
8 a.m.-12 p.m./2-6 p.m.

City Museum
(Museu da Cidade)
Lgo. do Pelourinho, 3
Tel: (071) 242-8773
8 a.m.-12 p.m./2-6 p.m.

Monsignor Aquino Barbaso Museum of Sacred Art
(Museu de Arte Sacra Monsenhor Aquino Barbosa),
Basílica de N.S. da Cpnceição da Praia
Tel: (0710) 242-0545 Tues-Sun 8-12 p.m.

Museum of Modern Art
(Museu de Arte Moderna)
Av. Do Contorno
Solar do Unhão
Tel: (071) 243-6174.
Tues-Fri 10-12 p.m./2-6 p.m.
Sat/Sun/holidays
2-6 p.m.

Museum of Sacred Art
(Museu de Arte Sacra)
Rua do Sodré, 25
Tel: (071) 243-6310
Tues-Sat 1-6 p.m.

Women's Institute Foundation Museum
(Museu da Fundação do Instituto Feminino)
Rua Mons. Flaviano, 2
Politeama de Cima
Tel: (071) 245-7522
Mon-Fri 8-11 a.m./2-4.30 p.m.

ART GALLERIES

Those showing the work of contemporary artists abound in the larger cities, especially Rio de Janeiro and São Paulo. The art museums also organize periodic exhibits. Shows are listed in the papers under *Exposições*. The Bienal or Biennial Art Exposition held in São Paulo on odd-numbered years lasts from September to January and is Latin America's largest contemporary art show.

CONCERTS

It is Brazil's forte. A variety of musical forms has developed in different parts of the country, many with accompanying forms of dance. While the Brazilian influence (especially in jazz) is heard around the world, what little is known of Brazilian music outside the country is just the tip of an iceberg.

Take in a concert by a popular singer or ask your hotel to recommend a nightclub with live Brazilian music: bossa nova, samba, choro and seresta are popular in Rio and São Paulo—each region has something different to offer. If you are visiting at Carnival, you'll hear and see plenty of music and dancing in the streets, mostly samba in Rio and frevo in the Northeast. There are also shows all year long designed to give tourists a taste of Brazilian folk music and dance. If you like what you hear, get some records or tapes to bring back with you.

The classical music and dance season runs from Carnival through mid-December. Besides presentations by local talents, major Brazilian cities (mainly Rio, São Paulo and Brasília) are included in world concert tours by international performers. One of the most important classical music festivals in South America takes place in July each year in Campos do Jordão in the state of São Paulo.

THEATERS

Some Brazilian cinema is very good — Brazil has in fact exported films quite successfully to North America and Europe. Without a knowledge of Portuguese, however, you may as well watch the exported films back home with subtitles in your language. But the majority of movies shown in Brazil are foreign-made, mostly American, all in the original language with Portuguese subtitles. Check out what's playing under the cinema heading in the local papers. An international film festival, FestRio, is held annually in Rio de Janeiro, and another takes place in São Paulo every October.

In order to enjoy the theater, you really would have to understand the language. Rio de Janeiro and São Paulo, especially, have busy seasons starting after Carnival and running through about November.

SHOPPING

WHAT TO BUY

Most visitors to Brazil just can't resist the stones. One of the major attractions of shopping for **gemstones** in Brazil, besides the price, is the tremendous variety not found anywhere else. Brazil produces amethysts, aquamarines, opals, topazes, the many-colored tourmalines—to name just a few of the most popular buys—as well as diamonds, emeralds, rubies and sapphires. Some 65 percent of the world's colored gemstones are produced in Brazil, also one of the world's major gold producers. Brazil today is one of the top jewelry centers in the world and costs are attractive because the operation is 100 percent domestic, from the mining of the gems to the cutting, crafting and designing of jewelry.

The value of a colored gemstone is determined mostly by its color and quality, not necessarily by size. Things to look for when choosing a gem: color, cut, clarity and cost. The stronger the color, the more valuable the stone. For example, a brilliant blue aquamarine is worth more than an icy pale stone. The cut should bring out the clarity, the stone's inner light of "fire".

Although you may find some tempting offers, unless you are an expert gemologist, it's wiser to buy from a reliable jeweler, where you will get what you pay for and can trust their advice, whether you are selecting a gift for someone (or treating yourself) or you have an investment in mind. The three leading jewelers operating nationwide are H. Stern, Amsterdam Sauer and Roditi, but there are other reliable smaller chains. The top jewelers have shops in the airports and shopping centers and in most hotels.

Another good buy in Brazil is **leather** goods, especially shoes, sandals, bags, wallets and belts. Although found everywhere, some of the finest leather comes from Brazil's South. Shoes are plentiful and handmade leather items can be found at handicraft street fairs.

Besides the street fairs, some cities have covered markets, sometimes run by the local tourism board. Among the typical and traditional craft items on sale at the markets:

Ceramics, especially in the Northeast, where clay bowls, water jugs, etc. are commonly used in the home; also from the Northeast, primitive clay figurines depicting folk heroes, customs and celebrations; **marajoara** ceramic pieces decorated with distinctive goemetric patterns come from the island of Marajó at the mouth of the Amazon river.

Beautiful **handmade lace** and **embroidered clothing** are produced mostly in the Northeast, especially in the state of Ceará while Minas Gerais is a traditional producer of handmade weavings and tapestries.

Cotton **hammocks** are popular all over Brazil, but used extensively instead of beds in the North and Northeast, the best place to buy them—sometimes finished with lacy crocheted edgings.

Brazil has beautiful **wood**. Gift shops sell items such as salad bowls and trays; woodcarvings can be found at the crafts fairs. Difficult to fit into your suitcase, but very unusual are the grotesque **carranca** figureheads unique to São Francisco river boats.

Straw and a variety of natural fibers (banana leaves, palm bark) are fashioned into baskets, hats, bags, mats, slippers, etc., especially in the Northeast.

Indian handicrafts, mostly from the northern Amazon region, include adornments (necklaces, earrings), utensils (sieves, baskets), weapons (bows, arrows, spears) and percussion instruments (like the

intriguing "rain sticks" that imitate the sound of falling rain) made out of wood, fibers, thorns, teeth, claws, colorful feathers, shells and seeds.

In Minas Gerais, **soap stone** items are on sale everywhere. Both decorative and utilitarian objects—cooking pots, toiletry sets, quartz and agate bookends and ashtrays—can be found in souvenir stores.

Paintings can be bought at galleries as well as at crafts fairs and markets. Brazilian primitive or naif paintings are popular.

A fun thing to take home are the peculiar percussion **instruments** that you hear the samba bands playing, usually on sale at street fairs. If you enjoy Brazilian music, buy some **records** or **tapes** at a record shop. Video films of the big Carnival parade in Rio, available quite soon after the celebration, make good gifts.

If fashion is your interest, boutiques in most cities are clustered in certain districts. Shopping malls also enable you to visit many shops in less time. Most clothes are 100 percent cotton—you may want to pick up some inexpensive cotton material at a fabric store. If you want something uniquely Brazilian to wear back home, buy something with lace or embroidery from the Northeast, a tiny bikini or a **kanga** beach cover-up (a big piece of printed fabric that can be wrapped on in a variety of ways—ask the shop girl for some suggestions).

Stores that sell religious articles are interesting to visit. Popular **amulets** include the **figa** (a carved clenched fist with the thumb between the index and middle fingers) and the Senhor do Bonfim ribbons (to be wrapped around a wrist or ankle and fastened with three knots) from Salvador.

Ground roasted coffee can be found at any supermarket or bakery—the vacuum-packed variety will stay fresh longer. Or you can get those packaged in a handy carton at the airport.

SPORTS

SPECTATOR

Soccer (futebol): This is Brazil's national sport and a passion that unites all ages and classes. During World Cup season, the country comes to a halt as everyone tunes in to watch the cup matches on T.V. If you're a soccer fan, arrange through your hotel to see a professional game—there are organized tour groups. The boisterous fans are often as interesting to watch as the game itself.

Especially exciting are the games between top rival teams in Rio's giant Maracanã Stadium, which squeezes in crowds of up to 200,000. There is rarely any violence, but it is to recommended that you get a reserved seat (around \$5-\$8) rather than sit in the packed bleachers (about \$1.50). Most weekend afternoons or in the early evening you can see a "sandlot" match between neighborhood teams on the beaches or in the city parks of Brazil.

Private clubs are big in Brazil and besides the socializing this is where most upper and middle class Brazilians practise sports. Although you can usually visit as a guest, many of the same sports facilities can also be found in top class hotels.

PARTICIPANT

Aquatic sports: As is to be expected in a land which has such an extensive coastline and major inland waterways as well as a mild climate, a variety of aquatic sports can be enjoyed in Brazil.

Ocean swimming is a delight, especially in the North and Northeast, where the water is warm all year round. Many hotels have swimming pools, as do the private clubs, but there are no public pools in Brazil.

Sailing/boating—Almost any coast town has boat rental facilities and many resort hotels have sailboats, fishing tackle, diving gear and surf and windsurf boards. Sailboats, speedboats or schooner-like Brazilian saveiros can be rented complete with equipment and crew at prices starting around $100 per day. In Rio go to the in-town Marina da Gloria.

Surfing and windsurfing are popular and rental equipment is available.

Fishing: There is a large variety of fish, both ocean and freshwater varieties, all along the coast as well as in the rivers and the flooded Pantanal marshlands. The equipment can be rented along with a boat and guide and special fishing excursions are organized. Professional fishermen in the Northeast will sometimes take an extra passenger or two on their jangada rafts.

Diving equipment can be rented and instructors are available. Some of the more spectacular places to dive include Fernando de Noronha island off Brazil's northeasternmost point and the coral Abrolhos archipelago off the coast of southern Bahia. More accessible are the "Sun Coast" east of Rio de Janeiro (Cabo Frio, Búzios) and the "Green Coast" between Rio and São Paulo (Angra dos Reis, Parati).

Other Sports: Some of the larger hotels have tennis courts. There are a few public courts, but the game is played mostly at clubs.

Golf is not a big sport in Brazil and is played mostly in Rio and São Paulo. There are no public golf courses, but although country clubs are quite exclusive, it is possible to make arrangements (through your hotel) to play as a visitor.

Horse racing is popular and several cities have tracks. The top prize event, called the Grande Premio do Brasil, is held at the Rio de Janeiro track on every first Sunday in August.

Brazil is on the world Grand Prix Formula 1 auto racing circuit. The Rio de Janeiro (or more recently, São Paulo) race is scheduled in March or April.

Handgliding is popular, especially in Rio, where modern Daedalus' leap off the mountains and soar on air currents before landing on the beach below. Inexperienced flyers can go tandem with an instructor.

Joggers have a beautiful place to keep in shape while in Rio: the in-town beaches have wide sidewalks, with the "mileage" marked in kilometers along the way. In São Paulo, Ibirapuera Park is a favorite spot for runners. The biggest foot races are the Rio Marathon and the Sao Silvestre race held in São Paulo on December 31, with the starting line in one year and finishing line in the next.

Hunting is forbidden by law throughout Brazil. The only shooting of wildlife that is allowed is with a camera.

Nature sports: There are plenty of peaks to climb in Brazil, if you enjoy mountaineering or rock climbing. In Rio, you can even climb the city's landmarks—Sugarloaf mountain and Corcovado. There are excursion clubs which arrange outings to nearby mountainous regions and areas where you can go spelunking, white-water canoeing, kayaking and sailing. Rapids-shooting rafting excursions can be arranged through hotels in Rio.

If you want to go biking and camping, contact the Camping Clube do Brasil. They organize treks in out-of-the-way parts of Brazil. If you prefer to go backpacking on your own, check out the maps available from the IBGE—Brazilian Institute of Geography and Statistics.

***Capoeira*:** An uniquely Brazilian sport, it is a relic from slavery days, when fighting, and especially training for fighting, by the slaves had to be dissimulated. *Capoeira* is a stylized fight-dance, with its own accompanying rhythms and music, using the feet a great deal to strike out with and requiring a graceful agility. This tradition has been kept alive chiefly in Salvador and Rio, where there are academies. Arrange through your hotel to see a presentation or you may catch a street group performing on a beach or a busy square.

PHOTOGRAPHY

Both Kodakcolor and Fujicolor film for color prints can be bought and developed in Brazil, as well as Ektachrome slide film. Kodachrome is not available nor is it developed in Brazil. Hotel shops will have film and specialty shops (easily spotted by signs out front advertising the brands of film they sell) carry equipment and accessories, and handle film processing. Developing is quick and of good quality. In the larger cities you will find 24-hour finishing and even one-hour service (in Rio at the Rio-Sul shopping center). Reliable labs include Kodak, Fuji, Multicolor and Curt. Find out from your hotel where you can take your film to be developed. *Revelar* = to develop; *revelação* = developing; film is *filme*.

Although it is often easier just to wait and have your pictures developed when you return from your trip, if you are going to be traveling around a great deal, remember that exposure to heat and multiple X-ray security checks at airports could ruin your film.

For tourists entering with photographic equipment that is obviously for vacation picture-taking, there are no customs restrictions. Professional equipment, if brought in substantial quantities, must be registered with customs for temporary entrance; but they leave the country with you. Contact a Brazilian consulate before traveling—depending on what you bring, you may need written authorization from a diplomatic mission outside Brazil.

Avoid taking pictures during the middle of the day when the sun is strongest and tends to wash out colors. Light in the tropics is very white and bright and you may want to use an appropriate filter. Mornings from nine to 11 are the best time for photography, or wait until the sun has set a little in the afternoon.

Don't walk around with your camera hanging around your neck or over your shoulder—there's nothing more conspicuous than a foreign tourist with a camera—an easy target for a snatcher. Carry it discreetly in a bag slung round in front of you. Never leave a camera unattended at the beach. If you have expensive equipment, it's a good idea to have it insured.

LANGUAGE

GENERAL

Although Portuguese, and not Spanish, is the language of Brazil, if you have a knowledge of Spanish, it will come in handy. You will recognize many similar words and most Brazilians will understand you if you speak in Spanish. Although many upper-class Brazilians know at least some English or French and are eager to practice on the foreign visitor, don't expect the man on the street to speak your language. An effort by a foreigner to learn the local language is always appreciated.

While at large hotels and top restaurants you can get by with few problems in English. If you like to wander around on your own, you might want to get one of the pocket dictionaries available in several languages to and from Portuguese. If you are unable to find one at home, they are on sale at airport and hotel shops and book stores in Brazil.

First names are used a great deal in Brazil. In many situations in which English-speakers would use a title and surname, Brazilians often use a first name with the title of respect: *Senhor* for men (written Sr. and usually shortened to Seu in spoken Portuguese) and *Senhora* (written Sra.) or Dona (used only with first name) for women. If João Oliveira or Maria da Silva calls you Sr. John, rather than Mr. Jones, then you should correspondingly address them as Sr. João and Dona Maria.

There are three second-person pronoun forms in Portuguese. Stick to *você*, equivalent to "you," and you will be all right. *O senhor* (for men) or *a senhora* (for women) is used to show respect for someone of a different age group or social class or to be polite to a stranger. As a foreigner, you won't offend anyone if you use the wrong form of address. But if you want to learn when to use the more formal or informal style, observe and go by how others address you. In some parts of Brazil, mainly the Northeast and the South, *tu* is used a great deal. Originally, in Portugal, *tu* was used similarly to the German "*Du*," among intimate friends and close relatives, but in Brazil, it's equivalent to *você*.

If you are staying longer and are serious about learning the language, there are Portuguese courses for non-native speakers. Meanwhile, here are some of the most essential words and phrases:

GREETINGS

Tudo Bem, meaning "all's well," is one of the most common forms of greeting: one person asks, "*Tudo bem?*" and the other replies, "*Tudo bem.*" This is also used to mean "OK," "all right," "will do," or as a response when someone apologizes, as if to say, "That's all right, it doesn't matter." Other forms of greetings are:

Good morning/Good afternoon
Bom dia /Boa tarde

Good evening/good night
Boa noite

How are you?
Como vai?

Well, thank you
Bem, obrigado

Hello
Alô (used mostly to answer the telephone—*bom dia*, *boa tarde* etc. are a more common form of greeting)

Hi, hey!
Oi (informal form of greeting also used to get someone's—like the waiter's-attention)

Goodbye
Tchau (very informal, most used), *até logo* (literally "until soon"), *adeus* (similar to "farewell")

My name is ... / I am ...
Meu nome é ... / Eu sou ...

What is your name?
Como é seu nome?

It's a pleasure
É um prazer, or frequently just *prazer* (used in introductions as, "Pleased to meet you").

Good! Great!
Que bom!

(To your) Health!
(the most common toast) *Saúde*

Do you speak English?
Você fala inglês?

I don't understand / I didn't understand
Não entendo / Não entendi

Do you understand?
Você entende?

Please repeat more slowly
Por favor repete, mais devagar

What do you call this (that)?
Como se chama isto (aquilo)?

How do you say ... ?
Como se diz ... ?

Please/Thank you (very much)
Por favor/(Muito) Obrigado
(or Obrigada, for a woman speaking)

You're welcome
De nada ("it's nothing)

Excuse me
Desculpe (to apologize)/*Com licença*
(to take leave or get past someone who is in your way)

PRONOUNS

Who?
Quem?

I/We
Eu /Nós

You
Você (singular)
Vocês (plural)

He/ She/They
Ele/Ela/Eles (*Elas*)

My/Mine
Meu/Minha (depending on gender of object)

Our/Ours
Nosso/Nossa

Your/Yours
Seu /Sua

His/Her, hers/Their, theirs
Dele / Dela / Deles (*Delas*)
(also *Seu*, *Sua* in all three cases)

GETTING AROUND

Where is the ... ?
Onde é ...?

...beach
...a praia

...bathroom
...o banheiro

...bus station
...a rodoviária

...airport
...o aeroporto

...train station
...a estação de trem

...post office
...o correio

...police station
...a delegacia de polícia
...

...ticket office
...a bilheteria

...marketplace/street market
...o mercado / a feira

...embassy /consulate
...a embaixada / o consulado

Where is there a ... ?
Onde é que tem ... ?

...currency exchange
...uma casa de câmbio

...bank
...um banco

...pharmacy
...uma farmácia

...(good) hotel
...um (bom) hotel

...(good) restaurant
...um (bom) restaurante

...bar
...um bar

...snack bar
...uma lanchonete

...bus stop
...um ponto de ônibus

...taxi stand
...um ponto de taxi

...subway station
...uma estação de metrô

...service station
...um posto de gasolina

...newsstand
...um jornaleiro

...public telephone
...um telefone público

...supermarket/shopping center
...um supermercado/um shopping center

...department store/boutique
...uma loja de departamentos /uma boutique

...jeweler
...um joalheiro

...hairdresser/barber
...um cabeleireiro/um barbeiro

...laundry
...uma lavanderia

...hospital
...um hospital

Do you have ...?
Tem ... ?

I want ... please.
Eu quero ... por favor

I don't want ...
Eu não quero ...

I want to buy...
Eu quero comprar ...

Where can I buy ...
Onde posso comprar ...?

...cigarettes
...cigarro

...film
...filme

...a ticket for ... (entertainment)
...uma entrada para ...

...a reserved seat
...um lugar marcado

...another (the same/different)
...um outro (igual / differente)

...this/that
...isto /aquilo

...something less expensive
...algo mais barato

...postcards
...cartões postais

...paper/envelopes
...papel /envelopes

...a pen/a pencil
...uma caneta /um lápis

...soap/shampoo
...sabonete/xampu or *shampoo*

...toothpaste/sunscreen
...pasta de dente/filtro solar

...aspirin
...aspirina

I need ...
Eu preciso de ...

...a doctor
...um médico

...a mechanic
...um mecânico

...transportation
...condução

...help
...ajuda

Taxi/Bus/Car
Taxi /ônibus /Carro

Plane/Train/Boat
Avião /Trem /Barco

A ticket to ...
Uma passagem para ...

I want to go to ...
Quero ir para ...

How can I get to ...?
Como posso ir para ...?

Please take me to ...
Por favor, me leve para ...

Please call a taxi for me.
Por favor, chame um taxi para mim.

What is this place called?
Como se chama este lugar?

Where are we?
Onde estamos?

How long will it take to get there?
Leva quanto tempo para chegar lá?

Please stop here./Stop!
Por favor, pare aqui./ Pare!

Please wait.
Por favor, espere.

I want to rent a car.
Quero alugar um carro.

What time does the bus (plane, boat) leave?
A que horas sai o ônibus (avião, barco)?

Where does this bus go?
Este ônibus vai para onde?

Does it go by way of ...?
Passa em ...?

Airport (Bus station) tax
Taxa de embarque

I want to check my luggage (on bus, etc).
Quero despachar minha bagagem.

I want to store my luggage (at station).
Quero guardar minha bagagem.

SHOPPING

How much?
Quanto?

How many?
Quantos?

How much does it cost?
Quanto custa? Quanto é?

That's very expensive.
É muito caro.

A lot, much (also very)/ Many
Muito /Muitos

A little / Few
Um pouco, um pouquinho / Poucos

AT THE HOTEL

I have a reservation.
Tenho uma reserva.

I want to make a reservation.
Quero fazer uma reserva.

A single room/ A doubleroom
Um quarto de solteiro/ Um quarto de casal

...with air conditioning
...com ar condicionado

I want to see the room.
Quero ver o quarto.

Suitcase/Bag, purse
Mala/Bolsa

Room service
Serviço de quarto

Key
Chave

The manager
O gerente

AT THE RESTAURANT

Waiter
Garçon

Maitre d'
Maitre

I didn't order this.
Eu não pedi isto.

The menu/The wine list
O cardápio/A carta de vinhos

Breakfast / Lunch / Supper
Café da manhã / Almoço / Jantar

The house specialty
A especialidade da casa

Mineral water (carbonated / uncarbonated)
Água mineral (com gás/sem gás)

Coffee/Tea/Beer
Café/Chá/Cerveja

White wine/Red wine
Vinho tinto /Vinho branco

A soft drink/Juice
Um refrigerante / Suco

A drink (alcoholic)/A cocktail
Um drink /Um cocktail

Ice
Gelo

Salt/Pepper/Sugar
Sal /Pimenta/Açucar

An appetizer/A snack
Um tira-gosto / Um lanche

Beef/Pork/Chicken/Fish/ Shrimp
Carne/Porco/Frango/ Peixe /Camarão

Well done/Medium rare/ Rare
Bem passado/Ao ponto/ Mal passado

Vegetables/Salad/Fruit
Verduras / Salada / Fruta

Bread/Butter/Toast/Eggs
Pão/Manteiga/Torradas / Ovos

Rice/ (French-fried) Potatoes/Beans
Arroz/Batatas (Fritas)/ Feijão

Soup/Sandwich/Pizza
Sopa/Sanduiche/Pizza

Dessert/Sweets
Sobremesa/Doces

A plate/A glass/A cup
Um prato /Um copo /Uma xícara

A napkin
Um guardanapo

The bill, please.
A conta, por favor.

Is service included?
Está incluido o serviço?

I want my change, please.
Eu quero meu troco, por favor.

I want a receipt.
Eu quero um recibo.

MONEY

Cash
Dinheiro

Do you accept credit cards?
Aceita cartão de crédito?

Can you cash a traveler's check?
Pode trocar um traveler' s check? (cheque de viagem)

I want to exchange money.
Quero trocar dinheiro.

What is the exchange rate?
Qual é o câmbio?

TIME

When?
Quando?

What time is it?
Que horas são?

Just a moment please.
Um momento, por favor.

What is the schedule?
(Bus, tour, show, etc.)
Qual é o horário?

How long does it take?
Leva quanto tempo?

Hour / day / week / month
Hora / dia / semana / mês

At what time?
A que horas?

At 1:00, at 2:00, at 3:00
A uma hora / as duas horas / as três horas

An hour from now
Daqui a uma hora

Which day?
Que dia?

Yesterday/Today/Tomorrow
Ontem/Hoje/Amanhã

This week/last week/next week
Esta semana/a semana passada/a semana que vem

Monday
Segunda-feira
often written *2a*

Tuesday
Terca-feira
often written *3a*

Wednesday
Quarta-feira
often written *4a*

Thursday
Quinta-feira
often written *5a*

Friday
Sexta-feira
often written *6a*

Saturday
Sábado

Sunday
Domingo

The weekend
O fim de semana

NUMBERS

one
um

two
dois

three
três

four
quatro

five
cinco

six
seis (or often meia, meaning "half" for half dozen)

seven
sete

eight
oito

nine
nove

10
dez

11
onze

12
doze

13
treze

14
quatorze

15
quinze

16
dezesseis

17
dezessete

18
dezoito

19
dezenove

20
vinte

21
vinte e um

30
trinta

40
quarenta

50
cinqüenta

60
sessenta

70
setenta

80
oitenta

90
noventa

100
cem

101
cento e um

200
duzentos

300
trezentos

400
quatrocentos

500
quinhentos

600
seiscentos

700
setecentos

800
oitocentos

900
novecentos

1,000
mil

2,000
dois mil

10,000
dez mil

100,000
cem mil

1,000,000
um milhão

Commas and periods in numbers take an inverted form in Portuguese: 1,000 is written 1.000 and one and a half (1.5) is written 1,5.

ADDRESSES

To help you understand the addresses in this appendix, here's what the Portuguese words mean: *Alameda* (abbreviated *Al.*) = lane; *Andar* = floor, story; *Av.* or *Avenida* = avenue; *Casa* = house; *Centro* = the central downtown business district, also frequently referred to as *a cidade* or "the city"; *Cj.* or *Conjunto* = a suite of rooms or sometimes a group of buildings; *Estrada* (abbreviated *Estr.*) = road or highway; *Fazenda* = ranch, also a lodge; *Largo* (*Lgo.*) = square of plaza; *Lote* = Lot; *Praça* (*Pça.*) = square or plaza; *Praia* = beach; *Rio* = river; *Rodovia* (*Rod.*) = highway; *Rua* (abbreviated *R.*) street; *Sala* = room.

Ordinal numbers are written with ° or a degree sign after the numeral, so that *3° andar* means 3rd floor. BR followed by a number refers to one of the federal interstate highways, for example BR-101, which follows the Atlantic coast.

Telex and telephone numbers are given with the area code for long-distance dialing in parentheses. *Ramal*=telephone extension.

FURTHER READING

GENERAL

Andrade, Manuel C. *The Land and People of Northeast Brazil.* Albuquerque, NM: U. of NM Press, 1980.

Aguiar, Neuma, ed. *The Structure of Brazilian Development.* New Brunswick, NJ: Transaction Books, 1979.

Bastide, Roger. *Brasil: Terra de Contrastes.*

Brandt, Chico. *Minas Gerais.*

Bruce, G. *Brazil and The Brazilians.* New York, NY: Gordon Press Pubs., 1976.

Cooke M. *Brazil on the March.* New York, NY: Gordon Press Pubs., 1976.

Denis, Pierre. *Brazil.* New York, NY: Gordon Press Pubs., 1977.

Dickenson, John P. *Brazil: An Industrial Geography.* Boulder, CO: West-view Press, 1978.

Dos Passos, John. *Brazil on the Move.*

Durant, Will. *Caesar and Christ.*

Felix, Anísio. *Bahia Pra Começo de Conversa.*

Hall, Frederick A., et. al., trs. from Portuguese. *Dialogues of the Great Things of Brazil.* Albuquerque: U. of NM Press., 1986.

Hunnicutt, Benjamin H. *Brazil Looks Forward.* New York, NY: Gordon Press Pubs., 1978.

Hunnicutt, Benjamin H. *Brazil: World Frontier.* New York, NY: Gordon Press Pubs., 1979.

Knight, Peter T. and Moran, Richard J. *Brazil.* Washington, D.C.: The World Bank Pubn. Dept., 1981.

Luccoc, John. *Notes on Rio de Janeiro and the South of Brazil.* New York, NY: Gordon Press Pubs., 1976.

Matthiessen, Peter. *The Cloud Forest.* New York: 1961.

Momsen, Richard. *Brazil, A Giant Stirs.*

Poppino, Rollie. *Brazil, Land and People.*

Raine, Philip. *Brazil: Awakening Giant.* Washington D.C.: Public Affairs Press, 1974.

Sabino, Fernando. *Crónicas.*

Saunders, John V., ed. Modern *Brazil: New Patterns and Development.* U. Presses Fla., 197

Shurz, William. *Brazil.*

Shoumatoff, Alex. *The Capital of Hope.* New York: 1980.

Shoumaroff, Alex. *The Rivers Amazon, San Francisco.* New York: 1978.

Stone, Roger D. *Dreams of Amazonia.* New York: 1985.

Wagley, Charles. *Introduction to Brazil.* New York, NY: Columbia U. Press, rev. ed. 1971.

Waugh, Evelyn. *Ninety-Two Days.* London: 1934.

Wellington, R.A. *The Brazilians.*

Wetherell, James. *Brazil: Stray Notes from Bahia.* New York, NY: Gordon Press Pubs, 1976.

Wigder, Roberta C. *Brazil Rediscovered.* Bryn Mawr, PA: Dorrance & Co., 1977.

Wright, M. *The New Brazil.* New York, NY: Gordon Press Pubs., 1976.

HISTORY/HISTORICAL TRAVEL NARRATIVES

Atkins, John A. *A Voyage to Guinea, Brazil and the West Indies with Remarks on the Gold, Ivory and Slave Trade.* Arlington Heights, IL: Metro Books Inc., 1972 reprint of 1735 ed.

Bates, Henry Walter. *On the River Amazon.*

Bourne, Richard. *Assault on the Amazon.*

Burns, Bradford. *A History of Brazil.*

Burns, Bradford. *Manaus 1910.*

Burton, Richard F. *Explorations of the Highlands of Brazil, with a Full Account*

of the Gold and Diamond Mines, Including Canoeing Down Fifteen Hundred Miles of the Great River São Francisco, from Sabara to the Sea. Westport, CT: Greenwood, 1968 reprint of 2nd vol. of 1869 ed.

Churchward, Roberto. *Wilderness of Fools*.

Collier, Richard. *The River that God Forgot*.

Costa, Rosa, *Histórias da Amazónia*.

Cunha, Euclides da. *Rebellion in the Backlands (Os Sertões)*. Chicago: 1944.

Fawcett, P.H. and Brian. *Lost Trails, Lost Cities*.

Ferreira, Barros. *Verdades e Mistérios da Amazónia*.

Ferreira, Rodrigues. *Nas Selvas Amazónias*.

Fleming, Peter. *Brazilian Adventure*. Norwood. PA: Norwood Editions, 1978 reprint of 1933 ed.

Fonseca, Gondin de. *Santos Dumont*.

Gardner, George. *Travels in the Interior of Brazil*. Wolfeboro, NH: Longwood Publishing Group, Inc., 1977 reprint of 1846 ed.

Graham, R.B. *A Brazilian Mystic: Life and Miracles of Antonio Conselheiro*. New York, NY: Gordon Press Pubs., 1976.

Haring, C.H. *Empire in Brazil*.

Machado, Carlos. *Memórias de Maquiâgem*.

Mauro, José. *Café Society*.

Roosevelt, Theodore. *Through the Brazilian Wilderness*.

Silva, Ernesto. *História de Brasília*. Brasília: 1985.

St. Claire, David. *The Mighty, Mighty Amazon*.

Staden, Hans. Burton, R.F., ed. Captivity of Hans Staden of Hesse, 1547-55: *Among the Wild Tribes of Eastern Brazil*. New York, NY: Burt Franklin Publ., 1964.

Villares, Henrique Dumont. *Santos Dumont: Father of Aviation*.

Wallace, Alfred Russel. *Narratives of Travels on the Amazon and Rio Negro*. Brooklyn, NY: Haskell Booksellers, Inc., 1964 reprint of 1889 ed.

Woodroffe, Joseph. *The Upper Reaches of the Amazon*.

CIVILIZATION, SOCIAL CONDITIONS & CUSTOMS

Araújo, Alceu. *Cultura Popular Brasileira*.

Batley, Richard. *Power Through Bureaucracy: Urban Political Analysis in Brazil*. New York, NY: St. Martins Press, 1983.

Carneiro, Edison. *Folguedos Tradicionais*. Rio de Janeiro: Edições FUNAR-TE. 1982.

Cascudo, Luis de Camara. *Dicionário do Folclore Brasileiro*. Belo Horizonte, MG, Brazil: Editora Itatiaia, 1984.

Cohen, Youseff, et. al. *Representation and Development in Brazil*, 1972-1973. Ann Arbor MI: ICPSR, 1980.

Flory, Thomas. *Judge and Jury in Imperial Brazil, 1808-1871: Social Control and Political Stability in the New State*. University of Texas Press, 1981.

Freye, Gilberto. *The Mansions and the Shanties (Sobrados e Mucambos): The Making of Modern Brazil*. University of California Press, 1986.

Freyre, Gilberto. *The Masters and the Slaves (Casa Grande e Senzala): A Study in the Development of Brazilian Civilization*. Berkeley, CA: University of California Press, 1986.

Freye, Gilberto. *New World in the Tropics: The Culture of Modern Brazil*. Westport, CT: Greenwood, 1980 rev.ed. of 1958 ed.

Gregor, Thomas. Mehinaku: *The Drama of Daily Life in a Brazilian Indian Village*. Univeristy of Chicago Press, 1980.

Harrison-Brose, Phyllis. *Behaving Brazilian: A Comparison of Brazilian and Northern American Social Behavior*. Cambridge, MA: Newbury House Pubs., 1983.

Levi-Straus, Claude. *Tristes Tropiques*. New York, NY: Antheneum Publs., 1974 trans.

McDonough, Peter and De Souza, Amaury. *The Politics of Population in Brazil: Elite Ambivilence and Public Demand*. University of Texas Press, 1981.

Pastore, José. *Inequality and Social Mobility in Brazil*. Madison, WI: University of Wisconsin Press, 1982.

Prado, Caio. *The Colonial Heritage of Modern Brazil*.

BLACK CULTURE/ RACE RELATIONS

Fernandes, Florestan. *The Negro in Brazilian Society*. Columbia University Press, 1969.

Margolis, Maxine L. and Carter, William E., eds. *Brazil: Anthropological Perspectives*. Columbia University Press, 1979.

Pierson, Donald. *Negroes in Brazil: A study of Race Contact at Bahia*. Southern Illinois University Press, 1967.

Reis, João José. *Rebelião Escrava no Brazil*. São Paulo: Editora Brasiliense, 1986.

Rodrigues, Nina. *Os Africanos no Brazil*. São Paulo: Editora Brasiliense, 1986.

Toplin, Robert B. *Freedom and Prejudice: The Legacy of Slavery in the United States of Brazil*. Westport, CT: Greenwood, 1981.

RELIGION

Bastide, Roger. *The African Religions in Brazil: Toward a Sociology of the Interpenetration of Civilizations*. Baltimore, MD: Johns Hopkins University Press, 1978.

Brown, Diana D. Umbanda: *Religion and Politics in Urban Brazil*. Ann Arbor, MI: UMI Research Press, 1985.

Brustolini, Júlio. *Nossa Senhora de Aparecida*.

Carneiro, Edison. *Candomblés da Bahia*. Rio de Janeiro. *Edições FUNARTE*, 1982.

Cook, Guilherme. *The Expectation of the Poor: Latin American Base Ecclesial Communities in Protestant Perspective*. Maryknoll, NY: Orbis Books, 1985.

Riserio, Antonia. *Carnaval Ijexá*. Salvador, Bahia: Currupio, 1981.

ART, ARCHITECTURE, MUSIC, DANCE & LITERATURE

Alencar, Edigar de. *Claridade e Sombra na Música do Povo*. Rio de Janeiro: Editora Francisco Alves, 1984.

Alvarenga, Oneyda. *Música Popular Brasileira*. New York, NY: Gordon Press Pubs., 1976.

Andrade, Mário de. *Pequena História da Música*. Belo Horizonte, MG, Brazil: Editora Itatiaia, 1980.

Campos, Augusto de. *Balanço da Bossa e Outras Bossas*. São Paulo: Editoria Perspectiva, 1984.

Editora Abril. *Arte Brasileira*. São Paulo.

Editora Abril. *Arte no Brazil*. São Paulo.

Editora Abril. *A Pintura no Brazil*. São Paulo.

Gardel, Luis. *The Escolas de Samba*.

Golberg, Isaac. *Brazilian Literature*. New York, NY: Gordon Press Pubs.

Hulet, Claude L. *Brazilian Literature* (3 vols.) Washington D.C.: Georgetown University Press.

Maura, Geraldo de. *As Festas Populares do Brazil pelos Pintores Populares*.

Niemeyer, Oscar. *A Forma na Arquitetura*.

Tinhorão, José Ramos. *Pequena História da Música Popular*. São Paulo: Art Editora, 1986.

Vasconcellos, Sylvia de. *António Francisco Lisboa*.

NATURAL HISTORY

Mors, Walter B. and Rizzini, Carlos T. Useful Plants of Brazil. Ann Arbor, MI: UMI Books on Demand.

Ruschi, Augusto. Aves do Brasil (Birds of Brazil). Portuguese/English edition in two vols.

GUIDE BOOKS

Bandeira, Manuel. *Guia de Ouro Preto*.

Câmara, Helder, ed. *Dicionário das Coisas de Rio de Janeiro*.

Editora Abril. *Guia Quatro Rodas Brasil*. São Paulo. Available on newsstands. Includes road map of Brazil.

Editora Abril. *Guia Quatro Rodas Camping*. São Paulo. Available on newsstands. Lists Camping Clube do Brasil campgrounds.

Editora Abril. *Guia Quatro Rodas Rio*. Available on newsstands. Includes city map.

Editora Abril. *Guia Quatro Rodas São Paulo*. Available on newsstands. Includes city map.

Frota, Guilherme de Andrea. *Um Guia Histórico do Rio de Janeiro*.

Pickard, Christopher. *The Insider's Guide to Rio de Janeiro*. Rio de Janeiro, Streamline Ltda. Available at book stores. Updated every year.
Ribeiro, Aor. *As Velhas Igrejas do Rio de Janeiro*.
Telles, Augusto Carlos da Silva. *Atlas dos Monumentos Históricos do Brazil*.
Torres, Heloisa A. *Museums of Brazil*. New York, NY: Gordon Press Pubs., 1976.

USEFUL ADDRESSES

TOURIST INFORMATION

Brazil's national tourism board, Embratur, headquartered in Rio de Janeiro, will send information abroad. Write to: Embratur, Rua Mariz e Barros, 13, 9º andar, Praça da Bandeira, 20000 Rio de Janeiro, RJ, Brazil.

Embratur has also recently re-opened their New York bureau, their only foreign office to-date. (Address follows).

In Brazil, each state has its own tourism bureau. Addresses for some of these in the main tourism cities are listed below. If you would like the address for a tourism board in an area not listed here, you can obtain it through Embratur. Your hotel should also be able to direct you.

GOVERNMENT TOURISM OFFICES

In Brazil

National
Embratur
Rua Mariz e Barros, 13
Praça da Bandeira
Rio de Janeiro, R.J.
Tel: (021) 293-0060

Belém
Detur
Av. Nazaré, 231
Tel: (091) 223-5802

Belo Horizonte
Belotur
Rua Tupi, 149
17° andar
Tel: (031) 222-5500
Information Centers: Praça Sete, Bus Station

Brasília
Detur
Setor de Divulgação Cultural
Centro de Convenções
Cetur
3° andar
Tel: (061) 225-5053
Information Center at Airport

Florianópolis
Citur/Embratur
Rua Esteves Junior, 74A
Tel: (0482) 22-6300

Fortaleza
Emcetur—Rua Sen. Pompéia, 350
Tel: (085) 231-3566

Manaus
Emamtur
Av. Tarumã, 379
Tel: (092) 234-2252
Information Center: Airport

Porto Alegre
CRtur
Rua das Andradas, 937
6° andar
Tel: (0512) 25-3877
Information Centers: Airport, Bus Station

Recife
Embratur
Rua Crus Cabuga, 533
Tel: (081) 231-4104 ramal 26
Information Centers:
Airport, Bus Station, Casa da Cultura

Rio de Janeiro
Riotur—Rua da Assembleia, 10
8-9° andares
Tel: (021) 242-1947/
242-8000;
Flumitur—Rua da Assembleia, 10
8° andar
Tel: (021) 398-4077
Information Centers: International Air-

port, Bus Station, Corcovado, Sugar Loaf, Cinelândia Subway Station, Marina da Gloria

Salvador
Bahiatursa—Praça
Municipal
Palácio do Rio Branco
Tel: (071) 241-4333
Information Centers: Airport, Bus Station, Mercado Modelo, Porto da Barra

São Paulo
Anhembi Centro de Feiras e Congressos
Av. Olvavo Fontoura, 1209
Tel: (011) 267-2122
Information Centers: Praça da República, Praça da Liberdade, Sé, Praça Ramos de Azevedo, Av. Paulista in front of Top Center and at corner of Rua Augusta, Shopping Morumbi, Shopping Ibirapuera.

EMBASSIES & CONSULATES

The following is a list of Brazilian missions abroad and foreign missions in Brazil's capital, Brasília, and the consulates in Rio de Janeiro and São Paulo. Many countries also have missions in several other cities. If you need to find a consulate nearer to where you are, enquire at your hotel or call your country's consulate in Rio or São Paulo or the embassy. It's a good idea to call before visiting—diplomatic missions frequently do not keep normal business hours. If you're coming to Brazil on business, remember that your consulate's commercial sector can be of great help.

BRAZILIAN MISSIONS ABROAD

Australia
Canberra House
40 Marcus Clarke Street
Canberra

Austria
Am Sugeck 1/V/15
1010 Vienna

Belgium
350 Avenue Luise
150 Brussels

Canada
255 Albert Street, Suite 990
Ottawa KIP 6A9

Denmark
Ryvangs Alle 24
2100 Copenhagen

East Germany
1071 Berlin, Pankow
D.R. Ebenstrasse

France
34 Cours Albert Ler
75008 Paris

Holland
Mauritskade 19
The Hague

Israel
Hei Beyar 14
Kikar Hamedinah
Tel Aviv

Italy
Palazzo Pamphilj
14 Piazza Navona
00186 Rome

Japan
11-13 Kita - Aoyama
2 Chome Minato-ku
Tokyo 107

Norway
Drammensvein 82-C
Oslo 2

South Africa
182 Balmoral Ave.
Aze Arcadia
Pretoria 0083

Sweden
Sturegalan 12
11456 Stockholm

Switzerland
Habsburgstrasse 6
3006 Bern

West Germany
Marienbura Parkstrasse 20 West
5000 Koln

CONSULATES ABROAD

The Brazilian consulate general in the United States is at: Brazilian Consulate General, 630 Fifth Avenue, New York, NY, 10020 U.S.A.
There are also Brazilian consulates located in Atlanta, Chicago, Dallas, Dayton, Houston, Los Angeles, Miami, New Orleans and San Francisco. Besides general information, if you are a U.S. citizen you will have to contact one of these missions to obtain a visa before traveling to Brazil.

In England, the Brazilian embassy is located at: Embassy of Brazil, 32 Green Street, London WTY 4AT England.

FOREIGN MISSIONS IN BRAZIL

Algeria
Brasília:
SHIS, QI 9, cj. 13, casa 1
Tel: 248-4039

Argentina
Brasília:
Av. W-3, quadra 51
bl. D, Edificio Imperador
E° andar
Tel: 273-3737
Rio de Janeiro:
Praia de Botafogo, 228 sobreloja
(Botafogo)
Tel: 5515198
São Paulo:
Rua Araújo, 216
8° andar (Centro)
Tel: 256-8555

Australia
Brasília:
SHIS. QI9, cj. 16, casa 1 Tel: 248-5569
Rio de Janeiro:
Rua Voluntários da Pátria, 45
5° andar (Botafogo) Tel: 286-7922

Austria
Brasília:
SES, Av. das Naçõe
lote 40
Tel: 243-3111
Rio de Janeiro:
Av. Atlantica, 3804
(Copacabana)
Tel: 227-0040
São Paulo:
Al. Lorena, 1271
(Cerqueira Cesar)
Tel: 282-6223

Bangladesh
Brasília:
SHIS, QI 9, cj. 2, casa 2 Tel: 248-0884

Belgium
Brasília:
SES, Av. das Nações
lote 32
Tel: 243-1133
Rio de Janeiro:
Av. Visconde de Albuquerque, 694
1° andar (Leblon)
Tel: 274-6747
São Paulo:
Av. Paulista, 2073
13° andar
(Cerqueira Cesar)
Tel: 287-7892

Bolivia
Brasília:
SCS, Edificio Camargo Correia, 10° andar
Tel: 223-2775
Rio de Janeiro:
Av. Rui Barbosa, 66
apt. 101 (Flamengo)
Tel: 551-2395
São Paulo:
Rua Quirino de Andrade, 219
3° andar (Centro)
Tel: 255-3303

Bulgaria
Brasília:
SEN, Av. das Nações
lote 8
Tel: 223-6193

Cameroon
Brasília:
SHIS, Q1 3, cj.5, casa 2 Tel: 248-4433

Canada
Brasília:
SES, Av. das Nações
Q 803
lote 16, s1. 130
Tel: 223-7515
São Paulo:

Av. Paulista, 854
5° andar
(Cerqueira Cesar)
Tel: 287-2122

Chile
Brasília:
SES, Av. das Nações
lote 11
Tel: 226-55445
Rio de Janeiro:
Praia do Flamengo, 344, 7° Andar
(Flamengo)
Tel: 552-5349
São Paulo:
Av. Paulista, 1009
10° andar
(Cerqueira Cesar)
Tel: 284-2044

China
Brasília:
SES, Av. das Nações
lote 51
Tel: 244-0277
São Paulo:
Rua Estados Unidos, 1071 (Jardim America)
Tel: 853-5195

Colombia
Brasília:
SES, Av. das Nações
lote 10
Tel: 226-8902
Rio de Janeiro:
Praia do Flamengo, 82
apt. 202 (Flamengo)
Tel: 225-7582
São Paulo:
Rua Marconi, 53
10° andar (Centro)
Tel: 255-6863

Costa Rica
Brasília:
SCS, Edificio Ceará, sls. 501/514
Tel: 226-7212
Rio de Janeiro:
Rua Jardim Botanico, 700
sl. 215 (Jardim Botanico)
Tel: 259-1748
São Paulo:
Av. Paulista, 2006
cj. 709 (Cerqueira Cesar) Tel: 251-5971

Cyprus
Rio de Janeiro:
Av. Rui Barbosa, 16
apt. 1601 (Botafogo)
Tel: 551-5446

Czechoslovakia
Brasília:
SES, Av. das Nações
lote 21
Tel: 243-1263
Rio de Janeiro:
Rua Maria Angelica, 503 (Jardim Botanico)
Tel: 266-2207
São Paulo:
Rua Barao de Itapetininga, 255
cj. 215 (Centro)
Tel: 231-4255

Denmark
Brasília:
SES, Av. das Nações
lote 26
Tel: 242-8188
Rio de Janeiro:
Praia do Flamengo, 284 apt. 101
(Flamengo)
Tel: 552-6149
São Paulo:
Av. Indianopolis, 382 (Indianopolis)
Tel: 571-6933

Dominican Republic
Brasília:
SHIS, Ql 3, cj. 2, casa 19
Tel: 243-1405
São Paulo:
Rua Dr. Oliveira Pinto, 85 (Jardim Paulistano)
Tel: 852-0097

Egypt
Brasília:
SEN, Av. das Nações
lote 12
Tel: 225-8517
Rio de Janeiro:
Rua Muniz Barreto, 741 (Botafogo)
Tel: 246-1852

El Salvador
Brasília:
SHIS, QI 9, cj. 14 casa 18 Tel: 248-0018
São Paulo:

Rua José Maria Lisboa, 744 (Jardim Europa)
Tel: 289-7313

Ecuador
Brasília:
SHIS, QI 10, cj. 1, casa 17 Tel: 248-5560
Rio de Janeiro:
Praia do Flamengo, 382 apt. 402 (Flamengo)
Tel: 552-4949
São Paulo:
Av. Paulista, 807
sl. 201 (Paraiso)
Tel: 289-9708

Finland
Brasília:
SES, Av. das Nações
lote 27
Tel: 242-8555
Rio de Janeiro:
Rua Paissandú, 7
4° andar (Flamengo)
Tel: 225-6145

France
Brasília:
SES, Av. das Nações
lote 4
Tel: 223-0990
Rio de Janeiro:
Av. Pres. Antônia Carlos, 58
6° andar (Centro)
Tel: 220-4529
São Paulo:
Av. Paulista, 2073
17° andar
(Cerqueira Cesar)
Tel: 285-9522

Gabon
Brasília:
SHIS, QL 10, cj. 8, casa 2 Tel: 248-6047

Germany (Federal Republic)
Brasília:
SES, Av. das Nações
lote 25
Tel: 243-7466
Rio de Janeiro:
Rua Pres. Carlos de Campos, 417
(Laranjeiras)
Tel: 285-2333
São Paulo:
Av. Brig. Faria Lima, 1383
12° andar
(Jardim Paulistano)
Tel: 814-6644

Germany (Democratic Republic)
Brasília :
SHIS, QL 6, cj. 8, casa 17
Tel: 248-1008

Ghana
Brasília:
SHIS, QL 10, cj. 8, casa 2 Tel: 248-6047

Greece
Brasília:
SHIS, QI 11, cj. 1, lote 11 Tel: 248-1127
Rio de Janeiro:
Praia do Flamengo, 382 apt. 802
(Flamengo)
Tel: 552-6849, 552-6749
São Paulo:
Av. Paulista, 1499
cj. 1104
(Cerqueira Cesar)
Tel: 285-5571

Guatemala
Brasília:
SHIS, QL 8, cj. 5, casa 11 Tel: 248-3318
Rio de Janeiro:
Rua Garcia d'Avila, 113 sl. 802
(Ipanema)
Tel: 294-1849
São Paulo:
Rua Veneza, 221
(Jardim Paulista)
Tel: 280-4318

Guyana
Brasília:
SDS, Edificio Venancio III, sls. 410/414
Tel: 224-9229
São Paulo:
Rua Beline, 280
(Alto de Pinheiros)
Tel: 831-0752

Haiti
Brasília:
SHIS, QI 7, cj. 16, casa 13 Tel: 248-6860
São Paulo:
Rua Bento Freitas, 178
sl. 24
Tel: 223-6122

Honduras
Brasília:
SBN, Edificio Paulo Mauricio Sampaio
sls. 1207/1211
Tel: 223-2773
Rio de Janeiro:
Praia do Flamengo, 66
sl. 1309 (Flamengo)
Tel: 205-0397
São Paulo:
Rua Beneficencia Portuguesa, 24, sl. 1014
(Santa Ifigenia)
Tel: 228-9740

Hungary
Brasília:
SES, Av. das Nações, 805 lote 19.
Tel: 243-0822

Iceland
Rio de Janeiro:
Praia do Flamengo, 66
sl. 1015 (Flamengo)
Tel: 285-1795

India
Brasília:
SDS, Edificio Venancio VI, 5° andar
Tel: 226-1545

Indonesia
Brasília:
SES, Av. das Nações, QD 405, lote 20
Tel: 243-0233

Iran
Brasília:
SES, Av. das Nações
lote 31
Tel: 242-5733

Iraq
Brasília:
SES, Av. das Nações
lote 64
Tel: 243-1804

Ireland
Rio de Janeiro:
Rua Fonesca Teles, 18 (São Cristovao)
Tel: 254-0960
São Paulo:
Av. Paulista, 2006
sl. 514 (Cerqueira Cesar)
Tel: 287-6362

Israel
Brasília:
SES, Av. das Nações
lote 38
Tel: 244-7675
Rio de Janeiro:
Av. N.S. de Copacabana, 680, cobertura
(Copacabana)
Tel: 255-5432
São Paulo:
Av. Brig. Faria Lima, 1766
(Jardim Paulistano)

Italy
Brasília:
SES, Av. das Nações
lote 30. Tel: 244-0044
Rio de Janeiro:
Av. Pres. Antonio Carlos, 40
7° andar (Centro)
Tel: 262-9090
São Paulo:
Av. Higienopolis, 436 (Higienopolis)
Tel: 826-9022

Ivory Coast
Brasília:
SEN, Av. das Nações
lote 9
Tel: 226-6525
Rio de Janeiro:
Av. Rui Barbosa, 870
apt. 1101 (Botafogo)
Tel: 551-0094
São Paulo:
Rua 7 de Abril, 261
sl. 1004 (Centro)
Tel: 231-0828

Japan
Brasília:
SES, Av. das Nações
lote 39
Tel: 242-6866
Rio de Janeiro:
Praia do Flamengo, 200 10° andar
(Flamengo)
Tel: 265-5252
São Paulo:
Av. Paulista, 475
7° andar (Paraiso)
Tel: 287-0100

Jordan
Brasília:
SHIS, QI 9, cj. 18, casa 14 Tel: 248-5407
São Paulo:
Av. São João, 755
sl. 42 (Centro)
Tel: 223-4302

Korea
Brasília:
SHIS, QI 11, cj. 3
casa 16, e 18
Tel: 248-4316
São Paulo:
Av. Paulista, 453
11° andar
(Cerqueira Cesar)
Tel: 288-3455

Kuwait
Brasília:
SHIS, QI 5, Chácara 30 Tel: 248-1634

Lebanon
Brasília:
Ses, Av. das Nações, 805 lote 17
Tel: 242-4801
Rio de Janeiro:
Rua Dona Mariana, 39 (Botafogo)
Tel: 266-6564
São Paulo:
Av. Paulista, 688
16° andar (Paraiso)
Tel: 288-2514

Libya
Brasília:
SHIS, QI 15, chéacara 26 Tel: 248-6710

Luxembourg
Rio de Janeiro:
Rua Alm. Mariath, 1
(São Cristóvão)
Tel: 248-2625

Malaysia
Brasília:
SHIS, QI 5, chácara 62 Tel: 248-5008

Morocco
Brasília:
SHIS, QI 11, cj. 5, casa 3 Tel: 248-3543

Malta
Brasília:
Av. W 3 Norte, quadra 507, bl. C
Tel: 272-0402

Mexico
Brasília:
SES, Av. das Nações
lote 18
Tel: 244-1011
Rio de Janeiro:
Praia de Botafogo, 28
sl. 301 (Botafogo)
Tel: 551-9696
São Paulo:
Rua Mexico, 706 (Jardim America)
Tel: 852-4933

Netherlands
Brasília:
SES, Av. das Nações
lote 5
Tel: 223-2025
Rio de Janeiro:
Rua Sorocaba, 570
(Botafogo)
Tel: 246-4050
São Paulo:
Av. Brig. Faria Lima, 1698
3° andar
(Jardim Paulistano)
Tel: 813-0522

Nicaragua
Brasília:
SCS, Edificio Antonia Venancio Silva
13° andar
Tel: 225-0283
Rio de Janeiro:
Praia de Botafogo, 28
sl. 602 (Botafogo)
Tel: 551-1497

Nigeria
Brasília:
SHIS, QL 6, cj. 5, casa 1 Tel: 248-6768

Norway
Brasília:
SES, Av. das Nações
lote 28
Tel: 243-8720
Rio de Janeiro:
Rua da Gloria, 122
sl. 102 (Gloria)

Tel: 242-9742
São Paulo:
Av. Sen. Queiroz, 605
sl. 405 (Centro)
Tel: 229-2764

Pakistan
Brasília:
SCS, Edificio Central
5° andar
Tel: 224-2922

Panama
Brasília:
SCS, Edificio JK
sls. 132/133
Tel: 226-0414
Rio de Janeiro:
Av. N.S. de Copacabana, 1183
sl. 601
(Copacabana)
Tel: 267-7999
São Paulo:
Av. Ipiranga, 795
sl. 512 (Centro)
Tel: 221-3252

Paraguay
Brasília:
SES, Av. das Nacões
lote 42
Tel: 242-3732
Rio de Janeiro:
Rua do Carmo, 20
sl. 1208 (Centro)
Tel: 242-9043
São Paulo:
Av. São Luis, 112
sl. 1001 (Centro)
Tel: 259-3579

Peru
Brasília:
SES, Av. das Nações
lote 43
Tel: 242-9933
Rio de Janeiro:
Av. Rui Barbosa, 314
2° andar (Flamengo)
Tel: 551-6296
São Paulo:
Rua Suécia, 114
(Jardim Europa)
Tel: 853-9372

Philippines
Brasília:
SEN, Av. das Nações
lote 1
Tel: 223-5143
São Paulo:
Rua Augusta, 2530
cj. 162 (Cerqueira Cesar)
Tel: 852-4255

Poland
Brasília:
SES, Av. das Nações
lote 33
Tel: 243-3438
São Paulo:
Rua Gabriel dos Santos, 124 (Santa Cecilia)
Tel: 66-2513

Portugal
Brasília:
SES, Av. das Nações
lote 2
Tel: 223-1090
Rio de Janeiro:
Av. Pres. Vargas, 62
3°/4° andares (Centro) Tel: 233-7574
São Paulo:
Av. da Liberdade, 602
2° andar (Liberdade)
Tel: 270-2555

Romania
Brasília:
SEN, Av. das Nações
lote 6
Tel: 226-0746
Rio de Janeiro:
Rua Cosme Velho, 526 (Cosme Velho)
Tel: 225-2212

Saudi Arabia
Brasília:
SHIS, QL 10, cj. 9
casa 20
Tel: 248-3525

Senegal
Brasília:
SEN, Av. das Nações
lote 18
Tel: 226-4405
São Paulo:
Rua Dr. Renato Paes de Barros, 33

19° andar (Itaim Bibi)
Tel: 883-1352

South Africa
Brasília:
SES, Av. das Nações
lote 6
Tel: 223-4873
Rio de Janeiro:
Rua Voulntários da Pátria, 45
9° andar (Botafogo)
Tel: 266-6246
São Paulo:
Av. Paulista, 1754
12° andar
Tel: 285-0433

Spain
Brasília:
SES, Av. das Nações
lote 44
Tel: 242-1074
Rio de Janeiro:
R. Lauro Müller, 116, Apto. 162
(Botafogo)
Tel: 541-2299
São Paulo:
Av. Bernardino de
Campos, 98
1° andar (Paraiso)
Tel: 284-0711

Surinam
Brasília:
SHIS, QL 12, cj. 2, casa 6
Tel: 248-1780

Sweden
Brasília:
SES, Av. das Nações
lote 29
Tel: 243-1444
Rio de Janeiro:
Praia do Flamengo, 344
9° andar (Flamengo)
Tel: 552-2422
São Paulo:
Rua Oscar Freire, 379
cj. 32 (Cerqueira Cesar) Tel: 883-3322

Switzerland
Brasília:
SES, Av. das Nações
lote 41
Tel: 244-5500
Rio de Janeiro:
Rua Candido Mendes, 157
11° andar (Gloria)
Tel: 242-8035
São Paulo:
Av. Paulista, 1754
4° andar
(Cerqueira Cesar)
Tel: 289-1033

Syria
Brasília:
SEN, Av. das Nações
lote 11
Tel: 226-1260
Rio de Janeiro:
Rua Emb. Carlos Taylor, 150 (Gavea)
Tel: 259-8893
São Paulo:
Av. Paulista, 326
6° andar (Paraiso)
Tel: 285-5578

Thailand
Brasília:
SEN, Av. das Nações
lote 10
Tel: 224-7943
Rio de Janeiro:
Av. Venezuela, 110
5° andar (Centro)
Tel: 291-5153)

Togo
Brasília:
SHIS, QI 11, cj. 9, casa 10 Tel: 248-4752

Trinidad-Tobago
Brasília:
SHIS, QL 8, cj. 4, casa 5 Tel: 248-1922

Tunisia
Rio de Janeiro:
Av. N.S. de Copacabana, 906, apt. 301
(Copacabana)
Tel: 235-4060

Turkey
Brasília:
SES, Av. das Nações
lote 23
Tel: 242-1850

United Kingdom
Brasília:
SES, Av. das Nações
Q 801, cj. K, lote 8
Tel: 225-2710
Rio de Janeiro:
Praia do Flamengo, 284
2° andar (Flamengo)
Tel: 552-1422
São Paulo:
Av. Paulista, 1938
17° andar
(Cerqueira Cesar)
Tel: 287-7722

Uruguay
Brasília:
SES, Av. das Nações
lote 14
Tel: 224-2415
Rio de Janeiro:
Rua Arthus Bernardes, 30 (Catete)
Tel: 225-0089
São Paulo:
Al. Campinas, 433
7° andar
(Cerqueira Cesar)
Tel: 284-5777

United States
Brasília:
SES, Av. das Nações lote 3
Tel: 223-0120
Rio de Janeiro:
Av. Pres. Wilson, 147 (Centro)
Tel: 292-7117
São Paulo:
Rua Pe. João Manoel, 933 (Jardim America)
Tel: 881-6511

Union of Soviet Socialist Republics
Brasília:
SES, Av. das Nações
lote A
Tel: 223-3094
Rio de Janeiro:
Av. Prof. Azevedo Marques, 50 (Leblon)
Tel: 274-0097

Vatican
Brasília:
SES, Av. das Nações
lote 1
Tel: 223-0794

Venezuela
Brasília:
SES 803, Av. das Nações lote 13
Tel: 223-9325
Rio de Janeiro:
Praia de Botafogo, 242
5° andar (Botafogo)
Tel: 551-5698
São Paulo:
Rua Jeronimo da Veiga, 164, 16° andar (Cidade Jardim)
Tel: 883-3000

Yugoslavia
Brasília:
SES, Av. das Nações
lote 15
Tel: 223-7412
São Paulo:
Rua Alm. Pereira Guimarães, 258
(Pacaembú)
Tel: 263-6433

ART/PHOTO CREDITS

Photographs	
240, 293R, 295	**Alves, Aristides (F4)**
102/103	**APA Photo Agency**
314	**Araújo, Zeca (F4)**
60, 167, 168, 170	**Augusto, Daniel Jr. (F4)**
25L, 182, 193, 215L, 238, 239, 254, 255, 312	**Azoury, Ricardo (F4)**
20/21, 74, 101, 268/269	**Benedicto, Nair (F4)**
56	**Brito, Cynthia (F4)**
77R	**Cytrynowicz, Salomon (F4)**
52, 53	**Fridman, Paulo**
252	**Gusmão, Antonio**
76L, 210/211, 212, 214L, 216R, 217, 219, 273R, 323	**House, Richard**
49R, 50, 51,	**Jornal do Brasil**
273L	**Lena**
34/35, 36/37, 68, 69L, 70R, 71L, 92R, 96L, 97L&R, 99L&R, 100, 104/105, 108, 110/111, 112/113, 114, 115, 116, 117, 118, 119L, 120R, 122L&R, 123, 125R, 126R, 127, 130, 131L&R, 132, 133, 136/137, 138/139, 140, 143, 144, 145, 146L&R, 147L, 148, 149, 150, 151, 156, 169R, 186/187, 188L, 192R, 202R, 206R, 247, 248, 249R, 256, 247L, 258R, 260, 261, 282/283, 284/285, 286, 288, 290, 291, 292, 300R, 301, 303L, 304R, 305, 306/307, 308	**Maier, John H. Jr.**
14/15, 166, 279, 296, 315	**Malta, Ricardo (F4)**
63	**Martins, Delfim (F4)**
163, 174L, 198, 203, 205, 206L, 207, 324	**Martins, Juca (F4)**
128, 129	**Meyer, Claus**
38/39, 40, 42, 43, 44R, 45L, 46L, 47R, 48, 80/81, 82, 84, 85, 86, 93L, 164, 175, 313, 317, 318, 319L	**Milliet, Vanja**
13, 16/17, 18/19, 22, 24/25, 26/27, 28/29, 32/33, 58, 61, 62, 65, 66, 72L, 73R, 85, 89, 90, 94, 95R, 152/153, 154/155, 160, 176, 179, 180L, 181, 184, 185, 190L&R, 191, 194, 195, 209, 218, 222, 224R, 226, 227, 228, 229, 230R, 231, 232, 233R, 234R, 235, 236, 241, 242, 243, 244/245, 253L&R, 258L, 262/263, 264, 265, 266, 270, 272, 274L, 275, 276R, 277, 278, 281, 298, 302, 309L, 310, 320, 322, 326, 327, 328	**de Nanxe, Vautier**
286/287, 325	**Ripper, João R. (F4)**
59, 96, 162, 214R, 251	**Simonnetti, Mauricio (F4)**
79	**Small, Michael**
294	**Speranza, A.G.**
54/55, 196/197, 259	**Tony Stone Worldwide**
204	**Veiga, Luis**

INDEX

A

B

C

D

H

I

M

N

O

P

Q – R

S

T

U – V

W

X – Z